Syria

the Bradt Travel Guide

Diana Darke

edition

I

www.bradtguides.com

Bradt Travel Guides Ltd, UK
The Globe Pequot Press Inc, USA

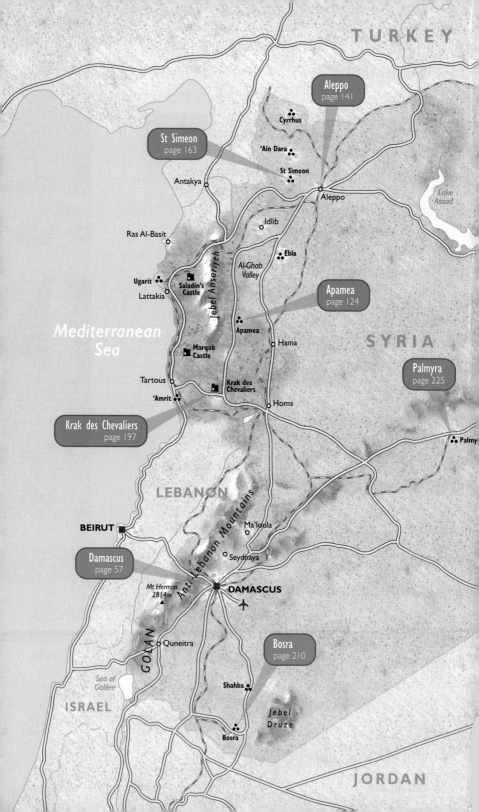

TURKEY

Cyrrhus

'Ain Dara

St Simeon

Antakya

Aleppo

Lake
Assad

Idlib

Ras Al-Basit

Ebla

Al-Ghab
Valley

Ugarit

Saladin's
Castle

Jebel Ansariyeh

Lattakia

Apamea

SYRIA

Mediterranean
Sea

Hama

Marqab
Castle

Tartous

Krak des
Chevaliers

'Amrit

Homs

Palmy

LEBANON

Anti-Lebanon Mountains

Ma'loula

BEIRUT

Seydnaya

Mt Hermon
2814m

DAMASCUS

GOLAN

Quneitra

Sea of
Galilee

Shahba

ISRAEL

Jebel
Druze

Bosra

JORDAN

Resafe
page 251

Raqqa

Resafe

Deir Ez-Zour

Qasr Al-Hayr Ash-Sharqi

Doura Europos
page 258

Doura Europos

Mari

Tigris

N

Bradt

IRAQ

KEY
Capital city ■
Main town ○
Airport ✈
Main road
Other road
Railway
International boundary

0 ————— 50km
0 ————— 50 miles

Syria
Don't
miss...

Great Umayyad Mosque
Ablution Fountain and mosaics
(JW) page 75

Ruins of Palmyra
Caravan city of the desert
(PS) page 225

Krak des Chevaliers
World's best-preserved
Crusader Castle
(FJ) page 197

Souks
Lanterns,
Aleppo souk
(AB) page 145

Bosra
Perfectly preserved
Roman theatre
(LM) page 210

top left **Bait Jabri courtyard restaurant, Damascus Old City** (AB) page 68

top right **Street near Bait Nizam, Muslim Quarter, Damascus Old City** (DD) page 90

left **Dates at Palmyra Oasis** (PS) page 234

PUBLISHER'S FOREWORD

Hilary Bradt

The first Bradt travel guide was written in 1974 by George and Hilary Bradt on a river barge floating down a tributary of the Amazon. In the 1980s and '90s the focus shifted away from hiking to broader-based guides covering new destinations – usually the first to be published about these places. In the 21st century Bradt continues to publish such ground-breaking guides, as well as others to established holiday destinations, incorporating in-depth information on culture and natural history with the nuts and bolts of where to stay and what to see.

Bradt authors support responsible travel, and provide advice not only on minimum impact but also on how to give something back through local charities. In this way a true synergy is achieved between the traveller and local communities.

* * *

My only visit to Syria was in 1963 when I hitchhiked round the Near East. I remember the utter otherness of Damascus compared with the Westernisation of Lebanon and Israel. My memory still holds the sensation of silk between my fingers, the vibrant colours and smells of the *souk*, and the unexpected hospitality of the people. I remember also the Roman ruins, impressive even to my immature mind. Diana Darke, who is a frequent visitor to the country, has brought it all back. Her descriptions of present-day Syria set my memories into a context of modern hotels and restaurants in a country that seems to have changed little in the things that matter most. What a treat!

above   **Beehive houses, northern Syria** (AB) page 123
below left   **St Simeon, City of the Dead** (LM) page 163
below right   **19th-century decorated door inside a restored Arab palace** (PS)

Reprinted December 2007 First published July 2006

Bradt Travel Guides Ltd
23 High Street, Chalfont St Peter, Bucks SL9 9QE, England; www.bradtguides.com
Published in the USA by The Globe Pequot Press Inc, 246 Goose Lane,
PO Box 480, Guilford, Connecticut 06475-0480

British Library Cataloguing in Publication Data
A catalogue record for this book is available from the British Library
ISBN-10: 1 84162 162 5   ISBN-13: 978 1 84162 162 3

Photographs Ádám Balogh (AB), Diana Darke (DD), Farhat Jah (FJ), Laurence Mitchell (LM), Patrick Syder (PS), John Wreford (JW)
Front cover Bedouin girl (JW)
Back cover Palmyra with the Arab Fort on the hill (JW), Crescent and Cross, Straight Street, Damascus (JW)
Title page Spice Souk, Damascus (JW), Corinthian carving, Palmyra (PS), Mosaic decoration, Sayyida Zainab Mosque (JW)

Illustrations Carole Vincer   **Maps** Dave Priestley, Steve Munns (colour map)

Typeset from the author's disc by Wakewing
Printed and bound in Malta by Gutenberg Press Ltd

above   **Waterwheels on Orontes River, Hama** (PS) page 118
below left   **Euphrates River near Doura Europos** (PS)
below right   **Barada River gorge, Zabadani area** (DD)

Author

Diana Darke graduated in Arabic from Oxford University and has specialised in the Arab World for the last 25 years. She has lived in a range of Arab countries, working as an Arabic translator and writing guidebooks. This guide to Syria is her tenth book. She first visited the country in 1978, while based in Lebanon studying Arabic, and because travel within Lebanon was very restricted during the civil war, she spent most weekends and language breaks exploring neighbouring Syria in her old Citroën 2CV. In 2005, following leads established during her research trips for this book, she bought an 18th-century Arab courtyard house in the Old City of Damascus, which she is now in the process of restoring. She is the first British person to to brave the Syrian bureaucracy and buy property in Syria in her own right as opposed to through a Syrian representative.

FEEDBACK REQUEST

Tourism in Syria is in its infancy and sources of information outside the country are few and far between. There is not even at present a Syrian National Tourist Board with overseas tourist offices, though there is talk of such a body being created. All the more valuable then is first-hand feedback from visitors to the country and the author would greatly appreciate any comments and information from readers to help keep the guide as up to date as possible. Please write or email via the publishers at: Bradt Travel Guides, 23 High Street, Chalfont St Peter, Bucks SL9 9QE; **e** info@bradtguides.com

Acknowledgements

Diana Darke would like to thank Dr Saadallah Agha Al-Kal'aa, Sawsan Jouzy and Nedal Machfeh from the Syrian Ministry of Tourism for their help in kindly putting a car at my disposal during my research trips and in patiently answering many questions. She would also like to thank Ahmad Yasseen; Raghad Khouri; 'Ali Najib of Syrian Air, Rawa Batbouta of the Cham Palace Group; Talal Chamsi-Pasha; Penelope Makins; Penny Clark; Dr Donald Rees; John and Tita Shakeshaft for their great help, good spirits and patience during research trips.

DEDICATION

To my parents, with gratitude

Contents

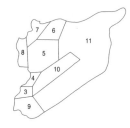

LIST OF MAPS

CHAM
PALACES & HOTELS

Chahba
Cham Palace
Aleppo

Ebla
Cham Palace
Damascus

Côte d'Azur
de Cham Resort
Lattakia

Cham Palace
Damascus

Palmyra
Cham Palace
Palmyra

Palmyra
Cham Palace
Palmyra

Apamea
Cham Palace
Hama

Fourat
Cham Palace
Deir Ezzor

Amman
Cham Palace
Amman, Jordan

Safita
Cham Palace
Safita

Côte d'Azur
de Cham Residence
Lattakia

Bosra
Cham Palace
Bosra

Badia
Cham Palace
Deir Ezzor

Central Reservation : Tel : (+963 11) 223 2320 – Fax : (+963 11) 222 6180
email : chamresa@net.sy – web : www. chamhotels.com

Introduction

Like so many countries of the Middle East, Syria owes its present boundaries to the vagaries of British, French and American foreign policy after the collapse of the Ottoman Empire at the end of World War I. Before then, the word 'Syria' was used to describe a much looser area covering not only the current state of Syria, but also Lebanon, Israel and Jordan. Both the Romans and the Ottomans knew this region as the Province of Syria, which had to the east and west the natural boundaries of the Euphrates and the Mediterranean, and to the north and south, the hills of Turkey and the Sinai Desert.

Suffering at present from an unfairly harsh image and generally painted very black in the Western media, the reality of Syria comes as a pleasant surprise. The people are relaxed, dignified and on the whole remarkably friendly towards Westerners. Exceptionally, there can be isolated incidents, such as the Danish Embassy in Damascus being burnt down in February 2006 following the surge of protest that swept the whole Muslim world against the cartoons of the Prophet Muhammad depicted as a terrorist in a Danish newspaper. The landscapes are full of contrasts and the country can boast the finest antiquities and sites of any country in the Levant. This book aims to encourage an enlightened form of tourism to Syria and to help visitors appreciate the colossal variety and cultural richness it has to offer. Contrary to widely held beliefs, Syria is an extremely safe tourist destination, with no petty crime. No foreigner has ever been kidnapped, raped or assaulted here, not even a Dane.

Oleander

Part One

GENERAL INFORMATION

Official name Syrian Arab Republic (Arabic Al-Jumhuriya Al-'Arabiya As-Souriya)

Location On the eastern Mediterranean coast, bordered by Turkey to the north, Iraq to the east, Jordan and Israel to the south and Lebanon to the west

Area 185,180 km² (less than half Iraq, about the same as Italy)

Climate Mediterranean on the coast, mild cool winters and hot dry summers in the interior

Status Republic: President, Prime Minister, with legislative power vested in the People's Assembly of 250 elected members

Head of state President Lt General Bashar Al-Assad, since 17 July 2000

Ruling party Ba'ath Socialist Party (as in former Iraqi regime)

Independence 17 April 1946

Population 20 million: 52% male, 48% female

Life expectancy Male 69.3, female 72.4

Capital Damascus, estimated population 4–5 million

Other main towns Aleppo, Homs, Hama, Lattakia

Economy Agriculture, forestry, fishing, phosphate mining, state-run industries, gas, oil and oil pipeline revenues

Language Arabic; English widely spoken and the first language learnt at school

Adult literacy rate Male 88.3%, female 60.5%

Religion Officially secular; 75% are Sunni Muslim, 10% Shi'a Muslim, 10% Christian, 5% Druze and 'Alawi minorities

Ethnic diversity Core population is Semitic, mainly Aramean; Bedouin represent the pure Arab race from the Arabian deserts; Kurds; Circassians; Armenians

Currency Syrian pound (S£) pegged to a basket of currencies including the euro as of February 2006.

Rate of exchange £1 = S£100.90, €1 = S£70.05, US$1 = S£48.85 (November 2007)

International telephone code +963

Time Summer, 1 April–30 September, GMT +3; winter, 1 October–31 March, GMT +2

Electrical voltage 220v, 50AC, two-pin sockets and plugs Continental-style

Flag Red, white and black horizontal stripes with two green stars in the white band (exactly the same as the former Iraqi regime except that had three green stars)

Public holidays See page 45

Background Information

Wisdom has lighted on three things: the brain of the Franks, the hands of the Chinese and the tongue of the Arabs.

HISTORY

The frontiers of present-day Syria are largely artificial, reflecting to a considerable extent the interests and prestige of the post-World War I powers of Britain, France and the United States. The northern boundary with Turkey is delineated by a single-track railway line, while the southern and eastern borders are arbitrary straight lines drawn for convenience and neatness by the post-war powers between salient points.

Before 1918 the term 'Syria' referred to the whole area that now comprises the modern states not just of Syria, but of Lebanon, Israel and Jordan as well. For both the Ottomans and the Romans the Province of Syria stretched from the Euphrates to the Mediterranean, and from the foothills of Turkey to the deserts of Sinai. When references are made to 'Greater Syria' this is the region that is meant, and aspirations to return to these 'more natural' borders used to underpin some aspects of political thinking under the late President Hafez Al-Assad till relatively recently. The young President Bashar has a more progressive outlook and is trying slowly and carefully to move his country on into a more liberal and open outlook through gradual economic and banking reforms. He has to walk a tightrope of introducing new reforms without destabilising the government. Faced with US sanctions and hostility, he is keen to establish good relations with Europe, and has made successful visits to Spain and China. Relations with Turkey are now especially good. He and his wife are on the whole widely liked and respected.

ANCIENT HISTORY In ancient times Syria was an important part of the Hittite, Assyrian and Persian empires, before being conquered by Alexander the Great in 332BC. After Alexander's death, Syria was part of the Seleucid Empire run by one of Alexander's generals Seleucus, and in the Roman expansion it became a province of the Roman Empire based on Antioch. The Byzantines ruled the area from AD300 to AD634, but towards the end of their rule they were severely weakened by a series of devastating raids launched from the east by the Persian Sassanids from 602 onwards, resulting in the Persian occupation of much of Syria, Palestine and Jordan. In 622 the Byzantine emperor Heraclius led a counter-attack over the next six years which was to drive them out again, but by the time the Muslim armies invaded from the south in 636 in a wave of conquest spilling out from the Arabian Peninsula, the Byzantine Empire was on its knees. Syria converted to Islam with little resistance and in 661 the Caliph Mu'awiya founded the Umayyad dynasty with his capital in Damascus. This was the golden era for the city which lasted until the Umayyads were overthrown by the 'Abbasid caliphs, in

- It is a secular state with no official religion, except that the head of state must in theory be Muslim. The perceived atheism of the regime provoked riots in the 1970s and 1980s which were brutally put down. Ayatollah Khomeini issued a fatwa (religious edict) after the 1979 Iranian Revolution declaring the 'Alawis to be within the pale of Islam, which helped give them legitimacy.
- 10% of the population is Christian. Tolerance of religious minorities is deep rooted and non-Muslim worship is encouraged. Christians reach high positions with no discrimination in the workplace.
- The mood of the country is relaxed; people are generally content with their lot. There is virtually no violent crime. Even honour killings are extremely rare and generally linked to blood feuds, so are nothing to do with foreigners. The strength of family ties means that no-one would bring dishonour or shame on their family by stealing.
- The country is agriculturally self-sufficient with excellent quality produce. Of the total area 45% is considered arable. It is also self-sufficient in oil, and in labour. Syrians do all their own work throughout society, which gives the country great social cohesion.

750 who moved their capital eastwards, first briefly to Kufa, then to Baghdad (for more detail on the Umayyads see page 63).

From the 12th to the 14th century coastal parts of Syria were ruled by Crusader principalities, till the emergence from Egypt of the powerful Mameluke sultanate which spread northwards to encompass Syria. In 1516 Syria was annexed by the Turkish Ottoman Empire, a state of affairs which prevailed until 1917 when a combined British–Arab army was led into Damascus by Prince Faisal Ibn Hussein, encouraged and inspired by T E Lawrence. In 1920 the independence of 'Greater Syria' was declared (including modern-day Lebanon and Palestine) with Faisal as its king, but later the same year the victors of World War I handed Syria to France as a mandated territory and French troops occupied Damascus.

Full independence was finally gained in 1946, with political instability both before and after. The pan-Arab, secular, socialist Ba'ath Party engineered Syria's unsuccessful union with Egypt (1958–61). Syria fought wars with Israel in 1948–49, 1967 and 1973, losing the Golan Heights to Israel in the 1967 war, and they remain under Israeli occupation today. Hafez Al-Assad came to power in 1970, a pragmatic Ba'athist leader under whose tight grip Syria was allied closely to the USSR and heavily involved in Lebanon and its civil war. He died in 2000 and was succeeded by his son Bashar Al-Assad who has been thwarted in many of his attempts to reform Syria and bring it into the 21st century, by the old guard who were loyal to his father and who are unwilling to embrace change. Syria was forced to withdraw its troops from Lebanon following huge international pressure after the assassination of former Prime Minister Rafiq Hariri on 14 February 2005. The UN investigation into the assassination under the German police officer Detlev Mehlis reported in October 2005 that key figures in the Syrian regime were implicated in the assassination, including Bashar's younger brother Maher, who runs the Republican Guard, and Bashar's brother-in-law, Assef Shawkat, who runs the military intelligence apparatus. The president himself is not directly implicated and was thought to be against the assassination. The Bush administration is putting colossal pressure on the regime to comply with its own foreign policy objectives, and Syria has responded by switching its foreign currency transactions away from the US dollar to the euro.

above   **Beehive houses, northern Syria** (AB) page 123

below left   **St Simeon, City of the Dead** (LM) page 163

below right   **19th-century decorated door inside a restored Arab palace** (PS)

above **Waterwheels on Orontes River, Hama** (PS) page 118

below left **Euphrates River near Doura Europos** (PS)

below right **Barada River gorge, Zabadani area** (DD)

PUBLISHER'S FOREWORD

Hilary Bradt

The first Bradt travel guide was written in 1974 by George and Hilary Bradt on a river barge floating down a tributary of the Amazon. In the 1980s and '90s the focus shifted away from hiking to broader-based guides covering new destinations – usually the first to be published about these places. In the 21st century Bradt continues to publish such ground-breaking guides, as well as others to established holiday destinations, incorporating in-depth information on culture and natural history with the nuts and bolts of where to stay and what to see.

Bradt authors support responsible travel, and provide advice not only on minimum impact but also on how to give something back through local charities. In this way a true synergy is achieved between the traveller and local communities.

* * *

My only visit to Syria was in 1963 when I hitchhiked round the Near East. I remember the utter otherness of Damascus compared with the Westernisation of Lebanon and Israel. My memory still holds the sensation of silk between my fingers, the vibrant colours and smells of the *souk*, and the unexpected hospitality of the people. I remember also the Roman ruins, impressive even to my immature mind. Diana Darke, who is a frequent visitor to the country, has brought it all back. Her descriptions of present-day Syria set my memories into a context of modern hotels and restaurants in a country that seems to have changed little in the things that matter most. What a treat!

Reprinted December 2007 First published July 2006

Bradt Travel Guides Ltd
23 High Street, Chalfont St Peter, Bucks SL9 9QE, England; www.bradtguides.com
Published in the USA by The Globe Pequot Press Inc, 246 Goose Lane,
PO Box 480, Guilford, Connecticut 06475-0480

Text copyright © 2006 Diana Darke
Maps copyright © 2006 Bradt Travel Guides Ltd
Illustrations copyright © 2006 individual photographers and artists

British Library Cataloguing in Publication Data
A catalogue record for this book is available from the British Library
ISBN-10: 1 84162 162 5   ISBN-13: 978 1 84162 162 3

Photographs Ádám Balogh (AB), Diana Darke (DD), Farhat Jah (FJ), Laurence Mitchell (LM), Patrick Syder (PS), John Wreford (JW)
Front cover Bedouin girl (JW)
Back cover Palmyra with the Arab Fort on the hill (JW), Crescent and Cross, Straight Street, Damascus (JW)
Title page Spice Souk, Damascus (JW), Corinthian carving, Palmyra (PS), Mosaic decoration, Sayyida Zainab Mosque (JW)

Illustrations Carole Vincer   **Maps** Dave Priestley, Steve Munns (colour map)

Typeset from the author's disc by Wakewing
Printed and bound in Malta by Gutenberg Press Ltd

Author

Diana Darke graduated in Arabic from Oxford University and has specialised in the Arab World for the last 25 years. She has lived in a range of Arab countries, working as an Arabic translator and writing guidebooks. This guide to Syria is her tenth book. She first visited the country in 1978, while based in Lebanon studying Arabic, and because travel within Lebanon was very restricted during the civil war, she spent most weekends and language breaks exploring neighbouring Syria in her old Citroën 2CV. In 2005, following leads established during her research trips for this book, she bought an 18th-century Arab courtyard house in the Old City of Damascus, which she is now in the process of restoring. She is the first British person to to brave the Syrian bureaucracy and buy property in Syria in her own right as opposed to through a Syrian representative.

FEEDBACK REQUEST

Tourism in Syria is in its infancy and sources of information outside the country are few and far between. There is not even at present a Syrian National Tourist Board with overseas tourist offices, though there is talk of such a body being created. All the more valuable then is first-hand feedback from visitors to the country and the author would greatly appreciate any comments and information from readers to help keep the guide as up to date as possible. Please write or email via the publishers at: Bradt Travel Guides, 23 High Street, Chalfont St Peter, Bucks SL9 9QE; e info@bradtguides.com

Acknowledgements

Diana Darke would like to thank Dr Saadallah Agha Al-Kal'aa, Sawsan Jouzy and Nedal Machfeh from the Syrian Ministry of Tourism for their help in kindly putting a car at my disposal during my research trips and in patiently answering many questions. She would also like to thank Ahmad Yasseen; Raghad Khouri; 'Ali Najib of Syrian Air, Rawa Batbouta of the Cham Palace Group; Talal Chamsi-Pasha; Penelope Makins; Penny Clark; Dr Donald Rees; John and Tita Shakeshaft for their great help, good spirits and patience during research trips.

DEDICATION

To my parents, with gratitude

Contents

LIST OF MAPS

CHAM PALACES & HOTELS

Chahba
Cham Palace
Aleppo

Ebla
Cham Palace
Damascus

Côte d'Azur
de Cham Resort
Lattakia

Cham Palace
Damascus

Palmyra
Cham Palace
Palmyra

Fourat
Cham Palace
Deir Ezzor

Apamea
Cham Palace
Hama

Amman
Cham Palace
Amman, Jordan

Safita
Cham Palace
Safita

Côte d'Azur
de Cham Residence
Lattakia

Bosra
Cham Palace
Bosra

Badia
Cham Palace
Deir Ezzor

Introduction

Like so many countries of the Middle East, Syria owes its present boundaries to the vagaries of British, French and American foreign policy after the collapse of the Ottoman Empire at the end of World War I. Before then, the word 'Syria' was used to describe a much looser area covering not only the current state of Syria, but also Lebanon, Israel and Jordan. Both the Romans and the Ottomans knew this region as the Province of Syria, which had to the east and west the natural boundaries of the Euphrates and the Mediterranean, and to the north and south, the hills of Turkey and the Sinai Desert.

Suffering at present from an unfairly harsh image and generally painted very black in the Western media, the reality of Syria comes as a pleasant surprise. The people are relaxed, dignified and on the whole remarkably friendly towards Westerners. Exceptionally, there can be isolated incidents, such as the Danish Embassy in Damascus being burnt down in February 2006 following the surge of protest that swept the whole Muslim world against the cartoons of the Prophet Muhammad depicted as a terrorist in a Danish newspaper. The landscapes are full of contrasts and the country can boast the finest antiquities and sites of any country in the Levant. This book aims to encourage an enlightened form of tourism to Syria and to help visitors appreciate the colossal variety and cultural richness it has to offer. Contrary to widely held beliefs, Syria is an extremely safe tourist destination, with no petty crime. No foreigner has ever been kidnapped, raped or assaulted here, not even a Dane.

Oleander

Part One

GENERAL INFORMATION

Official name Syrian Arab Republic (Arabic Al-Jumhuriya Al-'Arabiya As-Souriya)

Location On the eastern Mediterranean coast, bordered by Turkey to the north, Iraq to the east, Jordan and Israel to the south and Lebanon to the west

Area 185,180 km² (less than half Iraq, about the same as Italy)

Climate Mediterranean on the coast, mild cool winters and hot dry summers in the interior

Status Republic: President, Prime Minister, with legislative power vested in the People's Assembly of 250 elected members

Head of state President Lt General Bashar Al-Assad, since 17 July 2000

Ruling party Ba'ath Socialist Party (as in former Iraqi regime)

Independence 17 April 1946

Population 20 million: 52% male, 48% female

Life expectancy Male 69.3, female 72.4

Capital Damascus, estimated population 4–5 million

Other main towns Aleppo, Homs, Hama, Lattakia

Economy Agriculture, forestry, fishing, phosphate mining, state-run industries, gas, oil and oil pipeline revenues

Language Arabic; English widely spoken and the first language learnt at school

Adult literacy rate Male 88.3%, female 60.5%

Religion Officially secular; 75% are Sunni Muslim, 10% Shi'a Muslim, 10% Christian, 5% Druze and 'Alawi minorities

Ethnic diversity Core population is Semitic, mainly Aramean; Bedouin represent the pure Arab race from the Arabian deserts; Kurds; Circassians; Armenians

Currency Syrian pound (S£) pegged to a basket of currencies including the euro as of February 2006.

Rate of exchange £1 = S£100.90, €1 = S£70.05, US$1 = S£48.85 (November 2007)

International telephone code +963

Time Summer, 1 April–30 September, GMT +3; winter, 1 October–31 March, GMT +2

Electrical voltage 220v, 50AC, two-pin sockets and plugs Continental-style

Flag Red, white and black horizontal stripes with two green stars in the white band (exactly the same as the former Iraqi regime except that had three green stars)

Public holidays See page 45

Background Information

Wisdom has lighted on three things: the brain of the Franks, the hands of the Chinese and the tongue of the Arabs.

HISTORY

The frontiers of present-day Syria are largely artificial, reflecting to a considerable extent the interests and prestige of the post-World War I powers of Britain, France and the United States. The northern boundary with Turkey is delineated by a single-track railway line, while the southern and eastern borders are arbitrary straight lines drawn for convenience and neatness by the post-war powers between salient points.

Before 1918 the term 'Syria' referred to the whole area that now comprises the modern states not just of Syria, but of Lebanon, Israel and Jordan as well. For both the Ottomans and the Romans the Province of Syria stretched from the Euphrates to the Mediterranean, and from the foothills of Turkey to the deserts of Sinai. When references are made to 'Greater Syria' this is the region that is meant, and aspirations to return to these 'more natural' borders used to underpin some aspects of political thinking under the late President Hafez Al-Assad till relatively recently. The young President Bashar has a more progressive outlook and is trying slowly and carefully to move his country on into a more liberal and open outlook through gradual economic and banking reforms. He has to walk a tightrope of introducing new reforms without destabilising the government. Faced with US sanctions and hostility, he is keen to establish good relations with Europe, and has made successful visits to Spain and China. Relations with Turkey are now especially good. He and his wife are on the whole widely liked and respected.

ANCIENT HISTORY In ancient times Syria was an important part of the Hittite, Assyrian and Persian empires, before being conquered by Alexander the Great in 332BC. After Alexander's death, Syria was part of the Seleucid Empire run by one of Alexander's generals Seleucus, and in the Roman expansion it became a province of the Roman Empire based on Antioch. The Byzantines ruled the area from AD300 to AD634, but towards the end of their rule they were severely weakened by a series of devastating raids launched from the east by the Persian Sassanids from 602 onwards, resulting in the Persian occupation of much of Syria, Palestine and Jordan. In 622 the Byzantine emperor Heraclius led a counter-attack over the next six years which was to drive them out again, but by the time the Muslim armies invaded from the south in 636 in a wave of conquest spilling out from the Arabian Peninsula, the Byzantine Empire was on its knees. Syria converted to Islam with little resistance and in 661 the Caliph Mu'awiya founded the Umayyad dynasty with his capital in Damascus. This was the golden era for the city which lasted until the Umayyads were overthrown by the 'Abbasid caliphs, in

- It is a secular state with no official religion, except that the head of state must in theory be Muslim. The perceived atheism of the regime provoked riots in the 1970s and 1980s which were brutally put down. Ayatollah Khomeini issued a fatwa (religious edict) after the 1979 Iranian Revolution declaring the 'Alawis to be within the pale of Islam, which helped give them legitimacy.
- 10% of the population is Christian. Tolerance of religious minorities is deep rooted and non-Muslim worship is encouraged. Christians reach high positions with no discrimination in the workplace.
- The mood of the country is relaxed; people are generally content with their lot. There is virtually no violent crime. Even honour killings are extremely rare and generally linked to blood feuds, so are nothing to do with foreigners. The strength of family ties means that no-one would bring dishonour or shame on their family by stealing.
- The country is agriculturally self-sufficient with excellent quality produce. Of the total area 45% is considered arable. It is also self-sufficient in oil, and in labour. Syrians do all their own work throughout society, which gives the country great social cohesion.

750 who moved their capital eastwards, first briefly to Kufa, then to Baghdad (for more detail on the Umayyads see page 63).

From the 12th to the 14th century coastal parts of Syria were ruled by Crusader principalities, till the emergence from Egypt of the powerful Mameluke sultanate which spread northwards to encompass Syria. In 1516 Syria was annexed by the Turkish Ottoman Empire, a state of affairs which prevailed until 1917 when a combined British–Arab army was led into Damascus by Prince Faisal Ibn Hussein, encouraged and inspired by T E Lawrence. In 1920 the independence of 'Greater Syria' was declared (including modern-day Lebanon and Palestine) with Faisal as its king, but later the same year the victors of World War I handed Syria to France as a mandated territory and French troops occupied Damascus.

Full independence was finally gained in 1946, with political instability both before and after. The pan-Arab, secular, socialist Ba'ath Party engineered Syria's unsuccessful union with Egypt (1958–61). Syria fought wars with Israel in 1948–49, 1967 and 1973, losing the Golan Heights to Israel in the 1967 war, and they remain under Israeli occupation today. Hafez Al-Assad came to power in 1970, a pragmatic Ba'athist leader under whose tight grip Syria was allied closely to the USSR and heavily involved in Lebanon and its civil war. He died in 2000 and was succeeded by his son Bashar Al-Assad who has been thwarted in many of his attempts to reform Syria and bring it into the 21st century, by the old guard who were loyal to his father and who are unwilling to embrace change. Syria was forced to withdraw its troops from Lebanon following huge international pressure after the assassination of former Prime Minister Rafiq Hariri on 14 February 2005. The UN investigation into the assassination under the German police officer Detlev Mehlis reported in October 2005 that key figures in the Syrian regime were implicated in the assassination, including Bashar's younger brother Maher, who runs the Republican Guard, and Bashar's brother-in-law, Assef Shawkat, who runs the military intelligence apparatus. The president himself is not directly implicated and was thought to be against the assassination. The Bush administration is putting colossal pressure on the regime to comply with its own foreign policy objectives, and Syria has responded by switching its foreign currency transactions away from the US dollar to the euro.

CHRONOLOGY In this guide, historical background is woven into the text as and when relevant. For a concise overview however, the following detailed chronology is provided as a handy reference.

8500–4500BC	Neolithic revolution: settlement, development of agriculture and villages. Sites of 'Ain Ghazal, Beidah and Tell Halaf. Worship of the Earth Mother, the bull and ancestors.
4500–3200BC	Copper Age: spread of settlement on Mesopotamian model. Traditional date of Creation according to Jewish calendar. Clay used in pottery, dry brick used in construction, copper smelting. Crops diversified from wheat and barley to dates, olives and lentils. Earliest palaces and temples identified.
3200–1200BC	Bronze Age: development of city states, invention of writing, little cuneiform symbols on clay tablets. Sites of Mari, Ebla and Qatna. Akkadian Empire under Sargon of Akkad 2340–2284BC. Mari and Ebla razed by Akkadians c2250BC. Semitic tribes known as Amorites arrive, contemporary with Middle Kingdom in Egypt. Ebla and Mari rebuilt. Hammurabi of Babylon razes Mari. Hittites destroy Ebla c1600BC. 1400–1365BC Ugarit golden age under Canaanites, development of first alphabet. Battle of Qadesh 1286BC, Ramses II vs Hittites.
1200BC	Invasions by the mysterious Sea Peoples, destroying coastal towns and Hittite Empire.
1200–539BC	Iron Age: Exodus of the Israelites, new Semitic people called Arameans arrive in Syria 1200–1150BC. Solomon King of Israel 970–931BC. Aramean, Phoenician and neo-Hittite city states in the north, 'Ain Dara, Arwad.
900–539BC	Assyrian domination, capture Damascus 732BC. Neo-Babylonian domination (Chaldean) under ruler Nebuchadnezzar.

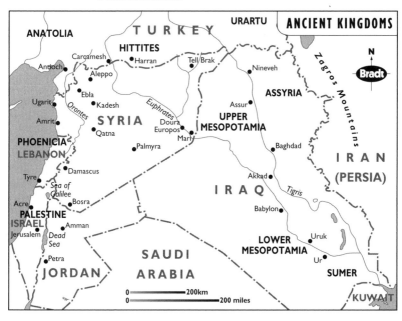

539–332BC	Persian domination under Darius I and Xerxes.
332–363BC	Conquest by Alexander the Great, defeats Persians under Darius III at Battle of Issus. Death of Alexander 323BC. Rivalries between the Seleucids and the Ptolemids. Site Doura Europos.
63–20BC	Conquest by Pompey. Syria becomes a Roman province. Expansion and prosperity under Rome. Mark Antony Governor of Syria 43–36BC. Cleopatra rules in Egypt 51–30BC. Sites Apamea, Bosra. Only resistance to Roman rule is from the Nabateans, nomadic people originally from northern Arabia, whose capital was at Petra.
AD46–58	St Paul evangelises after his conversion in Damascus. Rise of Christianity.
AD106	Annexation of the Nabatean kingdom to the Roman Empire by Emperor Trajan. Provincia Arabia is created with Bosra as its capital.
AD150–200	Major Roman building phase in Syria, Apamea, Palmyra, Husn Suleyman.
AD187	Emperor Septimius Severus marries Julia Domna, daughter of High Priest of Emesa (Homs).
AD244	Philip the 'Arab' Emperor.
AD256	Doura Europos falls to Persian Sassanians, and anarchy in Syria.
AD272	Queen Zenobia from Palmyra tries to free the East from Roman domination. Emperor Aurelian retaliates and captures Palmyra.
AD324–630	Disintegration of Roman Empire, rise of Christianity, establishment of Byzantine Empire. Sites Resafe, St Simeon, Dead Cities. AD330 Emperor Constantine transfers capital of the Roman Empire to Byzantium, renamed Constantinople. Constantine converts to Christianity on his deathbed, Christianity becomes the official religion of the Byzantine Empire. AD392 All pagan cults are outlawed. AD395 Formal split between East and West Roman Empire. Period of prosperity, flourishing of Dead Cities, followed by waves of devastating raids in 6th and 7th centuries by Sassanid Persians.
AD630–661	Prophet Muhammad, Arab conquests and rise of Islam. AD636 Battle of Yarmuk where Arabs defeat Byzantines. Damascus taken. Little resistance by local people disenchanted with Byzantine rule.
AD661–750	Umayyad Empire established with Damascus as capital under Mu'awiya as caliph. Umayyads were wealthy and generous patrons, assimilated Byzantine and Sassanid art, and permitted Christianity to continue without persecution. Sites Damascus Great Mosque, desert palaces. Serious tension develops over the rightful succession, resulting in major split between the Sunnis (following Mu'awiya) and the Shi'a (following 'Ali who was murdered in AD661.) The Shi'a reject the first three Sunni caliphs in favour of 'Ali, the Prophet's son-in-law, and this continuing dispute provokes the downfall of the Umayyad dynasty. For more details on the Shi'i/Sunni split, see page 80.

AD750–968	'Abbasid dynasty eliminates the Umayyads (one Umayyad prince escapes and travels across North Africa to establish an Umayyad dynasty in Spain with centres at Cordoba and Seville.) The 'Abbasid capital is moved to Baghdad. Sites Raqqa, Aleppo Citadel. The 'Abbasids reach their peak under the Caliph Haroun Ar-Rashid, 786–809, a character in *A Thousand and One Nights* and a contemporary of Charlemagne. The Hamdanid dynasty under Saif Ad-Dawla rules Aleppo. Their court enjoys a cultural flowering with the great poets Al-Mutanabbi and Abu Firas.
AD909–1072	Fatimid dynasty based in Cairo controls southern Syria. Fatimid Caliph Al-Hakim, the Blue-Eyed, becomes the central figure of the Druze faith, viewed as the last embodiment of the divine spirit.
AD1055–1128	Seljuk period where Seljuks sweep in from Central Asia and take over northern Syria. Syria becomes a battlefield between the Seljuks and the Shi'a Fatimids based in Cairo.
AD1096–1291	The Crusades, followed by the Muslim reconquest under Nur Ad-Din, Saladin and Baibars. Sites Krak des Chevaliers, Marqab, Saladin's Castle. First Crusade takes Jerusalem 1099.
AD1128–74	Zengid period. First Crusader attack on Damascus 1128. Second Crusade – unsuccessful attack on Damascus 1147.
AD1176–1260	Ayyubid rule. Saladin's rule. 1187 Battle of Hittin Saladin defeats Crusader army and takes back Jerusalem. Third Crusade recovers coastal ports 1187–92. Richard the Lionheart's truce with Saladin, Christians allowed access to Jerusalem 1192. Major Ayyubid building programmes in Damascus for Islamic learning and fortification. Fourth Crusade takes Constantinople 1202–04. Fifth Crusade fails to take Egypt 1217–21. Mongols sack Baghdad, murder Caliph 1258.
AD1260–1516	Mameluke period. Known as fierce fighters, a military class of Turkish origin some from the steppes of southern Russia who selected their leader from among their ranks, many of whom had originally been slaves (hence 'mameluke' meaning 'he who is owned'). The two most famous, Baibars and Qalawun, succeed in gradually expelling the last of the Frankish Crusaders out of the East. Last Mongol invasion under Tamerlane (Timur Leng, a Chagatai Turk) Damascus sacked 1400. Mameluke capital was Cairo since 1260 but Damascus was endowed with many great monuments.
AD1516–1918	Ottomans take Syria and keep it for four centuries. (They had taken Constantinople in 1453.) Suleyman the Magnificent, whose reign is considered the climax of the Ottoman period, extends the empire to include Serbia, Hungary, Mesopotamia and all of north Africa except Morocco 1520–66. First Ottoman 'capitulation' treaties with European powers, leading to increased trading activity with European consulates opening in Aleppo. French authorities start to take charge of Christian minorities 1548. Druze/Maronite Christian tensions break out, culminating in the 1860 Druze massacre of Christians in Damascus.

At the end of the 19th century as the Ottoman Empire was in terminal decline a wave of Arab nationalism appeared. Then the Sublime Porte in Constantinople made the fatal error of siding with Germany in World War I. Encouraged and inspired by their friend and ally T E Lawrence, together with the British Army, the Arabs rose up against the Ottomans under the leadership of Prince Faisal, son of the Emir of Mecca. Together they stormed Aqaba in 1916 and marched triumphantly into Damascus, forcing the Turks to retreat to the Turkish heartland. Confident he had won freedom from domination for the Arab countries and that an independent Arab kingdom would now be established, Faisal travelled to Paris only to discover the true terms of the Sykes–Picot agreement. The Allies – Britain, France and the USA – had already decided that Syria and Lebanon would be ruled by the French as mandated territory and that Britain would get Palestine, Transjordan and Iraq in the same way. Prince Faisal found himself a mere pawn in the game, nominally responsible for overseeing a series of Arab governors and the Arab administration. The frontiers of these Arab countries were drawn up by the victorious Allies and then confirmed by the League of Nations in 1920.

1920–1946 French Mandate of Syria. Revolt against French rule begins in the Hawran. France gives the Hatay Province with Antioch and Alexandretta to Turkey, an action condemned by Syria and still ignored by most of its official maps 1939. Syria is admitted to the United Nations 1945. Last French troops leave, Syria becomes independent for the first time in its history 1946.

1946–1970 Difficult beginnings of independence: Syria is ill-prepared anyway and matters are exacerbated by the creation in 1948 of the state of Israel on its doorstep. A series of military coups finally end with the coming to power of Hafez Al-Assad in 1970. Before that Syria attempts a disastrous union with Egypt called the United Arab Republic that lasts from 1956-63. The Ba'ath Party (Arabic 'Renaissance') comes to power as a pan-Arab, secular and socialist ideology. Syria begins nationalisation of the banking sector and of industry. It allies itself closely with the Soviet Union which provides its military equipment and train its military personnel. Most of the Syrian middle classes leave the country. Syria loses the Golan Heights to Israel in the Six-Day War.

1970–2000 General Hafez Al-Assad comes to power at the head of a less dogmatic Ba'ath Party, and Syria enjoys its first stability after half a century of turmoil. The Ba'ath Party relies heavily on the army and the security services. Assad liberalises the economy and creates a large state sector. Syria under him remains the last confrontation state against Israel, fights in the 1973 Yom Kippur War and is heavily involved in the Lebanese civil war from 1975. It insists on the return of the Golan before any peace talks with Israel can begin. In 1982 a Muslim Brotherhood revolt is totally crushed in Hama with thousands of casualties. In the first Gulf War in 1991 Syria fights with the US against Iraq and has a rapprochement with America.

1994 Basil, eldest son of Hafez Al-Assad, is killed in a car crash, and so Bashar, the next eldest, is recalled from Britain where he was studying ophthalmology, to be groomed for the succession.

2000–2006 Hafez dies and Bashar succeeds, aged 34. Young and inexperienced he is nevertheless keen to introduce change and reform. He marries Asma, an ethnically Syrian British Sunni Muslim, who is well educated and is beginning to emulate a Queen Nour of Jordan-style of involvement in women's issues, and cultural and environmental programmes to benefit the country. Bashar runs into difficulties over his reforms, known as the 'Damascus Spring', which are seen as too fast by the 'old guard' close to his father. The pace of change slows, though Bashar remains keen to modernise. In April 2005 Syrian troops withdraw from Lebanon after colossal international pressure following the assassination of Rafiq Hariri, former prime minister of Lebanon. The UN-conducted report accuses senior Syrian regime figures of direct involvement in the assassination. Syria awaits its fate at the hands of the international community, feeling isolated but defiant. The spectre of international sanctions depresses the economy, while oil output and exports decline. In February 2006 Syria switches its foreign currency transactions to the euro from the US dollar to avoid possible complications in the event of US interference in the Syrian economy. Syria is accused by the US of aiding the insurgents in Iraq. Since 2004 it has been inundated by huge numbers of refugees from Iraq, but its infrastructure can no longer cope and in late 2007 it imposes tough visa restrictions on Iraqis. The challenge facing the country is not to allow the hostility of the Bush administration and the Israeli government to derail its ambitious plans to reform the political and economic landscape of the country. The hope is that this can be achieved through deepening its ties to Europe and Turkey in particular.

GOVERNMENT AND POLITICS

The Syrian constitution was adopted in 1973 and defines Syria as a 'Socialist popular democracy'. The president has powers to appoint and dismiss government ministers and is also commander-in-chief of the armed forces. Legislative power is vested in the People's Assembly ('Majlis Ash-Sha'ab'), a body of 250 members elected by universal adult suffrage. On the death of Hafez Al-Assad on 10 June 2000, the constitution had to be amended to lower it from 40 the minimum age of the president, to enable his 35-year-old son, Bashar Al-Assad, to take over. Like his father before him, he is commander-in-chief of the armed forces and secretary-general of the Ba'ath Socialist Party. Besides the dominant Ba'ath ('Renaissance'), a revolutionary party based on the ideals of Arab nationalism and socialism, there are a number of other political parties such as the Arab Socialist Unionist Party and the Socialist Unionist Democratic Party which have a small number of seats in the People's Assembly.

Modern Syria gained its independence from the French Mandate in 1946 but has had a turbulent recent history. Since independence the longest period of political stability has been from 1963, when the Ba'ath Party took control. In 1966 a radical wing of the party took over and expelled the original party founders who subsequently established themselves in Iraq, setting up a rivalry between Damascus and Baghdad that persists even now. In 1967 Syria lost the Golan Heights to Israel in the Six Day War and its position remains steadfast that no peace talks with Israel can begin till these occupied territories are returned. Syria has however repeatedly said that if the Middle East Roadmap to Peace is acceptable to the Palestinians, then it will be acceptable to the Syrians. Hafez Al-Assad became president in 1971, at the head of a more moderate and pragmatic wing of the Ba'ath, and remained in control till his death in 2000, having been elected to power in five consecutive seven-year terms. Since 2000 under his successor and son Bashar Al-Assad, there has been considerable modernisation and a domestic anti-corruption drive. The Ba'ath is characterised by authoritarian rule at home and controls most of Syria's print and broadcast media. After Bashar came to power there was a short-lived flowering of press freedom, the 'Damascus Spring', with a few private publications, the first in 40 years, but that was then clamped down on. The domestic and foreign press are censored for material considered threatening or embarrassing to the government, and criticism of the president and his family is not permitted.

Syria is a member amongst other things of the IMF (International Monetary Fund), Intelsat, Interpol, the United Nations, the Non-Aligned Movement, the International Atomic Energy Agency, UNESCO, the International Federation of Red Cross and Red Crescent Societies, the International Criminal Court, the World Health Organisation and the World Trade Organisation. Syria and the EU are pursuing closer relations and an Association Agreement has been ratified with the potential for 100 million euro in development funds. Though the funds have yet to be released, blocked, some say by the United States, the hope is that such an agreement will lead to greater liberalisation in the Syrian economy long term.

Syria's relationship with Britain has improved steadily since diplomatic relations were restored in 1990. Tony Blair visited in October 2001 and Britain is keen to develop better relations and offer help towards reform wherever it can. It believes Syria matters and can play a constructive role in the region. President Bashar visited the UK in December 2002, calling on Tony Blair and the Queen. Sir Gavyn Arthur, Lord Mayor of London, visited in July 2003, along with delegations from the Bank of England and the UK's private banking sector. He had a private audience with Bashar which reinforced the need for banking reform in Syria and offered the help of the UK financial services industry. The current areas of difference are over Iraq, support for terrorists and human rights. In August 2004 Syria signed the Convention against Torture and other Cruel, Inhuman or Degrading Treatment or Punishment.

If readers would like more detail on politics they can go to the various recent publications listed in *Appendix 3*, the Foreign and Commonwealth Office Country Profile: Syria (*www.fco.gov.uk*) or the BBC News Country Profile: Syria (*www.bbc.co.uk*).

JUDICIAL SYSTEM

The French system introduced under the French Mandate is the main model. Damascus has a supreme court of appeal (court of cassation) and there are courts of appeal in each province or *muhafaza* in addition to lower level courts. The Islamic law system, the *Shari'a*, rules on matters of personal status such as inheritance, marriage and divorce. Christian churches have their own separate courts for such matters.

ECONOMY

Syria's economy is in the early stages of what is expected to be a major overhaul. The economic activities of the country are closely related to the climate. High rainfall levels along the coast and in the Orontes valley mean cotton, cereals, vegetables and fruit are extensively grown. Lower rainfall in the arc that runs from Jordan north and west through Syria into Iraq, known historically as the Fertile Crescent, means that with the help of irrigation schemes, this steppe land covered in seasonal grass can be converted into a rich and productive agricultural area. As a result some 45% of the country can be considered arable, while the remainder of bare mountain and desert can only sustain nomadic populations.

There has been a continuous drift towards the cities since the 1960s when some 40% of the population was classified as urban, so that now the proportion is in excess of 50%. The public sector employs about 31% of the Syrian labour force, the industrial and mining sector employs another 30%, while agriculture, forestry and fishing also employ about 33%. The country's main exports are crude petroleum, gas, cotton, fruit and vegetables, and phosphates. Agriculture is the mainstay of the Syrian economy, with the main crops being wheat, sugar beet, olives, lentils, chickpeas, cotton, tobacco, tomatoes, oranges and grapes, all of which are grown organically. Stock raising is another important branch of agriculture, with sheep, goats, chickens and cattle comprising the main livestock. Syria is self-sufficient in food, which should help protect it should outside sanctions be imposed in future.

Syria was thought to have no petroleum reserves after the Iraq Petroleum Company failed to find any in 1951. Concessions were then granted to a US operator and to a West German-led consortium in the northeast corner of the country, which resulted in discoveries later in the 1950s, albeit in small quantities and of low quality, and then in the 1980s large reserves of high-quality crude oil were found near Deir Ez-Zour by a consortium of foreign companies. Royal Dutch Shell, Elf Aquitaine and the US company Marathon are the main companies involved, and large gas reserves have also been found in the Palmyra area and other northeast regions. Views as to the chances of future discoveries are mixed, but many Western experts remain convinced that Syria does have the potential for further reserves. The government points out that only 40% of the 800 or so potentially hydrocarbon-bearing structures in Syria have been drilled so far. Known gas reserves are expected to last for another 30 years. The country also earns substantial transit revenues from the Iraqi Kirkuk–Baniyas oil pipeline, and there are other gas pipeline projects with Egypt, Lebanon and Turkey. Most of the country's refineries and industrial plants are centred on Homs and Hama.

The centrepiece of Syria's power production is the Tabqa Euphrates Dam project, completed in 1978 with Soviet financial and technical assistance, which created Lake Assad. Designed to hold some 12,000 million cubic metres of water, operating eight turbines and enabling the long-term irrigation of much extra land, the project has in fact not always lived up to expectations, due to increased water exploitation by Turkey upstream on its Atatürk Dam and associated Southeast Anatolia Project with a series of further dams on the Euphrates. There have been on and off agreements to construct nuclear power stations with help from the Soviet regime since the early 1980s, but nothing concrete has yet transpired. Power cuts remain common especially in the summer when demand is at its peak. In winter demand is less because most heating is via diesel fuel, known locally as *mazoot*. Water is also in scarce supply, with cuts to supply in summer in the capital usually overnight, so people cope by simply making sure their tanks are full. Long-term plans to increase water supply to major urban areas include the construction of desalination plants and long-distance pipelines.

The country's principal trading partners for imports in size order are: Germany, France, Italy, Turkey, USA, Japan, China, South Korea, Belgium, Saudi Arabia, UK, Ukraine and Russia. For exports they are Italy, France, Turkey, Saudi Arabia, Iraq, Spain, Lebanon, UK, Kuwait, USA and Russia. The EU is a major partner for agricultural trade, taking about 22% of exports, mainly cotton. Syria bulk exports olive oil to Spain and Italy for blending.

Syria's long-term economic prospects depend on new discoveries that would boost its proven oil and gas reserves, and on its ability to attract substantial foreign investment in the tourist infrastructure. This in turn will depend on the country's delivery of real liberalisation in its administrative and legal reforms in line with its recent promises. Syria is keen to enter the European Customs Union.

INVESTMENT AND FINANCE Syria has received subsidies from other Arab countries since 1967 when it lost the Golan Heights. Saudi Arabia has been the most consistent in honouring its aid commitments. The EU has also pledged a generous aid package, but its payment is linked to Syrian reforms which have yet to take place. In 2002 legislation was introduced allowing private banks to operate for the first time, and in early 2005 a series of radical banking reforms were introduced to encourage foreign investment. President Bashar Al-Assad is keen to move towards a more liberal financial system with plans to open a stock market in Damascus. Import duty on cars was also slashed in 2005 to make car ownership more accessible.

TOURISM There are ambitious plans to increase the number of tourist beds from 40,000 to 100,000 over the coming years, and investment laws have been passed to encourage foreign companies to build new hotels and tourist projects. Several such projects are already in the pipeline. Foreigners may now own property 100% in Syria with no need for a Syrian partner, and all investments in tourist infrastructure are exempt from tax for the first seven years of operation, and taxed on only 50% of profit for the next seven years. In reality most foreign investment has been from other Arab companies, especially Saudi Arabia, though both Germany and Russia have also recently invested. Arab visitors to the country account for about 75% of all tourists, the majority from Lebanon and Jordan. Arab tourists also spend more than Western visitors, as they stay longer, often the whole summer, and are always eating and drinking and buying stuff to pile up in their cars and drive home again. Iranians and Turks also come in large numbers. According to official figures, six million Arab and foreign tourists visited in 2004.

Pre-9/11 quite large numbers of American tourists used to visit but now they are few and far between. Of the Europeans the Spanish are the most numerous, followed by the Italians, the French, the Germans and the British. British tourism to Syria increased by 20% last year. Longer term the hope is that revenue from tourism will grow to help offset a potential decline in oil revenue. There is no doubt that Syria has great tourism potential but it needs to get the right infrastructure in place first and to resolve its environmental pollution issues before that potential can be realised. Imaginative tourist projects are required where interesting hotels of a high standard are constructed, and local people need to be involved in making handicrafts to sell to visitors *in situ*, so they can stay in their villages and not leave for the cities. Political stability is also key, so that people perceive it as the safe tourist destination which it historically always has been for foreigners. No Westerner has ever been kidnapped or harmed in any way in Syria.

GEOGRAPHY AND CLIMATE

Although much of the country is generally assumed by outsiders to be desert, it is important to realise that 80% of Syria's population lives to the west of a line drawn from Damascus to Aleppo, in a complex of mountain ranges and valleys, some of which are a continuation of the mountain ridge of the island of Cyprus. The highest mountain in Syria, Mount Hermon at 2,814m, is some 50km southwest of Damascus on the edge of the UN buffer zone to the Golan Heights. Snow can lie on the mountains that demarcate Syria's boundary with Lebanon (the Anti-Lebanon range) from late December till May or even June. Further north the next mountain range called Jebel Ansariye, whose highest point is 1,728m, runs parallel to the Mediterranean coast and also has important climatic effects, producing surprising amounts of rainfall. Parts of Syria have higher rainfall than parts of England.

Immediately east of the Jebel Ansariye is the flat river valley of the Orontes, whose fertile plain, the Ghab, floods regularly in winter and in summer used to be a malarial marsh. Now through reclamation and irrigation projects it is Syria's most productive agricultural area. Both Damascus and Aleppo lie in basins fed by small streams which dry up in summer; Damascus is watered by five such streams.

In the extreme southwest is another mountainous area, the Jebel Druze, a vast outpouring of lava, covered now in its distinctive volcanic black basalt rock.

The east of the country is largely steppe or desert, except for the river valleys of the Euphrates, the Tigris and their larger tributaries like the Khabour where irrigation schemes have extended the cultivable areas considerably in recent years. The triangle-shape region between the Tigris and the Euphrates is known as the *Jezira* (Arabic for 'the island').

CLIMATE The geographical differences in the country are reflected in the climate, with the eastern desert regions having Continental temperatures, very hot (above 38°C, 100°F) in summer, and cold winters with frequent frosts. The western areas have something closer to a Mediterranean climate, with milder rainy winters and less hot summers. The best time to visit is generally from late March to early June, before it gets too hot, then again from mid-September to mid-November before the rains start.

NATURAL HISTORY AND CONSERVATION

OVERVIEW The extraordinary contrast in Syria between the mountains, rivers and desert has shaped the dynamics of the country and its centres of population. The entire history of the region can be seen through its natural topography, above all through the famous 'Fertile Crescent'. This broad arc of land stretches up from southern Jordan, northwards through the Jordan valley, the Beqaa valley, the coastal plains of Syria and Lebanon, and the Orontes valley, then eastwards and southwards following the bend of the Tigris and Euphrates river valleys all the way down to the Persian Gulf. In these sheltered well-watered lowlands the world's first settled societies developed from around 8000BC: the Babylonian, the Assyrian and the Phoenician. It was the perfect environment for agriculture and a stable, permanently settled lifestyle.

In direct contrast to this was the desert, with its nomadic populations who would swarm in successive waves from the south, displacing the indigenous people of the Fertile Crescent and imposing themselves upon those that remained. In the heartland of the Arabian peninsula the population would reach the limit of what the land could sustain, and in recurrent cycles of about a thousand years the overflow would spill out northwards into the fertile areas watered by the rivers. The whole history of the region can be distilled into the conflicts and struggles between the sedentary populations already settled in the Fertile Crescent and the nomadic Arabians who came and imposed themselves and their Semitic language.

This was the setting and impetus for so many inventions and developments of early humans, stimulated by the blend of different peoples and their conflicts. So while Arabia was the cradle of the Semitic people, the Fertile Crescent was the setting of the Semitic civilisation and its achievements. The last and most important of these waves was the Muslims from central Arabia, coming with their new religion which shaped the region and which has remained in place to this day.

GEOLOGY During the Jurassic and Cretaceous periods (60–130 million years ago), what is now the Mediterranean was immensely larger and was called the Thetys Sea, after a sea nymph of Greek mythology. All of Syria and Palestine was underwater throughout that time, but in the following Tertiary Age (1–40 million years ago), extensive earth movements took place and the sea bed uplifted forming great mountain systems. The Lebanon, Anti-Lebanon and Jebel Ansariye ranges date from then, along with many other mountains round the world including the Alps and even the Himalayas. After emerging from the sea, the mountains were subjected to weathering and other forms of erosion, meaning that fossils which had been buried under thousands of feet of sedimentary rocks were exposed to view. In Syria many can still be found just lying on the surface in the desert, because their harder composition resisted the forces of erosion and weathering which dissolved the surrounding rock or reduced it to sand. Some scholars have even speculated that these fossils are relics of Noah's Flood. If you want to acquire some, the best place is one of the two Baghdad Cafés, the only stopover places in the desert en route between Damascus and Palmyra, where the young brothers sell a good range of fossils in their shops.

The rocks of Syria belong to the Jurassic and Cretaceous periods, both of which fall into the Mesozoic era, also known as the Age of Reptiles, and some fossils of dinosaurs have been found in Syria, usually fragmentary bones. The commonest fossils are molluscs, found in the sedimentary limestone rocks and deposited in the sea by rivers.

Further south major volcanic activity in the later Pliocene and Lower Pleistocene period (1–2 million years ago) led to the strong tectonic movements which caused the creation of the African Rift valley, the northernmost part of which is the Jordan valley, the Dead Sea, the Golan Heights and the Ghab Depression in the Orontes river valley. The volcanic eruptions spewed out the black, dense, finely grained igneous rock basalt so characteristic of the area. The Golan was associated with 'Bashan' of the Bible and the oak forests of the Golan used to be the most impressive forests in the whole region. In the Bible the 'oaks of Bashan' were used to make ships' oars, the cedars of Lebanon were used for the masts and the fir trees of Mt Hermon for the ships' planks. Most of the Golan oaks have long since been cut down and massive deforestation has taken place. The basalt soil which covers most of the Golan is fertile but not a good aquifer. After the first rains it gets quickly saturated and unable to soak up more, so most of the Golan's rainfall becomes surface run-off that finds its way into the river gorges and leads to further erosion.

The forests that originally covered the slopes of the Golan, the Jebel Ansariye and other hill areas of the country have long since disappeared, replaced by a scrub growth of conifers like the wild jujube (*Zizyphus spina-christi*) and the Aleppo pine and by shrubs like broom (*Retama roetan*) and mimosa. In the river gorges trees such as oleander (*Nerium oleander*), sharpened willow (*Salix acomphylla*) and Abraham's balm (chaste-tree, *Vitex Agnus-Castus*) thrive. Throughout the steppe areas desert-like bushes grow and make good animal fodder, notably salsola (*Salsola vermiculata*) which is able to regenerate with as little as 70mm of rain, a major benefit in areas that are subject to periodic drought or overgrazing. In spring from mid-February till late May many of the sites like Apamea and Palmyra are enhanced by delicate wild flowers in yellows, orange and blue. Fruit trees like apricot, cherry and apple and nut trees like pistachio and walnut also burst into blossom from mid to late February onwards, covering the hillsides in shades of pink and white. Even in the cities, especially Damascus, the air can be heavy with the scent of jasmine, damask rose and citrus flower, from late March to late May.

WILDLIFE

Birds Birdlife in Syria is relatively limited, and there has been little systematic fieldwork, with many areas never having been visited by birdwatchers. Informed estimates reckon there are around 380 species in 47 families, some 12 of which are globally threatened. The richest concentrations are in the mountains and forests of the Ansariye range inland from the coast, the Euphrates valley and the seasonal salt lakes in the desert, popular with migrants. There is one protected wetland, the Sabkhat Al-Jabbul Nature Reserve, a saline lake 30km southeast of Aleppo, where water birds such as the greater flamingo feed during migrations. Three pairs of bald ibis, a large and extraordinary bird on the verge of extinction and currently the subject of a WWF rescue operation, have recently been discovered in northern Syria, and there is a special reserve for them just over the border in Turkey near Birecik, between Gaziantep and Urfa.

Syria's endangered birds are listed as: Breeding – great bustard, lesser kestrel and bald ibis; Non-breeding – corncrake, Dalmatian pelican, imperial eagle and white-headed duck.

Rare speciality birds to watch out for are the cream-coloured courser, crimson-winged finch, desert finch, Houbara bustard, sand partridge, Syrian serin (small yellow and brown finch with a dancing flight), Syrian woodpecker (black and white, similar to great spotted woodpecker, found in the mountain forests), Temminck's lark, Upscher's warbler, white-tailed lapwing and white-throated robin.

General species to be seen are doves, pigeons, cuckoos, owls, nightjars, swifts, rollers, bee eaters, lapwings, larks, swallows, plovers, wagtails, pipits, snipe, bulbul, thrush, warblers, whitethroats, redstarts, flycatchers, wheatears, tits, nuthatch, finches, shrikes, magpies, jackdaws, ravens, crows, starlings, buntings, grebes, shearwaters, pelicans, cormorants, heron, storks, gulls, terns, flamingo, geese, ducks, teal, moorhens, coots, osprey, kite, vultures, harriers, buzzards, hawks, falcons, kestrels, partridge, bustards and quail.

The most readily available field guide is Collins' *The Birds of Britain and Europe with North Africa and the Middle East* by Heinzel, Fitter and Parslow. The website www.bsc-eoc.org/links has checklists of all bird species found in Syria.

Recommended birdwatching

Damascus area In the mountains west of Damascus is a good selection of eastern Mediterranean species including the Syrian serin and crimson-winged finch. Specifically:

- around the village of Abu Zad, altitude 1,500m, 50km northwest of Damascus, above the resort of Bludan
- North of the Damascus–Beirut road, 1-2km southwest of Jdeideh near the Lebanese border, on a steep hillside at the northwest end of Wadi Al-Qarn
- around Burqush on Mt Hermon.

Palmyra area As a desert oasis it is good for migrants and the seasonal salt lake Sabkhat Muh to the south supports wintering Eurasian dotterel and Finsch's wheatear.

At the ruined Umayyad palace complex of Qasr Al-Hayr Ash-Sharqi northeast of Tadmur (Palmyra) there have been sightings of lesser kestrel, cream-coloured courser, pin-tailed sandgrouse, Temminck's and desert larks.

Euphrates Valley, from Aleppo to Deir Ez-Zour Especially for waterbirds and waders:

- Large salt lake of Sabkhat Al-Jabbul 30km southeast of Aleppo, south of Al-Jabbul village
- The ruined Byzantine cities of Halabiye and Zalabiye 40km northwest of Deir Ez-Zour
- Shumaytiye, an ox-bow lake 20km northwest of Deir Ez-Zour
- Mayadin Pool, 46km south of Deir Ez-Zour near Qal'at Ar-Rahba, 2km southwest of Mayadin
- Small marsh 10km south of Jisr Al-Ashara southeast of Deir Ez-Zour towards the Iraqi border.

Animals Animal life used to include wolves, hyenas, boar, deer, bears and polecats in the days when the forests were more prevalent, as their abundant depiction in the mosaics of Roman times illustrates, but now animal life is limited to livestock of horses, cows, donkeys, goats, sheep and camels, along with poultry. Syria was famed as the home of the golden Syrian hamster (*Mesocricetus auratus*) since the first one was caught near Aleppo in 1930 and sent back to Britain, pregnant with her pups, the source of all future generations of pets. Only a handful more have been caught since then, so they are still very rare. Syrians, like all Arabs, do not have a pet-keeping culture. There is no 'sentimentality' towards animals which are seen as simply serving a purpose. They are certainly not required as companions, since the extended family system makes sure that loneliness is not an issue. Caged birds like canaries may be kept in the home for their song. Otherwise a man may have a relationship of respect with his horse, his camel or his falcon, but dogs, cats and hamsters do not enter the frame.

A small number of wildlife reserves, like the Talila Reserve near Palmyra, has been created to reintroduce species to the steppe lands such as oryx and gazelle, but these projects are in their infancy, though the necessity of extending such work is widely recognised in official circles.

ENVIRONMENTAL ISSUES The Ministry of the Environment was created only in recent years and awareness of environmental pollution is in its infancy. Schemes like the Talila Wildlife Reserve near Palmyra (see page 247) are encouraging first steps, and President Bashar himself is also a keen environmentalist. In spring 2005 he introduced a poster campaign all over the country urging citizens to plant as many trees as they could. In April 2005 in Damascus there was a drive to plant thousands of jasmine plants all over the city, in an attempt to recreate Damascus' epithet 'City of Jasmine' which the great modern Syrian poet Nizar Qabbani, who died in 1998, immortalised in his poems about the city. There is however a very long way to go and the scale of plastic bag and bottle pollution is horrendous throughout the country and along the shoreline. The Ministry of Tourism is trying to devise incentives for local people to clear up the rubbish themselves and keep their environment clean.

PEOPLE

Everyone who visits Syria returns with an abiding impression of the people, often talking more about them than about the country itself or its sights. This is because, contrary to all expectation, they find the Syrian people to be so charming, friendly, open and tolerant, yet at the same time dignified and respectful. It is rare for example to be hassled in the way so rampant in most north African countries, such as Morocco, by shopkeepers urging you to come into their shop, as this is considered undignified behaviour. Indeed the minister of tourism himself, on hearing that some younger shopkeepers are guilty of this, becomes quite angry and says he will have their shops closed down if he catches them. The usual Syrian pattern of behaviour is to offer help if you look as if you need it, and withdraw if you assure them you are fine.

Young Syrians are remarkably Westernised, both in their dress and in their openness. Most are very technologically aware, have the latest mobile phones, digital cameras and are avid users of the increasing number of internet cafés. This is a trend actively encouraged by President Bashar Al-Asad, himself head for many years of the Syrian Computer Society. In the streets you will see young Syrian girls walking together, arm in arm, some in tight jeans and T-shirts, some in Muslim dress with headscarves. They mix effortlessly, as personal dress code is precisely that, a personal matter for each individual to decide. There is no external pressure to dress one way or the other. Men are almost entirely in Western garb and it is unusual to see anyone in Arab robes with headdress except in the countryside or desert areas where it is more suited to the climate.

Ethnically, 90% of Syrians are Arab and the remaining 10% are the various ethnic minorities, predominantly Kurds and Armenians. About 300 Jews remain in Syria, living mainly in Damascus. The 5,000 or so who used to live here were given permission to emigrate in 1992, and those that remain have freely chosen to do so. Most of the ethnic groups are fully integrated into Syrian society, except for the 250,000 or so Kurds, who live mainly in the northeast Al-Jazira region and have no civil or political rights and are not entitled to Syrian nationality (see box, page 264). Palestinians resident in Syria on the other hand have all the same legal rights as Syrians, except for the right to vote. Ethnic background is not stated on the identity card which every Syrian has to carry, with the exception of the Palestinians. Most Palestinians are Sunni Muslim but some are Christian. They came as refugees from the 1948 and 1967 Arab–Israeli wars and settled originally in camps around Damascus. These camps have become increasingly permanent and have evolved gradually into proper residential quarters. Educated in the special schools set up by UNWRA (United Nations Relief and Works Agency for Palestinian Refugees in the Near East), their level of education is often higher than the national average. Most Palestinians resident in Syria will tell you it is the best of the Arab countries in which to live, as they are so well integrated.

The Kurds account for about 6% of the Syrian population, grouped mainly in the Kurd-Dagh Massif northwest of Aleppo and the Qamishli region along the Turkish border. Aleppo too has a large Kurdish population. The 20 million or so Kurds are scattered between Turkey, Iran, Iraq and Syria. They are Sunni Muslims but have their own language, Kurdish, which is Indo-European and unrelated to Arabic. With the Kurds recently gaining a measure of autonomy in Iraq, the Syrian government has been more uneasy about strong Kurdish nationalist aspirations in Syria.

Syria's Armenian community is based mainly in Aleppo, where they are heavily involved in the business community, and thought to number about 150,000. They are Christian – Armenia was in fact the first nation to adopt Christianity as its official religion in the early 3rd century. Of the seven million Armenians worldwide, most are now settled in the Republic of Armenia, free of Soviet rule since 1991, and about one million are in the United States of America.

There are also small communities of Circassians (known in Arabic as 'Shirkass'), Caucasians who were expelled by the Imperial Russian army in the 19th century.

They are Muslim and found refuge in the Ottoman Empire, yet have retained their own language and customs.

The Arabs who make up the majority of the population can be subdivided according to religion, with the most important group being the Sunni Muslims (see page 21), accounting for 74%, the 'Alawites of Shi'ite origin who account for some 13% (see page 80), the Arab Christians who account for about 10% (see page 110) and the Druze (see pages 218–19) who account for around 3% of the population.

SOCIAL PROBLEMS Syria's social problems are overpopulation, the expense of marriage and the lack of trained personnel. Unemployment is high at about 20% and the socio-economic challenge is to provide jobs for the 200,000 young people coming onto the job market each year. The average age of marriage has risen from 22 to 28 and the average family size has fallen from six to five. The government is keen to see it reduce to four. On the plus side drugs and crime hardly exist at all, half because of the culture of shame and bringing dishonour on the family if caught, and half because of the strict police state where it is always felt someone from the security services may be watching. On the rare occasions when criminals do perpetrate a crime, the security apparatus is quick to parade them very publicly on TV and radio. Foreign visitors need have no fear of the police as long as they do not get violent or high on drink or drugs in public and do not photograph in military areas.

Syria is very poor at its own publicity and PR and appears quite incapable of projecting a good image of itself on the international stage for the benefit of outsiders, in marked contrast to Israel for example. From its years of Soviet involvement and dependence it lacks experienced people who are competent at these increasingly important skills. Another major problem the country has to address is its 'brain drain', the exodus of highly educated and skilled people to earn better money outside the country. Syria needs to keep these people and make it more attractive for them to stay. One of the very few who comes across well on the media is a lady called Buthaina Sha'aban, the immigration minister, who succeeds in presenting herself as a balanced and sympathetic spokesperson. Her current job is to encourage some of these people to return by offering incentives and exemption from military service. Syria's silence on so many US accusations against it is generally seen as guilt, as the Western view is that if the country were innocent it would defend itself. Since Rafiq Hariri's assassination in February 2005 Syria has been forced to come much more centre stage and managed to conduct a remarkably orderly withdrawal of its troops from Lebanon after a 29-year stay at the end of April 2005 within a space of seven weeks. It remains in deep trouble however over its accused involvement at senior regime level in the assassination.

One of the most significant aspects of Syria's population is its virtually total absence of imported foreign workers. Syrians do all jobs from top to bottom in the social hierarchy. Its neighbour Jordan, by contrast, would collapse without aid and support, while the Gulf countries depend heavily on Indian and Pakistani labourers. Palestinians displaced from Palestine agree that Syria is the best Arab country to live in as a Palestinian. It is a very tolerant society with no religious or ethnic discrimination.

ARABIC LANGUAGE AND TRANSLITERATION

Arabic is the official language of the country, but English is widely spoken and understood. French is the next language after English, but English has become the dominant foreign language in schools and everyone wants to practise it. This

Writing Arabic using the English alphabet, known as transliteration, is a vexed subject on which Arabic scholars and academics become extremely exercised. The important thing to understand is that there is no one correct universally accepted system of transliteration from Arabic to English, and all attempts to impose such a system have run into the sand. Even if there is a preferred system in one Arab country, the reality is it is never consistently used. Consistency is not an Arab forte; indeed it is worth pointing out there is not even a word for 'consistency' in Arabic, it being a rather alien concept. Syria is no exception, and while it does consistently use the conventional French transliteration 'ch' to represent the English 'sh' sound (for example, Cham Palace, pronounced 'Sham Palace', Sham being the original Arabic word for both Syria and Damascus), in other areas Syrian transliteration is utterly random. Sometimes for example it uses the phonetic so-called sun-letter system where certain letters are elided into the definite article 'al-' , such as Deir Az-Zour as opposed to Deir Al-Zour, and sometimes it does not. Strictly speaking the letters 'o' and 'e' do not exist in Arabic, yet they are widely used throughout the Levant in transliteration. Thus Deir Ez-Zour, the spelling most widely used within Syria, could be equally well written Dair Al-Zur, Dayr Al-Zur, Deir Al-Zour, Dair Az-Zour, Dayr Az-Zur and so on, and no-one could insist on a particular spelling being right.

Because of these massive inconsistencies the author has tended to follow the transliteration as found in Syria on signposts etc, however inconsistent it may appear to an academic purist, since this is after all what visitors will see around them, and it is important to recognise signposts. The Arabic letter 'ayn, very difficult for foreigners to pronounce, is represented as a high inverted comma eg 'Ali, 'Alawi. By way of illustrating more inconsistencies, the signs for Krac des Chevaliers over the last few kilometres vary from Crak des Chevaliers to suddenly Qal'at Al-Husn or Husn Citadel. At least there are signs.

makes it fairly difficult for anyone trying to use a bit of Arabic and unless you are already fairly advanced it is hard to find people prepared to speak to you in Arabic.

Syrian-spoken Arabic is similar to the Levantine dialect spoken in Lebanon and Jordan, though there are differences of pronunciation and usage. In sound it is quite soft and sing-song, compared with the rather harsh guttural dialects of the Gulf and Egypt. Written Arabic is the same all across the Arabic world, with no dialectal differences, thanks to the unifying force of the Koran, so newspapers printed in Iraq can be happily read by an Algerian or a Moroccan, whereas the spoken dialect of Iraq at the extreme eastern end of the Arab world is virtually unintelligible to an Algerian at the western end and vice versa. For practical details, and greetings and basic vocabulary, see *Appendix 1*, page 271.

EDUCATION

There is free state-provided education which is compulsory till the age of 16 for boys and girls. There is then a baccalaureate-style qualification taken at 18, on the basis of which places at the state universities are awarded free to the top students. The education system is strongly influenced by the French model with a primary school, a middle school (*collège*) from ages 13-16, then secondary school (*lycée*). Both schools and universities have now become heavily oversubscribed because of the growing population, and private universities have begun to appear to fill the gap, though obviously only the well-off can afford them. There are also private schools, notably in the big cities, where the wealthy prefer to send their children as the IT facilities are better and more languages are taught beyond English, such as French, Spanish and German.

At university those with the highest grades go into medicine, the next level into engineering and IT, and the next level into law. Women account for 40% of students at university. Over 56% of the population is under 20, and class sizes are frequently over 30. Military service for men is still compulsory after education has finished, but was reduced in 2005 from two-and-a-half years to two years. Women may volunteer. Military service is still, however, seen as a big deterrent for graduates to stay in the country, as if they take higher-paid jobs in the Gulf for five years they can buy themselves out of their military service obligations. Many of them simply decide not to return as Syrian salaries, even in the private sector, cannot compete with Gulf salaries. Even neighbouring states like Jordan offer high salaries to well-qualified people, with private universities for example offering as much as US$1,000 a month to IT graduate teachers for a two-day week, thereby leaving them free to earn extra by doing private consulting as well.

RELIGION

Syria has a tradition of religious tolerance which is quite unusual in the Middle East. On the ID card which everyone has to carry religion is not even specified, and the government is expressly secular. Religion is considered a private and personal matter and no-one is judged on the basis of it. By way of example the author, in the process of purchasing her house in the Old City, grew to know the bank manager, who turned out to be Christian, a fact that only became evident after she was invited to the bank manager's home to celebrate a Christian festival. The author's lawyer, a Muslim, had known and had dealings with this lady bank manager for several years and had never realised she was Christian. Throughout Syrian society there are Christians at high levels in government, banking, the law, medicine and education.

All three great monotheistic religions – Judaism, Christianity and Islam, to list them in chronological order – began in the Middle East, and their development, clashes and schisms over the centuries have shaped the region of today. Islam is easily the dominant religion of the area, and in Syria 10% of the population is Christian, while Jews are almost non-existent. The dominant Muslim sect is the Sunni, regarded as the orthodox branch (Sunni means adherent of the Sunna or traditional path), accounting for over 75% of the population, while 10% belongs to the Shi'a sect, Shi'a meaning the split, the faction that split off from the orthodox (see box on the Sunni/Shi'a split on page 80). The remaining 5% belongs to the Druze and 'Alawi minorities (see pages 218–19 and 188).

Islam began in the 7th century through the Prophet Muhammad. Born around AD570 in Mecca he was an illiterate shepherd. He married Khadija, a wealthy merchant 15 years his senior, when he was 25 and worked for her on trading caravan routes as far afield as Syria. When he was 40 he had a series of visitations from the Angel Gabriel, telling him to recite. The words he recited, as God's mouthpiece, became, once they were later written down by his disciples, the Koran, which is so holy and powerful as a unifying force throughout the Arab world precisely because it is thought of as 'the Word of God'. The evocative language of the Koran is lost in translation, where it comes across as pompous and over-theatrical, but in Arabic it has a tremendous power and rhetorical pull which makes it almost entrancing when read aloud. It is still regarded by a fifth of humankind as the embodiment of all wisdom, theology and science: it is all

One of the very noticeable aspects of Islam that strikes most foreigners is how actively it is practised by young men everywhere, breaking off from their work or leisure to go to the mosque to pray. What average young man would be seen dead attending church in the West regularly? Church-going is widely seen as for old ladies, not the young. Islam, which means 'submission' in Arabic, has five so-called Pillars of Faith, one of which is to pray five times a day at the fixed times. The unmistakable call to prayer from the mosque minarets is the prelude to these prayers which take place at dawn, early afternoon, later in the afternoon when the sun is halfway set, straight after sunset and finally in the evening before bedtime. Prayers can be said anywhere and simply involve facing in the direction of Mecca and performing the ritual prostrations. Prayers must be said in a state of bodily purity which is why shoes must be removed and washing ablutions performed beforehand, to reflect purity of the soul. These prostrations, given the regularity and the sheer number of times they are performed every day, are better than any exercise or gym routine at keeping the older population supple and fit, and are the prime example of incorporating your daily exercise into your everyday lifestyle. The Friday noonday prayer is the only public one, compulsory for all adult males. Women generally pray at home, though some mosques have an area reserved for women only. The sermon or *khutba* at this weekly prayer is delivered by the imam and is very powerful in the shaping of public opinion.

The other four pillars are the *Shahada* or declaration of faith, which is what someone has to state on converting to Islam: 'There is no God but God and Muhammad is the Messenger of God'; observing the fasting month of Ramadan; giving alms (Arabic *zakat*) to the poor; and completing the pilgrimage to Mecca (Arabic *Hajj*) at least once in your lifetime.

Beyond these Five Pillars of Faith, Islam also stipulates no drinking of alcohol and no eating of pork or of meat that has not been slaughtered in the *halaal* way, that is throat-cutting and exsanguinations without pre-stunning. Gambling and money-lending are also forbidden, which means there will never be a national lottery and Islamic banking is a highly specialised field that does not include mortgages or loans. Muslims acknowledge Jesus as a prophet and 21 of the 28 prophets mentioned in the Koran appear in the Bible.

the more remarkable therefore that it came out of the mouth of an illiterate shepherd. Muhammad was driven out of Mecca by the angry Quraysh tribe who perceived him as a threat, and in AD622 he was invited to Yathrib, later renamed Medina, with his band of followers. This emigration or breaking of ties, Arabic *hijra*, is the date from which the Islamic calendar begins, which is why Islamic dates are about 580 years behind our Gregorian calendar, the current Islamic year being AH1427, standing for 'after *Hijra*'. The disparity in dates is due to the Muslim year being lunar and therefore approximately ten days shorter than the Gregorian solar calendar. The end of each of the 12 Muslim months is determined by the sighting of the new moon and hence the exact dates cannot be predicted in advance. Geography also comes into it, as the new moon gets spotted in different countries at different times so the exact Islamic date can vary by up the three days depending on the country. Saudi Arabia likes to take the lead, as the keeper of the holy sites of Mecca and Medina, and has been known to send up a helicopter to make sure the new moon is spotted on the day it prefers. Neighbouring Oman, not wanting to appear subordinate to Saudi Arabia, generally goes for a different day on principle.

Background Information RELIGION

Snippets from the Aramco School where Americans were being prepared for their postings in Saudi Arabia reveal a shocking level of ignorance about the culture. To questions like 'What is Islam?' replies were 'A game of chance, like bridge', 'A mysterious sect founded in the south by the Ku Klux Klan' and 'An organisation of American Masons who dress in strange costumes'. When asked about the Prophet Muhammad, their replies were 'He wrote *The Arabian Nights*', 'He was an American negro minister who was in competition with Father Divine in New York City' and 'Muhammad had something to do with a mountain. He either went to the mountain, or it came to him.'

Few other cultures have matched the Islamic in extent, longevity, resilience and tenacity. The speed with which the new religion of Islam swept out of the Arabian Peninsula was dramatic, and just 100 years after Muhammad's death his Muslim followers found themselves in possession of an empire that extended from the Bay of Biscay to the Indus and from China and the Aral Sea to the lower cataracts of the Nile. This empire was already larger than that of Rome at its zenith, and Damascus was its capital. Visually it is represented by many beautiful buildings, from the Alhambra in Spain to the Taj Mahal in India, and in the tilework and calligraphy of the mosques of Istanbul. But most experts agree that Islamic genius shows itself most clearly in its literature.

Great damage has been done to Arabic literature in the realm of translation. It has been made monstrous either by excessive literalism or made ridiculous by doggerel. Many great works of Islamic literature have not been translated at all and those who approach it as novices are generally surprised to discover within it unimagined quantity and an equally unimagined wealth of form and content. Poetry is the most beloved art to the Arab, especially when read aloud, as the beauty is in the rhetorical power and craftsmanship of the language. There is also a thread of deep ethical concern that is intricately woven into most Arabic literature, be they works of humour or religious treatise. (see *Further Information*, pages 281–2, for suggested books).

For all the world's Muslims the Koran is the greatest work of literature. Yet very few non-Muslims have ever read it, even though it is shorter than the New Testament, and could be read in a single day. Poor translation is the main reason, and the other problem is that it is that it is presented in what is generally considered to be reverse chronological order. It is recommended therefore to start at the back with the short dramatic suras (chapters) mainly revealed while Muhammad was still in Mecca, to set the scene, before attempting the longer suras at the front of the Koran revealed in Medina, which concern themselves with rather dry aspects of law-giving and on which the Shari'a, Islamic law, is largely based.

Pre-Islamic poetry is also very powerful and beautifully crafted, composed according to strict patterns of rhythm. It was originally an oral tradition, used to entertain around desert camp fires. After the death of the Prophet Muhammad, the Koran needed to be recorded and this was the impetus for Arabic to develop a proper written form, the Arabic script, on which all subsequent literature was based. Because of its genesis in the Koran, the Arabic script has always had sacred, even mystical associations, which led to its being extensively used in mosque decoration and tilework as calligraphic styles evolved, especially since representation of the human or animal form was forbidden under Islam. Under the Umayyad and 'Abbasid caliphates literature of all sorts flourished, poetry and prose, and many of the best-known poets were attached to the courts, like Al-Mutanabbi, considered the greatest ever Arab poet (see box page 142). Umayyad poetry abounds with experiments, new moods and themes. It was an age of anxiety, full of tensions, with society moving steadily towards a more urban way of life. The anxiety expressed itself in an attitude of escapism and self-indulgence. A new artistic freedom was born, a painful freedom, still looking for a focus in the age. Here by way of example are some words of Al-Akhtal, (c640 – c710), a Christian poet of the Umayyad court:

> When I saw the world full of constraint,
> Terror sent me riding on an endless journey.
> and
> The Euphrates, when its waves swell, and uprooted trees float along its length and
>   breadth,
> The summer winds playing on it, and fountains dancing on the crest of its waves,
> Flowing swiftly from the Byzantine mountains,
> Winding its way in many a turn and curve,
> Is not more generous than he.
> (panegyric to the Caliph, his master)

The Middle Ages under the Ottomans produced less great literature, with far more concentration on prose than on poetry, but the 20th century then witnessed a new flourishing with local poets like Adonis and Nizar Qabbani at the forefront of new methods of expression. Adonis is known as a poet of conflict and contradictions. With a dazzling linguistic flair he describes a deep vision of his culture and his country and the forces that have shaped it. His motto was that we must have a 'commitment to freedom, creativity and change'. He bemoaned the fact that the marriage of modernity imported from the West and the local culture, has produced 'a vast desert of imports and consumption'. Nizar Qabbani began as a love poet, but later in life wrote too of the challenges facing the Arab world, with such memorable expressions as: 'No regime could arrest my poems for they are dipped in the oil of freedom,' 'Each day we regress a thousand years' and 'History is a river that never flows backwards'. Some of these works exist in translation, notably *Victims of a Map: a bilingual anthology of Arabic Poetry* and *On Entering the Sea: the Erotic and Other poetry of Nizar Qabbani* both of which are highly recommended (see *Appendix 3*). Such is the power of the written word in Arabic that the script itself, even today, often forms the focus of modern art in the region, with astonishingly varied paintings based around particular letters, words or Koranic phrases, a natural evolution from calligraphy. In decorative Islamic art so-called Arabesque designs evolved, based round complex geometric shapes and patterns. Such designs were not used simply because the Prophet Muhammad, keen to steer his followers away from worship of idols, prohibited representational art, but also because of the positive effect of enhancing closeness to God. Liberated from the distraction of earthly images, the mind of the believer was free to focus exclusively on the concepts of infinity and to enter a pious hypnotic state similar to meditation.

PROVERBS Throughout the centuries proverbs have always been central to Arabic literature, far more widely used on a daily basis in everyday speech than in the West. In one small Levantine village alone a scholar recorded more than 4,000 proverbs. Due to this remarkable prevalence of the proverb, one is used at the front of each chapter of this book to add local colour and flavour. Here are a few more to end on:

> To understand a people, acquaint yourself with their proverbs.

> The whole world is nothing but the scraping of a donkey.

> When one door closes, a hundred others open.

Climb like a cucumber, fall like an aubergine.

One hundred years of tyranny is preferable to one night of anarchy.

If you wish to be obeyed, do not ask the impossible.

The man who cheats you once will cheat you a hundred times.

Too soft and you will be squeezed; too hard and you will be broken.

After 40 years the Bedouin took revenge and said: I have been quick about it.

Better than beauty is a camel.

Who does not think his fleas are gazelles?

If you are patient in a moment of anger, you will escape a hundred days of sorrow.

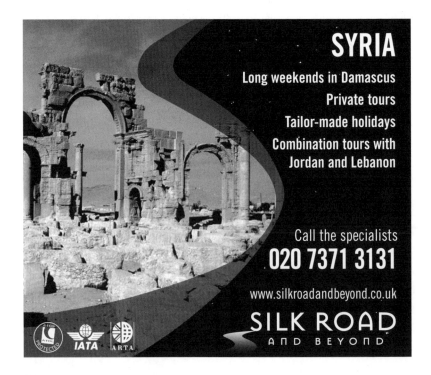

2

Practical Information

The pleasure of food and drink lasts an hour, of sleep a day, of women a month, but of a building a lifetime.

WHEN TO VISIT

Spring and autumn are the best times to visit when temperatures are around 25°C. The best months are April, May, June, September and October when sunshine is guaranteed and there is unlikely to be any rain. The summer months of July and August are very hot by Western standards with temperatures as high as 40°C, making it difficult to walk round sites except in the early morning or late afternoon. In the winter months it can be cold and wet but there will be beautiful clear sunny days as well. Daylight hours are very short though, with sunset as early as 16.20 in December, and sunrise at 06.40. Even in late March sunset is at 17.45, with sunrise at 05.30, so you should take this into account when planning itineraries. In high summer it gets dark at 20.00 and light at 05.15, so all in all it pays to be an early riser. In Ramadan opening hours are foreshortened, with museums, sites and monuments tending to close at 15.00, so this must be taken into account in your itinerary planning as well.

HIGHLIGHTS

- Palmyra, especially at sunrise or sunset, legendary Roman caravan city of the desert, guarded by its Arab fort, see pages 225–47
- Krak des Chevaliers, best-preserved Crusader castle in the world, see pages 197–202

AVERAGE MONTHLY TEMPERATURES AND RAINFALL

Damascus	J	F	M	A	M	J	J	A	S	O	N	D
Min °C	2	4	6	9	13	16	18	18	16	12	8	4
Max °C	12	14	18	24	29	33	36	37	33	27	19	13
Days with rain	7	6	2	1	1	0	0	0	2	2	5	5
Monthly rain (mm)	43	43	8	3	3	0	0	0	18	10	41	41
Aleppo	J	F	M	A	M	J	J	A	S	O	N	D
Min °C	1	3	4	9	13	17	21	21	16	12	7	3
Max °C	10	13	18	24	29	43	36	36	33	27	19	12
Days with rain	11	10	7	4	2	0	0	0	0	4	8	10
Monthly rain (mm)	89	64	38	28	8	3	0	0	0	25	56	84

- Damascus, its walled Old City like another world, rich in palaces, *souks* and churches, the awe-inspiring Great Umayyad Mosque at its heart, see pages 57–103
- Aleppo citadel, a military masterpiece, with the most authentic medieval *souk* in the Middle East at its foot, see pages 147–50
- Bosra, its superbly preserved Roman theatre concealed inside a 13th-century Arab fortress, see pages 210–17
- Cities of the Dead, early Byzantine ghost towns in the hills around Aleppo, see pages 130–7, 163–8, 172–3
- Waterwheels of Hama, still working on the Orontes river, see pages 118–23
- Saladin's Castle, most dramatically sited Crusader castle in the world, see pages 174–7
- Apamea, Roman city with a superb colonnaded street even longer than that of Palmyra, in a rural setting, see pages 124–8

SUGGESTED ITINERARIES

It would take a good four weeks to see all the places described in this book, which very few visitors will have the time to do. The following is a selection of itineraries according to your available schedule.

ONE WEEK (1,200KM EXPRESS TOUR)
1 night Damascus: Old City and *souks*
1 night Lattakia, via Ma'loula and Krak des Chevaliers
2 nights Aleppo, via Ugarit, Saladin's Castle and St Simeon; Old City and *souks*
1 night Hama, via Cities of the Dead and Apamea
1 night Palmyra
1 night Damascus

ONE WEEK
1 night Damascus: Old City and *souks*
1 night Hama, via Krak des Chevaliers
2 nights Aleppo, via Apamea and Dead Cities: St Simeon, Citadel, Old City
2 nights Palmyra
1 night Damascus

TWO WEEKS
2 nights Damascus: Old City and *souks;* National Museum
1 night Hama, via Ma'loula
3 nights Aleppo, via Apamea and Dead cities; St Simeon; Citadel, Old City, Jdeideh
1 night Lattakia, via Qalb Lozeh and Saladin's Castle
1 night Krak des Chevaliers, via Ugarit and Marqab
1 night Hama, via Husn Suleyman and Masyaf
2 nights Palmyra, via Masyaf and Qasr Ibn Wardan
2 nights Bosra, via Shahba and Qanawat; via Salkhad and Mushannaf
1 night Damascus, via Ezraa

THREE WEEKS
2 nights Damascus: Old City and *souks;* National Museum, Tekkiye Suleymaniye, Jebel Qassioun
2 nights Bosra, via Quneitra and Ezraa; via Salkhad and Suweida
3 nights Hama, via Mushannaf and Shahba; via Apamea and Dead Cities; via Husn Suleyman and Masyaf

1 night Krak des Chevaliers

3 nights Lattakia, via Amrit, Tartous and Marqab; via Ugarit and Ras Al-Basit; beach rest

4 nights Aleppo, via Saladin's Castle and Qalb Lozeh; Citadel, Old City, Jdeideh; Dead Cities circuit; St Simeon, 'Ain Dara and Cyrrhus

2 nights Deir Ez-Zour, via Resafe and Halabiye; via Mari and Doura Europos

2 nights Palmyra, via Qasr Al-Hayr Ash-Sharqi; Talila Reserve

2 nights Damascus, via Dmeir, Ma'loula and Seydnaya; revisit National Museum and Old City

TOUR OPERATORS

Andante Travels Ltd The Old Barn, Old Rd, Alderbury, Salisbury SP5 3AR; ✆ 01722 713800; f 01722 711966; e tours@andantetravels.co.uk; www.andantetravels.co.uk. Specialists in archaeology and ancient history, running 2 tours a year in Apr and Oct, with a max group size of 18. 11-day tours cost c£1,850.

Andrew Brock Travel Ltd 29A Main St, Lyddington, Oakham, Rutland LE15 9LR; ✆ 01572 821330; e abrock3650@aol.com; www.coromandelabt.com ACE Study Tours (Association for Cultural Exchange), Babraham, Cambridge CB2 4AP; ✆ 01223 835055; f 01223 837394; e enquiries@acestudytours.co.uk; www.study-tours.org. Archaeology-focused tours 3 times a year in Apr and Oct, usually incorporating Baalbek in Lebanon. Tours last 10–15 days with group size ranging between 15 and 25.

Cox and Kings ✆ 0207 873 5000; www.coxandkings.co.uk. Culture and history-focused tours from Mar to Nov. Group size around 15. Lebanon and Syria: the Grand Tour, 11 nights, 10 departures a year, £1,295 per person; Syria Journey to Palmyra, 8 nights, 7 departures a year, £1,045 per person; Jordan and Syria the Ancient Lands, 11 days, 9 departures a year, £1,375 per person.

Hinterland Travel 12 The Enterdent, Godstone, Surrey RH9 8EG; ✆/f 01883 743584; e hinterland@btconnect.com; www.hinterlandtravel.com.

Martin Randall Travel Ltd Voysey House, Barley Mow Passage, London W4 4GF; ✆ 020 8742 3355; f 020 8742 7766; e info@martinrandall.co.uk; www.martinrandall.com. The most upmarket tours available, offering 6 nights for £1,550 and 9 nights for £1,900, complete with guest lecturer. They usually travel 2 or 3 times a year, in Apr, and in late Oct.

Silk Road and Beyond 371 Kensington High St, London W14 8Q2; ✆ 020 7371 3131; e sales@silkroadandbeyond.co.uk; www.silkroadandbeyond.co.uk.

The Traveller and Palanquin 92–93 Great Russell St, London WC1B 3PS; ✆ 020 7436 9343; f 020 7436 7475; e info@the-traveller.co.uk; www.the-traveller.co.uk. Cultural tours with guest lecturer, 6-night Taste of Damascus tour including Palmyra and Krak des Chevaliers, and 16-night Ancient Syria tour, covering all the major ancient sites.

Voyages Jules Verne 21 Dorset Sq, London NW1 6QG; ✆ 0845 166 7068; www.vjv.com Since 2005 the company has been offering a succession of 6-night tours which whiz round Bosra, Palmyra, Lattakia and Krak des Chevaliers. The basic price is low at under £500 but be prepared for all the extras which get sprung on you after arrival as it transpires many items are not included.

ADVENTURE TOUR OPERATORS Look at www.responsibletravel.com to see some small group tours (4–20 people) through Syria and Jordan, starting in Damascus, ending in Aqaba, including short camel treks in Wadi Rum and camping or simple village accommodation. Hiking and trekking are offered, with tours of 14–18 days. Also www.imaginative-traveller.com offers a nine-day grassroots adventure tour in simple accommodation. Local tour operators based in Damascus, like Adonis (*www.syriaadonistravel.com*) and Abinos Travel (*www.abinostravel.com*), will also arrange tailor-made adventure tours in 4x4 vehicles with camping and simple hotels.

There are no organised facilities for hikers, or indeed proper maps, but the terrain in the mountains inland from the coast is spectacular, especially in April/May with the spring blossom and in September/October with autumnal colours. To lend purpose and goal, the adventurous could attempt to walk for example between the Crusader castles, *à la* T E Lawrence (though he did it in the blazing heat of August). The best map for this is the free Ministry of Tourism leaflet, 'Syria: the Coast', which you can pick up at the airport on arrival.

TOURIST INFORMATION

The Ministry of Tourism is planning to open a network of tourist offices in key European capitals which will certainly help matters. At the moment nothing is available outside the country except a few vague brochures from the embassies. Within the country there are tourist offices at Damascus airport and in downtown Damascus and in the main towns. Office hours are erratic and they can often be shut for no obvious reason. The members of staff are friendly and well meaning but often not very well informed. You can usually pick up a map and some general leaflets on the different regions of the country if you happen to find them open. Often the hotel reception desks are more useful places for general information and for arranging excursions or booking accommodation. See *Appendix 3* for useful websites to browse before travelling to Syria.

RED TAPE

Visas must be obtained from the Syrian embassy in your home country before departure. In London visas take four working days to process but it is best to allow a week. The whole process can be done efficiently by post using Special Delivery envelopes to ensure safe arrival and return of your passport. Obviously you must have no Israeli stamp in your passport. Visas are always valid for 15 days but can be extended relatively simply once you are inside the country at the Ministry of the Interior. The cost is based on a reciprocal scheme, according to what your home country charges Syrians for a visa to enter. For UK passport holders the cost at the time of writing was £36 for a single entry visa which is valid for three months from the date of issue, and £50 for a multiple entry which is valid for six months from the date of issue. If sent by post, payment must be in the form of a postal order; if in person, then cash only. Visa application forms must be submitted in duplicate with two passport photos and a letter from your employer confirming your identity and your travel to Syria as a tourist. If you are retired or have no employer a letter on any official letterhead will suffice. All visas allow for a stay of 15 days only, and if you stay longer you must apply in person with at least two further passport photos for a visa extension at a passport and immigration office in Damascus, Aleppo, Homs, Lattakia or Tartous. There is a small fee of about S£50 and the normal pattern is you submit it one day and come back to collect it the next, so make sure you apply in time before it expires and that you plan to be in the same place for two days. There is no Passport office in Palmyra.

Visas for Lebanon can be purchased at the border, as long as your passport has no entry/exit stamps from the border crossings between Jordan and Israel and between Egypt and Israel. The cost is also lower than if you get it beforehand in your own country. A 48-hour transit visa is free.

Ⓔ FOREIGN MISSIONS AND ASSOCIATIONS IN DAMASCUS

French Cultural Centre Bahsa, Damascus; ☏ 2316181/82; www.ccf-damas.org
British Council Shaalan, Maysaloun St ☏ 3310631; f 3321467; e

general.inquiries@bc/damascus.bcouncil.org. Library, internet access and café.
Goethe Institute 60 Adnan Malki St, PO Box 6100; ☏ 3336673; f 3320849

Danish Institute (Bait Al-'Aqqad), 8-10 Souq Al-Souf, Souq Midhat Pasha, PO Box 1262, Damascus; ℡ 2238038; f 2249014: e did@scs-net.org; www.damaskus.dk
Dutch Cultural Centre PO Box 36103 Mezzeh; visitors' address: East Mezzeh, Al-Farabi St No:85, Damascus; ℡ 61249791, 6117622; f 6120515; e director@niasd.org; www.niasd.org.
British Embassy Malki PO Box 37: ℡ 3739241/2; f 3739236, Open 08.00–15.15. Closed Fri and Sat.
United States Embassy Abu Roumaneh PO Box 29: ℡ 3333052, 3330788, 3332815
French Embassy Ayoubi Street PO Box 769; ℡ 3327993, 3327995

German Embassy Malki PO Box 2237: ℡ 3323801/2
Australian Embassy Mezzeh PO Box 3882: ℡ 6111226, 6132424
Canadian Embassy Mezzeh PO Box 3393: ℡ 6116692, 6116851
Danish Embassy Abu Roumaneh PO Box 2244: ℡ 3337853
Italian Embassy Malki PO Box 2216: ℡ 3338338, 3332621
Netherlands Embassy Abu Roumaneh: ℡ 3336871
Spanish Embassy Abu Roumaneh PO Box 392: ℡ 6132900/1

GETTING THERE AND AWAY

✈ **BY AIR** This is the way the vast majority of visitors will arrive, mainly at Damascus International Airport, though there are now also direct international flights into Aleppo. The national airline, Syrian Arab Airlines (*27 Albemarle St, London W1X 3HF;* ℡ *020 7493 2851;* f *020 7493 2119; www.syriaair.com*), has a fleet of about 14 aircraft, most of them purchased in the 1980s, and flies direct to most European and Arab capitals. It offers the cheapest deals from most European capitals and also flies direct from London. Prices range from as little as £200 return in low season (January and February) to £360 return in high season in July and August, with the average price around £300 return. From London there are three flights a week to Damascus on Tuesdays, Thursdays and Sundays, with direct return flights on Saturdays, Mondays and Wednesdays. Flight timings are excellent, with outward flights leaving at 10.00 in summer. 09.00 in winter, arriving c16.30. Return flights to London leave c15.30, arriving c19.30. In low season especially during January and February flights are sometimes rather annoyingly diverted via Manchester at short notice to collect a few extra passengers, when numbers are too low to justify running the extra flight from Manchester. The flight itself takes around four and a half hours, but the apparent discrepancy in landing times is due to the two-hour time difference with Damascus being that much ahead of London. In-flight food is basic but adequate. Alcohol is served erratically, even in first class, and usually in the form of whisky or gin. Wine is very rarely available. There is no in-flight entertainment so come equipped with your own stock of books, puzzles or whatever. Their flight number code is RB, rather confusingly, and in Damascus their head office is at Youssef Al-Azmeh Square (℡ *+963 11221 4923*). It is not, at the time of writing, possible to book direct through the website. Bookings still have to be in person with cash or debit card, or by cheque in the post, allowing ten days for clearing. If you use a credit card there is an extra charge. You can also collect booked tickets at the airport by paying in cash. On the return, especially in high season, flights have to be reconfirmed in person at one of the Syrian Air offices, as many tickets have open dates, with local Syrians changing their times at the last minute, so flights can sometimes be overbooked. In low season it is not strictly necessary, though it is always worth double checking the timings have not changed.

Other airlines like British Airways, Air France or KLM also fly to Damascus but are more expensive, and involve a change of plane in Paris or Amsterdam or at the very least a stopover on the tarmac in Beirut. Timings are often poor and frequently involve arriving and departing in the early hours of the morning. In-flight food and entertainment goes some way to compensating, depending on your

2

priorities. To research prices on these other airlines you can check the following websites: www.travelocity.com, www.expedia.co.uk and www.lastminute.com. Syrian Airlines does not yet feature on these websites so it is easily overlooked. Damascus International Airport is some 30km south of the city at the end of a specially built dual carriageway, and the drive into the centre takes about 30 minutes. The fixed fare for taxis is S£500 (cUS$10) irrespective of whether you buy a taxi ticket at the special desk in the Arrivals hall or just go out of the terminal building yourself and get your own yellow taxi. Taxis are always in abundant supply, and apart from at peak season times in July and August when planes are packed with visitors from other Arab countries, the airport is not that busy. It is rare to find more than two or three flights arriving simultaneously.

On arrival all foreigners have to complete an entry/exit card, the colour of which varies randomly from yellow to blue and green, before they can proceed to passport control and go to collect luggage. This card must then be shown at passport control and stamped, and you must be careful to keep it on you to show again as you leave at the departures passport control kiosks. In the arrivals area before passport control there is also a money-changing booth which offers a better rate than the hotels. Certain nationalities, such as Indians and Pakistanis, can also obtain visas here on arrival, but all European visitors must have obtained their visa in their own country before departure.

It is essential to reconfirm your flight at least 72 hours before leaving. Sometimes this can be done by your hotel on the phone, but the surest way is to go in person to the local airline office and get the confirmation sticker put in your ticket, especially if you are flying in busy high season times. On departure, make sure you have some Syrian cash left: the fare back out to the airport from Damascus city centre will be S£500; a luggage trolley costs S£75; if a porter helps you he will expect S£25; then there is a plastic cling-film wrapping service you can pay for if you are worried about the condition of your bags or cases in their stuffed-to-bursting state, costing around S£200 per bag; and finally there is the departure tax, currently S£200 (cUS$4), to buy your departure tax stamp, which will then be stuck in your passport by the passport control officials, before they let you through into the departures area. The departure tax rates for Syrians are very high at S£1,700, while other Arab nationalities' rates are also high at S£800. The departures area is surprisingly comfortable, with good duty free shops up the escalators, and the pleasant self-service restaurant café area has huge picture windows. Last-minute presents can be bought here in the duty-free gift shop, as well as cigarettes and alcohol, and there is even a stall beside the restaurant selling CDs and tapes of Arabic and Western music. Another good stall for gifts is the excellent Ghraoui chocolate and sweets shop, where you can mix and match from a large range of exotically named sweets, all locally made from chocolate, nuts, dates and dried fruits. There are internet facilities both in the main airport foyer before check-in, and in the departures area after check-in.

BY BOAT Syria's main ports for commercial traffic are Lattakia and Tartous, both on the eastern Mediterranean with frequent services to Cyprus, Greece and Turkey. By virtue of its 'Alawi connections and the former President Hafez Al-Assad's family links to the town, Lattakia's port has, since 1975, seen heavy investment, becoming Syria's premier port. There is a commercial ferry, Helas Ferries, that transports lorries from Volos near Thessaloniki in Greece to Tartous, that will take normal cars if it has room. Facilities are basic in the extreme, with scarcely edible food, but the virtue is cheapness. There is also a weekly commercial ferry to Lattakia from Alexandria via Beirut, stopping in Cyprus in the summer.

BY TRAIN Trains are not widely used except for commercial traffic. The state railway company has about 140 diesel locomotives, mainly Soviet built. In 1997 a team of Iranian consultants began feasibility studies on the construction of a metro system in Damascus. Work has begun on a major upgrading of the country's rail network and ambitious plans have been drafted for expanding port infrastructure. The Ministry of Transport is also attempting to increase rail usage for both freight and long-distance passenger services and to improve commuter train services. For the moment they are extremely slow and unreliable, from whatever direction you choose to enter, and therefore not recommended.

 BY CAR Border crossings are slow and tedious with many stages, tending to take at least an hour, irrespective of whether your entry is from Turkey, Lebanon or Jordan. You can drive your own vehicle into Syria with no *carnet de passage* as used to be required. You simply have to buy a temporary customs waiver at the border which costs cUS$50, together with third party insurance, roughly US$40 per month. The road network is pretty good, with dual carriageways linking the main cities.

 BY BUS Long-distance intercity luxury buses are an efficient and extremely cheap way to travel but you need to have obtained your visa in advance as it is not possible to purchase a Syrian visa at the border. Exiting Syria, however, it is possible to buy a tourist visa at the border for any of the three neighbouring countries to which travel is an option, namely, Turkey, Jordan and Lebanon. From Turkey the buses come direct from Antakya, crossing at the Bab Al-Hawa border point, arriving at Aleppo bus station or at the Pullman Harasta bus station 5km northeast of Damascus city centre. From Jordan JETT, the national bus carrier, and Karnak, one of the Syrian bus companies, run from Amman, crossing at the Jabir–Nasib border. The journey between Amman and Damascus takes four to five hours depending on how busy the border crossing is, and costs S£300.

From Lebanon buses run every one or two hours from Beirut to Damascus and the journey takes three to four hours depending on border times and costs S£200, so cheap you can probably afford to buy two seats to stretch out, as your seat tickets are numbered. The other bonus of the Lebanese crossing is the duty-free shop on the Syrian side of the border, before the long no-man's land, where cheap alcohol, cigarettes, perfume, chocolate and other duty-free goods can be bought but only in US dollars. It has excellent modern toilet facilities.

BY TAXI FROM LEBANON If you want to do the whole process more quickly, you can simply take a taxi from Beirut to Damascus for about US$40. The taxi to the border from Beirut takes roughly an hour, the border procedures with filling in the exit and entry documentation takes between 30 minutes and an hour depending on traffic, and the final stretch on to Damascus takes a little over half an hour. All taxis have permits, so can cross the border with no problem, just stopping at customs for the car to be checked. To catch a taxi back again from Damascus to Beirut costs cUS$30, and a Lebanese visa costs US$33 for one month, or less for shorter periods.

 HEALTH *with Dr Felicity Nicholson*

WATER Whilst tap water is considered drinkable in Syria, it is highly recommended that you drink the very cheap and ubiquitously available mineral water which Syria produces itself from its mountain springs. There are several makes and all are fine.

Dr Jane Wilson-Howarth

Long-haul air travel increases the risk of deep vein thrombosis (DVT). Although recent research has suggested that many of us develop clots when immobilised, most resolve without us ever having been aware of them. In certain susceptible individuals, though, large clots form and these can break away and lodge in the lungs. This is dangerous but happens in a tiny minority of passengers.

Studies have shown that flights of over five and a half hours are significant, and that people who take lots of shorter flights over a short space of time form clots. People at highest risk are:

- Those who have had a clot before – unless they are now taking warfarin
- People over 80 years of age
- Anyone who has recently undergone a major operation or surgery for varicose veins
- Someone who has had a hip or knee replacement in the last three months
- Cancer sufferers
- Those who have ever had a stroke
- People with heart disease
- Those with a close blood relative who has had a clot

Those with a slightly increased risk:

- People over 40
- Women who are pregnant or have had a baby in the last couple of weeks
- People taking female hormones or other oestrogen therapy
- Heavy smokers
- Those who have very severe varicose veins
- The very obese
- People who are very tall (over 6ft/1.8m) or short (under 5ft/1.5m)

VACCINATIONS The only official vaccine required is yellow fever for those travelling from an infected area and over one year old. However, it is sensible to be up to date with tetanus, diphtheria and polio (ten yearly), typhoid (three yearly) and have been immunised against hepatitis A. Vaccines such as Havrix Monodose or Avaxim give protection for one year and can be boosted to extend this for 20 years. It can be used even up to the day before departure,

For longer trips (more than four weeks) or for those working in medical settings or with children, then hepatitis B vaccination will be recommended. Three doses of vaccine can be given over as little as 21 days if time is short (Engerix only).

Rabies vaccination may also be suggested for longer trips or if you are going to be more than 24 hours from medical help. Again three doses of vaccine can be given over 21 days.

MALARIA The risk of malaria in Syria is from May to October and exists along the northern border in the northeast of the country. Very few travellers do more than just pass through this area either to or from Turkey but if you are planning to linger then malaria tablets (chloroquine taken once weekly) will be recommended. These should be started a week before going to the area, whilst there and continued for four weeks after leaving. The tablets are best taken with the evening meal and at any rate never on an empty stomach. They may not be suitable for people with bad psoriasis and should be avoided if you are epileptic, taking Zyban (an anti-smoking drug) or certain heart medications.

A deep vein thrombosis is a blood clot that forms in the deep leg veins. This is very different from irritating but harmless superficial phlebitis. DVT causes swelling and redness of one leg, usually with heat and pain in one calf and sometimes the thigh. A DVT is only dangerous if a clot breaks away and travels to the lungs (pulmonary embolus). Symptoms of a pulmonary embolus (PE) include chest pain that is worse on breathing in deeply, shortness of breath, and sometimes coughing up small amounts of blood. The symptoms commonly start three to ten days after a long flight. Anyone who thinks that they might have a DVT needs to see a doctor immediately who will arrange a scan. Warfarin tablets (to thin the blood) are then taken for at least six months.

PREVENTION OF DVT Several conditions make the problem more likely. Immobility is the key, and factors like reduced oxygen in cabin air and dehydration may also contribute. To reduce the risk of thrombosis on a long journey:

- Exercise before and after the flight
- Keep mobile before and during the flight; move around every couple of hours
- During the flight drink plenty of water or juices
- Avoid taking sleeping pills and excessive tea, coffee and alcohol
- Perform exercises that mimic walking and tense the calf muscles
- Consider wearing flight socks or support stockings (see www.legshealth.com)
- Take a meal of oily fish (mackerel, trout, salmon, sardines, etc) in the 24 hours before departure to reduce blood clotability and thus DVT risk
- The jury is still out on whether it is worth taking an aspirin before flying, but this can be discussed with your GP.

If you think you are at increased risk of a clot, ask your doctor if it is safe to travel.

Basic sensible precautions include using DEET-containing insect repellents such as Repel on all exposed skin from dusk till dawn, and sleeping under permethrin-impregnated mosquito nets at night. Prompt investigation of a fever is vital and any high fever occurring more than seven days into the area and up to one year after leaving (most especially in the first three months) should be reported to a doctor. For those travelling in more remote areas, standby treatment may be recommended. Discuss this with your doctor before you go.

INSURANCE Make sure you have travel insurance that covers you for medical emergencies. The best way is to have an annual worldwide policy so that you are always covered wherever you go, and family policies of this type usually cost less than £120 for the whole year.

MEDICAL ADVICE AND CHECKLIST Syria is not a disease-ridden country and by being sensible in what you eat and do, you are most unlikely to have any problems. Salads are freshly prepared and are fine as hygiene standards in restaurants are basically good. Salads in the hotels can be less fresh, so exercise your judgement when choosing. Squeezing lemon juice over the salad (lemon wedges are liberally added as garnish anyway in most places) also helps to sterilise. Avoid too much olive oil in the first few days as your digestive system is likely to protest just from the unaccustomed extra oiliness. Eat plenty of the good flat Arabic bread to help soak up the oil. As in most Middle Eastern countries, antibiotics can be bought over the counter at any chemist. However it is always best to be prepared and so you would be wise to carry with you the following medications:

- Anti-diarrhoea pills. If your over-the-counter drugs bought in your home country do not work, you can go to any chemist and buy Ercefuryl capsules which work wonders. For really desperate cases you can buy over the counter a drug called Lamutile (formerly Lomotil) which is guaranteed to stop diarrhoea in its tracks, but should not be taken for more than two or three days. These drugs, combined with a day of no food, just fizzy lemonade or Coke every hour, will sort out virtually every case.
- Antihistamine tablets. Something like Clarityn will protect you against every allergic reaction, such as to dust, insect bites or even heat rash.
- Insect repellent wipes or spray to prevent any mosquito bites. Syria is not generally mosquito-ridden, as the climate is dry not humid, but prevention is simple and easy.
- Paracetamol. It is always useful for unexpected headaches or other aches and pains which could otherwise detract from your holiday.
- Plasters and antibacterial cream, to make sure a little cut does not turn into anything else.
- Sore throat lozenges. It is often quite windy and dry in Syria and it is best to suck a lozenge the moment you feel your throat getting uncomfortable.
- Eye drops. The wind and dust combined with strong sunlight can cause irritation and redness to those with sensitive eyes, so something soothing is a good precaution. If you get an actual eye infection, antibiotic eye drops can be bought over the counter.
- Sun cream, at least factor 15, preferably 25 or above for the face. Try to keep out of the strongest sun between 11.30 and 15.00, or if you have to be out then, wear a hat.

TRAVEL CLINICS AND HEALTH INFORMATION A full list of current travel clinic websites worldwide is available from the International Society of Travel Medicine on www.istm.org. For other journey preparation information, consult www.tripprep.com. Information about various medications may be found on www.emedicine.com.

UK

Berkeley Travel Clinic 32 Berkeley St, London W1J 8EL (near Green Park tube station); ☎ 020 7629 6233
British Airways Travel Clinic and Immunisation Service 213 Piccadilly, London W1J 9HQ; ☎ 0845 600 2236; www.ba.com/travelclinics. Walk-in service (no appointment necessary) Mon, Tue, Wed, Fri 08.45–18.15, Thu 08.45–20.00, Sat 09.30–17.00. As well as providing inoculations and malaria prevention, they sell a variety of health-related goods.
Cambridge Travel Clinic 48a Mill Rd, Cambridge CB1 2AS; ☎ 01223 367362;
e enquiries@cambridgetravelclinic.co.uk; www.cambridgetravelclinic.co.uk. Open Tue–Fri 12.00–19.00, Sat 10.00–16.00.
Edinburgh Travel Clinic Regional Infectious Diseases Unit, Ward 41 OPD, Western General Hospital, Crewe

Rd South, Edinburgh EH4 2UX; ☎ 0131 537 2822; www.link.med.ed.ac.uk/ridu. Travel helpline (☎ 0906 589 0380; open weekdays 09.00–12.00). Provides inoculations and antimalarial prophylaxis and advises on travel-related health risks.
Fleet Street Travel Clinic 29 Fleet St, London EC4Y 1AA; ☎ 020 7353 5678; ww.fleetstreetclinic.com. Vaccinations, travel products and latest advice.
Hospital for Tropical Diseases Travel Clinic Mortimer Market Building, Capper St (off Tottenham Ct Rd), London WC1E 6AU; ☎ 020 7388 9600; www.thehtd.org. Offers consultations and advice, and is able to provide all necessary drugs and vaccines for travellers. Runs a healthline (☎ 0906 133 7733) for country-specific information and health hazards. Also stocks nets, water purification equipment and personal protection measures.

Interhealth Worldwide Partnership House, 157 Waterloo Rd, London SE1 8US; ☎ 020 7902 9000; www.interhealth.org.uk. Competitively priced, one-stop travel health service. All profits go to their affiliated company, InterHealth, which provides health care for overseas workers on Christian projects.

MASTA (Medical Advisory Service for Travellers Abroad) London School of Hygiene and Tropical Medicine, Keppel St, London WC1 7HT; ☎ 0906 550 1402; www.masta.org. Individually tailored health briefs available for a fee, with up-to-date information on how to stay healthy, inoculations and what to bring. There are currently 30 MASTA pre-travel clinics in Britain. Call ☎ 0870 241 6843 or check online for the nearest. Clinics also sell malaria prophylaxis memory cards, treatment kits, bednets, net treatment kits.

NHS travel website www.fitfortravel.scot.nhs.uk. Provides country-by-country advice on immunisation

and malaria, plus details of recent developments, and a list of relevant health organisations.

Nomad Travel Store/Clinic 3–4 Wellington Terrace, Turnpike Lane, London N8 0PX; ☎ 020 8889 7014; travel-healthline (office hours only) ☎ 0906 863 3414; ℮ sales@nomadtravel.co.uk; www.nomadtravel.co.uk. Also at 40 Bernard St, London WC1N 1LJ; ☎ 020 7833 4114; 52 Grosvenor Gardens, London SW1W 0AG; ☎ 020 7823 5823; and 43 Queens Rd, Bristol BS8 1QH; ☎ 0117 922 6567. For health advice, equipment such as mosquito nets and other anti-bug devices, and an excellent range of adventure travel gear.

Trailfinders Travel Clinic 194 Kensington High St, London W8 7RG; ☎ 020 7938 3999; www.trailfinders.com/clinic.htm

Travelpharm The Travelpharm website, www.travelpharm.com, offers up-to-date guidance on travel-related health and has a range of medications available through their online mini-pharmacy.

Irish Republic

Tropical Medical Bureau Grafton Street Medical Centre, Grafton Buildings, 34 Grafton St, Dublin 2; ☎ 1 671 9200; www.tmb.ie. A useful website specific

to tropical destinations. Also check website for other bureaux locations throughout Ireland.

USA

Centers for Disease Control 1600 Clifton Rd, Atlanta, GA 30333; ☎ 800 311 3435; travellers' health hotline: 888 232 3299; www.cdc.gov/travel. The central source of travel information in the USA. The invaluable *Health Information for International Travel*, published annually, is available from the Division of Quarantine at this address.

Connaught Laboratories PO Box 187, Swiftwater, PA 18370; ☎ 800 822 2463. They will send a free list

of specialist tropical-medicine physicians in your state.

IAMAT (International Association for Medical Assistance to Travelers) 1623 Military Rd, 279, Niagara Falls, NY14304-1745; ☎ 716 754 4883; ℮ info@iamat.org; www.iamat.org. A non-profit organisation that provides lists of English-speaking doctors abroad.

International Medicine Center 920 Frostwood Dr, Suite 670, Houston, TX 77024; ☎ 713 550 2000; www.traveldoc.com

Canada

IAMAT Suite 1, 1287 St Clair Av W, Toronto, Ontario M6E 1B8; ☎ 416 652 0137; www.iamat.org

TMVC Suite 314, 1030 W Georgia St, Vancouver BC V6E 2Y3; ☎ 1 888 288 8682; www.tmvc.com

Australia, New Zealand, Singapore

TMVC ☎ 1300 65 88 44; www.tmvc.com.au. 31 clinics in Australia, New Zealand and Singapore, including: *Auckland* Canterbury Arcade, 170 Queen St, Auckland; ☎ 9 373 3531
Brisbane 6th floor, 247 Adelaide St, Brisbane, QLD 4000; ☎ 7 3221 9066

Melbourne 393 Little Bourke St, 2nd floor, Melbourne, VIC 3000; ☎ 3 9602 5788
Sydney Dymocks Bldg, 7th floor, 428 George St, Sydney, NSW 2000; ☎ 2 9221 7133
IAMAT PO Box 5049, Christchurch 5, New Zealand; www.iamat.org

South Africa and Namibia

SAA-Netcare Travel Clinics P Bag X34, Benmore 2010; www.travelclinic.co.za. Clinics throughout South Africa.
TMVC 113 D F Malan Dr, Roosevelt Park,

Johannesburg; ☎ 011 888 7488; www.tmvc.com.au. Consult website for details of other clinics in South Africa and Namibia.

IAMAT 57 Chemin des Voirets, 1212 Grand Lancy, Geneva; www.iamat.org

SAFETY

Contrary to its image, Syria is probably one of the safest countries in the world. Violent or petty crime towards foreigners is virtually non-existent, and at the time of writing no foreigner had ever been the target of violence. Such violence as does exist is usually in the context of a family feud where honour is implicated and retaliation is considered necessary to safeguard the family reputation. To steal something from a foreigner would be regarded as shameful and against the principle of hospitality to the guest. That said, there have been occasional cases of pickpocketing and passport theft in the Damascus and Aleppo *souks,* though visiting Russians renewing their Turkish visas are the prime suspects rather than local people.

The concept of 'health and safety' is one which has yet to take hold in Syria. Such matters are entrusted to God. Consequently motorcyclists never wear helmets and many motorists do not wear seatbelts (most cars do not even have them in the back seat). It is not unusual to see an entire family crowded onto one moped, each member perched nonchalantly in some precarious position. A helmet would in any event be difficult to reconcile with a headdress. In rural areas up to 30 members of the extended family are routinely transported to and from the fields in the back of a pick-up trucks often with animals bundled in, too.

POLICE Police are not in evidence in Syria, except the traffic police who stand at busy junctions and control the traffic flow. There are no police checkpoints except in areas of military sensitivity, and as a tourist the only ones you are ever likely to come across are at Mari, close to the Iraqi border, where there is a simple checkpoint at which your passport has to be produced, and at the approach to Quneitra in the Golan Heights near what is now the Israeli border. The police are courteous and friendly, never aggressive unless you have done something you shouldn't, like photograph military installations.

WOMEN TRAVELLERS Women travelling alone are not bothered or hassled in the way that they are in the north African Arab countries like Morocco. Such behaviour is considered shameful and most Syrians have a natural dignity which prevents them going down that road. Syria is very tolerant of the Western habit of women travelling alone, though most will wonder quite why there is no man in tow and some will indeed unashamedly ask outright. Syrian women would certainly be most unlikely to go on holiday abroad alone, and if they were not married, they would travel with other relations. Wearing something that can pass as a wedding ring helps, though they will still ask why your husband is not with you. If you are an older woman, you can always say you are a widow, and the more children you can claim to have the better. Body language is very important and eye contact with men should be kept to a minimum. As long as you act modestly and do not appear to be actively looking for a man, you will be accepted and welcomed. In restaurants there are often family areas, and as a single woman you should aim to sit as close as possible to other women, not near groups of men.

FACILITIES FOR SPECIFIC TRAVELLERS

TRAVELLING WITH FAMILIES AND CHILDREN Syrians, like all Arabs, adore children, and families with all ages of children will always be made to feel very welcome everywhere, including hotels and restaurants. Family rooms in hotels are a rarity though, with rooms having either a big double bed or twin beds, and the Arab approach is that children just pile in with their parents. In restaurants local children even of very young ages stay up till late at night, happily fiddling or playing at the table with no screaming or tantrums. There is no specific kiddies' food on offer on menus. Children just eat smaller versions of whatever the adults have. Chips and bread are always good staples and most children also love *falafel* (deep-fried chickpea balls) and the various dips. The fact that so much eating takes place with fingers using the flat Arab bread as a scoop rather than with cutlery also appeals. Pavements and alleys are often uneven in the cities, so pushchairs can be a struggle and are best left at home. Child-carrying harnesses are much more practical for very little ones. Older children need to be good walkers, as much time will be spent exploring on foot both in the cities and on sites in the countryside. Protection from the sun is vital for young skins, with high-factor suncreams and hats that you should bring with you from home, as you cannot rely on finding them inside the country. Children love mosques, especially the big ones like the Umayyad Mosque in Damascus, which are treated by local children like an open playground. You can picnic in them, or climb anything climbable, and no-one will bat an eyelid or dream of ticking you off. Public loos are few and far between, so in the cities you have to use restaurant facilities and in the countryside the nearest rock or bush.

DISABLED TRAVELLERS Syria has no disabled facilities and exploring the cities in a wheelchair, with the uneven pavements, would be a major challenge. Many restaurants are on the ground floor, but often with small steps up or down. The big five-star hotels are better, with lifts and even the occasional ramp, but the smaller hotels are simply not equipped for disabled visitors.

WHAT TO TAKE

Sun cream is essential, at least factor 15, and apart from the medical items listed earlier, a torch and binoculars can be useful, and make sure you always have toilet paper to hand in your pocket or your bag. A small calculator is useful to help convert currencies. Insect repellent in the form of wipes or sprays guarantees no bites and ear plugs guarantee no interrupted sleep from the dawn call to prayer. A torch for dark recesses of castles like Krak des Chevaliers is recommended (but remember to keep it on you all the time, not in your bag in the hotel). There is virtually no shade in many extensive sites like Palmyra or Apamea, so a sunhat and sunglasses to protect from the very bright light are important. After dusty journeys and picnics wet wipes are also a good idea and very easy to keep in a pocket at all times.

MAPS The best two maps are those by Freytag & Berndt and by Geoprojects. The best place to buy maps in the UK is Stanfords (*12–14 Long Acre, London WC2E 9LP* ✆ *020 7837 2121*). Inside the country the Ministry of Tourism has some basic maps which you can pick up at their desk in Damascus airport arrivals hall on the far right as you exit from the customs area, and you can also buy local maps in Avicenne, the best foreign bookshop in Damascus, located in Brazil Street, the same street as the Omayad Palace Hotel, near the Cham Palace Hotel. Car hire firms will also give tourist maps out for free with your car.

CAMERA ADVICE It is best to bring with you as much film as you think you will need, as it will not only be cheaper but probably better quality than film bought in Syria. Shops in five-star hotel chains like the Cham Palace group tend to sell

Ariadne Van Zandbergen

EQUIPMENT Although with some thought and an eye for composition you can take reasonable photos with a 'point-and-shoot' camera, you need an SLR camera if you are at all serious about photography. Modern SLRs tend to be very clever, with automatic programmes for almost every possible situation, but remember that these programmes are limited in the sense that the camera cannot think, but only make calculations. Every starting amateur photographer should read a photographic manual for beginners and get to grips with such basics as the relationship between aperture and shutter speed.

Always buy the best lens you can afford. The lens determines the quality of your photo more than the camera body. Fixed fast lenses are ideal, but very costly. Zoom lenses are easier for change composition without changing lenses the whole time. If you carry only one lens, a 28–70mm (digital 17–55mm) or similar zoom should be ideal. For a second lens, a lightweight 80–200mm or 70–300mm (digital 55–200mm) or similar will be excellent for candid shots and varying your composition. Wildlife photography will be very frustrating if you don't have at least a 300mm lens. For a small loss of quality, tele-converters are a cheap and compact way to increase magnification: a 300mm lens with a 1.4x converter becomes 420mm, and with a 2x it becomes 600mm. Note, however, that 1.4x and 2x tele-converters reduce the speed of your lens by 1.4 and 2 stops respectively.

For photography from a vehicle, a solid beanbag, which you can make yourself very cheaply, will be necessary to avoid blurred images, and is more useful than a tripod. A clamp with a tripod head screwed onto it can be attached to the vehicle as well. Modern dedicated flash units are easy to use; aside from the obvious need to flash when you photograph at night, you can improve a lot of photos in difficult 'high contrast' or very dull light with some fill-in flash. It pays to have a proper flash unit as opposed to a built-in camera flash.

DIGITAL/FILM Digital photography is now the preference of most amateur and professional photographers, with the resolution of digital cameras improving the whole time. For ordinary prints a 6 megapixel camera is fine. For better results and the possibility to enlarge images and for professional reproduction, higher resolution is available up to 16 megapixels.

Memory space is important. The number of pictures you can fit on a memory card depends on the quality you choose. Calculate in advance how many pictures you can fit on a card and either take enough cards to last for your trip, or take a storage drive onto which you can download the content. A laptop gives the advantage that you can see your pictures properly at the end of each day and edit and delete rejects, but a storage device is lighter and less bulky. These drives come in different capacities up to 80GB.

it at inflated prices, and even have disposable cameras in case your own is lost or malfunctions. Standard AA batteries are available, but not the good-quality ones like Duracell or Panasonic, so again it is best to bring what you need with you. For digital cameras, remember to bring your adapter if you have rechargeable batteries, and a memory card big enough to store all your holiday photos till you get home and can load them into your computer. Museums, especially the bigger ones like the Damascus National Museum, either ask you to leave your camera at the entrance or else forbid the use of flash photography. If you need to get film developed locally there are several shops in Damascus along Barada Street and on Martyr's Square which have modern, fully automated processing and printing labs.

Bear in mind that digital camera batteries, computers and other storage devices need charging, so make sure you have all the chargers, cables and converters with you. Most hotels have charging points, but do enquire about this in advance. When camping you might have to rely on charging from the car battery; a spare battery is invaluable.

If you are shooting film, 100 to 200 ISO print film and 50 to 100 ISO slide film are ideal. Low ISO film is slow but fine grained and gives the best colour saturation, but will need more light, so support in the form of a tripod or monopod is important. You can also bring a few 'fast' 400 ISO films for low-light situations where a tripod or flash is no option.

DUST AND HEAT Dust and heat are often a problem. Keep your equipment in a sealed bag, stow films in an airtight container (eg: a small cooler bag) and avoid exposing equipment and film to the sun. Digital cameras are prone to collecting dust particles on the sensor which results in spots on the image. The dirt mostly enters the camera when changing lenses, so be careful when doing this. To some extent photos can be 'cleaned' up afterwards in Photoshop, but this is time-consuming. You can have your camera sensor professionally cleaned, or you can do this yourself with special brushes and swabs made for the purpose, but note that touching the sensor might cause damage and should be done only with the greatest care.

LIGHT The most striking outdoor photographs are often taken during the hour or two of 'golden light' after dawn and before sunset. Shooting in low light may enforce the use of very low shutter speeds, in which case a tripod will be required to avoid camera shake.

With careful handling, side lighting and back lighting can produce stunning effects, especially in soft light and at sunrise or sunset. Generally, however, it is best to shoot with the sun behind you. When photographing animals or people in the harsh midday sun, images taken in light but even shade are likely to be more effective than those taken in direct sunlight or patchy shade, since the latter conditions create too much contrast.

PROTOCOL In some countries, it is unacceptable to photograph local people without permission, and many people will refuse to pose or will ask for a donation. In such circumstances, don't try to sneak photographs as you might get yourself into trouble. Even the most willing subject will often pose stiffly when a camera is pointed at them; relax them by making a joke, and take a few shots in quick succession to improve the odds of capturing a natural pose.

Ariadne Van Zandbergen is a professional travel and wildlife photographer specialising in Africa. She runs the Africa Image Library. For photo requests, visit www.africaimagelibrary.co.za or contact her on ariadne@hixnet.co.za.

ELECTRICITY Power supply is 220v, 50Hz; plugs and sockets are the Continental two-pin type. Power cuts are rare these days.

WEIGHTS AND MEASURES

Syria uses the metric system, so distances are given in kilometres. The table below gives conversions to the imperial system:

1cm	0.4 inch
1m	3.3 feet
1m	1.09 yards

1 litre	1.06 quarts								
1 litre	0.22 gallon								
1 kg	2.2 pounds								
Degrees Celsius		–5	0	5	10	15	20	25	30	35
Degrees Fahrenheit		23	32	41	50	59	68	77	86	95

TIME

Syria is two hours ahead of the UK all year round except for the month of October when clocks in Syria have gone back at the end of September, while in the UK they do not go back till the end of October, so then it is only one hour ahead. Winter GMT+2, summer GMT+3.

$ MONEY AND BANKING

The Syrian pound, variously abbreviated as SY, SYP, SL or S£ (again, no one way can be regarded as the right way) was until February 2006 pegged to the US dollar and consequently prices in hotels for example have tended, especially at the upper end of the market, to be quoted in US dollars. At the time of writing however, it was pegged to the euro, so if this turns out to be a permanent rather than a temporary move, prices will increasingly be quoted in euro. The official exchange rate in June 2006 was US$1 = S£50, £1 = S£93 and €1 = S£64.

Many shops selling carpets and souvenirs will exchange foreign currency on the spot, offering the same rate as the official one, which is posted in the papers, in the banks and on the Commercial Bank of Syria website www.cbs-bank.com. Banking hours have been dramatically increased to 08.00–18.00 daily except Fridays and computerisation has been introduced in banks, aiming for a paperless system in future.

Avoid travellers' cheques as they are difficult and time-consuming to change and only certain banks will accept them. US dollars in cash are the best and most stable, though euros and pound sterling in cash are also accepted but less desirable and the shop owners do not always know the up-to-date rates. ATMs (usually in purpose-built kiosks) are also spreading fast, especially in Damascus, where there is one inside the walls beside Bab Sharqi in the Christian quarter, and one just outside the walls in front of the citadel, across the road from the Souk Al-Hamadiye pedestrian underpass, opposite the law courts. These will accept most Western credit and debit cards and give you the official rate in Syrian cash instantly. Credit cards are increasingly accepted in four-star hotels and upwards and in many of the more upmarket restaurants in the cities. Petrol stations do not accept them, neither will the smaller hotels, but the bigger car hire firms like Chamtour/Hertz will.

Syrian cash will be needed for entry fees, taxi fares, restaurants and small purchases in the *souk*. Notes come in S£1,000, 500, 200, 100 and 50 denominations. The smaller notes like S£100 and 50 are very useful for taxis and entry fees. Coins come in S£25, 10, 5 and even 2, and are very useful for small tips. In some public toilets in the cities S£10 is actually charged for both men and women so it is always a good idea to keep some coins on you.

BUDGETING The cost of living in Syria is basically low. Food is cheap and this is reflected in the cost of eating out, where a meal for two without alcohol in a good class of restaurant will cost S£300–500 (US$6–10). If you want alcohol the cheapest is 'araq, the local aniseed spirit, similar to but smoother than the Greek *ouzo* and the Turkish *raki* at only S£50 (US$1) per glass, followed by beer, where a 500ml bottle of local beer is S£100 (US$2) and a 300ml can of imported, usually

Lebanese or Egyptian beer is S£150 (US$3). Wine is the most expensive form of alcohol, with local wine around S£500 (US$10) and Lebanese wine from S£800–1,400 (US$16–24) depending on make and vintage. Car hire costs around US$50 per day including insurance and tax for an average four-door saloon car, a double room in a three to four-star hotel costs around US$80, and the standard entrance fee at sites and museums is S£75 for minor sites and S£150 for major sites. It is therefore reasonable to budget US$10 per day per person for food, US$40 per day per person for accommodation and US$5 per day per person for entry fees and taxi fares, making a total daily budget per person of US$55, not including car hire. If you are on an organised package, you will need no more than a bit of incidental spending money, say US$5 per day, but maybe some spare cash for presents in case the shops where you buy do not take credit cards. *Souk* stallholders take cash only, Syrian pounds for small items, though most are happy to take US dollars for more expensive items. Cash in euros or pounds sterling is increasingly accepted by shops.

Entry fees Entry fees for sites and museums are set for foreigners at either S£150 each for major sites such as Palmyra and the Damascus National Museum, or S£75 for more minor sites like Resafe and small museums. Local people pay a fraction of this, in line with their level of income.

Tipping On the whole Syrians expect tips less than many Arab countries where it is endemic, certainly less than Egypt or Morocco, but a tip is always appreciated. This is not just for foreigners, it is a general principle that the better off give a bit of extra to the less well off who have done a service. In restaurants, 5% extra to the bill is fine. A guardian who has come specially to open something should get S£100 (US$2) and so on. Guides, if they are employed officially by your tour operator, appreciate foreign currency, and should be tipped, anything from US$5 to US$25, depending how pleased you are with their service, how long they have been with you, and how big your group is. Taxi drivers, however, do not expect tips. Just give S£50 for any fare in town, and for any further distance the agreed amount only. Never give money to someone from whom you ask directions or who invites you to drink a cup of tea, as that would be insulting and cause offence. In hotels the luggage carrier should get S£25-50 depending on the amount of your luggage and the class of your hotel.

GETTING AROUND

PUBLIC TRANSPORT Yellow taxis are plentiful and cheap in the cities and no fare within the city should cost more than S£50 (US$1). City buses are crowded and dirty and to be avoided. There is no metro in Damascus though there have been feasibility studies, so once the funds are available it will probably happen. A taxi up to Jebel Qassioun will cost S£200–300 depending on your bargaining powers.

For travel further afield yellow taxis are still remarkably cheap by European standards, so even a taxi from Damascus to Homs for example, a journey of 162km, costs only S£2,000 (US$40). A lot cheaper but requiring more organisation, are the very comfortable buses which travel frequently between the main towns, but you have to buy your ticket the day before to be sure of a seat, from the bus station which in Damascus is in Baramkeh, north of Martyr's Square. The journey from Damascus to Aleppo takes five hours. Trains are very slow and not even worth enquiring about. From Baramkeh microbuses (white minibuses seating about ten people)) run to all the local destinations around Damascus, as far as Zabadani (a 45-minute journey costing S£20) and Khan Arnabeh (the closest

Syria has an excellent and efficient bus network, provided by competing deluxe bus companies linking all the main cities and beyond into the neighbouring countries of Turkey, Lebanon and Jordan. There is no need to book ahead unless you are travelling over busy holiday times, and tickets are so cheap you may well feel it is worth buying the numbered seat next to you for leg room and stretching space. There are short tea-stops en route at places with good toilet facilities. Approximate journey times from Damascus are five hours to Aleppo, three hours to Palmyra, three to four hours to Beirut and four to five hours to Jordan, depending on border traffic. Costs range from S£200 for a three to four hour journey such as for Beirut or Palmyra, up to S£500 for a longer journey such as Aleppo or Antakya in Turkey. Each city has its own bus station, but the hub of the whole system is in Damascus, where buses operate out of two stations: Baramkeh for all destinations south including Bosra, Beirut and Amman, and Pullman/Harasta for all destinations north including Tartous, Lattakia, Palmyra, Deir Ez-Zour and Aleppo. Baramkeh is 400m south of the National Museum in a huge chaotic open space divided into three sections, one for deluxe buses, one for microbuses and one for service taxis. There are many companies to choose from, such as Karnak, Al-Ahlia and Qadmous, and all are of a similar standard, so the simplest option is to choose on the basis of which timing suits you best. All offer water and snacks and some even have television. There is never a shortage of touts offering to help you find your way, as it can be rather confusing, with each bus company having its own ticket office. The Pullman/Harasta bus station is inconveniently located 5km north east of the city centre, and the same system applies, with a range of companies competing for the same routes, so you choose the best timing and buy your ticket at that company's office.

place for Quneitra), a journey of an hour costing S£20. Service taxis are a bit more expensive than the deluxe buses, costing S£350 to Beirut and S£400 to Amman.

CAR HIRE Car hire is readily available from companies like Chamtour/Hertz and Europcar, usually offering various sizes of Renault, Peugeot or Ford. Three days is usually the minimum car hire period, and the cost is around US$50 a day with unlimited kilometres for a standard-size car, including comprehensive insurance. An International Driving Licence is recommended but not essential, as UK and European national licences seem to be acceptable, and the minimum age is 23 or sometimes 25 depending on the firm. There is a choice of limited or unlimited kilometres, limited being cheaper if you are not going far. The deposit is usually taken by credit card, then torn up on safe return of the car. Always make sure you have the telephone number to call in the event of breakdown or accident, and check the seat belts work, both front and back (if any). If you are too daunted by the prospect, it is not hugely more expensive to hire a car with a chauffeur, at a cost of about US$90 a day. The driver also expects a tip of cUS$10. If you do this for more than a day trip, make sure the price includes the chauffeur's meals and accommodation as well as the petrol. Hire cars cannot cross borders into neighbouring countries.

DRIVING Petrol is incredibly cheap as it is heavily subsidised, and diesel is even cheaper. Petrol stations outside the cities can be quite widely spaced so never let the fuel gauge fall below quarter full. Motoring is on the right and speed limits are 90kmh on normal roads and 110kmh on dual carriageways. Seat belts in the back are very rare. They generally work in the front though are not worn much by local people. The road network is pretty good on the whole, but signposting can leave something to be desired and is sometimes only in Arabic. You must be prepared to stop and ask frequently. You will find people very helpful. Drivers are generally quite well behaved, better than in Lebanon, Egypt and some European countries like Italy or Portugal. Night-time driving should be avoided if possible, as verges are often not marked and many vehicles have faulty lights. It gets dark early in Syria, as early as 16.30 in winter, and in the summer around 19.00.

✈ **BY AIR** Syrian Airlines has domestic flights from Damascus to Aleppo (as many as ten a day) for around US$20 one-way. A return ticket costs US$38. There are also cheap daily flights to Lattakia and Deir Ez-Zour.

ACCOMMODATION

Syria has a surprising number of five-star luxury-class hotels, especially in Damascus, such as the Meridien, the Sheraton, the Semiramis and the newest addition, the Four Seasons. The only five-star hotel to have a chain all round the country though is the Cham Palace group, owned by Syrian millionaire and benefactor Osmane Aidi. He also owns Cham Car (Hertz agency) and Cham Tour. Prices in these five-star hotels start from around US$100 and go as high as US$325 for the best category of double room in high season. In Damascus in high season there is an acute shortage of accommodation, so booking ahead is essential. These hotels have all the usual five-star facilities like swimming pool, tennis courts, health club, etc and several restaurants to choose from.

There is also rock-bottom accommodation, very cheap at around S£600 per night (US dollars are not used at these establishments) with shared bathroom facilities and poor hygiene standards. What Syria lacks is enough accommodation in the middle category, in the three- and lower four-star class. Notable exceptions are places like the Omayad Palace, heavily used by businessmen, costing around US$90 for a double room, or the three-star Carlton Hotel, both in Damascus, and the Baron in Aleppo, costing around US$40 for a double room. In places like these your bathroom is en suite and there is usually an adequate restaurant, but there is no pool or gym or business centre with internet facilities, for example.

One category of hotel that is just beginning in Syria and will be the key to high-quality tourism in future, is the bijou style of old renovated Ottoman houses. There are several in Aleppo, all in the Christian quarter of Jdeideh, and one or two in the Old City of Aleppo. In the Old City of Damascus a handful have now opened. The first (April 2005), is near Bab Touma, called Beit Al-Mamlouka, with eight beautifully restored rooms round a courtyard, and in early 2006 the extraordinary Talisman Hotel opened in the Jewish quarter, on a lavish scale and with a huge pool in its courtyard. Prices for the existing places are currently high, in the five- star bracket, but in future it is to be hoped that more in the three and four star bracket will appear to help fill the accommodation gap in Damascus. In time and given political stability many such establishments will doubtless appear, along the lines of the Moroccan *riads* in Marrakesh, offering a similar kind of experience, of an intimate handful of rooms round a courtyard, breakfast taken on the roof terrace or beside the courtyard fountain, and often with a private *hammam*.

✗ EATING AND DRINKING

Syrian food is excellent and may be familiar to you through both Lebanese and Turkish restaurants in your own country. The ingredients are of superb quality and the fruit and vegetables all freshly harvested and local. No food is imported and flown halfway round the world. Almost all restaurants serve Syrian rather than foreign food and you tend only to find such things as Italian or Chinese restaurants in the five-star hotels. Every meal begins with *mezze*, a selection of starters, some hot, some cold, which are various salads, such as *muhammara* ('reddened'), an excellent walnut paste spiced with hot chilli pepper; *tabbouleh*, finely chopped mint, tomatoes, onion and cracked wheat; *baba ghanouj*, a chunky aubergine dip; *moutabbal*, smooth aubergine dip with sesame paste mixed in; and *hummus*, chickpea dip which the Greeks have tried to claim as their invention. Among the hot *mezze*, the best are the various types of *kibbeh*, minced lamb with onion and pine nuts served either flat or in conical balls or even raw, only for the brave. The main courses are various chicken kebabs or lamb kebabs, the best of which are *shish taouk*, *kebab halabi* (Aleppo kebab), served between flat Arab bread and with a tomato sauce, and *kebab urfali* (Urfa kebab from Turkey). When a menu mentions 'meat' it means lamb. Beef is relatively rare and the most expensive form of meat. Chicken is always listed separately under 'chicken'. Fish is also rare and is just called 'fish'. It is probably true to say that most Arabs do not really understand fish or appreciate its diversity. The furthest they tend to go is to call it white fish as opposed to red fish. Desserts are either plain fruit – grapes, strawberries, cherries, apples, bananas, oranges – or sweet sticky pastries soaked in honey with pistachio or almond, reminiscent of Greek *baklava*, and the ubiquitous crème caramel.

In the big hotels an open buffet is the usual style in the restaurants, so tour groups can go and select whatever they want in whatever order they want. At the other end of the scale, Syrian fast food has been around on the street for centuries, long before the Americans, with stalls selling falafel, hot chickpea balls stuffed into pitta bread with salad, and *shawarma*, thinly sliced lamb or chicken from a revolving spit like the Turkish *döner* kebab, again stuffed in bread with salad, to be eaten on the move by other shop owners and stall holders. Since they are so freshly prepared they are always safe to eat in the main towns.

Arabs have a very sweet tooth and drink their tea and coffee heavily sugared. Tea is always drunk black in little glasses, and mint tea is popular after meals as a *digestif*. Coffee is either Turkish with thick dregs, or clear greenish cardamom coffee as drunk by the Bedouin. Cardamom coffee is always drunk unsweetened but Turkish can be ordered with lots of sugar, *sukkar kateer,* medium sugar, *mutawassit,* or no sugar, *saadeh.* Coffee with milk is available only with Nescafé. They also like

ARAB FOOD AND DRINK INVENTIONS

The concept of the three-course meal, consisting of soup, followed by fish or meat, then fruit and nuts, was brought to Córdoba in Spain in the 9th century by Ali Ibn Nafi, nicknamed Ziryab (the Blackbird), from Iraq. He also introduced crystal glass, which had been invented in the Arab world by Abbas Ibn Firnas in the 9th century after experiments with rock crystal. We can thank the Arabs too for the accompanying drinks of coffee and alcohol. Arabic 'qahwa' became the Turkish 'kahve', then the Italian 'caffe' and then the English coffee. The first coffee beans were exported from Ethiopia to Yemen, where Sufis (Islamic mystics) boiled the bean and drank the liquid to stay awake all night on special occasions. By the late 15th century it reached Mecca, then Turkey via Damascus on the Hajj route, and found its way to Venice in 1645. It was brought to England in 1650 by a Turk who opened the first coffee house in Lombard Street in the City of London. As for alcohol, the process of distillation was invented around 800 by Jabir Ibn Hayyan, Islam's foremost scientist, even though drinking the product was forbidden (*haram*) in Islam.

sweet fizzy drinks and there are local versions of Cola, lemonade and orangeade which are a touch sickly for the European palate. There are even now locally made diet versions. Fresh juices are another favourite, with freshly squeezed orange juice the commonest, but also lesser-known combinations like fresh lemon juice with mint, called *laymoun bi-na'na'*. On the alcoholic front, there is local beer called Barada, an imported beer called Al-Maza from Lebanon which costs a bit more and even an alcohol-free local beer. The main spirit is *'araq*, the aniseed flavoured clear drink that goes cloudy when water or ice is added, which is very cheap and sold in small bottles. The local wine is usually St Simeon, available in red or white, and considered rather inferior to the more expensive Lebanese wines such as Ksara and Kfreya. The choice in restaurants is not big, never usually more than three or four types if you are lucky.

PUBLIC HOLIDAYS AND FESTIVALS

The following are fixed public holidays, when government offices close, but shops stay open:

New Year	1 January
Revolution Day	8 March
Mothers' Day	21 March
Evacuation Day	17 April (evacuation of the French in 1946, national day)
Labour Day	1 May
Martyrs' Day	6 May
Christmas Day	25 December

In addition to these there are the variable Muslim holidays which are fixed according to the lunar calendar and therefore move backwards by about 11 days each year. In 2005 they fell as follows:

Eid Al-Adha (Feast of the Sacrifice)	21–24 January
Al-Hijra (Muhammad's flight from Mecca)	10 February
Mawlid An-Nabi (Prophet's birthday)	21 April
Eid Al-Fitr (Feast at the end of Ramadan)	3–5 November

In 2006 they are estimated to be on:

Eid Al-Adha	10–13 January
Al-Hijra	30 January
Mawlid An-Nabi	10 April
Eid Al-Fitr	23–25 October

In 2007 they are estimated to fall on:

Eid Al-Adha	30 December–2 January
Al-Hijra	19 January
Mawlid An-Nabi	31 March
Eid Al-Fitr	12–14 October

The various Christian holidays like Easter and saints' days are celebrated by the relevant Christian sects, their dates all varying slightly, so their own businesses or shops will close on those days, but all other offices, shops and businesses stay open as usual. Make sure you have enough money to last during the three to four day bank and office closure of the major religious festivals. The bigger hotels will change money all the time anyway, but they may simply run out due to demand.

RAMADAN Visiting Syria during Ramadan, the ninth month of the Islamic lunar calendar, is not a problem as most restaurants continue to serve food and drink during the day. Out of respect it is advisable not to smoke, eat or drink publicly in the streets during daylight hours, and you will not see many Syrians breaking this rule. But again the view taken is that this is a private matter and what you do in private is your own affair. Office and shop hours are shortened, and most sites will shut around 15.00 so it does have the effect of foreshortening your day, which you must take into account in your itinerary planning. Once daylight is over of course, Ramadan is a time of great feasting and partying. Ironically for the month of fasting, more food is consumed during Ramadan than at any other time of year and shopkeepers always see it as their boom time, when everyone is buying gifts, visiting each other and entertaining at home. Sales of meat are always especially high in Ramadan. Most Syrian Muslims look forward to Ramadan as the highpoint of the year.

SHOPPING AND BARGAINING

Syria is an excellent place for buying good-quality souvenirs and gifts that are still made by local craftsmen. The best places to buy are the *souks* in the old cities of Damascus and Aleppo, and both also have a specially designated handicrafts market in Damascus beside the Tekkiye Suleymaniye complex, near the National Museum, and in Aleppo in Souq Ash-Shouneh at the beginning of the *souk* opposite the citadel. These areas are more sanitised for Western tourists and prices are fixed, but the range and choice are very good. Damascus is particularly noted for its embroidered tablecloths and napkins, and its *pashmina* shawls in beautiful elegant colours and traditional designs. Carpets and rugs are not made in Syria itself but you can buy here old and new rugs from Iran, Turkey or Turkmenistan at reasonable prices. Along Straight Street in the Old City of Damascus beyond the Roman Arch in the Christian quarter, you will find many shops selling antiques, and wooden marquetry pieces old and new, which is the great specialty of the Damascene cabinet makers. They make boxes, games, mirrors, pedestal tables that can be dismantled for easy transportation, and larger items of furniture like chests and wardrobes. There is also copper and brassware for sale, old and new, and many jewellery shops selling all types of gold and silver trinkets. Many of the more Bedouin-style items, like silver earrings with semi-precious stones such as jade, turquoise, lapis and coral are very beautiful and reasonably priced, costing around US$8, and make very good presents, easy to pack away in your luggage with little extra weight. Damascus tiles in their characteristic blues, greens and black are excellent value – modern, but made to look old. Traditional clothing for both men and women is another good buy, and old gowns in embroidered silk can still be found, though increasingly rarely. In the *souks* it is also fun to buy perfumes from the stall holders after trying what seems like hundreds, and spare some time in Damascus' Souk Al-Bezuriye for the fresh herbs and spices, which make easy, light gifts, though make sure they are properly sealed before packing in your luggage. Aleppo is famous additionally for its silk scarves and also the wonderful Aleppo dark green soap made from olive and laurel, packaged into all different shapes and sizes for gifts.

Bargaining is standard and you should aim to knock off around 20-30% of the originally quoted price. This is the norm for locals too, though they will be more

ARAB LIFESTYLE INVENTIONS

Numerous concepts that have influenced our lifestyle in the West originated in the Arab world, yet most of the time we remain in blissful ignorance of our debt. Carpets for example were regarded as part of paradise by medieval Muslims, who developed advanced weaving techniques, new colours and complex arabesque patterns which formed the basis of Islam's non-representational art. Floors in England, as Erasmus recorded, were 'covered in rushes, occasionally renewed, but so imperfectly that the bottom layer is left undisturbed, sometimes for 20 years, harbouring expectoration, vomiting, the leakage of dogs and men, ale droppings, scraps of fish, and other abominations'. The Arabs too first developed the idea of the garden as a place of beauty and meditation, creating the first royal pleasure gardens in 11th century Spain. Medieval Europe had only functional kitchen and herb gardens.

On the hygiene front Arabs perfected the recipe for soap which we still use today, combining vegetable oils with sodium hydroxide and aromatics such as thyme oil. Washing and bathing are religious requirements for Muslims, and a weekly visit to the *hammam* was de rigueur for men and women. The unwashed Frankish Crusaders arriving from Europe were distinctly pungent to Arab nostrils. Shampoo was first introduced to England by a Muslim who opened Mahomed's Indian Vapour Baths on Brighton seafront in 1759 and was subsequently appointed Shampooing Surgeon to kings George IV and William IV.

The practice of quilting came back to the West via the Crusaders. They saw Muslim warriors wearing straw-filled quilted canvas shirts instead of armour. As well as protection the quilted shirts also provided very effective insulation, and the idea for quilted bedding quickly transferred back to colder climates in northern Europe.

The list could go on and on, but includes the camera (Arabic 'qamara' meaning dark or private room), the fountain pen and the cheque (Arabic 'saqq' meaning a written vow to pay for goods when they were delivered, to avoid cash having to be transported across dangerous terrain). In the 9th century a Muslim businessman could cash a cheque in China drawn on his bank in Baghdad.

practised at the techniques of feigning indifference and then moving off to the next stall, to be called back with a lower price. In the specific handicraft *souks* in Damascus and Aleppo referred to above, prices are fixed, though there may be a bit of movement if you are buying in quantity.

 ## ARTS AND ENTERTAINMENT

There are cinemas in the big cities most of which show Western films with the original soundtrack and Arabic sub-titles. There is usually massive audience participation and it tends to be an all-male experience. Women would be well advised not to go alone as it would be seen to be inviting attention. For cultural entertainment there are concerts, operas and plays performed regularly at Dar Al-Assad, an impressive modern opera house set in grounds near Umawiyyeen Square. The Syrian National Symphony Orchestra plays at a high standard under its Armenian conductor, Missak Baghboudarian. Sometimes the cultural institutes like the Goethe Institute or the British Council sponsor a visiting performance. All entertainments and cinema showings are listed in the English-daily *Syria Times*.

SPORTS The five-star hotels offer tennis courts, swimming pools and fitness centres, and a few, like the Ebla Cham near Damascus airport, offer golf. On the coast the beach resort hotels offer waterskiing and windsurfing. The ubiquitous sport, played in all villages by all ages of youth, on whatever makeshift bit of ground can be found, is football. Some of the local tour operators can set up horseriding or camel-trekking tours.

❯ MEDIA AND COMMUNICATIONS

NEWSPAPERS The only daily English paper is the *Syria Times*, a flimsy and heavily controlled affair, but with useful practical information like exchange rates, emergency phone numbers and occasional interesting cultural items. There are three Arabic dailies: *Al-Ba'ath*, the political paper, *Ath-Thawra*, a government daily and *Tishrin* which has a little more independence. Once a week it runs a page called 'Hurra' (Free) which solicits articles from writers outside the paper, including members of opposition parties. Bashar himself is in favour of what he calls 'a calm, logical and balanced style that respects the intelligence of the audience'. He has also asked newspaper editors to stop referring to him as 'al-ra'id al-khalid' (the immortal leader).

RADIO AND TELEVISION BBC World Service can be reached at certain times of day on the following frequencies: SW6195kHz, 9410kHz, 12095kHz, MW1323kHz (227m).

Voice of America can be reached at certain times of day on these frequencies: SW 792kHz, 1260kHz, 1546kHz, 3985kHz, 5995kHz, 6040kHz, 7170kHz, 11965kHz and 15205kHz.

There are two Syrian TV channels whose programmes are listed in the *Syria Times*, and Channel 2 has many foreign programmes. The staple fare which Syrians love is Egyptian films, sitcoms and soaps. Most of the bigger hotels have satellite television, as do many private homes, so the simplest way to keep up with the news while away is by tuning in to BBC World or CNN. There are two Syrian radio channels which are both state-run. Most Syrians tune in to the Qatar-based Al-Jazeera news agency for coverage of the war in Iraq.

INTERNET The internet has hit Syria big time in the last few years and is growing at a ferocious pace, estimated at 45% per year. Bashar Al-Assad, the president, is the head of the Syrian Computer Society, so has always been keen to promote it and increase its accessibility. Syrians love technology and as the cost of computers gets lower and lower more and more individuals have their own facilities at home. Internet cafés are springing up everywhere, even in some of the restored courtyard houses of the Old City in Damascus like Bait Jabri and are very popular with the young. Many of these are based on dial-up systems rather than broadband, but rates are very low at S£50 (US$1) per hour. Increasing numbers of hotels and businesses have email addresses and websites. There is no censorship of websites any longer and it is very easy to access your emails. Both Yahoo and Hotmail websites were banned until late 2004 as potentially subversive, but those days mercifully are now over.

MOBILES The telephone system was modernised in 1996 and in 2000 Ericsson of Sweden installed a GSM system for mobiles which has been hugely successful. There are now two competing GSM networks, one operated by Ericsson the other by Syriatel, equipped by Siemens, and market penetration has soared in recent years, as Syrians love to talk and rates are relatively low. Mobile telephones have taken Syria by storm and adverts and billboards for the two networks dominate the cityscapes even more than the omnipresent pictures of the Assads, either Hafez the father, or now increasingly, Bashar the son, or else groupings with both or with the trio including Basil the dead brother who would have become president had he not been killed in a car crash. Smiling young faces beam out from the billboard adverts for Syriatel with Arabic slogans like 'Every Eid, may you be near', a clever twist on the standard Arabic Eid (religious festival) greeting 'Every year, may you be well.'

Coverage across the country is excellent and it is very satisfying to send a text home to the UK from the middle of the Syrian desert and then to receive a reply within minutes. UK mobiles work perfectly here and if you want to speak locally but not go the expense of buying a new handset, you can buy a Syrian SIM card for S£400, then buy a limited amount of charge credit starting from S£300 for a week. Locally costs are very low at S£4 per minute mobile to mobile, and S£6 mobile to landline. Remember to bring your charger and travel plug so that you can use the local two-pin standard European-style plug socket in your hotel room. Texting as a foreign visitor is by far the best way to keep in touch with friends and family back in your home country. It is cheap, simple and quick. International phone calls on land lines have been rendered virtually obsolete as a result, partly because of cost and partly because the international land line system is dodgy with poor line quality and many attempts required to get through. Shops specialising in mobile phones are all over the place in the cities and you will find the shop owners very knowledgeable and helpful. Note that a Blackberry will not work inside Syria because Syria is still on the GSM, not the GPRS network.

TELEPHONE CODES AND NUMBERS Calling Syria from overseas you must dial 00 + 963 + regional code without the 0 + the number itself. International phone calls from hotel rooms are extremely expensive. A fax sent back to your home country is much cheaper. Friends or relations attempting to ring through to you from abroad in your hotel room will experience great difficulty and huge patience is required by the caller, not to mention the expense.

Common country codes (from within Syria)
UK	00 + 44 + the number itself minus the 0
USA and Canada	00 +1 + the number itself
Australia	00 + 61 + the number itself

Local codes within Syria
Damascus	011	Bosra	015
Aleppo	021	Ma'loula	012
Homs	031	Palmyra	031
Hama	033	Safita	043
Lattakia	041	Tartous	043
Deir Ez-Zour	051		

International directory enquiries	☏ 149
National directory enquiries	☏ 147
Damascus airport	☏ 5445983/9

Emergency numbers
Ambulance	☏ 110
Fire	☏ 113
Police	☏ 112

Private hospitals in Damascus
Al-Chami Hospital (takes VISA,   ☏ (011) 373 4925
  MasterCard and American Express)

French Hospital	☏ (011) 444 0460
Italian Hospital	☏ (011) 332 6030
Central 24-hour Pharmacy	☏ (011) 445 2074

Arabic language schools in Damascus

ASP Centre, University of Damascus	☏ (011) 211 9853
Arabic Teaching Institute for Foreigners	☏ (011) 662 2268
IFEAD	☏ (011) 333 1962
Abu Nur Arabic Centre	☏ (011) 277 7158

POST Stamps to Europe cost S£18 for letters and S£10 for postcards. Stamps are sold by bookshops, newsagents and some souvenir shops and hotel receptions, as well as post offices, but these are difficult to find and very busy.

BUSINESS

Syria is a country riddled with the many-layered bureaucratic legacies of the Ottomans and the French and doing business successfully is all to do with being patient and developing the right contacts who will help you negotiate your way round or through it. If you can get through all the bureaucracy, there are generous taxation laws to encourage foreign investment.

Employment law is fiendishly complex and if you can keep your number of employees below five you will escape the need for complicated social security schemes. Labour is cheap by Western standards, with the daily rate for a manual labourer being about S£400 (c£4), or S£600 (£6) for a skilled labourer. A middle-range manager would expect to be paid in US dollars at around US$300–350 a month.

Now that private banks have opened as part of the banking liberalisation policy, it is possible to get a business loan from either BEMO or Bank of Syria Overseas. BEMO is a joint venture between Lebanon's Banque Europeene pour le Moyen Orient, Saudi Fransi Bank and local Syrian investors, and is one of Lebanon's larger foreign banks with a strong Syrian heritage, controlled by the Obeiji family – originally from Aleppo. Business is brisk and there are now several branches in Damascus, expanding to Aleppo, Homs and Lattakia. Bank of Syria Overseas, the first private bank to open in 2004, is a joint venture between Banque du Liban et d'Outre Mer (BLOM), the World Bank's International Finance Corporation and local investors. BLOM is Lebanon's largest bank, controlled by the Azhari family. It too has several branches in Damascus, expanding to Aleppo, Homs and Lattakia. Both banks take local and foreign currency deposits, offer short-term trade financing and issue letters of credit and guarantee. The third private bank, International Bank for Trade and Finance (IBTF), has strong Jordanian credentials, with 49% owned by Jordan's second-largest bank, the Housing Bank for Trade and Finance (*www.the-housingbank.com*). Its lead branch has a prominent location on the same square as the Hijaz railway station in Damascus' commercial centre, and plans to move quickly into retail banking, mirroring Housing Bank in Jordan. It was the first bank to have its own ATM, and offers a range of retail products including interest-earning current accounts, instant access deposit accounts, mortgages, education and car loans and even unsecured personal loans. Current banking rules mean that interest can be paid only on local currency accounts, not foreign currency accounts. There are cautious plans to open a stock market in Damascus, inspired by President Assad's visit to Turkey where he was impressed by the new Istanbul bourse.

Apart from the private banks, the government has implemented cuts in corporate taxation, down to the lowest rate of 20%, which compares favourably with neighbouring countries, Egypt 35%, Turkey 30% and Jordan 25-35%: all further evidence of its attempts to create a better business environment with more investor friendliness. Foreign investors may also repatriate their dividends and capital. Tourism projects and other important projects are allowed to be 100% foreign-owned, with no requirement to have a Syrian partner.

Syria has six free zones, three in Damascus, one each in Aleppo, Lattakia and Tartous, where business activities are not subject to Syrian law and regulations, being treated as activities conducted outside Syrian territory.

OPENING HOURS Friday is the weekly holiday when all banks, *souks*, government departments and most offices are closed. In Christian quarters shops close on Sundays instead and are open Fridays. Over the two major religious holidays of Eid Al-Fitr (after Ramadan) and Eid Al-Adha (Feast of the Sacrifice) all government offices, banks and most shops close for three days, but tourist sites stay open. See *Public holidays and festivals* (page 45) section for exact dates in 2006 and 2007.

Banks Banking hours were greatly extended in Aril 2005 and now all banks are open 08.00 till 18.00 daily except Friday.

Shops Shop hours are variable but are usually 09.30–19.00, though shops may often shut for two or three hours in the middle of the day, around 14.00-16.00 especially in summer, when many shop owners will go home for a late lunch and then have a sleep. *Souks* are closed Fridays.

Restaurants Lunch is generally served late, after 13.30, though most restaurants will open from 12.00, and dinner is also late, from around 21.00 to 23.00, though most restaurants will open at about 19.30 and not close till after midnight. In the Old City of Damascus most of the restaurants in the converted palaces and houses like Beit Jabri are open continuously from 12.00 to 24.00.

Offices Government departments and embassies are open approximately 08.00–15.00, while the private sector is more like 10.00–19.00. In Ramadan office hours are generally restricted, closing an hour or two earlier.

Museums and sites Museums across the country are closed on Tuesdays, but most sites are open daily, especially the major places like Palmyra and Krak des Chevaliers. Summer opening hours (1 Apr–30 Sep) are usually 09.00–18.00, while winter hours (1 Oct–31 Mar) are usually 09.00–16.00 because of failing daylight hours. In Ramadan hours are foreshortened and most places will close around 15.00.

BUYING A PROPERTY

The law in Syria recently changed to allow foreigners to buy property, part of a general liberalisation policy to encourage foreign investment. That said it is nevertheless a lengthy and complex bureaucratic process that takes at least a year before you will receive official papers saying the property is transferred to your name, even though you will have parted with the money many months earlier. There are at present no conventional estate agents offices where you can go and view the market. All is done by word of mouth, and various shopkeepers tend to double as middle men between vendor and purchaser and it is just 'known' who is considering selling. Knowledge of Arabic is an enormous help, though not essential if you have a translator you trust. Very occasionally there are adverts in the local papers, but these are generally in Arabic. At present in the Old City of Damascus you can buy a small house with say five rooms and an area of 150m², for about S£5.5 million (c£60,000), but for a bigger more elaborate house you can pay up to S£20 million (£210,000). Most will then require restoration which has to be completed according to stringent conservation controls and will cost at least half as much again. It is essential to have a lawyer you trust and to agree the fee in advance. The negotiating process with the family which is selling is often lengthy, involving several meetings, and once the price is agreed, a contract will be signed usually specifying payment in two or three instalments over a period of months. A cash deposit of around 10% is always expected on signature of contract, and if either side withdraws, that money may be lost. Your papers and the signed contract then have to pass through many stages and many government departments, including stringent security checks conducted by the 'Mukhaabaraat', the intelligence services. On completion of all the administrative paperwork you will finally be issued, usually about a year after the process was begun, with a Green Card, known locally as the 'Taaboo', which is the document showing the property officially registered in your name. At this stage you can apply for residence status, which relieves you of the necessity of obtaining a visa each time you enter the country.

CULTURAL ETIQUETTE

The golden rule is to stay polite, patient and calm at all times. If you lose your temper with a Syrian Arab you will have immediately lost their respect. Keep a sense of humour and be sociable and friendly. The social niceties are very important and Syrians would never launch straight into a serious topic or business matter, American-style, before the requisite greetings and enquiries after health and family have been completed. This is just regarded as basic good manners, and the fact that Americans do not adapt their usual direct approach to this part of the world helps earn them their bad reputation and unpopularity with Arabs in general.

RULES OF ETIQUETTE
- Always remove shoes before entering a mosque. Some mosques have a place where all shoes are deposited in exchange for a numbered token. In others, like the Umayyad Mosque, you simply carry them round with you. If you are fretful about sullying your socks, you can bring along 'mosque socks' to put on over your other socks, though it is surprisingly easy to forget to remove them at the end, thereby rather destroying the point.
- Men and children are generally happy to be photographed, but women should be asked first.
- Profuse thanks for a gift is not the Arab way, so do not expect it if you give a gift and do not make a fuss over a gift you have received.
- Outward displays of affection like kissing and petting are frowned on. A couple holding hands is acceptable but that is as far as it should go in public. Arab men often hold hands with each other and kiss each other on the cheek. It is normal friendship, not a sign of homosexuality.
- Do not flatter or compliment people on their children. You will be suspected of putting the 'evil eye' (the eye of the devil which brings bad luck) on them. The Arabic phrase you can use to ward off the evil eye is *'Ayn Allah yaHrasak*, meaning 'May the eye of God protect you' or *Al-Hasoud laa yasoud*, meaning 'The envious will not prevail'. A symbol of a blue eye is also a good luck symbol to keep you safe from the evil eye.
- Do not eat with your left hand or take a present with your left hand.

- As a woman do not make the first move to shake hands with a man. Wait till he offers it directly. If, on greeting, he holds his right hand to his chest instead of offering his hand, it means he is a practising Muslim and does not touch any woman who is not his wife or relation. Contact would also make him unclean before his prayers.
- Do not waste water.
- Set a good example by never throwing out your litter.
- In restaurants women travelling singly or in groups should eat in the family area, not out in the general area.
- Never go behind the iconostasis in Eastern churches. It is for priests only.
- Never take photos near borders, airports, dams or bridges.
- Do not provoke unwanted political discussions.
- As a man do not enquire after the health of women members of another man's family.
- As a man, do not flirt or make any physical contact with Syrian women.
- Avoid cynicism when discussing serious issues. To joke about such matters as death, tragedy, poverty or illness is regarded as very disrespectful.
- Avoid attempting to bribe an official of any sort. You could end up in jail.

DRESS AND BODY LANGUAGE Dignity is the key word here and it is important to dress respectfully and in a way that it not viewed as provocative. Shorts and sleeveless tops are best confined to the beach resorts, though short sleeves and trousers are fine for both sexes as long as they are not too tight or transparent. That said, some Syrian girl teenagers will themselves wear tight jeans and T-shirts, yet be walking along the street arm in arm with a veiled girlfriend of the same age. On the whole Syria is a tolerant society and the view is taken that such matters are personal and it is up to each individual to dress and behave in ways they feel comfortable. It is probably true to say that Christian women dress in a more Western fashion than Muslim women, and this is noticeable for example as you walk round the Old City of Damascus and move from the Muslim quarter into the Christian quarter.

Body language should be dignified too, and as a woman, the key rule is to avoid too much eye contact with men as you walk around; it will then be clear that you are not inviting attention. You need to maintain a balance and remain friendly and polite yet unavailable. It is very important to keep a proper distance in order to avoid confusion and embarrassment. If you accept hospitality as a woman and then appear too friendly and solicitous, the signals can easily be misread.

GIVING SOMETHING BACK

You should always be conscious, when visiting somewhere like Syria, that it is important to put back into the country more than you take out. Try to minimise your ecological footprint by being moderate in your water and electricity usage and always set a good environmental example by not throwing out plastic rubbish after picnics. Use local services wherever possible rather than foreign, so that your expenditure goes back into the economy. Fly with the national carrier, Syrian Airlines, which in any event offers the cheapest flights direct to Damascus from most European capitals, and at reasonable times of day rather than arriving in the middle of the night after a stopover en route like so many of the foreign carriers such as British Airways and Air France.

A certain amount of street begging goes on in the cities, and local people do generally give a few coins, especially to those with evident handicaps or disabilities, because there is no social security to help them. Islam advocates the giving of alms to the poor, *zakat* as it is called in Arabic, which is one of the Five Pillars of Islam.

Part Two

THE GUIDE

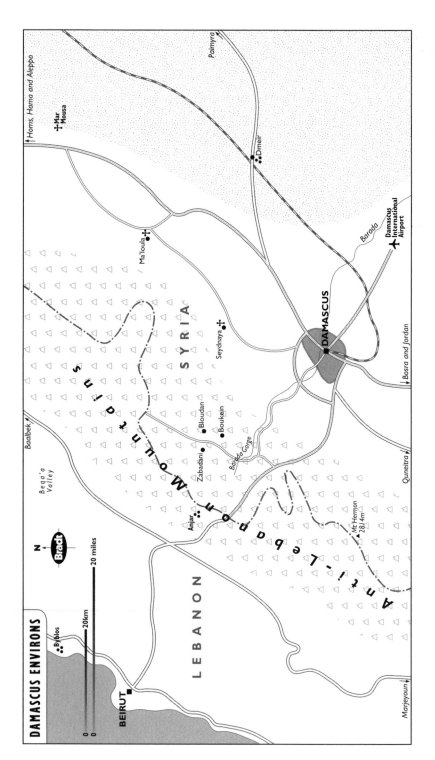

DAMASCUS ENVIRONS

N

Brad

0 20km
0 20 miles

BEIRUT

Byblos

LEBANON

Bega'a
Valley

Baalbek

Anjar

Zabadani

Mt Hermon
2814m

Anti-Lebanon Mountains

Marjeyoun

Quneitra

Bloudan

Boukein

Barada Gorge

Seydnaya

S Y R I A

Ma'loula

Mar
Mousa

Homs, Hama and Aleppo

Palmyra

Dmeir

Barada

DAMASCUS

Damascus
International
Airport

Bosra and Jordan

3

Damascus دمشق

If God did not forgive, Paradise would be empty.

Damascus is a timeless city, throbbing with life and vibrancy, seemingly at one with its past and present. Its people are calm and accepting, open to outside influences yet satisfied with the limitations of their daily lives. It is not a frantic or aggressive city. For a capital with a population estimated at four million, its mood is remarkably serene. They are not a people in a hurry to get somewhere. They are content to enjoy whatever pleasure or joy life offers, content with the moment they find themselves in. They appear to have an instinctive understanding of the local proverb: *As-Sabr Miftah al-Faraj*, 'Patience is the key to happiness.'

Nowhere is this mood of the city more apparent than in the Great Umayyad Mosque in the heart of the Old City. As soon as you enter, a wave of timelessness engulfs you. Syria was always a melting pot of people from Egypt, Asia Minor, Assyria, Babylon, Persia, Greece and Rome, and there is a sense here of the tides of history that have washed over the city, each leaving some mark, but each co-existing with its neighbour, an eclectic collection of styles, yet joining together to form one cohesive whole. Mark Twain wrote on his visit to Damascus in *The Innocents Abroad*:

> She measures time not by days and months and years, but by the empires she has
> seen rise and crumble to ruin. She is a type of immortality... Damascus has seen all
> that ever occurred on earth and still she lives. She has looked upon the dry bones of a
> thousand empires, and will see the tombs of a thousand more before she dies.

And so it is with the city itself. As the Great Umayyad Mosque is a symbol of how elements from disparate origins can come together to form a harmonious grouping, so the city itself, especially the Old City, combines old, new and renovated, Muslim, Christian and Jewish, religious, secular and touristic, all living side by side. In short it is a city at ease with itself, able to accept its shortcomings, accommodate its differences, and indeed be enriched by them.

SETTING

The reason for Damascus' location is less clear today than it was to early travellers, for the orchards and gardens that once covered some 30 square miles, called the Ghouta Oasis and fed by the waters of the Barada River (ancient Abana), have been swallowed up by the invasive sprawl of modern concrete, leaving just 15% of it behind. Visualising the earthly paradise here described by many early travellers is quite a feat of the imagination these days. But from Jebel Qassioun, the bare dramatic outcrop that rises abruptly to the north of Damascus, sheltering it from the elements, you can still glean a sense, especially at night when the concrete disappears into a sea of lights, of how this huge well-watered spot was like a port on the edge of the desert, the first haven of fertility, greenness and water, after the harshness of the unforgiving desert to the east. To the west the view is dominated by the high mountains of the Anti-Lebanon range, the highest of which at 2,814m, Mount Hermon, mentioned 15 times in the Bible, retains its snow-covered summit till June, whence its Arabic name Jebel Ash-Shaikh (Mountain of the Shaikh), like a white-haired elder.

The Barada River, source of Damascus' great fertility, was and still is fed by the melt-waters of Jebel Ash-Shaikh, flowing strongly through the city in the spring, skirting the northern walls. Tents were pitched along its green and grassy banks where merchants would refresh themselves and their animals till as late as the 20th century. Every house in the city had its own water supply in Ottoman times through a complex network of waterways and channels leading off from the river. According to well-documented traditions the Prophet Muhammad once came to the edge of Damascus accompanying a trading caravan owned by his wealthy merchant wife Khadija, 15 years his elder. The place where he stopped is still called Qadam, Arabic for 'foot', the last place he put his foot before refusing to go further. On his first glimpse of Damascus he said that if man could have but one paradise, he would have to give up the earthly paradise of Damascus in order to be able to enter the paradise of heaven.

Early in the 20th century the horseride from Salihiye on the slopes of Jebel Qassioun to the centre of Damascus was a half-hour of passing through cool gardens and orchards, full of roses, jasmine and citrus flower. Even today, long after most of the gardens and orchards have been covered over in concrete and roads, the scent of jasmine and citrus flower is powerfully present in the streets of Damascus in April and May. Nizar Qabbani, Syria's greatest modern poet called Damascus 'City of Jasmine', and in April 2005 the municipality had a drive to plant thousands more jasmine flowers around the city.

ORIENTATION FROM JEBEL QASSIOUN جبل قاسيون

As a foreign visitor your focus will be almost entirely on the Old City and the cluster of sights around the National Museum. For an overview of Damascus it is a good idea as early as possible in your stay, to catch a taxi up to Jebel Qassioun (expect as a foreigner to pay around S£250 each way, though a local would pay no more than S£150). Ideally this would be just before sunset so you can sit at one of the cafés and watch the night descend upon the city. In the morning and midday it is liable to be foggy with poor visibility. Damascus itself already sits at an altitude of 690m and Jebel Qassioun rises a further 300m, high enough for eagles and other birds of prey to be seen regularly circling overhead. Early travellers, Arab and European, all had their first sight of Damascus from the slopes of Jebel Qassioun, and all were smitten. The 12th-century Spanish Muslim traveller Ibn Jubair wrote: 'If Paradise be on earth, it is, without a doubt, Damascus; but if it be in Heaven, Damascus is its counterpart on earth.'

Tradition held that Damascus itself was founded by the grandson of Shem, son of Noah, and in some sources it is also named as the Garden of Eden. Muslim tradition associated the refuge described in the Koran (23:51) for Jesus and Mary with Jebel Qassioun: 'and We made the son of Mary and his mother a Sign, and gave them shelter on a pleasant plateau with springs of running water.' Abraham was said to have dwelt in its caves and had the oneness and unity of God revealed to him here.

Today the concrete jungle is testimony to the wealth that exists in Damascus. Those with money pour it into new buildings rather than invest it in something less safe and less tangible like stocks and shares. Property remains no matter what

THE MUSHROOMING SUBURBS

Since the industrial revolution a radical social change has taken place in Syria, as elsewhere. No longer will three generations live together in one house, sharing the childcare and all eating together. Now they all have different jobs, will return from work at different times, will eat differently, and as a result the old system has been disintegrating. The solution was found to be a move out of the family house into apartments. Laws were introduced to facilitate this, as beforehand rental law was very much in favour of the tenant, with rents fixed unrealistically low and no landlord powers to evict. To overcome these laws, landlords had to find ingenious solutions, such as coming to a deal with their tenants to sell the apartment and share the proceeds 50:50, which then enabled both tenant and landlord to buy a bigger place and start afresh. Another landlord might have a three bedroom apartment rented out on a fixed low rent set in the 1970s. As long as the same tenant or another member of his family lived there, the rent could not be raised. One landlord, despairing of his lack of income from the property, converted a garage that was attached which then rented out at four times the rent of the three bedroom apartment. The effect of these tenant-favoured laws was to slow down construction. Landlords were frightened of getting trapped into a low fixed rent and therefore often even refused to rent their properties out, preferring to keep them empty and just gain from the capital appreciation. Now that the protected rent law has gone, the construction industry has gone wild, making up for lost time, and hence the mushrooming suburbs of Damascus.

and parents here like to build houses for their children if at all possible. The result is the uncontrolled sprawl you see before you, and the extra demand on water supplies has sapped the Barada River almost dry, except in the spring melt-water season when the flow increases noticeably, especially beside the National Museum.

Though the Barada River, once the lifeblood of the city, is no longer visible from up here, swallowed up along with the orchards and gardens by the inexorable urban sprawl, the Old City, still walled in its entirety and classified in 1979 as a UNESCO World Heritage Site, is readily distinguishable by its dense cluster of minarets and by the unmistakable shape of the massive Great Umayyad Mosque, once Roman temple, once Christian cathedral. For centuries and centuries the Old City was Damascus. It was later rulers like the Turks and the French who expanded beyond its walls, the Turks with their Tekkiye Suleymaniye complex along the banks of the Barada and the present Shari' Quwatli, and the French filling the space between Jebel Qassioun and the Turkish city, creating the wealthy leafy suburbs and wide avenues of Malki and Abu Roumaneh where embassies are mainly clustered. The Old City however, far from being dead and supplanted by the modern city, is one of the few Middle Eastern cities (along with Cairo and a handful of the north African cities like Marrakech) to have preserved its commercial life. Indeed, it is even undergoing something of a revival in its fortunes, as more and more of its wonderful old buildings are being restored and converted into splendid restaurants and hotels for use by locals as much as tourists. And for nightlife the Old City has now become the place to be.

From Jebel Qassioun the road continues eastwards, if you want to drive from here direct to visit the Christian villages of Seydnaya and Ma'loula (described later), winding across the ridge with extensive views to both sides, before dipping down into Damascus' northeast suburbs. These suburbs, now considered quite posh and respectable, used to be scruffy village encampments of poor traders who had come to the city to sell their wares. The wealthy folk of Damascus, if they

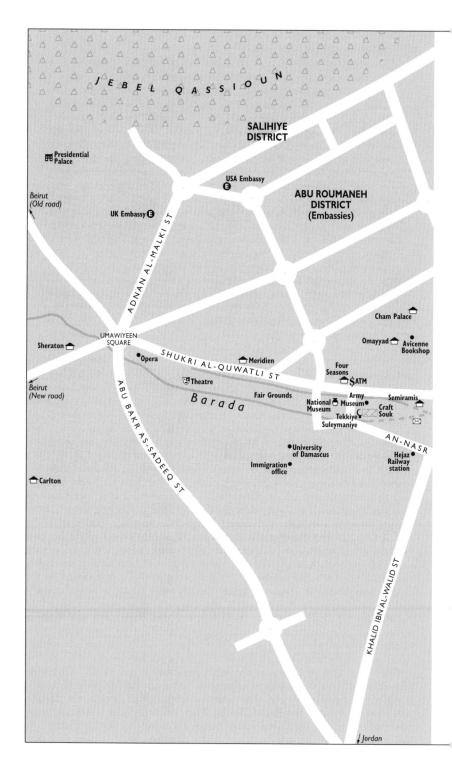

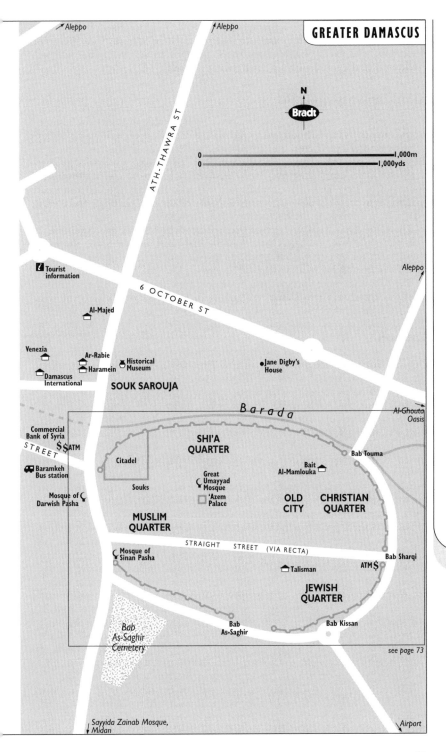

N

Bradt

0 ————————— 1,000m
0 ————————— 1,000yds

Aleppo

Aleppo

Aleppo

ATH-THAWRA ST

6 OCTOBER ST

i Tourist
information

Al-Majed

Venezia

Ar-Rabie

Haramein

Historical
Museum

Damascus
International

SOUK SAROUJA

Jane Digby's
House

B a r a d a

Al-Ghouta
Oasis

Commercial
Bank of Syria

STREET

$ $ATM

Baramkeh
Bus station

Mosque of
Darwish Pasha

Citadel

Souks

SHI'A
QUARTER

Great
Umayyad
Mosque

'Azem
Palace

Bab Touma

Bait
Al-Mamlouka

OLD
CITY

CHRISTIAN
QUARTER

MUSLIM
QUARTER

STRAIGHT STREET (VIA RECTA)

Mosque of
Sinan Pasha

Talisman

Bab Sharqi

ATM $

JEWISH
QUARTER

Bab
As-Saghir
Cemetery

Bab
As-Saghir

Bab Kissan

see page 73

Sayyida Zainab Mosque,
Midan

Airport

wanted to insult someone's appearance, would say: 'You look like a tramp from such and such village encampment.' Now that these suburbs have become respectable, the name of the village keeps changing to an ever more outlying encampment, the more outlying being the more scruffy.

HISTORICAL OVERVIEW

Excavation in any systematic sense has never been possible in Damascus because of its continuous inhabitation and so the earliest remains have been buried under successive waves of occupation. In Al-Ghouta Oasis round the city, however, fragments of Neolithic chance finds have proved that the oasis was settled as early as the 4th millennium BC, giving rise to Damascus' claim to be one of the earliest continuously inhabited urban centres in the world. Its first recorded historical mention is in the Mari tablets (see page 263) in c2500BC as Dimashqa, and then a little later as Dimaski in the Ebla archives (see pages 137–9).

Thereafter Damascus was settled from around 2000BC by the Amorites, a Semitic people from the desert interior of the Arabian Peninsula. Some 500 years later it came under Egyptian influence and was mentioned in the ancient Egyptian Tell Al-Amarna archives in the reign of Thutmosis III.

The Arameans were the next great power and from the 10th to the 8th century BC it was known as Aram-Damascus, famous for its Temple of Hadad on the site of what is today the Great Umayyad Mosque, and for its repeated clashes with the biblical kingdoms of Israel and Judaea, as chronicled at length in the Old Testament.

Then, after repeated attacks, the Assyrians from northern Mesopotamia took the city in 732BC under the great Assyrian king Tilgath Pileser III, who in turn fell to the Neo-Babylonians in 572BC led by King Nebuchadnezzar, conquering all of Syria and Palestine and even what is now eastern Turkey.

Next came the Achaemenid Persians who, under their King Cyrus, made Damascus the seat of a Persian satrap or governor in 539BC. But when Alexander the Great defeated the Persians at the famous Battle of Issus in 332BC, Damascus came under Greek control. Now for the first time the visible effects of the historical vicissitudes were left as the city had the classic Hellenistic grid pattern applied to its layout. After Alexander's death in 323BC Damascus was tugged between the rival Seleucid and Ptolemaic empires of Alexander's generals, and in the weakening of Greek control that followed, the Nabateans, from their capital at Petra, Jordan, extended their influence northwards to include Damascus.

Such was the scene when the Romans entered centre-stage in 64BC, conquering all of Syria, and their long reign, lasting 700 years, has left many of its relics in the Old City as we see it today. From this period date the Via Recta (Straight Street), the walls and gateways of the Old City, the triumphal arches and above all, the massive Temple of Jupiter built on the site of the 9th-century BC Temple of Hadad, the Aramean deity who was then merged with Roman Jupiter. From this period too dates the city's impressive water system, with an ambitious series of tunnels and aqueducts still visible today in parts of the Barada Gorge, bringing the water from the Barada down into the homes and baths of the city's inhabitants. Trade flourished and Damascus reaped the rewards of its location on the crossroads of major caravan routes south to Cairo and east to Baghdad. The city was declared a metropolis by Hadrian in AD117 and a colony by Alexander Severus in AD222.

The early events of Christianity, with the conversion of St Paul and his Damascene moment, in fact took place before Roman rule was fully in place, but later, after Christianity was adopted as the imperial religion by Constantine in the 4th century AD, the Temple of Jupiter was converted to the Cathedral of St John

Although Umayyad rule was to last only a hundred years till the rival 'Abbasid tribes took power and moved the capital to Baghdad, the Umayyad period was responsible for a cultural outburst which left its permanent mark in the Great Umayyad Mosque, Islam's holiest place after the Ka'aba at Mecca and the Dome of the Rock in Jerusalem and one of the most magnificent works of early Islam. Other Umayyad monuments, such as the Great Palace, have been lost over the centuries. The Umayyads were Islam's first dynasty. Up till then the first four caliphs, known as the *Rashidoun* (Rightly Guided Ones), had been chosen by consensus in line with the sheikh elder system where the person whose qualities most distinguished him for leadership was selected. Now power lay in the hands of one family, the Umayya. From the new capital in Damascus the new dynasty could control the eastern Mediterranean coastlands and the desert to the east. They advanced across northern Africa and into Spain, where they were responsible for such gems as Seville and Córdoba, and eastwards to the Oxus Valley and into northwestern India. Damascus itself with its fertile orchards and good water supply was able to produce the surplus needed to maintain a court, an army and a government for the first time in Islam's history.

Later regimes widely criticised them for losing the purely religious motivation of the early Rightly Guided caliphs and for becoming worldly and self-interested. Certainly the realities of governing an expanding empire changed the style of leadership and brought it face to face with tough decisions and compromises. The new Umayyad rulers were army leaders and tribal chiefs, not members of leading families in Mecca and Medina as before. Mu'awiya himself was a superb military organiser and transformed his Syrian army into the first disciplined and ordered force in Islamic warfare, abolishing many archaic tribal relics. An ordered Muslim society emerged out of seeming chaos. He created the first bureau of registry and a postal service, and appointed many Christians to high positions, including the poet laureate, financial administrator and his own doctor. He presided over disputes between early Christian sects and even rebuilt a church in Edessa (modern Urfa in southeast Turkey), the centre of Syriac-speaking Christianity.

He demonstrated that supreme Arab virtue of *Hilm*, a concept translated as grace, clemency, forbearance and the ability to resort to force only when absolutely necessary and to use peaceful means in all other situations. 'I apply not my sword', he said, 'where my lash suffices, nor my lash where my tongue is enough. And even if there be one hair binding me to my fellowmen, I do not let it break: when they pull I loosen, and if they loosen I pull.'

This supreme self-control made him master of all situations. Mu'awiya was however a controversial figure, vilified by many later Arab historians as the first Arab *malik*, king, a title so abhorrent to puritanical Muslims it was only ever used for non-Arabs, and he was consequently accused of secularising Islam.

the Baptist and Damascus became the seat of a bishop second in importance only to the patriarchate of Antioch.

The 700 years of Roman rule were brought to an abrupt end by the expansion of the Muslim Empire from its heartland in the Arabian Peninsula. Following the Prophet Muhammad's death in AD632 the early caliphs and their armies surged northwards at phenomenal speed and first took Damascus in 636. Initially it was just a northern outpost, but when its governor Mu'awiya proclaimed himself the next caliph in 661 in direct rivalry to 'Ali, the all-important Sunni/Shi'a split in Islam was born (see page 80) and Mu'awiya as the Sunni (orthodox) caliph founded the Umayyad dynasty with Damascus as its administrative capital, thereby making the city the centre of the Arab world.

During the 10th, 11th and 12th centuries Damascus entered a period of turbulence with successive Tulunid (Egyptian), Ikhshidid (north African), Fatimid (Egyptian), Hamdanid (Aleppian) and Seljuq (Turkish) dynasties, but no specific remnants of those dynasties survive in the city today. However it was gradually over this period that the inhabitants began to segregate themselves for protection into quarters, based on their religious faith. The Sunni orthodox Muslims gathered round the Great Umayyad Mosque, the Citadel and the western parts of the Old City, the Shi'a grouped northeast of the mosque in the Amara district, the Christians centred themselves round Bab Touma (St Thomas' Gate) to the northeast, and the Jews congregated in the southeast. The Graeco-Roman grid street pattern also began to be dissipated by the addition of winding narrow alleyways.

The city regained its strength and purpose in the 12th century under Nur Ad-Din, Zengid ruler of Aleppo, and then under Salah Ad-Din (Saladin), who had made his reputation by overthrowing the Egyptian Fatimids and establishing his own Ayyubid dynasty. The citadel of Damascus became Saladin's headquarters and though the Crusaders made three attempts over a 20-year period to take it, they never succeeded. The citadel, walls and gateways were reinforced and the population spread at this point up into the Salihiye district on the lower slopes of Jebel Qassioun. The city is recorded at this time as being larger than either Paris or Florence.

Ayyubid rule in Syria was terminated by the Mongol invasion of 1258, with Damascus itself devastated in 1260, but the Mamelukes, the slave dynasty who were even fiercer fighters than the Mongols, then extended their dynasty northwards from their base in Cairo and retook Syria, expelling the last of the Crusader presence into the bargain. Damascus flourished as the Mamelukes' second capital after Cairo, under Sultan Baibars (ruled 1260–77) and his successor Qalaun (ruled 1280–90), and many of the Islamic monuments of the city today date from this period. In 1400 a second wave of savage Mongol incursions took place under their leader Tamerlane, destroying much of the city and killing huge numbers.

When the Ottomans took over Syria in 1516 the amenities of the city gradually began to improve, especially under enlightened governors such as As'ad Pasha Al-'Azem in the 18th century. Its importance to the Ottomans was less as a caravan trading centre than as a staging post in the journey from Constantinople to Mecca on the annual Hajj or pilgrimage, where the pilgrims could stock up with provisions. They would begin to gather in their thousands, camped on the banks of the Barada, spending sometimes three months acquiring camping material, camels and food before setting out en masse on the arduous three-week desert crossing. It was important to the credibility of the Ottomans as guardians of the Holy cities of Mecca and Medina, to be able to guarantee the safety of the pilgrims and to ensure the Hajj was completed successfully each year.

As the 400 years of Ottoman rule drifted on into the 19th century the economy began to stagnate and Beirut took over as the intellectual and economic regional centre. A low point was reached in 1860 when tensions between Druze (see pages 218–19) and the Maronite Christians in Lebanon led to a massacre of the Christian community in Damascus, a massacre which Lady Jane Digby (see box page 239) survived, her house being outside the walls and therefore not in the Christian area.

Arab nationalism was on the rise in the late 19th century, but when the Ottoman Turks allied themselves with the Germans in World War I, Damascus was once again an important strategic centre. It fell to the Allies in 1918 and the Ottoman

Empire was in its final throes, but the Arab nationalist dream of an independent Syria was betrayed by the Allies and Syria was handed over instead to the French as mandated territory in 1920. The French Mandate was not popular and in 1925 the city rose up against the French authorities, provoking a bombing campaign of Damascus which caused extensive damage in the Old City. Only after World War II did the French leave and Damascus became in 1946 the capital of the independent Syrian Arab Republic.

GETTING THERE AND AWAY

Damascus International Airport lies 30km south of the city, connected by a specially built dual carriageway, and therefore taking only 30 minutes by taxi. The set fare for all taxis into Damascus is S£500 and you can either take any of the yellow taxis waiting outside the airport building or pay the S£500 at the taxi ticket desk on the right as you emerge from the customs check into the arrivals area, which then means you are escorted out of the airport and have to wait while your numbered car arrives. The price is the same either way.

Damascus airport is not big and the processing on landing does not usually take very long as a result. On arrival, before queuing up at passport control, you must fill out one of the coloured entry/exit cards (any colour, they are all the same), giving all your personal data, passport details and flight number, so have a pen to hand. This card is stamped by passport control and you then keep it with your passport throughout, till it is collected on departure at the airport. Unless you arrive very late at night there is also a money-changing booth in front of the passport control desks, which gives a better exchange rate than the hotels.

On your departure, remember to keep enough money back for the taxi fare of S£500, the departure tax of S£200 and the trolley fee of S£75. Porters are on hand and expect *baksheesh* of something between S£15 and S£25. The departure tax must be paid for with Syrian currency, and you are handed a stamp which you must then take to passport control so they can stick it in your passport. Once through into the departures area, the duty-free zones are surprisingly extensive and modern, with a full range of perfumes, makeup, cigarettes and alcohol. There is also an excellent upmarket chocolate and sweet stand called Ghraoui, an area selling music CDs and a pleasantly open restaurant and café area.

GETTING AROUND

Taxis are plentiful and cheap and there is little point using anything else. The fare into the city from the airport is fixed at S£500, and any fare within the city should not exceed S£50. Microbuses are cheaper but run only on fixed routes and from certain places. There are no trains, trams or metro service. As a foreigner taxi fares are higher and a taxi up Jebel Qassioun for example will cost S£250–300, even though a local would only pay S£150.

Walking in Damascus is easy and straightforward. You have no need to worry about pickpockets or other molesters as there is virtually no street crime. You are safer here late at night alone than in any Western city. As a woman you will not be bothered unless you invite attention by being too scantily dressed or by too much eye contact. At all busy crossroads there are stairs with overpasses to get you to each of the corners. At many other major roads there are traffic lights with a pedestrian green man just as in Europe to let you know you can cross safely. Traffic is obedient and always follows the signals and policemen's directions. Traffic police are strongly in evidence to guarantee total compliance with the rules, though their touch is light if you as a foreigner inadvertently get it wrong.

LOCAL TOUR OPERATORS

All the bigger hotels have links into the various locally based tour operators and will set up tours to suit all budgets and preferences, thereby taking the administrative strain off the individual traveller. Alternatively you can contact any of the following operators directly and browse their websites to get an idea of what is on offer.

Abinos Travel and Tourism PO Box 30422, Damascus; ☎ +963 11 23 22730; www.abinostravel.com. A full range of services from airport collection to tailor-made adventure tours.
Adonis Travel PO Box 34–36, Al-Moutanabi St, Damascus; ☎ +963 11 5134850; www.syria.adonistravel.com. Offers a full range of services from airport collection to à la carte itineraries, classical programmes, business travel and themed tours, eg: religion.
Jasmin Tours Damascus ☎ +963 11 2317597;

f +963 11 2313176; e jasmine@jasmintour.com; www.jasmintour.com. Offers 8-day hiking tours combined with culture and nature, and 10-day classical tours.
Silk Road Travel and Tourism Fardoss St, PO Box 12958, Damascus; ☎ +963 11 2230500; f +963 11 2231138; e hanano@silkroad-tours.com; www.silkroad-tours.com. Offers a range of tours from 3 to 12 nights, in combination with Lebanon, Jordan and Egypt.

TOURIST INFORMATION

There are three tourist offices in Damascus where you can collect the occasionally useful Ministry of Tourism free maps and leaflets on the country and the region, but the staff, though willing, are not usually well-informed on anything practical and do not for example make hotel bookings. The most conveniently located one is in the Arrivals Hall at Damascus International airport, on the far right corner as you emerge from Customs. The other two are both in modern downtown Damascus, one near the entrance to the Handicrafts Souk by the Tekkiye Suleymaniye complex, supposedly open 09.00–14.00 except Friday, though in practice closed most of the time, and the other, the main tourist office, in Shari' 29 Mai, just north of Youssef Al-Azmeh Square, near the Cham Palace Hotel (*open 09.30–19.00 except Fri*).

WHERE TO STAY

HOTELS Damascus is well provided with five-star hotels belonging to international chains like the Sheraton and the Meridien. These are located in the new commercial districts and can be a bit far from the centre, certainly no longer within walking distance of the main attractions like the National Museum and the Old City. The newly opened Four Seasons is an exception, very well-located directly opposite the National Museum, but very expensive, too. In the middle category there is something of a dearth, with the Omayad Hotel standing out as by far the best at the moment. In the Old City the first few imaginative small 'boutique' hotels have been created out of restored Ottoman mansions. At the bottom end of the market there are a just a couple of one star backpacker level hotels, both located outside the Old City, and both tending to be pretty full.

The following is not a comprehensive list, but covers a good selection of the better choices, starting with the most expensive.

🏠 **Four Seasons** (381 rooms) PO Box 6311; ☎ 3391000; f 3390900; e reservations.dam@fourseasons.com; www.fourseasons-syria.com. Damascus' latest addition

at the top end, opened late 2005, built with Saudi money in a good central location overlooking the Barada and the National Museum, 2km from the Old City. Locals complain it has lost them one of their nicest city parks, and certainly its massive 23-storey green and white hulk now dominates the skyline and has become a major landmark viewed from Jebel Qassioun. It boasts all the usual 5-star facilities including 5 restaurants, nightclub, health club, pool and business centre. *US$320–390 dbl, US$280–355 sgl.*

🏠 **Cham Palace** (400 rooms) Maisaloun St, PO Box 7570; ✆ 2232300; f 2212398; e chamresa@net.sy; www.chamhotels.com. The premier hotel in this Syrian luxury chain which has branches in most of Syria's main cities. It is the best located of the 5-star hotels in the heart of the commercial district and 1.5km from the Old City. The lobby is quite magnificently grand with huge ceiling height and is worth having a drink in even if you are not staying. As well as its 5 restaurants, indoor pool and fitness centre, it has 24-hr money changing, business centre, a bookshop and the Chamtour car hire agency (linked to Hertz) just next door. Its Etoile D'Or restaurant on the top floor is Damascus' only revolving restaurant, a real treat for your final night, maybe. *US$160–240 dbl, US$150–210 sgl, depending on exact room size and location.*

🏠 **Ebla Cham** (440 rooms) PO Box 6416; ✆ 2241900; f 5427275; e chamebla@net.sy; www.chamhotels.com. Out near the airport this massive 5-star luxury place is used mainly by businessmen. It boasts an 18-hole golf course (par 72, 6,111m), pool, fitness centre and 4 tennis courts. *US$220–260 dbl, US$170–200 sgl.*

🏠 **Meridien** (350 rooms) Shukri Al-Quwatli St, PO Box 5531; ✆ 3738730; f 3738661; www.lemeridien.com. Pleasantly located in its own greenery east of Umawiyeen Square, this was Damascus' first luxury hotel, built in the 1970s. Most rooms have now been refurbished and it has the usual clutch of 5-star facilities with shopping mall, pool, tennis, business centre, car hire linked to Europcar and 5 restaurants; 500m from the National Museum. *US$240–260 dbl, US$205–220 sgl.*

🏠 **Sheraton** (278 rooms) Umawiyeen Square, PO Box 4795; ✆ 3734630/2229300; f 2243607; e resv_sheraton@net.sy; www.starwood.com. Terrible location well out of town beside a maze of main roads just west of Umawiyeen Square. All the usual 5-star facilities compensate. Car hire linked to Falcon and Europcar. *US$205–310 dbl, US$175–260 sgl.*

🏠 **Semiramis** (115 rooms) Victoria Bridge, PO Box 30301; ✆ 2233555; f 2216797; e semiramis@net.sy; www.semiramis-hotel.com. Well situated close to the Old City but on a busy square

with no views. Small rooftop pool (indoor and outdoor), health centre, car hire linked to Europcar. Nightclub with live singers and good Chinese restaurant among the 4 it offers. Cheapest of the 5-star hotels. *US$130–170 dbl, US$110–150 sgl.*

🏠 **Omayad** (80 rooms) Brazil St. PO Box 7811; ✆ 2217700; f 2213516; e omayad-hotel@net.sy; www.omayad-hotel.com. Very well located in a quiet side street close to the Avicenne bookshop and the Cham Palace and a short walk from the National Museum, this hotel is classed as 4-star with a plush foyer and spacious rooms. The Lebanese management is very IT literate and all rooms have wireless internet connectivity and there is a permanent facility on the computer in the foyer free of charge. Rooftop restaurant used for functions. Good breakfast buffet served in the bar. Much used by businessmen. Member of Swiss International Hotels and Resorts. *US$100–105 dbl, US$86–91 sgl.*

🏠 **Venezia** (75 rooms) PO Box 9; ✆ 2316631; f 2314030; e info@venezia-syria.com; www.venezia-syria.com. This 3-star hotel is quite swish after a recent facelift. It is well located on a main road near the Cham Palace and tends to have lower-level tour groups from Spain and Sweden. One restaurant, rooms adequate if uninspiring. *US$60/65 sgl/dbl.*

🏠 **Al-Majed** (100 rooms) PO Box 13152; ✆ 2323300; f 2323304; e majed@almajed-group.com; www.almajed-group.com. Tucked down a side street not far from the Cham Palace, this hotel caters mainly for Lebanese and Arab visitors. The rooms are quite small and simple but have a huge fridge reflecting the Arab tendency to eat prolifically in their rooms. The rooftop restaurant is very Arab and a bit kitsch. There are pleasant sitting-out areas for eating and drinking lining the driveway to the entrance. Next door is the sister hotel Al-Khayyam. *US$35/50 sgl/dbl.*

🏠 **Beit Al-Mamlouka** (8 rooms) Bab Touma, PO Box 34049; ✆ 5430445; f 5417248; e almamlouka@mail.sy; www.almamlouka.com. Opened April 2005, this is the first restored Arab courtyard house in the Old City offering accommodation. Beautifully done in authentic style by a lady from Aleppo, it is rated 5-star with exquisite furnishings and each room in a different theme, from Suleyman the Magnificent to Haroun Ar-Rasheed. There is no restaurant as such, but meals can be taken by special arrangement if required. *US$180–250, including buffet b/fast taken in the old stable.*

🏠 **Hotel Talisman** (15 rooms) ✆ 963 92 9333478; e youseftakla@yahoo.fr; www.hoteltalisman.net. In the Jewish quarter in a street running parallel to Straight St, 200m to the south. Opened March 2006 and built from an 18th-century ruin, this remarkable fantasy hotel is conceived on a grand scale and has involved major reconstruction. The extremely spacious courtyard has a 1.8m-deep pool which can be used for swimming. Public reception areas are extensive, there is a *hammam* and all rooms have wireless internet connection, plasma TV screens and expensive furnishings down to every detail, even specially monogrammed towels. The first Talisman Hotel opened in Cairo last year. € *200 for a dbl,* € *240 for a junior suite and* € *280 for an exclusive suite including b/fast.*

🛏 **Ar-Rabie** (15 rooms) Bahsa St, Souk Sarouja; ☎ 2318374; f 2311875; no email or website. Classed as 1-star and set in a run-down 19th-century house, this is a friendly place for backpackers, students and lone travellers on a budget. Shared facilities and basic rooms. Simple b/fast. Large covered courtyard. Usually full. *S£250/675 sgl/dbl.*

🛏 **Al-Haramein** (15 rooms) Bahsa St, Souk Sarouja; ☎ 2319489; f 2314299; e alharamain_hotel@yahoo.com. Also classed as 1-star and tucked up the same alley as Ar-Rabie, this is a very similar 19th-century house and with very similar clientèle. Its courtyard is smaller but still covered. Shared facilities, simple b/fast. Usually full. *S£600/175 dbl/sgl.*

✖ WHERE TO EAT AND DRINK

RESTAURANTS Damascus' eating scene has been transformed in recent years by the revolution that has taken place in the Old City. Upwards of 70 restaurants now exist within the walls, set in restored 18th- and 19th-century Arab houses, each one different, each one beautiful in a different way. Most serve typical Syrian food with an excellent range of *mezze*, all freshly prepared and using wonderful natural ingredients. No sign of junk food here. In fact, a Kentucky Fried Chicken outlet tried to open a few years ago with all the usual hype; huge queues of young people built up on the first day curious to see exactly what this American fare was like. On discovering they paid high prices to receive a few pieces of precooked chicken in a cardboard box, they soon abandoned it in favour of local fast food where you can eat a whole freshly cooked chicken for half the price. The outlet was forced to rename itself and serve local food instead. For alcohol with the meal you tend to have to go to places in or close to the Christian quarter. Other eating places outside the Old City are plentiful as well, but only those with a special ambience are given mention here. All food is cheap and it is difficult to pay more than S£1,500 (US$30) for a three-course meal for two with wine. Without alcohol it is usually closer to S£700 for two (US$14). Unless otherwise mentioned, all the restaurants listed here open from around noon until midnight, eating being a national pastime.

Old City

✖ **Bait Jabri** ☎ 5443200; www.jabrihouse.com. One of the first to open and still probably the most popular. Quite tricky to find for the novice in a side alley southeast of the Great Umayyad Mosque, but well signposted. Beautifully set in the spacious courtyard of an 18th-century Ottoman mansion with a central fountain, the restaurant also has an internet café in one of its rooms off the *iwan* (open arch for summer seating) which has to be one of the most extraordinary settings for an internet café anywhere in the world. The Arabic food is cheap and unpretentious and this is one of the few places to serve falafel, hot fried chickpea balls. Service is excellent, by the all-male waiters, standard for this

part of the world. No female would work as a waitress, waiting on men. The clientèle is totally mixed in age, gender and nationality. Many local girls in groups come here to eat lunch, some in Western dress and tight jeans, some in traditional headdresses, according to their family background, blending together quite naturally. No alcohol is served, though local alcohol-free beer is on offer. In winter the courtyard is covered. The WC facilities are imaginatively kitted out and reasonably clean.

✖ **Leila's Restaurant and Terrace** ☎ 5445900. Located in the southeast corner of the lane that leads round the outer wall of Great Umayyad Mosque, this place must have the most stunning roof terrace in the city, directly beneath the Jesus Minaret of the mosque. At night when the mosque is floodlit the ambience is breathtaking. No alcohol is served because of the proximity to the mosque but the food is very good and freshly prepared: the usual full range of Arab fare. *Prices are moderate; reservations are advisable for the roof terrace on summer evenings.*

✗ **Al-Khawali** Located on Straight St on the corner of the lane that runs south to Bait Siba'i, this is a vast restored palatial house. Downstairs it has a courtyard with seating round the fountain, upstairs is an extensive galleried area with more seating, and then steps lead up to the very top terrace, from where there are magnificent views over the domes of Khan Assad Pasha, Damascus' grandest caravanserai. Main courses are very good as well as the *mezze*. Prices are moderate and service is excellent. There is also a bread oven in the downstairs courtyard so the bread is freshly baked and brought straight to the table. No alcohol is served. *Prices are average.*

✗ **Barjees** Down in the southern Muslim quarter near Bab As-Saghir, this is the only restaurant in this area at the time of writing. Tucked up a side street it is surprisingly large inside with a spacious restored courtyard complete with fountain and balcony terrace. Usual Arab food, no alcohol. The name Barjees comes from a game for two played with shells instead of dice, not unlike backgammon, but played on cloth, not wood. *Average prices.*

✗ **Narcissus Palace** ↘ 5431205. Attractive alcohol-free courtyard set in the heart of the Muslim area near Bait Jabri. Splashing fountain and lofty tarpaulin ceiling in winter. A flat TV screen is incongruously set in the old stone walls. Good range of *mezze*. Very popular with young Syrian women who come in groups to lunch and smoke *nargilehs* (water pipes). *Reasonable prices.*

✗ **Casablanca** ↘ 5419000, 5417598. Located in the Christian quarter in Hanania St, the street from Bab

Sharqi to the Ananias Chapel, this is a chic French-style cuisine place with prices to match. Set in a converted Ottoman house the atmosphere is somehow rather dead and it appears to be used largely by businessmen doing official entertaining. Alcohol available but no prices on the menu: always a bad sign. Check before you order. *Open for lunch 11.30–16.00, for dinner 19.30–00.30; live music from 22.30.*

✗ **Al-Dar** ↘ 5423232. In the Christian quarter set by itself this place is unusual in being completely modern, designed by an architect to look like an old courtyard house. The atmosphere is expensive yet the food and alcohol is surprisingly reasonably priced.

✗ **Arabesque** ↘ 5433999. In the Christian quarter, popular because of its attractive, heavily-foliaged roof terrace. Wine is expensive but the food is good and averagely priced. *Reservations preferred.*

✗ **Elissar** ↘ 5424300. Close to Bab Touma in the Christian quarter, this upmarket restaurant no longer offers the best food, though it still has a good reputation. The courtyard setting is attractive with a lot of plant life. Alcohol is served. *There are no prices on the menu.*

✗ **Oriental Restaurant** (formerly Zeitouna Restaurant) ↘ 5431324. In Zeitouna St, near Bab Sharqi, past the Greek Catholic Patriarchate and the Guitarre Restaurant, tucked up a side alley. Very attractive courtyard and fountain, with more seating on the terrace upstairs. Excellent food with such delicacies as freshly cooked artichoke hearts. Live solo singer downstairs playing the 'ud (lute).

✗ **Abou Al-'Izz** ↘ 2218174. Set upstairs up an unlikely looking staircase just off the Souk Al-Hamadiye and near the Great Umayyad Mosque, this large unassuming place is less sophisticated than the previously listed ones, but serves good-value Syrian food in quantity. No alcohol. The WCs are of the squat variety and could be cleaner.

New City

✗ **Etoile D'Or** ↘ 2232300. The revolving restaurant at the top of the Cham Palace Hotel, a magnificent dinner setting, hard to beat for sophistication and prices. It takes two hours to complete a revolution.

Jebel Qassioun

✗ **La Montagna** The best place on the mountain, imaginatively designed like a giant glasshouse, arranged in descending terraces from the entrance. Fabulous views down over the city, especially at night. Italian and international menu with big

Service can seem slow compared with the speed of the Old City restaurants, but then the expectation is that you want to linger. Good wine list.

selection of pasta and pizzas. No alcohol but good selection of freshly made juices. Try their lemon juice with mint. Quite pricey considering there is no alcohol.

ENTERTAINMENT AND NIGHTLIFE

Nobody comes to Syria for the nightlife, since it is virtually non-existent. As the capital city, Damascus obviously offers more than anywhere else in the country, but even so it is limited. There are no casinos and whilst there are a few independent nightclubs they are generally seedy and only frequented by men in search of eastern European or Russian prostitutes. These girls sit at the bar thinly disguised as escorts, waiting to have expensive drinks bought for them. The big luxury hotels like the Sheraton and the Meridien have nightclubs attached but apart from being very expensive, tend to be rather soulless and bland, though there will usually be live music. Nothing much swings into action till after 22.30.

The other forms of evening entertainment are the cultural events sponsored by the various foreign cultural institutes such as the British Council, the Goethe Institute and the French Cultural Centre. The Ministry of Culture also arranges concerts, theatrical performances and exhibitions which are held at the National Opera House in Damascus. The English-daily newspaper *Syria Times* gives listings of what's on.

For **cinema** showings of Western films the best bet is the Cham Cinema attached to the Cham Palace Hotel. Tickets are cheap at S£150 and there are two screens, one of which is usually showing in English. Big release films tend to arrive in Syria about a month after their initial release in the West.

Most local people's idea of a good night out is a family gathering or a group of friends eating together in leisurely fashion quite late (21.30–22.00 onwards), maybe in a restaurant with live music and singing. Almost all such places are now concentrated in the Old City which has seen an enormous revival in its fortunes with the restoration of many beautiful old houses and their conversion into atmospheric restaurants. There are at least 50 open now, mainly frequented by local people. Businessmen and wealthier local people go to the expensive places like Casablanca and the Piano Bar in the Christian quarter, where restaurants will freely serve alcohol. At the Nawfara Café behind the Great Umayyad Mosque, the oral tradition is kept alive by a *hakawati* or storyteller, holding forth in Arabic most evenings from 19.00, which will give you a flavour of the rhetorical power of the Arabic language, even if you do not understand a word.

SHOPPING

For souvenir and present shopping the best place to start is the Handicraft Souk in the alleyway that forms part of the Tekkiye Suleymaniye complex behind the Damascus National Museum. In addition to the alleyway itself the shops now line the arcaded courtyard of the attached caravanserai originally used by pilgrims stopping over in Damascus on their way to Mecca. Prices in all these shops are fixed and the quality and choice is good. If you can find what you like here, it is easier to buy and you will feel less pressurised into making a decision. It is particularly good for jewellery, inlaid wooden boxes, worry beads, Damascus fabrics beautifully made into tablecloths and napkins, old Bedouin clothing and modern local glass and pottery ware.

After you have seen what prices are like and what range there is on offer in the Tekkiye Suleymaniye handicraft market, you will feel more confident about buying in the *souks* of the Old City which obviously also offer a huge range of souvenir and gift shopping. Most of the stalls selling carpets, handicrafts, antiques and souvenirs are grouped along the Souk Al-Hamadiye and in the streets round the side and along the back of the Umayyad Mosque by the Nawfara Café. For antiques and metal ware the best shops are along the eastern half of Straight Street, beyond the Roman Arch in the Christian quarter. Many of these shops also have good carpets and Damascus tiles. The tiles, with their predominant blues and greens in abstract or floral patterns, are generally modern, but have been aged very effectively, and prices are very reasonable. Also in the Christian quarter the street leading up to St Ananias Chapel has a good range of tiles and pottery, much of it from Iran, along with fabrics and carpets. Prices are a little higher but the quality is very good.

Fresh spices and herbs also make very good presents and souvenirs, with the added advantage of being both light and cheap, though everything in your luggage will be impregnated by the time you return home. The place to go is the Souk Al-Bezuriye, a whole street full of spice merchants, the same street where the Khan As'ad Pasha is to be found. Even if you have no intention of purchasing, it is a wonderful place to linger and soak up the smells and fragrances. Perfumes distilled from all sorts of exotic plants and substances are also on offer.

OTHER PRACTICALITIES

HOSPITALS AND PHARMACIES See *Chapter 2*, pages 49–50 for a list of Damascus' private hospitals and the 24-hour pharmacy. Pharmacies are plentiful and well-stocked all over town, both inside and outside the walls, recognisable by their green cross. Many prescription drugs can be bought cheaply over the counter, and frequently are.

BANKS See *Chapter 1*, page 12 under *Investment and Finance* and *Chapter 2*, page 40 under *Money and Banking*. The Commercial Bank of Syria is the national bank, with branches all over the country. There are none inside the Old City, but there is one just outside the walls near the Souk Al-Hamadiye entrance, opposite the Law Courts, and there is another on Youssef Al-Azmah Square near the Cham Palace Hotel that displays the exchange rates electronically outside. The banks are generally chaotic places, to be avoided if possible, and if all you want is Syrian cash, the ATMs are a much better bet, with one just inside Bab Sharqi, one beside the Four Seasons Hotel and one outside the walls just in front of the Citadel.

CHURCH SERVICES Church services are held on Sundays by the churches of all the represented denominations in the Old City: Syrian Orthodox, Greek Orthodox, Armenian, Greek Catholic, Syrian Catholic, Maronite, Evangelical and Anglican. Communion is said to be highly enjoyable, with wine-soaked brioche served on silver spoons.

COMMUNICATIONS
Internet There is an increasing number of internet cafés in Damascus (as there is in Aleppo, too), and all the major hotels have internet facilities. Some enlightened hotels, like the Omayyad Palace Hotel, even have wireless internet connection in all hotel rooms, free of charge to all guests. Inside the Old City the internet cafés can be a bit slow, with dial-up connections, but the ones in the commercial districts have broadband. Costs are between S£100 and 200 per hour. Syria is becoming impressively computer-literate, a process encouraged by President Bashar Al-Assad, who is president of the Computer Society. Places like the French Cultural Centre also help by offering Syrians lots of courses on how to get started on the internet. More and more places and people have email addresses and more and more hotels have websites where you can even make online bookings.

Post There is a main post office on the road between the Semiramis Hotel and the Hijaz railway station. Do not rely on the hotel reception to post your letters and cards. Find a yellow letterbox, which are plentiful on the streets, and write 'BRITAIN' not 'UK' on the address.

THE OLD CITY

Entry to the Old City (*One full day minimum, avoid Fridays*) Covering an area of at least 2km by 1.5km within the walls, the Old City of Damascus is easily twice the size of the Old City of Aleppo, and with a much more cohesive feel to it, probably because the Umayyad Mosque is so clearly its heart and everything else follows on from that. Gai Eaton, in his book *Remembering God*, has a memorable way of bringing the Old City to life:

The parallels between the city and the human body are fairly obvious. The colleges and centres of learning are the head, the sanctuary (or, failing that the central mosque) is the heart, the market is the stomach, the gardens are the lungs, horses and donkeys are the legs, the people circulating in the streets are the blood cells, and so on.

The city walls, still for the most part in evidence, run for 5km in circumference, and had a total of nine gates, eight of which are still extant. Only Bab Al-Nasr, Victory Gate, has disappeared. Even the names of the gates evoke powerful associations: from the Arabic they translate into names like Gate of Paradise, Gate of Peace, Gate of Deliverance, and the Romans named them after their gods like Mercury, Venus, Saturn, Mars and Jupiter. Many of the original Roman stone blocks can still be seen at the base of these gates, despite the plundering and rebuilding of the last 2,000 years. It would take some three hours to walk the length of the walls today and is not recommended except to the dedicated and even then only in early morning or late evening. Remarkably the walled city today still follows almost exactly the same lines as the Roman/Hellenistic city, only one gate, Bab Al-Faradis, having been moved north to the bank of the Barada River, and this was under Nur Ad-Din in the 12th century.

If your hotel is close enough, walk to the Souk Al-Hamadiye entrance by the citadel. Walking in Damascus is a pleasure. The pace is unhurried, people appear relaxed and comfortable, and there is always plenty to look at. Pavements are often spread with extraordinary and unexpected street wares, from cheap Chinese watches to eye-catching ladies' underwear. You will not be bothered or hassled, unless you are indecently dressed. Damascus has seen foreigners come and go throughout its long history. You are just one more among the many.

If you cannot work out the route or are too far away, take one of the ubiquitous yellow taxis. You will not usually have to wait more than a few seconds to get one, and no taxi fare within the city should ever cost more than S£50. Ask for Souk Al-Hamadiye and you will be dropped by the pedestrian underpass, a relatively recent construction, together with the railings to prevent conventional street crossing, with steps down and escalators up. The escalators are still something of a novelty, and timid young women, fearful that their long robes will get caught in the mechanism, still occasionally have to be led giggling with embarrassment up the steps by their husbands or male relations.

Nothing will have prepared you for the sight that awaits you as you come up the escalator. This, the main entrance to the *souk,* will take your breath away as you are sucked into its innards. You have crossed into another world, and the sheer scale, the sheer height, is unrivalled anywhere in Turkey or the Arab world. The vastness of its arched roof is like an immense dark cavern, pierced with holes that let through bursts of sunlight almost like stars twinkling in the firmament. Do not even think about buying anything on this first entry to the *souk.* Focus instead on drinking up the atmosphere, letting the magic of the place wash over you. On subsequent visits you can go faster, enter from other streets or gateways, but this first entry into the Old City of Damascus should never be rushed and should always be done via the Souk Al-Hamadiye.

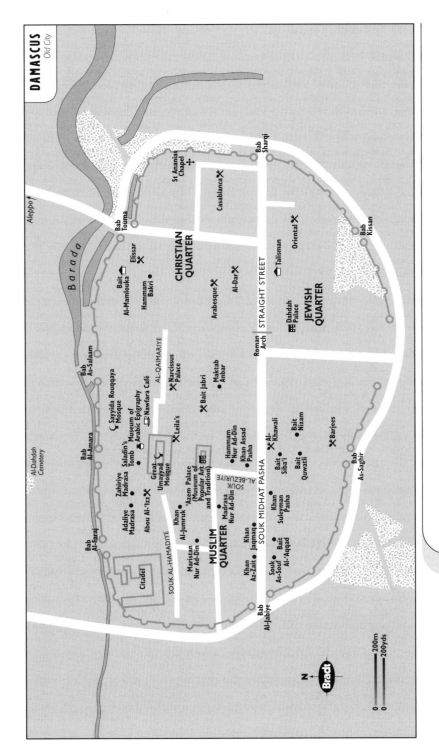

DAMASCUS
Old City

Aleppo

Barada

Al-Dahdah Cemetery

Bab Al-Faraj

Citadel

SOUK AL-HAMADIYE

Bab Al-Amara

Bab Al-Jabiye

Adaliye Madrasa
Zahiriye Madrasa
Abou Al-'Izz ✕

Khan Al-Jumruk

Maristan Nur Ad-Din

MUSLIM QUARTER

Khan Az-Zait
Khan Jaqmaq
Souk As-Souf
Bait Al-Aqqad

Khan Suleyman Pasha

Madrasa Nur Ad-Din

SOUK AL-BEZURIYE

SOUK MIDHAT PASHA

Saladin's Tomb
Museum of Arabic Epigraphy

Bab As-Salaam

Sayyida Rouqqaya Mosque

Great Umayyad Mosque

'Azem Palace (Museum of Popular Art and Tradition)

Leila's ✕
Nawfara Café

AL-QAIMARIYE

Narcissus Palace ✕
Bait Jabri ✕

Maktab Anbar

Hammam Nur Ad-Din
Khan Assad Pasha

Al-Khawali ✕
Bait Nizam
Bait Quwatli

Bait Siba'i

Barjees ✕

Bab As-Saghir

Bait Al-Mamlouka
Hammam Bakri

Elissar ✕

Bab Touma

CHRISTIAN QUARTER

Arabesque ✕
Al-Dar ✕

St Ananias Chapel ✝

Casablanca ✕

Bab Sharqi

Roman Arch
STRAIGHT STREET

Dahdah Palace

Talisman

JEWISH QUARTER

Oriental ✕

Bab Kissan

N

0 ——— 200m
0 ——— 200yds

Bradt

Souk Al-Hamadiye سوق الحمدية (*Open c09.00–c21.00 daily except Fri*) Dating to the late 19th century in its present form, the Souk Al-Hamadiye owes its name to the Ottoman Sultan Abdul Hamid II who refurbished the *souk* into its current format with high metal roof above double-storey shop façades, where the offices and storerooms are ranged on the upper storey. Always busy with local people of all ages, men and women, men in groups, women in groups, couples, this is where most Damascenes still choose to come for their shopping. Malls and department stores do not yet exist, mercifully, so shopping remains the social unhurried experience it used to be in the West in the 19th century. Elaborately costumed water sellers still ply the length of the *souk*, offering glasses of water, while other vendors without stalls try to sell stuffed eagles, all the rage at the moment. Foreigners blend into this *mêlée*, often looking a bit bewildered and self-conscious, but largely ignored by the tolerant crowds. In summer many Gulf Arabs are distinguishable by their white robes, strolling leisurely through the *souks*, ever watchful for bargains. They spend weeks if not months visiting to get away from the searing heat of their homeland in this the Arab world's most northerly and therefore also coolest country. They generally arrive by car and can therefore pile their vehicles high with purchases before driving home to the Gulf and Saudi Arabia.

The holes that pepper the corrugated iron roof are in fact bullet hole relics from the 1925 uprising against the French-imposed Mandate. The wide avenue of the 500m-long *souk* is built along the original axis and processional way of the Roman city that led to the massive Temple of Jupiter, now the Great Umayyad Mosque.

Roman gateway and forecourt As you emerge from the darkened *souk* areas into the daylight, the incongruous sight that awaits you is a series of Roman monumental archways, beautifully crafted out of warm golden-red stone, and blending seamlessly with their Ottoman surroundings. The monumental gateway to which they are joined marked the outer entrance of the Roman Temple of Jupiter and the 12m-high columns are topped with spectacularly carved Corinthian capitals. The outer compound perimeter of the temple was originally a massive 305m by 385m, with a monumental gateway on each side.

Beyond the gateway the space opens out in an expanse of golden paving stones that ends in the colossal inner precinct wall of the Great Umayyad Mosque, built from the same warm-coloured stones and whose huge lower blocks are clearly still the Roman stones from the original Temple of Jupiter. An arcaded row of columns from Byzantine times runs in front of a series of shops selling Korans and religious texts.

'Adaliye and Zahiriye Madrasas مدرسة العادلية ومدرسة الظاهرية (*Open 08.00–14.00; no entry fee*) The main entrance to the Great Umayyad Mosque that faces you (on the western wall) cannot be used by foreigners and non-Muslims, but the gateway itself, called Bab Al-Barid (Gate of the Post), deserves a close look at its huge bronze 15th-century doors. Foreigners have to enter from round the other (north) side by the tourist entrance. But do not be in too much of a hurry to enter the mosque: whet your appetite first with a handful of more minor monuments all grouped near that northern flank. Turning left along the western precinct wall, follow the alleyway to reach the pair of *madrasas* (religious schools), called the 'Adaliye and the Zahiriye, both built in the 13th century. Under the threat of the Christian Crusaders, Islam developed and strengthened its own orthodoxy, and there was a resulting flourishing of *madrasas*, to promote Islamic beliefs and institutions. Leading theologians, philosophers and poets were drawn to Damascus at this time, to escape the more unstable centres of Palestine and Baghdad. The 'Adaliye had been shut for restoration for many years, but finally reopened in March 2006. Its name derives from the fact that Al-'Adil, one of Saladin's brothers, is buried here, and it houses a rich collection of manuscripts.

Immediately opposite is the Zahiriye *madrasa* where the guardian will show you into the courtyard and the tomb chamber of the Mameluke Sultan Baibars to the right of the entrance. The beautiful green and gold mosaics follow the same colour scheme and style as those in the Great Umayyad Mosque, though they are more coarsely executed despite being created 500 years later. Baibars was the famously fierce and warlike leader who made certain of the Crusaders' final departure from the Middle East. He died here in Damascus in 1277. The building was originally the private house where Saladin's father, Ayyub (hence the Ayyubid dynasty), had lived, but Baibar's son converted it into a *madrasa* and added the spectacular beehive, honeycombed or stalactite shapes (known as *muqarnas*) above the entrance. This style of vaulting was a Muslim invention of the 10th century, designed to symbolise the honey promised to the believer in paradise. The name Zahiriye comes from the Arabic 'zahir' meaning the external or outward aspect of things, as opposed to the 'batin' meaning the interior or inside aspect.

Museum of Arabic Epigraphy *(Open 08.00–14.00 daily except Tue; S£75 entry fee)*
Continuing up the picturesque alleyway eastwards past many old houses with overhanging first floor balconies in typical Ottoman style, following the northern edge of the Great Umayyad Mosque precinct wall, you come after some 100m on your right, to the Museum of Arabic Epigraphy (inscriptions), housed in a 15th-century late Mameluke *madrasa* with colourful stained-glass windows. Oddly juxtaposed in the alley are stalls selling women's nighties, bras and aerobics body suits.

The museum itself, looked after by a friendly head-scarved lady caretaker, is a haven of peace and tranquillity with its fountain splashing soothingly in the central courtyard, and well worth a visit of half an hour or so, especially if you interested in the Arabic script and the origins of the alphabet (see box on *Early alphabet and the tablets*, page 186). There are some beautifully illuminated Qur'ans, illustrating the different styles of script.

Sayyida Rouqqaya Mosque جامع السيدة الرقية Wandering further along the same
alleyway you will come to a crossroads where signs to the left point to Sayyida Rouqqaya, a modern Shi'ite mosque, (see box on page 80) built in the Iranian style in 1993 with Iranian funds in this the Shi'ite district of the Old City, known as Amara. Rouqqaya was one of the daughters of the Shi'ite martyr Al-Hussein, whose tomb lies within the mosque. Shi'ite women are distinctive in this area by their totally black robes and veils, showing nothing at all, and looking rather sinister. You may enter the mosque, though the crowds are rather daunting, and women must be completely covered in the robes provided. Shoes must be carried by both men and women over to the counter on the left side only of the courtyard and handed to an attendant in exchange for a numbered token, then collected on leaving. Inside the mosque, men and women have to enter the shrine area by separate doorways labelled in Arabic only, so take care to watch who goes in where. Once inside, the areas do not meet up as the men's and women's areas are totally segregated with each having access to one side only of the elaborately, not to say garishly decorated tomb. All the surfaces inside the mosque are highly coloured, with tilework in blues and greens, and gold and green neon lighting. When Shi'a pray, they often use a small mud brick, said to be the mud of Mecca, which they take out of a green bag and place on the floor so that their foreheads touch it during prostration.

Great Umayyad Mosque الجامع الأموى الكبير *(Open to visitors 09.00–18.00 daily except
Fri; noonday prayers 11.30–14.00; S£50 entry fee)* Retrace your steps now to the

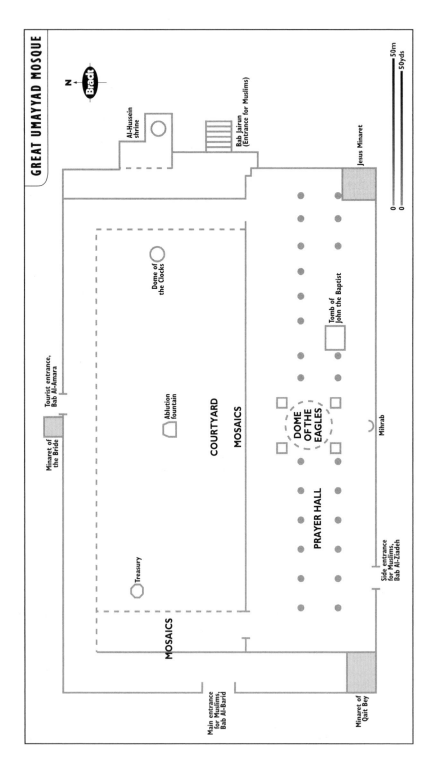

GREAT UMAYYAD MOSQUE

N

Al-Hussein shrine

Bab Jairun
(Entrance for Muslims)

Jesus Minaret

Dome of
the Clocks

Tomb of
John the Baptist

Tourist entrance,
Bab Al-Amara

Ablution
fountain

COURTYARD

MOSAICS

DOME
OF THE
EAGLES

Mihrab

Minaret of
the Bride

PRAYER HALL

Treasury

MOSAICS

Side entrance
for Muslims,
Bab Al-Ziadeh

Main entrance
for Muslims,
Bab Al-Barid

Minaret of
Qait Bey

50m
50yds
0
0

northern side entrance of the Great Umayyad Mosque where you can follow the signs into the little kiosk to the left, calling itself 'Putting on Special Clothes Room'. Here you buy your ticket for which you get a mini-pamphlet to the mosque and a hooded, grey full-length robe which all female foreigners must wear throughout their visit. The robes come in three different sizes, and are required only for the mosque itself, not for the Saladin mausoleum beside, though in practice everyone puts them on now. Having tied them in front and looking like Thomson and Thomson from the Tintin books, you may now set off towards Saladin's Tomb, a simple mausoleum with a distinctive dark red watermelon-shaped dome. Inside are two tombs: the original one in carved walnut, looking distinctly decayed, and a later one in elaborate white marble, a gift from the German Kaiser Wilhelm II in 1898 to curry favour with the Ottoman sultan of the time. The inscription reads: 'Oh Allah, be satisfied with this soul and open to him the gates of paradise, the last conquest for which he hoped.' The modesty of the tomb befits the man who died without personal wealth, a leader of great stature and grace (see *Saladin* box, page 83). Shoes must be removed and left at the entrance and arrows indicate the correct direction of circumambulation. The turquoise tilework on the walls is 17th-century Damascus-made and especially fine.

Continue now straight on through a marbled courtyard with fragmentary Roman columns to enter the mosque to the right, below the north minaret beside the orange-juice seller. Shoes must be removed and either left outside or carried round with you. The guardian will expect *baksheesh* if you leave your shoes with him. During your stay you should aim to see the mosque at least twice, once in daylight, once at night, spending as long here as you can. It is a massive, accepting place. Once inside the precincts you have entered a different world, a haven where time stands still, a sacred site since the 9th century BC when the Semitic Arameans built a temple here to their chief god Hadad, who was appeased by notoriously bloody sacrifices including the sacrifice of children. The Romans then incorporated Hadad into their huge Temple of Jupiter. The temple compound in the 1st century BC was far bigger than that of the current mosque, which probably equated more to the inner enclosure (*temenos*) with its central chamber and sacrificial altar.

When Christianity was adopted as the official religion of the Byzantine Empire in the 4th century AD the pagan temple was torn down and the building was converted to the Cathedral of John the Baptist, whose head is buried here, a distinction also claimed by three other places in Europe. The arrival of the Arabs in 636 did not initially change matters and the Muslims for nearly 100 years allowed the Christian community here to continue to worship freely in their churches, even sharing the extensive compound for a time, with the Muslims focusing their prayers on the south wall that faced Mecca, while the Christians continued to use the cathedral as the city's main place of worship.

In 708 the Caliph Al-Walid decided that the expanding Muslim population needed a larger space to worship in and he negotiated with the Christians for the church to be ceded and began the seven-year-long construction of the mosque which used up the state's entire revenue for that period. The Christians were compensated, according to early historians, with permanent rights to the four church sites elsewhere in the Old City, including the present Greek Orthodox Patriarchate. Byzantine influence is clear in the architecture and decoration of the building, and Byzantine mosaic specialists were said to have been drafted in from Constantinople to help create, alongside Syrian craftsmen, the exquisite green and gold mosaic work which originally covered all the courtyard wall and which now survives only in part. Records indicate that 12,000 workmen were employed.

The building was reorientated towards the south, the direction of Mecca, by the adding of a transverse aisle in the centre that led into the *mihrab* or prayer niche and a central dome was added to make this the focal point of the mosque. Even so the mosque today still has the feel of a basilica with three aisles separated by two rows of internal columns, yet the blending of the two only serves to enhance the special feel of the place. The great mosque at Córdoba, built by the Umayyads in Spain nearly a century later, also has some echoes of this, with its dome above the prayer room, forests of columns and gold mosaics in which Caliph Al-Hakam expressly set out to surpass the mosaics here.

Despite invasions, Mongol sackings, earthquakes and fire, the mosque's original plan has remained unchanged. The greatest damage was probably caused by the fire of 1893 which destroyed the inner fabric of the prayer hall, which is said to have been started by a workman engaged on repair work smoking his *nargileh* (water pipe). The subsequent fire caused the central dome to collapse. The Ottomans restored everything but in a simplified style, so the building we see today is still substantially the same as the original 7th-century structure.

The courtyard and mosaics No other building in Damascus embodies the complexity of the city's past as much as this Great Umayyad Mosque. Along with Jerusalem's Dome of the Rock it stands as one of early Islam's greatest and most sacred monuments. The sheer beauty of the green and gold mosaics on the main façades is mesmerising and the colossal space 50m by 122m was laid with the current pinky white marble flagstones in the late 19th century, replacing the original mosaic paving that had been damaged by fire and earthquake.

The delicate octagonal domed building freestanding to the right (western end), still decorated with exquisite green and gold mosaics, was the treasury of the mosque, raised up off the ground to protect it from theft by eight ancient recycled columns with Corinthian capitals. The Treasury is thought to date to the late 8th century, making it early 'Abbasid, whilst the mosaics are reckoned to be largely 13th- or 14th-century restorations. The real mystery though is how anyone got inside at all, as there seems to be no entrance. The ablution fountain in the centre of the courtyard is relatively modern, and most ablutions are in fact performed now in the two much more private separate men's and women's rooms off the northwestern corner of the portico near the treasury. The little domed pavilion on the left (eastern end) is known as the Dome of the Clocks because it was used until recently to store the mosque's clock collection. Dating from the 18th or 19th century it reuses, like the Treasury, eight columns with ancient capitals, no doubt relics rescued from the Roman Temple of Haddad. These wonderful fusions of building materials from different periods contribute greatly to the special atmosphere of the mosque.

Originally the mosaics would have covered all the surfaces of the arcaded walls and the main façade of the prayer hall. Nowhere else in the world has mosaic been used on such a massive scale, though the Sicilian cathedral of Monreale near Palermo built in the 12th century by the Norman king of Sicily William II, was clearly a borrowing from the Umayyad Mosque brought back by Crusaders and Arab craftsmen used on the construction. Much has been lost through the ravages of fire and earthquake over the past 12 centuries, with major restorations in 1929, 1954 and 1963. The unrestored sections are still recognisable as they form the darker patches in the mosaic. Despite all this, enough remains to convey still the sheer magnificence of the conception. The theme is thought to be a representation of the Koranic paradise: 'Such is the Paradise promised to the righteous; streams run through it; its fruits never fail; it never lacks shade.' (Koran 13:35)

The place where this vision is most clearly to be seen is in the so-called Barada Panel, the mosaic which runs along the inner arcade of the western wall (far right on entering from the tourist entrance), and this too has been least restored over the years. Thought to represent the river of paradise in the form of the Barada River flowing through the lush vegetation of orchards, groves, fields and lined here and there with palaces, pavilions, bridges and fantasy cities, the whole image is unlike anything else in the world, neither Arab, nor classical, possibly more reminiscent of Byzantine than anything else, yet the subject matter entirely different, with not a human figure, saint or deity in sight. God is implied but never represented in Muslim art. For humans to imagine they can represent God in any art form is presumptuous and blasphemous from the Muslim point of view.

Another theory on the purpose of the mosaics is that they depict the subjection of the world to Islam, a world with no representations of humans, only nature and buildings, and other scholars have suggested the mosaics may simply represent the city of Damascus in the 8th century. We will never know for sure, but maybe in fact they are a blend of all three theories, showing a fantasy vision of 8th-century Damascus as a heavenly paradise after the world has come to be dominated by Islam. The mosaics can be seen very well after dark, when they are floodlit, along with the finely painted 15th-century high wooden ceiling just inside the main entrance at Bab Al-Barid.

The mosaics everywhere in the mosque begin above 6.5m height on the walls. Below that the Umayyads used marble panelling for decoration. Much of this is 19th- and 20th-century renovation work, but fragments of the original Umayyad marblework can be seen in the east vestibule around the east side door of Bab Jairun on your way into the prayer hall. The complex geometric patterns used here are among the earliest examples of this style of decoration which was later to become the Islamic hallmark.

Minarets Of the three distinctive minarets of the mosque the two corner ones are thought likely to have been built on the site of earlier Roman/Byzantine towers. The earliest one is the Tower of the Bride (Madhanet Al-'Arous) on the north wall, immediately beside the tourist entrance. Its lower part is 9th century and the upper section dates to the 12th century. The name originates in a legend that the daughter of a merchant who gave enough lead to cover the minaret roof, became the sultan's bride. On its side is an astronomical clock.

Of the two corner minarets, the one to the left as you enter from the tourist entrance is the Tower of Jesus (Madhanet 'Issa), so called because this is the place according to Muslim tradition, from which Jesus will descend on the Day of Judgement to fight the Anti-Christ. Built on the site of an Umayyad structure, the current minaret is 13th century, with an Ottoman upper section. To the right corner as you enter is the Tower of Qait Bey built by the Egyptian Mameluke sultan of the same name in 1488.

The minaret was introduced by the Umayyads and Syria is therefore the first home of the minaret. Thought to have been built originally as watchtowers, these early Syrian minarets were always square and built of stone. It was only later that they were used by the muezzin for the call to prayer. The Arabic word *minaara* from which we take our word 'minaret' means lamp or lighthouse, confirming the watchtower role. Later minarets, as they were used ever more prolifically throughout the Muslim world, took on the traditional shape of towers in whatever country they arose, using local building materials, thereby introducing huge variety into the shapes and sizes.

Prayer hall On the way into the prayer hall to the far left, opposite the Dome of the Clocks, is a series of separate chambers behind the arcade called Mashad Al-Hussein, an important place of pilgrimage for the Shi'a. Muslim tradition holds that after the martyrdom of Al-Hussein, son of 'Ali and grandson of the Prophet

The main division in Islam between the Sunna (the right way or practice, based on Muhammad's behaviour as recorded in the *Hadith* or Sayings of the Prophet) and the Shi'a (faction or party) is more of a political than a religious divide, in that it goes back to the years immediately following the Prophet Muhammad's death in 632, when there was a radical disagreement about the succession. The Sunni (orthodox mainstream) believed the caliphate should pass to the person chosen by the *'ulema* or Islamic clergy, while the Shi'ites believed that 'Ali, husband of the Prophet's daughter Fatima, and his descendants were the rightful successors to the caliphate. Considered pious, brave and good-natured, 'Ali had in fact been proclaimed caliph after the previous caliph 'Uthman was murdered, but Mu'awiya challenged him and their conflicting claims were put to arbitration, a process that left 'Ali weakened and cost him his life two years later. This split has some similarities with the split in Christianity between the Protestants and the Roman Catholics, in which the latter, with their veneration of saints' shrines and love of ritual practices, are likened to the Shi'ites. For the Sunnis, the intermediary between God and humans was the Koran. For the Shi'ites it became the religious leader or imam himself, who they believed was divinely designated for the supreme office, and therefore qualified for *'ismah* or immunity from error. The extreme Shi'ites took this a stage further and considered the imam himself to be the divine incarnation. This later evolved into a *mahdi* hypothesis of a saviour-leader which was certainly influenced by the Judeao-Christian ideas of the Messiah. Iraq proved the most fertile soil for the flourishing of Shi'a doctrine and today the majority of Shi'ites are to be found in Iran and Iraq. In Syria only some 11% of the population is Shi'ite , while 74% is Sunni. Scores of different Shi'ite sects arose which became the natural centre of attraction for all sorts of political and religious non-conformists, economic and social malcontents Globally Shi'a account for 10% of the world's Muslims and number some 130 million. Traditionally they were the underdogs, oppressed and marginalized by Sunni ruling regimes, as in Iraq till recently. Regime change and the removal of the Sunni Saddam Hussein has resulted in the empowerment of the Shi'a majority there and disenfranchised the Sunni minority leadership that had ruled Iraq since 1932. The reverberations of the Shi'a victory will inevitably extend beyond Iraq's borders.

Muhammad, his head was brought here and put on display to humiliate the supporters of 'Ali, founder of the breakaway Shi'a sect. Some Umayyad accounts say the head was then buried here, while others say it was sent to Medina for burial. The Battle of Kerbala took place on 10th of Muharram AD680, the date on which Shi'ism can be considered to have begun, and is marked in the Islamic calendar by the Shi'ite festival of 'Ashoura, a day of great mourning and self-flagellation. It is worth making a quick detour into these rooms, despite the overwhelming smell of feet, to observe the large numbers of Shi'ite pilgrims who come here, many from Iran, the women in their black robes and the men in dark Western suits, devoutly fingering and kissing the various sacred places of the shrine.

The original prayer hall had no walls separating the courtyard, and the arches were simply open. The shape of the prayer hall is surprisingly long and thin, yet because its orientation is to the long south wall, it gives an impression of great space as you pass along the different sections.

Inside, for Westerners who have never been into a mosque before, the main surprise is how naturally and normally everyone behaves. There is none of the hushed awe and inhibition of a church. There is no furniture, only carpets, and men of all ages lie on the floor taking a nap, children play chase, women sit casually in groups resting and chatting, having picnics and pouring tea from thermos flasks. Even mobile phones are permitted. It is a place of relaxation, a haven from the bustle of the outside world. The smell of feet can be quite pervasive at times. A few older men may be seen sitting cross-legged devoutly reciting verses aloud from the Koran held open on its special cross-legged stand, oblivious to all else, but they are a small minority. You too can sit somewhere quietly leaning against the wall, drinking in the atmosphere.

Within the huge internal space the first thing to notice is the green-glassed domed building freestanding at the eastern end as you enter, which is said to be the tomb of John the Baptist. There is no concrete evidence that John the Baptist's head was brought to Damascus from Palestine where he was beheaded following Salome's dance, but one noted Arab historian related how the caliph Al-Walid discovered the head, then had a special column erected to mark the spot. The tomb inside is Ottoman and white marble, the previous wooden one having been cremated in the fire of 1893.

The massive dome built over the centre of the prayer hall is known as the Dome of the Eagles, because it is thought to represent the head and body of an eagle, with the wings represented by the long prayer halls stretching either side. Built of stone in rather austere style, it replaced the original wooden ceiling which was destroyed by fire. The earliest mosques erected in conquered countries were simple quadrangles built of clay and mud bricks. The first *mihrab* to indicate the direction of prayer towards Mecca is thought to have been in the mosque in Medina, and their use spread rapidly to all mosques, where they always represent the most sacred focal point of the building. They are always empty because obviously Islam does not permit human representation and anyway there is no worship of saints or prophets in Islam. They do however receive the greatest concentration of decorative effort and so became over the centuries a barometer to gauge the continually changing forms of Islamic decorative art. In addition to the main *mihrab* there are three other smaller and less elaborate *mihrabs* along the southern wall. These represent the other three schools of Sunni law, with the main *mihrab* being for the Shafi'i school, the dominant school in Damascus and the most moderate of the schools, and the others being for the Hanbalis, the Hanafis and the Malikis.

The craftsmen employed by Al-Walid to build the mosque were from Persia, India, Greece and Egypt and this blend of remarkable skills shows itself in the masterpiece of sumptuous marbles and mosaics of gold leaf representing trees and cities of paradise. Fragments of 11th-century mosaic can still be seen inside the prayer hall on the north wall of the transept, as can some of the original wooden panelling of the transept ceiling on the courtyard side. Though burnt down in 1069, and again in 1400 by the Chagatai Turk Tamerlane and for the last time in 1893, the mosque is still considered the fourth Wonder of the World by Muslims and the fourth sanctuary of Islam after the Harams (sacred places) of Mecca and Medina and the Dome of the Rock in Jerusalem. The Umayyad Mosque and the Al-Aqsa Mosque are the first two congregational mosques of Islam, not just places of worship, but also serving as general assembly halls and as political and educational forums.

The first *minbar* or pulpit in Islam was in Muhammad's first mosque in Medina, a simple palm trunk fixed in the ground for the Prophet to stand on while addressing the congregation. The *minbar* is used in all mosques for the imam to address the faithful, especially at the Friday noon sermon. In Umayyad times it tended to be a small platform of tamarisk wood with three steps, a style copied from those seen in churches in Syria. Throughout Syria Muslim architecture was influenced by the pre-existing Christian Syro-Byzantine style with its Greek and Roman antecedents.

The outside walls of the mosque As you leave the mosque and return your gown, go back out into the large open square on the west side of the mosque where the main entrance for Muslims is located, and turn left to skirt the southern wall. It is very apparent here that the stonework belongs to the original Roman temple and that the mosque windows were built so high up in order not to interfere with this. Look out in the centre of the wall for the blocked-up triple doorway and lintel, today partially obscured by the addition of an electrical substation with skull and cross-bones on it. This was the original southern entrance to the temple used by both Christians and Muslims for the 70-year period that they shared the temple compound for worship, before the mosque was built. Its reorientation towards Mecca meant that this entrance had to be blocked so as not to be in conflict with the *mihrab* and *minbar*. An inscription in Greek above the central doorway reads: 'Thy Kingdom, O Christ, is an everlasting Kingdom, and Thy Dominion endureth throughout all generations.'

Just opposite the electricity substation are some public toilets, kept relatively clean, with separate men's and women's entrances, costing S£10 for use.

Rounding the corner of the southeastern wall you come to the blocked-up Gate of the Fountain, Bab al-Nawfarah, which has given its name to the café and district immediately below it. In Roman times this was the monumental main entrance to the temple and the grandeur of its scale, with its Roman triple doorway and remnants of the pillared entrance approached by 15 wide steps, is still apparent. The street leading east from here led originally to the agora, and followed it past the café for some 100m, where you will see, largely buried below ground by the rise in ground level over the centuries, another Roman triple gateway that led originally to the outer temple compound, and from which it was another 250m to the agora, now entirely lost in the maze of streets and houses. The Umayyad royal palace, also now totally disappeared, is thought to have been in this area too.

Beyond the Roman gateway the main street running east is called Al-Qaimariye, a lively shop-lined street that leads off towards Bab Touma and the Christian quarter.

The citadel القلعة The massive citadel area which occupies the northwest corner of the Old City finally opened in April 2006 after completion of its long restoration project and will either be used as a war museum or a centre for cultural activities or both. A Franco–Syrian archaeological mission has been working here since 2000. Even though it is still not usually open to the public whilst its fate is being decided, a walk around its outer walls remains interesting for helping bring to life the military history of the city, and you can also cast a glance at the dwindling Barada River, Damascus' original lifeblood, now reduced to a fetid stream by years of overuse and abuse. Photos as recent as 1950 show a very different Barada, wide and magnificent, in flood in the centre of the city. Only in March and April, when the snows melt on the Anti-Lebanon range, does the river flow fast again for a time, a rare glimpse of how its might used to be.

Unlike most citadels which were built on hills or tells, the Damascus citadel is unusual in being built on the flat. The reason for its exact siting was that from here, immediately to the south of the Barada, the citadel could control the flow of water and its outlets, diverting it in times of danger into the defensive moat along the eastern, southern and western ramparts. These moats were 20m wide and 6m deep, affording great protection from attack.

The citadel was in the first instance built by the Seljuks between 1077 and 1157, and from that period the most remarkable room inside is the one with the four ancient columns recycled from antiquity. From the luxurious pottery finds and goblets of fine glass the archaeologists can tell that the meat served in the citadel

Known in Arabic as Salah Ad-Din, Reformer of the Faith, the name of the Muslim warrior chief we know as Saladin is apt, for his two ambitions were to bring back Sunni dominance, especially in Egypt which had been taken over by the Shi'ite Fatimids, and to expel Christian Crusaders from Jerusalem and the Levant. Ethnically Kurdish, his youth and early education were spent in Syria. He made his military reputation in Egypt, thwarting Crusader interests in the 1160s, and then moved north to Damascus, from where he fought sporadic battles against the Zengids in Aleppo. His first major defeat of the Crusaders was at the Battle of Hittin (west of the Sea of Galilee) in 1187 on a boiling July day.

During his lifetime he achieved an impressive unification of the Levant and Muslim territory against the Crusaders, but much of this was lost in the power squabbles and divisions that took place after his death. Far more than just a warrior and champion of Sunni Islam, Saladin also founded many religious schools, *madrasas*, and mosques, patronised scholars, encouraged theological studies and introduced advanced water systems with dykes and canals.

On his recapture of Jerusalem its Christian population was peacefully evacuated, a total contrast to the massacre of Muslims that the Crusaders had carried out when they took the city 88 years earlier. To this day he is considered a paragon of virtue, with a keen sense of honour and justice. Saladin fought only when absolutely necessary, was merciful towards his prisoners and accumulated no personal wealth, leaving on his death at the age of 54 in 1193, 47 dirhams and a gold piece. His modest tomb stands beside the Umayyad Mosque. He left 17 sons to quarrel over his dynasty, called the Ayyubids, and bequeathed to Damascus much beautiful architecture still extant today.

---

halls was mostly lamb, but that fish and game were also served, as well as gazelle, goose, duck and hare. At banquets it was not unusual for 3,000 sheep, 600 cows and numerous chicken and geese to be consumed, along with huge quantities of sugar.

Excavations have also shown that there were several cafés inside the citadel, following the lead taken by the first Damascus cafés along the Barada from around 1746 onwards, a habit that grew up here in Ottoman times to while away the time when the pilgrims gathered for the Hajj and camped along the river banks sometimes for months at a time, stocking up on provisions and waiting for the official start of the journey to Mecca.

On the walls and roofs an artillery platform has been found from which projectiles weighing 18–25kg (usually lead) were hurled using catapaults for distances of 180–220m. There are 12 defensive towers and a vast courtyard inside, most of which dates from the 12th century Ayyubid dynasty of Saladin. This citadel was his headquarters and Damascus became the key centre for resistance to the Crusader invasion of the Holy Land, Palestine and Syria. The citadel was his staging area, supply centre and chief arsenal for all his military operations, and as such it merited the highest level of fortification possible. The Ayyubid workmanship is evident in the typical large rough blocks of masonry, the use of machicolation boxes (crenellated overhanging openings on the tops of the walls for throwing down stones and other deterrents on the enemy), arrow slits and vaulted interiors. Outside the northwest corner of the citadel, facing the busy thoroughfare of Ath-Thawra Street, stands a massive bronze statue representing Saladin and his victory over the Crusaders. Saladin sits proudly astride his horse and behind him on foot are Renaud de Chatillon and Guy de Lusignan, both defeated by Saladin at the momentous Battle of Hittin. The Christian crown lies on the floor.

Walk from the Saladin statue along the northern course of the walls with the Barada River to your left. The stroll is pleasant and never too crowded or busy and makes an interesting alternative route to enter the Old City apart from the main Souk Al-Hamadiye entrance. The double gateway along this northern stretch, Bab Al-Hadid, (Gate of Iron), was the citadel's main entrance, originally guarded with heavy iron gates. Inside, the passageway does five twists and turns (like the Aleppo Citadel entrance), designed to slow any attackers' onslaught right down, so that deterrents such as stones and excrement could be rained on them en route. The ordinary soldiers' latrines were generally situated near the machicolations and entrances so that the excrement could be quickly and easily tipped onto the attackers. Hot oil, which some sources suggest was used, would have been prohibitively expensive and wasteful – excrement was free. Just inside the gateway is a long vaulted hall which was used as a prison as recently as 1985. At the far end it leads into the Great Hall with the four ancient pillars mentioned earlier.

Skirting round the eastern walls there is another gate far less defended than the exposed Bab Al-Hadid, whose entrance has lovely honeycombed stalactite vaulting (*muqarnas*), dating to 1213, one of the earliest examples of this north Syrian architectural feature. Continue along the eastern wall of the citadel to re-enter the Souk Al-Hamadiye just over halfway along its length.

Maristan Nur Ad-Din بيمارستان نور الدين (*Open 08.00–14.00 daily except Tue; S£75 entry fee*) A visit to this former hospital/lunatic asylum, now turned since 1978 into a Medical Museum, should be one of your highest priorities within the Old City after the Great Umayyad Mosque. Also used originally as a medical school and research centre, it was the most advanced medical institution of its time.

Cross over the Souk Al-Hamadiye thoroughfare, doing a little dog-leg right–left, and you will come after some 100m to the Maristan Nur ad-Din, entered through a white painted honeycombed arch above the gateway with an ancient lintel recycled from classical times. Note the fine metal handles of the iron-studded doors. Inside, the museum is attractively laid out in the 12th-century building in rooms round the central courtyard, and it will come as a real eye-opener to most to see how Arab medicine was the precursor to so much of what is now established medical practice, and how the principles of homoeopathy and aromatherapy for example, all began in the Arab world many centuries ago. A great deal of the wisdom expounded here strikes a remarkable chord in today's health-obsessed world. Arab medicine was a great deal more advanced than in Europe in the 12th century, and only after the early Arabic texts of Muslim scholars were translated into Latin in later centuries did Western medical knowledge begin to progress.

Opposite the ticket office is a rather random but nonetheless curiously fascinating room full of stuffed animals showing the range of wildlife which used to roam freely in the Damascus area. The whole building functioned as a hospital from its founding by Nur ad-Din in 1154 right through till the 19th century when a separate National Hospital was built by the Ottomans outside the Old City. Around the courtyard it has two *iwans* (open arches to the courtyard), the larger of which was used for lessons and medical consultations. The smaller has a *mihrab*, suggesting it was used as a mosque, and is elaborately decorated in marble with patterns of cornucopias, vines and grapes.

Most of the exhibits are labelled in English and French, and as you follow the rooms round the courtyard anticlockwise, the first is the Hall of the Sciences, where various Arab scientists from the 9th to the 15th century are listed and their researches and discoveries explained.

The earliest one, 'Abbas Ibn Firnas (died 886), was the first to conduct a flying experiment, Icarus-style. In 852, a thousand years before the Wright brothers, this

The numbering system used all over the world is probably Indian in origin but the first actual numerals to appear in print were Arabic, in the work of the Muslim mathematicians Al-Khwarizmi and Al-Kindi around 835. Algebra was named after Al-Khwarizmi's book *Al-Jabr wa-Al-Muqabilah*, much of whose contents are still in use. The work of Muslim maths scholars was imported into Europe 300 years later by the Italian mathematician Fibonacci. Algorithms and much of the theory of trigonometry came from the Muslim world, and Al-Kindi's discovery of frequency analysis made all the codes of the ancient world soluble and created the basis for modern cryptology.

By the 9th century many Muslim scholars knew the earth was a sphere, proved, said the astronomer Ibn Hazm, by the fact that the sun was always vertical to a particular spot on earth. Galileo realised this in Europe 500 years later. So accurate were the calculations of the 9th-century Muslim astronomers that their measurement of the earth's circumference was less than 200km out. In the 12th century the scholar Al-Idrisi took the first globe to the court of King Roger of Sicily.

One of the most important mechanical inventions in the history of humankind was the crank-shaft, invented by the Muslim engineer Al-Jazari. He devised it to raise water for irrigation. He also invented or refined the use of valves and pistons, and was the father of robotics. Among his 50 other inventions was the combination lock.

Muslim poet, astronomer, musician and engineer, hoping to glide like a bird, jumped from the minaret of the Grand Mosque in Córdoba using a loose cloak stiffened with struts. The cloak slowed his fall, creating the first parachute and leaving him with only minor injuries. In 875, aged 70, having perfected a machine of silk and eagles' feathers, he jumped from a mountain, staying aloft for ten minutes. He crashed on landing, and correctly concluded that he needed to give his device a tail to make it stall on landing. Baghdad International Airport and a crater on the moon are named after him.

Al-Biruni (died 1048) studied the difference between the weight of substances in air and in water, such as feathers or gold. Al-Farabi (died 950), a philosopher and musician, was the second master of logic after Aristotle. He made the first lute-like instrument and was also a doctor, mathematician and astronomer. Ibn Al-Haytham (died 1039) was an optician who conducted the first experiments with reflections. A hundred works are ascribed to him on mathematics, astronomy, philosophy and medicine. Al-Idrissi (died 1166) was a geographer and produced the first remarkably accurate map of the world. Among the other inventions were scales for weights and measures and the plumb line for obtaining straight lines in construction.

In the *iwan* notice the hanging pipes of irregular lengths, whose different soothing sounds were used to pacify mental patients. The next room is the Hall of Medicine housing a graphic collection of medical instruments such as scalpels for haemorrhoids and goitres, tweezers and pliers for tooth extraction. The dentist's chair of Al-Zahrawi (died 1013) is on display, a remarkable man who used gold and silver fillings and only used extraction as the last resort. The Arabs were also the first to invent anaesthetics in the form of alcohol soaked in a sponge mixed with hashish, opium and belladonna, then put on the nose for inhalation. There are also drawings of the anatomy of the eye, potties for night-time urination and separate bowls for food, as they were already very hygiene-conscious and realised that illness spread through contagion.

3

Ibn Sina (died 1037, known as Avicenna in the West, and famous as a philosopher and poet as well as a physician) is described along with his ideas on the importance of mother's milk and that before dentition the diet should consist of nothing else: first tooth, first meal. He was also against early forced sitting and walking for babies. Ibn Sina too was the first to talk of the relationship between spirit and body, and that emotional problems can manifest themselves in physical symptoms. His encyclopaedic book, *The Law in Medicine*, was translated into Latin in the 12th century and became the medical textbook for the schools of Europe.

Many other very modern ideas are elaborated, such as the necessity of not overeating, the importance of a balanced diet and regular physical exercise to maintain health. The use of kohl is encouraged to protect the eyes from dust and from the sun's rays. Smoke is to be avoided and its fumes must not be breathed in. The properties of figs are discussed, such as their guarding against poisoning and their dissolving of kidney stones. The final vitrine to the left of the door as you enter displays Ottoman circumcision scissors and recommends circumcision to protect boys from illness. Soap, as still made in Aleppo from olive oil, comes from the Arabic *saboun* and was used for impetigo. The benefits of baths are extolled: the importance of detoxification through the pores, which gets rid of impurities and aids sleep.

The final room is the Hall of Pharmacy of which the Arabs were the founders. There are over 80 medical words taken from Arabic into European languages, such as santal, tamarind, anis and amber. The Arabs made anti-toxins from plant extracts, adding orange and lemon juice to make them palatable. They made potions for constipation, migraines, jaundice and used dried lizard as an aphrodisiac.

There is a large vitrine of herbs and their properties. Garlic is described as a general antiseptic, anti-cancer, anti-flu, anti-hypertension aid. Tamarin is a gentle laxative, valerium calms nervous illnesses, parsley is a diuretic and evacuates kidney stones, pourpier activates the memory and tones the nervous centres. Myrrh is an antiseptic for diarrhoea, an anti-spasmodic, and good for skin diseases. Rose water was produced against headaches, eye pain, palpitations and to regain consciousness after fainting. There is also a whole table of aromatherapy, dating back to the 13th century.

Khans of the Old City There are 18 surviving *khans* (warehouses) in the Old City mostly dating to the Ottoman period. They flourished especially in the 18th and 19th centuries when trade in Damascus was at its peak and the warehouses grew up as places to store goods for trade and to accommodate the merchants themselves. They were bonded warehouses for use only by merchants entering or exiting the city, where the market inspector would set the city tax which varied according to the type of goods. Most are concentrated in the area between the Umayyad Mosque and Straight Street to the south, the area which took over as the commercial heart of the Old City. Over the centuries the commercial centre moved from the Roman agora which lay east of the Temple of Jupiter in the current Nawfara area, to the centre of Straight Street in the Arab Middle Ages, to the area southwest of the Umayyad Mosque where the Mameluke and Ottoman *khans* were built. Many *khans* were destroyed in the French bombardment following the 1925 revolt, particularly in the Hariqa area immediately to the south of Souk Al-Hamadiye.

Clearly marked just 10m south of the beginning of the covered part of Souk Al-Hamadiye past the Roman gateway, is the Khan Al-Jumruk, the Customs *khan*, unusual because of its L shape, the only such one in the Old City. It was built in 1608–09 and has a total of six domes, four along the east-west axis and two along

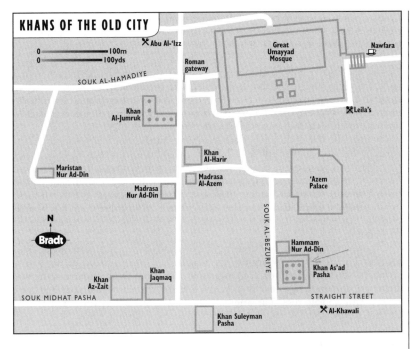

the north–south axis. Its arches all carry black-and-white striped decoration and all the domes are intact. Both sides are now lined with ladies' clothing and cloth shops, all with modern metal shutters. Tucked in a nearby side street, opening out into a *souk* selling sheets, towels and table linen, is the discreet entrance to the 12th-century theological school Madrasa Nur Ad-Din. This building also houses the tomb of Nur Ad-Din, governor of Aleppo and uncle to Saladin, whose leadership gave Syria the common purpose to fight the Crusaders and whose achievements paved the way for his nephew. His tomb can be seen through a metal grill behind the drinking fountain. It is still a working mosque and you should always check and ask permission before entering. Shoes will have to be removed at the threshold in the usual way and women will have to cover their heads with scarves.

By far the most spectacular and grandiose of the *khans* is Khan As'ad Pasha, built by one of the wealthy 'Azem family members from 1751-53. It is located at the far end of the Souk Al-Bezuriye (Spice Market), the *souk* that runs south from the open place in front of the 'Azem Palace to meet Straight Street. The design of the *khan*, with the main courtyard covered with a series of eight domes, is reminiscent of the Persian *khan* style. Even its entrance is the grandest in the city, with elaborately carved black and white stonework with geometric patterns, a stalactite niche above the gates and mock carved columns in twisted and spiral geometric shapes and a geometric frieze finely carved running all round the outer edge of the gateway. Despite this elaborate entrance it is still easy to miss the *khan* among the bustle and commotion of the Souk Al-Bezuriye, where your attention is likely to be distracted by all the fragrant herbs and spices. The landmark to spot the *khan* from the street is the green-painted pulpit sticking out at first-floor level overhanging the street. Its opening hours are sporadic and it is used today mainly as an exhibition space for local artists. In 1998 it served for a time as the Natural History Museum of Damascus. The ceiling is supported by four massive pillars and round the courtyard sides are two storeys of rooms, the ground floor for storage, the upper for sleeping.

Every notable businessman in Damascus rented a room here. The covered courtyard with its colossal ceiling height, gave protection from the extremes of weather, winter and summer. The original massive 600m central dome over the courtyard has collapsed and now there is just a huge piece of cloth covering it. Despite the huge ceiling height the predominantly grey and black stone gives it a rather daunting and forbidding feel inside, only occasionally alleviated by white stone. It has been likened in feel to St Peter's Basilica in Rome and certainly the internal space is of cathedral proportions. From any high vantage point its cluster of domes also makes a distinctive mark on the skyline of the Old City.

On the same side of the street but a few metres further north closer to the 'Azem Palace is the 12th-century public bath house called Hammam Nur Ad-Din, one of the oldest and grandest in Damascus. Still functioning today, it takes only men. From the street you will get only a tantalising glimpse through the entrance, as the really beautiful rooms lie hidden inside away from prying eyes, as with all these buildings of the Old City. If the ticket-office man is asked politely and it is not too busy, he may allow both men and women into the first room, the frigidarium, to take photos.

On the covered section of Straight Street on the north side are two *khans* close together. The first is Khan Jaqmaq, the smaller and more modest of the two, a rectangle which you enter on the longer side. At each of the shorter sides the two arches are supported by a huge thick pillar. The upstairs runs round a covered open gallery with wooden roof. The original courtyard paving is very fine, in black, red and beigy pink stone. A few of the shops still function but the whole place is very run-down. A massive *keena* tree gives shade all year round to one side. Khan Az-Zait, just a few metres further on, has a good entrance leading into its square black and white courtyard. The whole thing, top storey and bottom, even the walls and arches of the upper floor, is all still built of the original black and white stone. Some of the shops are still in use but all is distinctly scruffy.

Retrace your steps now to the next little turning on the right of Straight Street, that is the opposite side to the two *khans*. This leads you into a narrow street running parallel to Straight Street, known as Souk As-Souf (wool market), and about 50m along to it to the left is the Danish Cultural Institute, set in the former Bait Al-'Aqqad. This magnificent palace with elements going back as far as Mameluke times was the subject of a joint restoration project between the Danes and the Syrians and took nearly six years. The result is a stunning triple-courtyard cultural research centre used for lectures, students' Arabic courses and a wide variety of cultural events. It is well worth a look and if you ring the bell during office hours you will generally be allowed to look round.

Close by is the 18th-century Khan Suleyman Pasha, built by one of the 'Azem governors. If it happens to be open – it has been closed for restoration for some time and there is talk of it reopening as a hotel – you enter through a monumental doorway into a rectangular courtyard originally covered with two domes. A few metres further down the same street is Khan Az-Zeit (oil), centre of the olive oil trade, built at the end of the 16th century, with an elegant gallery raised on arches running round the first floor.

'Azem Palace قصر العزم (Museum of Popular Arts and Tradition) *(09.00–17.30 summer, 09.00–15.30 winter; open daily except Tue; closed Fri 12.00–14.00 summer, 11.00–13.00 winter; S£150 entry fee. The public toilets are surprisingly clean considering how often the palace is the venue of children's school outings.)* The 'Azem Palace is the largest and grandest of the Ottoman residences of the Old City. With characteristic Syrian modesty, in Arabic just known as Bait Al-'Azem (House of the 'Azem), as everything from a palace to a small house is called *bait*. A house is always named

after the family that lived there and the distinguished 'Azem family produced five governors of Damascus over nine different periods between 1725 and 1809.

Now configured as the Museum of Popular Arts and Tradition, the original 18th-century construction was built on the site of an earlier Mameluke governor's residence. It has been through many renovations over the years and was badly damaged by fire in the 1925 uprising. The Syrian government bought it off the 'Azem family in 1951 and converted it to a museum which opened in 1954, making it one of Damascus' first. Built between 1749 and 1752 by Assad Pasha Al-'Azem, governor of Damascus, who also built the palace of the same name in Hama, the palace displays all the notable features of Arab/Ottoman domestic architecture. But whilst the 'Azem Palace in Hama is a delightful compact gem of a place, the Damascus 'Azem Palace is very open with enormous courtyards, so that the whole is less intimate and loses its cohesion somewhat.

Go first into the smallest of the courtyards, to the right of the ticket office. This is the *salamlik*, the reception area where guests were received with its formal grand hall (*qa'a*) with its own central fountain and marble floors. The large *iwan* (open arch for summer seating) has an exquisitely decorated arch in *ablaq* pastework: to the right is the winter reception room with a lower ceiling and chimney for heating, while to the left is the summer reception room with much higher ceilings and a beautiful marble fountain to cool the room with ten delicate brass snake-head waterspouts. The colossal thickness of the walls helped to keep the heat out in summer and the heat in during winter. The complex marblework of the floor is especially beautiful. On the raised dais the display is rather incongruously of a man weaving belts, his huge loom behind him.

Retrace your steps now to the ticket office and go to the left side to enter the largest courtyard which is the *haramlik* or private family quarters. The marked tour of this huge space with its pool and citrus trees all around takes you clockwise round the rooms, coming first to the old school with its dressed dummies in costume. Among the many other rooms are a library, an arms room, a pilgrimage room complete with camel and *mahmal* on its back, and in the corner is a delightful bath complex (*hammam*) with domed roofs on a very intimate scale. There is a small simple café beside the *hammam* entrance where you can sit outside and sip tea. The servants' area (*khadamlik*) is off in another corner of the courtyard near the school and musical instruments rooms, but is closed to the public and used as administrative offices. The three courtyards of *salamlik, haramlik and khadamlik* always together formed the essential layout of the wealthier Ottoman homes of the Old City.

Leaving the 'Azem Palace by the street that runs straight from the entrance off towards the Maristan Nur Ad-Din, you will pass after 50m or so on your left a beautiful shop stuffed full of all types of antiques, housed in an old *madrasa* called Madrasa Al-'Azem. Its courtyard and fountain are lovely and you can climb the stairs to the terrace for an excellent view of the Umayyad Mosque. Some 200m further along the same street you will notice on your right a street running north which has the considerable remnants of a massive stone wall, built of limestone blocks which must have been Roman in origin, maybe part of a palace or temple complex, now absorbed into the modern city, its mystery intact and undiscovered.

Restored palaces of the Old City Slowly but surely more and more of the Old City's magnificent old houses and palaces are being restored and preserved. The body responsible for this is the Mudiriyat Dimashq Al-Qadima, the Council for Old Damascus, which takes its responsibilities very seriously and has a team of about 20 architects specialising in restoration work. It even has its headquarters in one such restored palace, Maktab 'Anbar, a grand 19th-century building spread over several courtyards, which is often used in film backdrops.

Nizar Qabbani, famous poet of Syria who died in exile in 1998, describes the magic of the old courtyard house of his childhood in Damascus thus:

That house marked, to me, the borders of the world; it was my companion, it was an oasis, a place for winter and summer alike. I can close my eyes and call up, thirty years later, my father sitting in its courtyard, his coffee in front of him, and his brazier and his can of tobacco and his newspaper. On the newspaper would fall, in intervals of five minutes, white jasmine flowers, as though they were love letters falling from the sky.

The Agha Khan is also involved in a series of restoration projects in the Old City, of three major palaces, Bait Nizam, Bait Siba'i and Bait Quwatli, which he hopes will get permission to be turned into a five-star luxury hotel complex. Bait Nizam and Bait Siba'i are now complete but the restoration of Bait Quwatli is still ongoing. Of the three Bait Nizam is the largest, with three courtyards in the usual pattern where the first one is the salamlik for receiving guests, the second is the haramlik for the private family quarters and the third is the khadamlik for the servants, usually off the haramlik. The normal pattern, as here, is that the salamlik is smaller than the haramlik, and the khadamlik is obviously the smallest of the three.

The opening hours of the houses are a bit erratic, but the best time to find their doors open is between 10.00 and 14.00. There is no entry fee at the time of writing and visitors are free to come in and wander round at leisure. Bait Nizam, signposted off Straight Street, was once the residence of the British consul, but before restoration was being used as a foam factory. From the street, as ever, nothing is given away, and the discreet entrance betrays nothing of the grandeur within. You step straight into the salamlik courtyard with its very pretty fountain and glorious seahorse waterspouts and magnificent marblework and stonework of the walls and courtyard flooring. The haramlik beyond is even more exquisite, more elaborately decorated, as was generally the case, since this is where the family spent most time.

These days this courtyard is used for regular functions and occasions, and often on Monday evenings at 19.30 from April onwards till August, talks are given on the restoration projects of the Old City by the architects involved, with slides shows and even whirling dervishes adding local colour.

Bait Siba'i in a nearby side street, also signposted from Straight Street, is a smaller and more modest affair than Bait Nizam, and was once used as the German consul's residence. Once again the largest courtyard, beautifully decorated and with lovely citrus trees and jasmine, was the haramlik, while the smallest courtyard to the left after you enter the modest door from the street, was the salamlik.

Among the palaces there is one, the Dahdah Palace, that is actually still lived in by its family descendants. Tucked away in a street very close to the Jewish quarter, it is number 9 in the street and has a small sign up high. Ring the bell anytime between 09.30 and 13.00 and the family will almost certainly come and let you in, showing you round the magnificent if slightly decaying rooms of the palace. George Dahdah died in 2002 in his 80s, but his daughter continues to live here with her family who have owned it for the last 70 years. The father collected much silver, copper and brassware over his lifetime which is on display in a magnificent room with high painted wooden ceilings. Most of this collection is available for purchase and proceeds help towards the cost of preserving the house. The family still uses the palace living rooms for special occasions like Christmas (they are Christian), but otherwise they live in a much more modernised section of the house beyond the main rooms, in the former servants' area or khadamlik, where the rooms are smaller and easier to heat. The whole place has a wonderful atmosphere of faded but lived-in grandeur, with a beautiful and mature courtyard garden.

The Christian quarter Bab Sharqi (Eastern Gate), along with Bab Touma (Thomas's Gate) are the two gates of the Old City that lead into the Christian quarter, and the better place to begin a tour of the Christian areas and the Jewish quarter is Bab Sharqi. Immediately inside Bab Sharqi to your left as you enter stands the silver-domed church which is used by Damascus' small Armenian Orthodox community (most Armenians in Syria live in Aleppo), a 19th and 20th century building. Continuing some 100m along Straight Street you come to the Syrian Catholic Cathedral of Mar Paulus (St Paul), a 19th- and 20th-century building on a large scale with rather grand and surprisingly effective concrete classical-style pillars which look like black basalt till you get up close. The plaque announces its consecration in 2001 and you can stroll freely in its large courtyard to the side.

Back on Straight Street you next turn left at the black and white minaret into a kind of square. To the right a little into the square is the attractive La Guitare Restaurant with open rooftop seating, though at night its garish neon lighting can be rather off-putting. Immediately opposite is the Greek Catholic Patriarchate, seat of the Melkite Patriarch of Antioch (see page 105), with school and monastery attached, and grand basalt arches set behind high railings but still open to stroll round. It has a fine clock tower with a distinctive chime that even plays a tune, and a bell tower beside which stays strangely immobile during the chimes. On the corner nearby is the Patriarchate bookshop selling tapes, books and CDs.

Returning to Straight Street continue now till you reach the Roman arch in the middle of the road, regarded as the edge of the Christian and Jewish quarters. Turn left (south) here to reach after some 200m the first junction to the right, where a small sign quite worn and high up announces 'Arabian Palace'. This is the Dahdah Palace described on the previous page, still lived in by the Dahdah family, right on the fringes of the Jewish quarter.

STRAIGHT STREET

Forget any romantic notions you may have about the biblical 'street called straight'. Mark Twain in his *Innocents Abroad* wrote: 'The street called Straight is straighter than a corkscrew, but not as straight as a rainbow.'

The Via Recta as the Romans called it, was the *decumanus maximus*, the main thoroughfare through the Old City, and so it is today with all that entails. In other words it is a busy heavily trafficked street with no special charm, and as a pedestrian you would do well to keep off it altogether. Its original width in Roman times was 26m, four times its current width, and it was lined with columns and stalls. The westernmost section, always referred to locally as Midhat Pasha, is still covered with its high-arched corrugated iron roof. Then there is a stretch of street running for some 400m till you reach the Roman arch thought to have been part of a tetrapylon that originally marked the major intersection in the Roman street plan between the decumanus maximus and the cardo maximus. It was discovered during the French Mandate, 4.25m below the present street level, then excavated and re-erected here. Today it marks the crossing point from the Muslim quarter into the Christian and Jewish quarters of the Old City. From this point eastwards the rest of the street is known as Bab Sharqi.

There is not a great deal to see in the Jewish quarter today as it is rather run-down and deserted, the last of Damascus' Jews having been encouraged to leave in the early 1990s under President Assad, most of them going to Israel. The Syrian government has plans to turn the Jewish area into an artists' quarter, with galleries and shops for local painters, sculptors and other artists, but so far this is in the very early stages. One such gallery can be seen however by continuing down the main alley southwards that the Dahdah Palace forked off from, then turning left at the next junction. A blue sign points towards the 'Sculptor Mustafa Ali Gallery Art Foundation', which you will come to some 100m later. There are about four abandoned synagogues in the area, all dating to the 19th and 20th centuries, all rather insignificant architecturally. Continue along the narrow road past the art gallery as it winds through the many ruined and dilapidated houses on both sides. The inspirational new Talisman Hotel here, marked only by a pair of lamps either side of the modest doorway and a pair of spruced-up shops opposite, represents what may be the beginning of the revival of the Jewish quarter proper. At one point the alley does a dog-leg through a narrow alley and to the left look out for the beautiful elaborately carved wooden-framed windows of Bait Lisbona, one of the loveliest 19th-century houses of old Damascus, but today in a sorry state of repair. Follow the alley onwards to rejoin Straight Street beside a little garden to your right.

Crossing straight over here you can stroll through the Christian areas north towards Bab Touma on a wide main road that takes you past the Palace of Abdul Nur on your right after 75m, closed to the public. Then just at the next major junction to the left you pass the large Lazarite Monastery, an imposing 19th-century church behind railings, locked except during services. The road here is one of the main driveable streets into the Christian quarter and is consequently often quite busy and crowded. A few metres beyond the left-hand junction which leads uphill is the Palais Ash-Shamiye to the left of the street, and 100m further on to the right on the corner of a street called Ad-Deir (the Monastery) is the Franciscan Convent.

Straight on is the square that opens up into Bab Touma, a busy place with the gate itself, the Gate of Thomas, disjointedly standing in the midst of the traffic, the walls having long ago been knocked down to make way for the roundabout. During the French Mandate and afterwards many such violations of the historic monuments of Damascus took place in the interests of free-flowing traffic. In the event the Bab Touma area is a major traffic bottleneck. To the left of the junction heading towards Hammam Bakri you come very soon to the distinctive pink façade of the grand and luxurious Beit Al-Mamlouka, a house converted by an enterprising lady from Aleppo into an exclusive eight-room hotel for the rich and famous. The Hammam Bakri immediately opposite is a small 500-year-old bathhouse that takes women between 10.00 and 16.00, and men from 17.00 till 22.00. Full scrubs and massages are offered to both sexes, and the modesty rating is high, with large wraps provided (see *Aleppo* chapter, page 150, for a full description of the *hammam* experience).

Turning right to continue the stroll through the Christian quarter, follow the street that runs inside the walls for some 200m till you have to fork right to avoid the dead end. Continue straight over the next crossroads and then turn left into Al-Azariye Street, then turn left again to reach the St Ananias Chapel, tucked in a corner but clearly signposted. There are many more dead ends in the Christian quarter and you may have to ask the way if you accidentally take a wrong turning and lose your sense of direction. Everyone is always happy to direct you.

St Ananias Chapel كنيسة حنانيا (*09.00–18.00 daily; S£150 entry fee*) This little church marks the house of Ananias, a Christian citizen of Damascus who helped Paul regain his sight. Paul, originally called Saul, was a Jew from Tarsus (modern Turkey), brought up a Pharisee, who persecuted Christians and who was authorised

by his leaders to arrest Christian converts in Damascus. As he approached the city, on a spot now marked by the Franciscans with a chapel in the southeast area of the walls, 'a light from heaven shone all around him'. He fell to the ground and a voice above spoke out: 'Saul, Saul, why are you persecuting me?' He was blinded by the light and led in a state of confusion into the city where he was taken to a house to recover. A local Christian called Ananias had a simultaneous vision telling him to go to that same house, where he met Saul, gave him shelter and initiated him into Christianity. Saul's sight returned and he was renamed Paul. With newly converted zeal he began preaching in the synagogues proclaiming Jesus as the Son of God. Once he came to the attention of the Jews, they gave instructions for him to be killed. Paul was warned and fled the city, spending the rest of his life travelling and proclaiming his mission elsewhere throughout the Middle East and Asia Minor (Turkey). He had had his 'Damascene moment'.

The ticket kiosk also has a little shop selling tacky souvenirs, but the chapel itself is interesting because it takes you down several metres to the original Roman street level where the house stood in the time of Christ, and even the stone blocks appear to be authentic.

Bab Sharqi باب شرقي From the House of Ananias the street that runs south towards Bab Sharqi is á kind of Christian *souk* with very good souvenir shops, the best in the Christian quarter, as well as the most upmarket night-time eating places such as Casablanca and le Piano.

Known by the Romans as the Gate of the Sun, Bab Sharqi ('Eastern Gate'), is the oldest surviving monument in Damascus, dating to the late 2nd, early 3rd century AD. It is the only one of the eight remaining gates of the Old City to retain its original form of a triple passageway, the large central one being for wheeled traffic and the two smaller flanking ones for pedestrians. The gate was restored under the French Mandate. It is also known to be the entrance through which the first Muslims, under the Arab commander Khalid Ibn Al-Walid, entered the essentially Christian city in 636. It was his decision to allow the Christians continued access to their churches in this area that was responsible for the gradual evolution of the Christian quarter, and likewise the Jewish quarter, based round its synagogues. The little mosque perched to the north of the gateway dates back to Nur Ad-Din's rebuilding of the walls in the 12th century.

St Paul's Church and Bab Kissan كنيسة مار بولس وباب كسان From Bab Sharqi it is a walk of some 400m round the outside of the walls to reach Bab Kissan (Roman Gate of Saturn), facing the big roundabout from which the main road heads out south to the airport. This is the spot where St Paul's Chapel has now been built beside the blocked-up gate, to mark where Paul is said to have been lowered in a basket down the walls to escape the Roman soldiers who were out to kill him. There is no actual historical evidence that this exact spot was the place, but since he would have lived in the Christian quarter and left in the direction of Jerusalem, here is as likely as any other spot along this stretch of wall. The chapel is a little kitsch with a replica basket displayed to help the imagination, but is nevertheless quite an evocative place. There is no entry fee but donations in the gift box are appreciated.

City Walls viewed from outside Still intact for at least 5km of their total 6km length, the walls to this day follow the Hellenistic and Roman course, with their original Roman stonework still clearly visible at the lower levels. The upper sections are mainly Arab work dating from the 11th century onwards when they were strengthened against Crusader and Mongol onslaughts. The modern gates still correspond with the original Roman gates, except for Bab Al-Faraj, Gate of

3

Deliverance, which is a purely Arab gate dating to Ayyubid times. The best-preserved and most impressive of the gates of the Old City is along the northern stretch of wall: Bab As-Salaam, meaning Gate of Peace, the original Roman Gate of the Moon. Heavily fortified with machicolation boxes to pour deterrents of various sorts on the enemy, the massive lintel above the door carries an Arabic inscription dedicated to the Ayyubid ruler who fortified it in 1243.

Al-Ghouta Oasis واحة الغوطة
If you want a stroll out of the Old City of about one and a half hours, there is, east of Bab Sharqi, a small patch of the Ghouta orchards left, getting smaller every year, but nevertheless enough to give you a flavour of what the surroundings of the city were like not so long ago. Tragically, the fertile land of the oasis is being swallowed up at a rate of about 500 acres (200ha) per annum. The best irrigated and most fertile zone, next to the northern suburbs and the villages of Mezzeh, Qadam and Berzeh, has gradually been urbanised through a process of illicit construction accelerated by an upsurge in immigration. The groundwater has been polluted due to excessive pumping and over-extraction from the Barada River.

To reach this last patch, take the underpass at Bab Sharqi to cross the busy main road outside the walls. In the middle of the tunnel is a remarkable chunk of unexcavated Roman wall deep under the modern ground level. On emerging, follow the sign to Al-Ghouta and walk along the long straight road past various factories and plant nurseries to finally reach a large open space where Damascus' rubbish is recycled and sold, reminiscent of the Zabbaleen district in Cairo, where you can find everything from nuts and bolts to kitchen sinks. From here you can follow a lane to the left leading down into the Ghouta, walking back in the direction of the city. Fragments of orchard remain here with walnut and apricot trees, and cows grazing in between, giving a brief glimpse of what the Ghouta would once have been like all around the city. The lane then joins a tarmac road that winds through a sheep slaughter area, very poor and squalid, heading towards a tall very thin minaret as your homing beacon, near a glass factory, to get you back to the main road.

Bab As-Saghir Cemetery مقبرة باب الصغير
Another remarkable and very atmospheric place to walk is the huge Bab As-Saghir Cemetery just a few minutes' walk south from Bab As-Saghir ('Small Gate', the Roman Gate of Mars). The cemetery is so big it is now cut into chunks by roads, but consult the map on pages 60–1 to reach the chunk that has the tombs of Fatima, daughter of the Prophet Muhammad, and the double tomb of Sukhaina and Zainab, daughters of Al-Hussein, whose death marked the start of Shi'ism. If you come on a Friday morning these tombs are heavily visited by hordes of black-veiled Shi'ite women, single-minded and oblivious, arriving in cars and microbuses. Street stalls are set up to capture the potential shoppers. Even as a foreign woman you will feel invisible. Enter through any one of the many gateways into the cemetery. Negotiating the gravestones can be quite tricky as they are so tightly packed and you need to be quite slender to squeeze between them. The atmosphere is further enhanced by the dramatic backdrop of Jebel Qassioun dominating the horizon to the north.

Sayyida Zainab Mosque جامع السيدة زينب
If you are interested in observing more of the Shi'ite phenomenon you can make a visit by taxi or microbus to this large mosque 10km southeast of the Old City. Like the Sayyida Rouqqiya Mosque in the Old City it is modern, Iranian funded, and very brightly coloured, not to say garish, with a gold-domed prayer hall and two tall round minarets. Chadors are available for women to cover up at the entrance and men must be discreetly dressed with no shorts or T-shirts. Avoid Fridays when it is packed with visiting

pilgrims. The tomb of Sayyida Zainab is in the middle of the heavily coloured, tiled prayer hall. Another tomb claimed to be hers is in old Cairo. She was the sister of Hussein and granddaughter of Muhammad.

BEYOND THE OLD CITY (*Half day minimum, avoid Tue*) Outside the Old City the other cluster of sights you should devote at least half a day to, is the grouping around the National Museum, located about 2km west from the Old City and fronting onto the Barada River, which will or will not be in evidence depending on the time of year. For those who find shopping in the Old City *souks* a bit daunting, not to say intimidating, this area also has the much more approachable Handicrafts Souk, attractively set along an alleyway behind the nearby Army Museum and extending into the courtyard of an Ottoman *khan* and *madrasa*. Prices here are reasonable and can still be slightly bargained down. It offers an excellent range of souvenir and gift shops and is particularly good for jewellery.

National Museum المتحف الوطني (*Open 09.00–16.00 winter, 09.00–18.00 summer daily except Tue; entry fee S£150 for foreigners, S£15 for Syrians, S£10 for students and military. Larger bags must be left at the ticket office. Cameras must be left in the vestibule with the guard, but you can photograph freely in the gardens. There is a small café in the grounds offering simple sandwiches and drinks. No alcohol. Adequate though certainly not pristine WC facilities beside the café. The ticket office has a good selection of books and postcards.*) Built on a manageable scale this, Syria's premier museum, merits a first visit of one to two hours. You can always take breaks if you feel the need in the attractively laid out gardens, heavily treed and flowered, in which you will always find a shady spot to sit and contemplate the basalt tomb doors, sculptural relics and miniature waterwheels that are liberally scattered throughout the gardens. If you can fit it in, make a quick first visit at the start of your trip, then return for a second trip at the end when the sites will mean more to you, and so that can linger over your particular favourites, having seen their provenance.

The museum covers the entire range of Syrian history, some 11 millennia, from antiquity to the Ottoman period, and also displays all the major finds from Mari, Ebla and Ugarit. The highpoint is the synagogue of Doura Europos, brought in its entirety from the Euphrates valley and reconstructed here. Indeed it was to house this unique treasure that the museum was built in the first place. As a result of further remarkable archaeological finds, it had to be expanded again in 1954 and in 1961. The quality of the labelling of the exhibits still leaves something to be desired, with most just giving a simple date and provenance, but there have been some improvements and the Qatna Hall is in a league of its own in the high standard of its explanatory panels.

Having walked up the path through the gardens to the main museum entrance, notice how this has been constructed to reuse wherever possible the decorative elements of the entry façade of the 8th-century Umayyad desert palace Qasr Al-Hayr Al-Gharbi, set between a pair of modern semi-cylindrical towers. The darker patches are original while the lighter patches are restored. The decoration is based on geometric and floral motifs and represents a weird blend of floral leaves, trees, rosettes and even, right at the top, a rearing horse, and the busts of young women on the capitals, showing how the Umayyads borrowed from Byzantine, Hellenistic, Roman and Persian Sassanid designs to create their own unique style. The tympanum (space between the lintel and the arch above the portal) is heavily decorated with niches, false windows and colonettes. The entire façade was rebuilt stone by stone thanks to the excavations conducted between 1936 and 1939. The palace was originally built out in the desert west of Palmyra between 724 and 727 in the reign of the caliph Hisham.

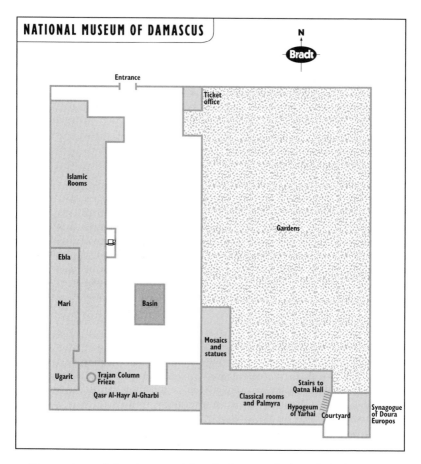

NATIONAL MUSEUM OF DAMASCUS

N

Bradt

Entrance

Ticket
office

Islamic
Rooms

Gardens

Ebla

Mari

Basin

Mosaics
and
statues

Ugarit

Trajan Column
Frieze

Stairs to
Qatna Hall

Qasr Al-Hayr Al-Gharbi

Classical rooms
and Palmyra

Hypogeum
of Yarhai

Courtyard

Synagogue
of Doura
Europos

On entering and showing your ticket, the large vestibule to the left and right is
devoted to more decorative stonework fragments from the Qasr Al-Hayr Al-
Gharbi. A very interesting wooden model of the palace shows how its layout
worked, all the more interesting because the site itself is so heavily ruined it is
impossible to get a feel for this when *in situ*. Everything worth seeing has been
brought here and reassembled.

Just to the right of the entrance desk your eye will be caught by a very life-like
copy of Trajan's Column Frieze, given as a gift to the museum in 2001 by the
Italian Cultural Institute in Damascus, on the 2nd millennium anniversary of the
Damascene architect Apollodorus (AD97–130), architect of the Column. It is well
labelled with explanations giving the subject matter of the detailed and delicate
frieze and the room opposite the Column is also given over to more elements of
the frieze. The original Trajan's Column was 30m high and still stands in Rome's
Trajan Forum. Finished in AD113 it was built to commemorate Trajan's victorious
military campaigns. The shaft was made of 18 Carrera marble drums of 4m
diameter each, and the frieze winds round the drum shaft 23 times. Inside was a
spiral staircase of 185 steps to a viewing platform on the top. There is also a plaster
cast taken in the 19th century now on display in the Cast Court of the Victoria and
Albert Museum in London, where a century of acid pollution is said to have made
the cast more legible in places than the original. This copy here is clearer still.

Since the displays are not arranged chronologically, you can now choose to head left out of the vestibule into the wing of Classical Antiquity housing Palmyra finds, Byzantine mosaics, the reconstructed Tomb of Yarhai and the Synagogue of Doura Europos, or to head to the right out of the vestibule into the rooms displaying the finds from the ancient sites of Ugarit, Mari and Ebla, then on into the Islamic display rooms where ceramics, pottery, manuscripts and decorated wood are displayed. If you have no preference, you can always let it be decided by which way looks less crowded.

To the left, up the steps you enter first of all the long thin room with collections of statuary and mosaics from the Hawran and Jebel Druze to the south of Syria. The new museum at Suweida, south of Damascus near Bosra, has the best collection of statues and mosaics from this region, but the collection here is nonetheless impressive. Of particular note here is, on the left wall, the superb late 3rd-century AD allegorical mosaic of Gée (Earth), one of the most important mosaics of the ancient Near East, in splendid colours of yellow, red, blue, green, orange and black. Earth is represented by a goddess sitting in the centre with a cornucopia in her hand surrounded by four babies holding baskets of fruit. To the left, Aion (Time) turns his wheel, symbol of the endless cycle of nature, while on the right Prometheus makes humans' first perishable garment, and behind, Hermes leads the human soul. The heads looking down from the clouds represent the winds and the dew. This mosaic illustrates well the philosophical theme popular at the time: human involvement, in spite of their mortality, in the eternal order of nature, but it is also a tribute to the fertile Hawran plain.

Moving on into the main hall, note on the right wall the mosaic with three allegorical women, dated to the early 4th century. The central one sitting on a throne is Eutekneia, representing Joy with Children, to the left is Philosophy with a basket of rolled parchments before her, and to the right is Justice (Dikaiosyne). The striking colours are violet, garnet, yellow and black. These mosaics were brought from their original locations in Roman villa floors using a complex and laborious process whereby they were lifted out in their entirety by a special glue-coated thick cloth covering the whole mosaic. The cloth was then carefully transported to the museum and laid down into a tailor-made cement frame, where the glue was dissolved with a chemical, and the cloth removed to reveal the mosaic once more. At the end of the hall you come now to an open landing, from which steps lead down into the reconstructed underground tomb of Yarhai from Palmyra, brought here in its entirety and reconstructed in 1934–35. Notice the two monolithic doors made to look like wood. Inside, the deceased presides over a funeral banquet to sustain him in the afterlife, while busts of members of his family look on from the niches. In style the tomb is very similar to the Tomb of the Three Brothers in Palmyra, the only underground tomb in Palmyra open to the public. Like that tomb, it is a mass grave with compartment shelves built into the walls for bodies from the same family, in use over a period of two centuries. As each compartment was filled, it was sealed by a funerary bust of the deceased, thereby creating an extraordinary series of family portraits. The women were shown partly veiled to represent death. An inscription tells us Yarhai had it built for his family in AD 108. The tomb is built of the characteristic pale yellow limestone from the quarries of Palmyra.

From the same landing you must now cross the open courtyard to the reconstructed synagogue of Doura Europos, the most unusual exhibit of the museum, and unique in the world. Discovered *in situ* on the banks of the Euphrates in 1932, it was so well preserved because it was accidentally filled in with earth when the Persian Sassanids took the town in the mid 3rd century AD. The most striking thing on entering the synagogue is the richness of colour of all the walls covered in frescoes. The whole building has an almost hauntingly weird atmosphere, unlike any other. All the surfaces are decorated and the ceiling too is heavily patterned with medallions and flowers and painted beams.

The wall immediately opposite the entrance is the Wall of the Torah, with a niche to hold the Jewish holy book, marking the direction of Jerusalem. The benches all round the walls were where the worshippers sat. The frescoes all illustrate scenes from the Old Testament with patriarchs and prophets in their human form, against all Talmudic tradition. This was not that unusual during the Roman period, however, when strongly Hellenised Jews did use the human form, as displayed in several mosaics of that time in Palestine with human figures, indicating the open and diverse cultural traditions to which Doura Europos was exposed during the 2nd century AD when the frescoes were painted. The cycle of paintings is arranged at four heights, with the lowest height given over entirely to animals, thought to be symbolic.

The Torah wall is the most complete. From right to left the scenes are:

Bottom: Moses as a baby in four scenes, being rescued from the Nile waters; David the King of Israel
On the other side of the Torah niche: story of Esther and Mordacai; Elias resuscitates the son of the widow Sarepta
Middle: the Ark in the hands of the Philistines, the Temple, the prophet Josiah
On the other side of the Torah niche: Aaron and his son in front of the Tabernacle; Moses giving water to the 12 tribes
Top: the Hebrew exodus from Egypt, in four scenes; the plagues descending on a city, Moses parting the waters of the Red Sea, the drowning of the Egyptians, Moses giving water to his people
Above the niche: Moses receiving the Law; the majesty of Solomon

On the left wall:

Bottom: the fire from the sky sets fire to the funeral pyre prepared by Elias; the vain prayers of the priests of Baal; Elias and the widow of Sarepta
Top: the triumphal return of the Ark to Jerusalem

On the right wall:

Bottom: the death of Joab, general and nephew of David, who was executed inside the very Temple where he had hoped to find refuge from the prosecution of Solomon; the vision of Ezekiel setting the stamp of shame on the sins of Israel
Middle: taking of the Ark by the Philistines
Top: Jacob's dream

Back in the landing from where the steps go down into the Tomb of Yarhai, be sure not to miss the recently opened spectacular Qatna Hall, professionally displayed now up the stairs here in a series of rooms. These are the fruits of the joint Syro–Italian–German mission, made between 1994 and 2004. The University of Tübingen has been responsible for the many excellent panels in English and Arabic explaining the project itself and the history and significance of the finds.

The site of Qatna is located 15km northeast of Homs on the eastern edge of the Orontes valley and is a very extensive 2nd-millennium BC city of the Early and Middle Bronze Age, contemporary with Mari and a little later than Ebla. Although the site has been dug sporadically since the 1920s, most of the really spectacular finds have been uncovered in the last ten years, especially during the excavation of the 80-room Royal Palace, one of the largest and most monumental palaces of ancient Syria.

Near the beginning of the Qatha Hall, one of the first exhibits is the skeleton of a 25–35-year-old man, thought from the great hole in his skull and the carelessly thrown position he was found in inside his grave, to have been murdered. His teeth are still remarkably good for a 30 year old, let alone a 4,000-year-old man.

As well as the exquisite workmanship of the beaten gold ornaments and jewellery, the two most spectacular finds are at the far end of the hall, namely the twin duck heads with the head of the Egyptian cow goddess Hathor between them, and the orangey red agate vessel, both beautifully illuminated in their own individual vitrines, both found on the dining bed of the dead king. The gold hand nearby is also very striking. Bristol University has been involved in the analysis of the substances found in the large clay pots on the site and has found traces of wine, beer and milk.

At the site itself the modern village of Mishrifiye is the result of Christian villagers being displaced from the ruins by the digs in the 1930s. Many of the families still come on Fridays to picnic within the site close to their abandoned houses, school, mosques and churches. A drivable track leads round the site.

In its heyday in the first half of the 2nd millennium BC the city controlled an important kingdom on the trade route between Mesopotamia and the coast via Palmyra, and in the mid 14th century BC the king here was loyal to Egypt and fought against the Hittites, thereby earning their wrath and later being pillaged by them, the population being deported to Egypt.

Returning to the hall and walking back down the other side of it, there are displays of some very interesting textiles from Palmyra dated from the 1st to the 3rd century AD. The importance of these textiles lies in the sophisticated patterns and designs found on them, some with human and animal motifs, some with floral, rosette and arabesque patterns that can be traced to architectural patterns of the time, too. The colours are still bright, with reds, blues, greens and dark yellow, and the silk from China shows how far flung the Palmyrene trading partners were. Note the quality of the cloth, especially the Chinese silk that was used for wrapping bodies in the tombs. The range of dyes used also reflects the diverse trade links: with the red taken from a cochineal insect found in Anatolia and the Caucasus, the light red taken from madder root found in Persia and the Mediterranean, the blue from indigo brought from India, the purple from a shell found on the coast and the yellow the only local colour, coming from a weld plant found in Syria.

In the Doura Europos room the most striking item on display, on the back wall, is the fresco representing a ceremony in the temple of the Palmyrene gods. Discovered in the ruins of the temple at Doura Europos the fresco dates to the 1st century BC and shows two priests in conical hats and long white tunics, behind whom stand the commander of the sacrifice, Conon and his daughter richly adorned in jewels. In the same room, to the right of the entrance, is another painting representing a temple priest dressed in a long white tunic, holding a plate and knife in one hand, while raising the other hand above a small altar.

Cross back over the vestibule entrance of the museum now to enter the Eastern Antiquities area, starting at the Ugarit Hall. This room contains a remarkable collection of objects, including some exceptionally delicate ivory work, notably the tray in vitrine number 3, finely carved with scenes of animals – gazelles, eagles with wings spread and a sphinx – set around a rosette. It was found broken in a million pieces and patiently reconstructed by Syrian archaeologists. In vitrine number 4 is the famous alphabet of Ugarit from the 14th century BC, which formed the basis of the Phoenician alphabet, then the Greek, and from that of all the Western languages. It was read from left to right and consisted of 30 letters. A total of over 17,000 tablets using this alphabet were found at Ugarit – administrative, legal, diplomatic and religious, as well as royal correspondence – and are displayed in the subsequent vitrines (see page 186 for box on the *Early alphabet*). In vitrines numbers 10,11 and 12, do not miss the remarkable ivory bust of an Ugarit prince (or princesse), a delicately carved ivory panel with scenes on both sides, and an elephant's tusk discovered in the Royal Palace at Ugarit, 53cm long, carved in the shape of a naked woman, probably a goddess.

Then comes the Ebla room, with a small collection of clay tablets, but the major Ebla finds are in the museums at Idlib and Aleppo. Far more spectacular is the Mari room, displaying some of the most famous pieces excavated at this important city state on the Euphrates that flourished in the 3rd and 2nd millennia BC. Vitrine 36 houses the so-called Treasure of Ur, found hidden in a jar, and identified by an inscription as a gift from the founder of Ur to the King of Mari. It consists of cylinder seals, a collection of bronze statues of goddesses, naked with arms outstretched, eyes of mother-of-pearl and blue lapis lazuli, and most spectacular of all, the eagle with lion's head, where the wings and body are a solid piece of lapis lazuli and the head and tail of gold leaf. This creature has become the emblem of the Mari digs. Note too the mummified fish and the elaborate stone weights in the shape of ducks and lions used for weighing gold and silver. In vitrine 41 look out for the famous alabaster statues, first of the dancer Ur-Nanshe, often mistaken for a woman, sitting cross-legged on a cushion, and then of Shibum, a votive offering praying standing up, hands clasped, head shaved, with long beard, and wearing only the puffy skirt made of sheep's wool called a *kaunake*. Many such stylised statues were found in the temples. In the middle of the room is a clay model of a 3rd-millennium BC house, circular, with nine rooms around a courtyard. Many such models were found, usually buried in the floors of the houses.

Moving on to the Islamic rooms you come first to the Raqqa room, where two models show the layout of the town and its palaces. In its own vitrine in the middle of the room note especially the fine 12th-century coloured ceramic statue of a horseman with Asiatic features, fighting the dragon that is entwined round the leg of his horse. Another vitrine against the wall displays a hoard of copper coins discovered by chance at Raqqa, weighing 50kg. Consisting of several thousand coins, both Arab and Byzantine mixed, it demonstrates the commercial links between the two rival empires, Christian and Muslim.

From the Raqqa room a long corridor leads off into a series of rooms exhibiting collections of 12th- to 14th-century coloured tiles and ceramics, followed by a room of illuminated Korans. Notice too the brass navigation instruments, scissors and circumcision tools. There is also an impressive display of gold Islamic jewellery, most of it from Raqqa or Aleppo dating to the 12th century, very delicate work including earrings, bracelets, rings and necklaces. In the final room is a collection of carved and painted wood, among which a magnificent cenotaph stands out, dated to 1265, ordered by the Mameluke Sultan, Baibars, to commemorate Khalid Ibn Al-Walid, the Muslim general who conquered Damascus in 636.

Right at the very end of the corridor is a reconstruction of a Damascene reception room of the 18th century, original elements of which were offered to the museum in 1958 by Prime Minister Jamil Mardam Bey. Note the marble chimney.

Army Museum متحف الجيش (*Open 09.00–14.00 daily except Tue; S£75 entry fee*) This extraordinary museum is located behind the National Museum in the buildings which were originally the kitchens and refectories for the Tekkiye Suleymaniye complex. Scattered about in the gardens in front of the old *tekke* or monastery with mosque attached, is an incongruous collection of planes and tanks used in Syria's various wars, and even an old Sputnik commemorating Syrian involvement in the former Soviet Union's space programme. Inside, there is an interesting collection of weapons among which the black satanic helmet with two horns from Crusader times is especially sinister-looking. There is also a very good model of Saladin's Castle, set on its spit with the gorge all around.

Tekkiye Suleymaniye Complex التكية السليمانية In the signs on the ground the spelling of this complex of buildings is 'Al-Takiya As-Soulaymaniya', where the first word, Al-Takiya, does not use the sun-letter system where the al- elides into the first letter of the next word, ie: At-Takiya, while the second word, As-Soulaymaniya, does: another example of the amazing inconsistency of the English transliteration in use everywhere.

One of the most attractive spots in Damascus, this beautifully designed complex was masterminded in 1553 by Turkey's most famous architect, Sinan, also referred to as the Ottoman Michelangelo, to whom he was a near contemporary. 84 of Sinan's buildings are still standing in Istanbul alone. He was nearly 50 when he completed his first mosque and died aged 97, beating Michelangelo's 88 by nearly a decade. Built on the site of Baibars' Ablaq Palace which the Chagatai Turk Tamerlane had razed to the ground over a century earlier, its purpose was to provide a gathering point for pilgrims preparing for their annual Hajj to Mecca, an event for which the governor of Damascus traditionally took responsibility. Surrounded by the bustling modern city it nonetheless manages to create an atmosphere of pleasant calm, set in abundant greenery beside the gardens of the Army Museum, and with its alleyway of handicraft shops, an easier place to shop than the Old City. The attached *madrasa* complex is approached through a discreet entrance in the handicraft alleyway, opening up into a lovely courtyard whose paving slabs are at appealingly drunken angles, set round a large fountain pond and now housing further handicraft shops selling an excellent selection of items from traditional clothing to paintings. These rooms would once have housed religious students. The mosque itself is still in use. Built in honour of Suleyman the Magnificent (1520–66), it was one of the total of some 335 buildings designed by Sinan, which include not only mosques and *madrasas* but also tombs, *hammams,* caravanserais, fortifications and aqueducts.

Hejaz railway station محطة الحجاز This remarkable relic of Ottoman times can be incorporated in the 15 minute-walk from the National Museum towards the Old City. Built in 1917 to transport pilgrims from Damascus to Mecca, it is now obsolete, awaiting development into a shopping mall complex. One of its old 1908 steam locomotives graces the front of the building, perched incongruously above the pavement. Some of the old wooden carriages of the private train of the last Ottoman sultan, Abdul Hamid, have also been converted to a bar and restaurant. With the outbreak of World War I the Ottoman and German troops used the railway as a vital transport link, which the Allies naturally made regular attempts to blow up. Inside the ticket office hall of the railway building the wonderful coloured glass windows and painted ceiling give a special atmosphere.

Historical Museum of Damascus متحف تاريخ دمشق (*Open 08.00–14.00 daily except Fri; S£75 entry fee; allow 30mins*) Set by itself in a side street tucked off Ath-Thawra Street, not on the way to anywhere and therefore very little visited, is this little gem of a museum, often pictured on the entry tickets to sites of the Old City. Once the home of the wealthy Khaled Al-'Azem, a former prime minister of Syria, it is all a little run-down and neglected now, but the ceilings of the reception rooms off the main courtyard are all in good condition, as are the elaborately carved shutters. The patterned marble flooring in white, black, pink, yellow and red is also exquisite throughout, and look out too for the unique fountain in the shape of a maze, the only one of its kind in Damascus. One of the rooms also houses some interesting models of old Damascus.

The Hajj was (and still is) a religious duty and turned every Muslim into a traveller at least once in his lifetime. But it was also very important for the dissemination of ideas, with rich and poor, high and low, Muslims from countries as far afield as China, Africa, Persia and Turkey fraternising and meeting together on the common ground of faith. Massive economic repercussions also followed in its wake. Every pilgrim took with him something to sell as he went along, to help pay for his journey. The items would include cereals, olive oil, arms, textiles, dried fruit and soap and on the return from Mecca pilgrims would bring back coffee from Arabia, muslin, silk, precious stones, spices, drugs, indigo, camphor and gum Arabic to be traded on from Damascus to Istanbul and the West. The journey was hazardous and took 35 days there and 35 back, plus one week to complete the Eid Al-Kabir rituals. There was always the danger of Bedouin raiding parties who had to be fought or bought off. They would block wells and leave pilgrims to die of thirst, then strip them naked. The pilgrims were also at the mercy of flash floods, snow storms, terrible heat and sometimes the caravans would get lost. Often they travelled at night to avoid the heat. Such were the dangers of the Hajj that when one group of 2,000 Persian pilgrims arrived in Damascus in 1711 to find they had missed the caravan's departure by a few days, they simply decided to stay and wait for the next year's departure, rather than risk going alone. Patience was most definitely a virtue. Damascus and Cairo were the two most important points of departure for the Hajj caravan, and pilgrims from Anatolia, Iran, Iraq and Syria would all gather in Damascus. It is estimated the caravan used to consist of something between 20,000 and 30,000 pilgrims. Most began to assemble in Damascus a few weeks ahead of time, and camped on the banks of the Barada or lodged in *khans* or *madrasas* while gathering supplies for the journey. This was when the first coffee shops developed on the banks of the Barada, the pilgrims sipping tiny cups of coffee and smoking *nargilehs*, and listening to the storytellers (*hakawati*) to while away the evenings.

The departure of the Hajj caravan was a magnificent sight to behold. They would set off in a carnival-like procession and all of Damascus would come out to see them off – dervishes whirling, drummers beating, women ululating, swordsmen dancing. The order of the procession was very particular, with the artillery and cavalry in front, then the Sunni pilgrims, followed by the camel bearing the *mahmal*, a splendidly decorated litter, symbolic of the caravan's dignity, in which sat the leader of the Hajj. After that came the treasurer and more cavalry, then the Shi'a and Persian pilgrims, with the dromedary riders bringing up the rear. The opening of the Hijaz Railway in 1908 specifically to take pilgrims to Mecca put an end to such colourful processions, though Damascus remained the gathering point for departure, till the advent of air travel put paid to that, too.

Souk Saroujah سوق ساروجة The area where the Historical Museum lies, north and west of the Old City, is known as Souk Saroujah, the Saddlemaker's Souk, and is a friendly if run-down area of shops and stalls. In Ayyubid times this area was a cemetery for wealthy Damascenes, with many tombs and mausoleums. In later Ottoman times space constraints meant that the cemetery was built over with houses for wealthy Turkish military officers and civil servants, but in recent years many of the fine old houses here have been demolished in the name of redevelopment and the two old hotels of Ar-Rabi' and Al-Haramein are among the few Ottoman buildings remaining.

Salihiye الصالحية If you are staying in Damascus a longer time and have a few hours to spare you can make an interesting excursion to the district of Salihiye, 2km to the north of the city centre, on the lower slopes of Jebel Qassioun. Here are concentrated 70 of the 250 or so officially recognised historical monuments of Damascus, pretty much all dating from the 13th and 14th centuries. Most of them are closed so the excursion is more in the nature of a walk than anything else, but it is still interesting to see the monuments from the outside, since this is where much of the architectural attention is focused, and to stroll at leisure for 1 or 2km through the bustling streets and market, getting a feel for a different part of the city.

Salihiye was also the part of town chosen by wealthier residents of Damascus, as the climate was fresher, with more greenery and orchards, like a kind of garden suburb. Foreigners favoured it for the same reason, and both Lady Jane Digby, the 19th-century English aristocrat who settled in Damascus, and Richard Burton, British Consul from 1869 to 1871, accompanied by his wife Isobel, lived here in neighbouring courtyard houses with fine roof terraces, preferring it to the more claustrophobic Old City, where the gates were at that time closed at night.

The name Salihiye is thought to have originated in the name Abu Salih Al-Hanbali, the early Muslim scholar who founded the Hanbali school of law, and whose followers built a Hanbali mosque here to keep it well away from the Shafi'i school of law which was dominant in the Old City. Salihiye therefore became a centre for Hanbalis in Damascus, all the more so once large numbers of Hanbali refugees fleeing the Mongol invasion arrived here from Harran in northern Mesopotamia in the 13th century. In Arabic the word *saalihoun* also means saints or righteous people, which could be taken as a reference to the large number of saints' tombs here.

Start your tour by catching a taxi through the modern concrete sprawl to Midan Jisr Al-Abyad, an open square on the edge of Salihiye, with a 13th-century Ayyubid *madrasa* called Madrasa Maridaniye in its northeast corner, fronting the busy road. It is usually closed but you can check by trying the entrance on the north side. From the square now take the left street that heads northwards up the hill for about 150m, passing in a side street to your left a pair of 14th-century mausoleums, one of which is of a Hanbali sheikh. Continuing just about 20m north uphill, you now turn right into the main street called Madares As'ad Ad-Din, walking along the flat west to east, parallel to the base of the mountain. This is the street, about 1.4km long, which most of the other monuments to be seen are clustered along, and the specific area is known as Ash-Sharqasiyye.

Strolling now at a leisurely pace you can inspect the succession of about 14 tombs, mausoleums, *madrasas* and mosques that you will pass to the right and left along the street, all closed, all dating from the 13th and 14th centuries, till you enter the fruit and vegetable market, bursting with fresh produce.

After the market the buildings are less clustered and the first one to see is the Hanbali Mosque built between 1202 and 1213, with its plain, rather austere façade. If it is not prayer time you can enter, observing the usual practices of removing shoes and covering bare skin and hair if you are female, and look out for the six classical columns recycled in the courtyard. Inside the prayer hall the fine *minbar* is 13th century.

After the Hanbali Mosque there are just three more *madrasas* and tombs to be seen from the outside, one of which, the Madrasa Omariye, the oldest building in the Salihiye district, now heavily ruined, was built by Muslim refugees who escaped from the Crusader massacre that followed the Christian capture of Jerusalem in 1099.

For a detailed account of all the buildings in this district you can consult Ross Burns' *Monuments of Syria* (see *Appendix 3*).

3

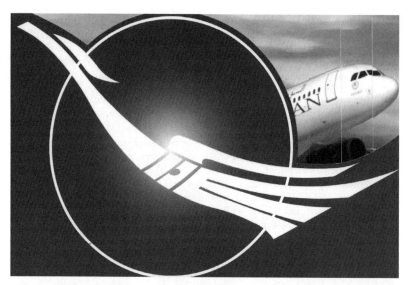

SYRIAN ARAB AIRLINES

- Syrian Airlines reaches 44 cities in three continents: Europe, Asia and Africa
- Syrian Airlines transports one millionn passengers every year
- Syrian Airlines gives low promotional offer fares in both domestic and foreign markets
- Syrian Airlines grant many advantages through its frequent flyer programme
- Syrian Airlines flies to Damascus three times a week from London and twice a week from Manchester

27 ALBEMARLE STREET, LONDON W1S 4BJ
SALES & INFO ☏ 020 7493 2851

4

Christian Villages of the Qalamoun Mountains

Dine with a Jew but seek shelter from a Christian.

HISTORICAL BACKGROUND

The 10% of Syria's population who are Christian are these days concentrated mainly in the cities, but north of Damascus, less than an hour's drive away from the capital, is a Christian enclave where several important churches and monasteries are clustered. Here you can still get a sense of how isolated it must have been living in a Christian community in a dominantly Muslim environment.

Much of the early development of the Christian church took place, not surprisingly, in what is present-day Syria, Turkey, Israel, Jordan and Lebanon. Christianity is after all a Middle Eastern religion. It was in Antioch (modern Antakya, now Turkey) that the followers of Christ were first called Christians. Early Christians were persecuted under the Roman Empire, with many martyrs who later became saints, but gradually the religion spread and became more accepted. The first official recognition came in 313 when Emperor Constantine issued the Edict of Milan, giving them the right to practise their faith, and then in 380 the Emperor Theodosius declared Christianity the official religion of the Roman Empire.

When the Roman Empire split into East and West, Constantinople became the capital of the Eastern Roman Empire or Byzantine Empire as it was known. Under the Byzantines Christianity in the Middle East divided into many different churches as a result of complex theological disputes over the nature of Christ, often reflecting power struggles within the empire as well. The main split was between the so-called Diophysites (who called themselves orthodox and who believed that Christ combined two natures, divine and human) and the Monophysites, who believed he was of one nature, divine only. By way of compromise, the Byzantine Emperor Heraclius (610–41) adopted a Monothelite view that Christ had a dual nature but one will. This view was in turn denounced as heresy in 680 by the Sixth Ecumenical Council (see box on page 170).

In the Byzantine Empire those who adhered to the orthodox Diophysite view were called Melkites (also Melchites or Malkites), meaning in Arabic the king's men, because their allegiance was with the Byzantine emperor in Constantinople. Those who adhered to the various heterodox views founded separate churches including the Syrian or Jacobite Church based at Antioch, the Egyptian Coptic Church based at Alexandria, the Armenian (Gregorian) Church, the Nestorian (Chaldean) Church and the Maronite Church.

Over the centuries doctrinal differences between the Eastern (Orthodox) Church and the Western (Latin Catholic) Church of Rome intensified, culminating in the great schism of 1054 when the Eastern Church refused to

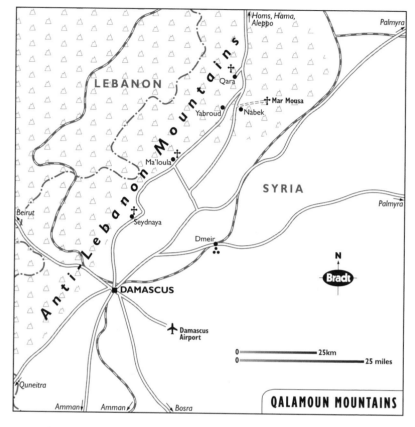

Map labels:

Palmyra

Homs, Hama, Aleppo

Qara ✝

LEBANON

✝ Mar Mousa

Yabroud • Nabek •

SYRIA

Ma'loula ✝

Palmyra

Beirut

✝ Seydnaya

Dmeir

N

Bradt

DAMASCUS

✈ Damascus Airport

Anti-Lebanon Mountains

0 ══════ 25km
0 ══════════ 25 miles

Quneitra

Amman↑   Amman↙   Bosra

QALAMOUN MOUNTAINS

---

accept the supremacy of the Pope, transferring its loyalty instead to the Patriarch of Constantinople. Later, in the 18th century, many of the independent Eastern Church recanted and once more acknowledged the supremacy of the Pope, and were called thereafter the Uniat Churches. These included the Melkites, the Maronites, the Syrian Catholics, the Greek Catholics, the Armenian Catholics and the Copts. They were allowed to retain their own languages, rites and canon law.

In Syria the Greek Orthodox of the Patriarchate of Antioch and the Greek Catholics in communion with Rome, are the most numerous, though in Aleppo the Armenian Catholics are the most important. There are still small communities in Syria of Armenian Orthodox, Syrian Orthodox, Syrian Catholics, Maronites, Roman Catholics, Protestants and Anglicans. Damascus is today the seat of the Greek Orthodox, Greek Catholic and Syrian Orthodox Patriarchs of Antioch.

SEYDNAYA صيدنايا

From Damascus the 26km drive north to these Christian enclaves takes only half an hour. It passes through a series of small villages, always climbing slightly, to reach Seydnaya ('Our lady' or 'Our Hunt', a reference to the local myth described later) at an altitude of 1,650m, a large village far from entirely Christian. Here you will see, set slightly above the village, the Greek orthodox Convent of Our Lady of Seydnaya, the second-holiest pilgrimage site to Greek Orthodox Christians after

Jerusalem. The convent comes under the Patriarchate of Antioch in Damascus and the Virgin Mary Festival is held here every year on 8 September. Their bishops are drawn from celibate clergy and monasteries and convents play an important role in the Church. They practise baptism by immersion, venerate icons and do not accept the doctrine of purgatory, unlike the Roman Catholics.

WHERE TO STAY AND EAT

Seydnaya Hotel (27 rooms) ✆ (11) 5950358. Simple hotel on the western outskirts of town, with a small open-air pool. Lovely views from the terrace over the snow-capped Mt Hermon from Feb to Jun. A favourite with Lebanese pilgrims. Avoid Sat nights when it is always full. *US$15–25 sgl/dbl.*

Seydnaya Monastery For independent travellers staying in the monastery itself is an option, offering basic but free and clean rooms, though you need to be a devout Catholic to pass muster.

✘ **Al-Tilal Restaurant** On the main Damascus road 1km after the turning off for Seydnaya. Syria's biggest restaurant with seating for up to 1,000 under the glass rotunda, with marble in abundance.

Middle Eastern, Chinese, Spanish, Italian and French cuisine of a high standard. Lebanese singers and concerts at weekends.

Safir Hotel, Ma'loula ✆ 7770250; f 7770255; e safir@net.sy. 4-star. Perched on the rocky outcrop above the town, beside St Sergius, with excellent views over the town. Swimming pool, tennis court. Expensive, but the only thing worth considering in the area. *US$80–110 sgl/dbl.*

✘ **Family Restaurant, Ma'loula** Down in the square this small simple restaurant is clean and good value, offering basic Syrian food like kebab, omelette and vegetable starters. It is even licensed, selling wine and beer. The local Ma'loula wine is very dark, cloudy and sweet, almost closer to sherry.

OTHER PRACTICALITIES There are no WC facilities at Seydnaya and no refreshments. At Ma'loula there are WCs and refreshments available in the village beside the convent. There is no entry fee for either place, though donations in the gift box are always appreciated.

WHAT TO SEE AND DO The devout, mainly women, come to this Syrian Lourdes from far afield to ask for cures for sick relations, and the intensity of their grief and pleadings can often lead to highly emotional scenes in the inner shrine sanctum, which can leave you, as a mere bystander, feeling rather voyeurist and awkward. The sanctity of the spot dates back to a vision of the Virgin Mary seen by the Emperor Justinian when out hunting. He was on the point of firing an arrow at a deer, when the deer transformed itself into an icon of the Virgin, and a voice came out of the image ordering the emperor to build a church on this spot. The miraculous icon was said to have been painted by St Luke and is credited with the power to perform miracles. Further icons of the Virgin Mary said to be painted by St Luke existed at Tartous in the Cathedral of Our Lady of Tortosa, in the Sumela Monastery of eastern Turkey and in the Chilandar Monastery of Mt Athos. In later traditions the number of icons of Mary attributed to Luke would greatly multiply, all derived from the story that such an icon was sent as a gift by Eudokia, the wife of Theodosius II (died 460), from Jerusalem to Pulcheria, daughter of the Emperor Arcadius. The icon is kept in a small grotto within the church, called 'Shaghoura' meaning the Famous in Syriac-Aramaic, and in Crusader times the Knights Templar used to collect oil that was supposed to ooze from it as a sacred relic to take back to Europe.

The first church on the site was cut into the rock below where the vision was seen, and this can still be seen as the approach road to the convent passes in front of it. The statues in the rock niches are now decapitated. The road ends in a large car park, and to the side of the long steps leading up to the convent is a school for orphans, run by the convent as a charity. The infirm can avoid the long climb up the steps by taking the lift newly constructed on the left-hand side.

Icons are extremely important in the Eastern Orthodox Church as they are regarded as the dwelling place of God's grace and therefore give the faithful a sense of the presence of God. The subject matter of the icon is very often the Virgin Mary and/or Christ. Mary is always shown with her hair and shoulders covered. Her veil has a golden fringe and three stars to symbolise her virginity before, during and after the birth of Christ. The other common iconic representations are of Mary on a throne holding Christ on her lap, Mary praying, raising her hands in adoration to God, often with the Infant Jesus portrayed with an adult head to symbolise his wisdom; Mary pointing to the Infant Jesus whilst looking at the onlooker; and Mary embracing the Infant Jesus with motherly compassion. The two commonest images of Christ are as Pantocrator (Ruler of All) and Deisis. The Pantocrator is usually found in the main dome of a church, his head with a halo and a cross inside. In his left hand he holds the Bible, and his right is raised to bless. The first two fingers of the right hand are joined to symbolise the two distinct natures of Christ, human and divine, while the other two fingers touch the thumb to symbolise the Trinity. The Deisis icon shows Christ surrounded by saints, disciples or archangels, though in some he is accompanied only by the Virgin Mary and John the Baptist. Other common subjects for icons are the 13 Great Feasts around which the Church's calendar revolves: the Nativity, the Presentation of Mary in the Temple, the Annunciation, the Dormition of the Mother of God, the Nativity, the Presentation of Jesus in the Temple, the Baptism, the Transfiguration, the Entry into Jerusalem, the Ascension, Pentecost, the Exaltation of the Cross and the Resurrection.

Entry to the convent is through a low door where you have to duck, and the Virgin's shrine is in the far right corner of the first courtyard. A notice in Arabic exhorts: 'Please no graffiti on the walls.' Shoes must be removed at the entrance, and inside the small dark room the walls are covered with icons, lamps, silver hands of Fatima (good luck symbols even for Christians, Fatima being the daughter of the Prophet Muhammad) silver trinkets of all sorts, offerings made to the Virgin Mary in gratitude for the fulfilment of a cure of their loved ones. Piety oozes from the old women who kiss and slobber profusely over the icon of the Virgin, praying for miracles.

Returning to the first courtyard and climbing the steps up onto the roof of the convent, you can sit on one of the benches and enjoy the peaceful ambience as you gaze out over the village and valley beyond. The original convent had many underground grottoes where Christians used to pray in secret, and over the centuries wars and earthquakes destroyed the early buildings, necessitating many restorations and rebuildings. The current buildings date from a hotchpotch of periods, each part having been added as and when a large donation made it possible. These donations and their donors are recorded in inscriptions on the buildings. Among the more recent is one made by an American couple from Wisconsin, Massachusetts in 1958.

Back down in the second courtyard the main church is the only part of the convent that can be visited. It is largely modern in feel. Notices in Arabic request visitors to dress properly before entering and to cover their heads. In practice few visitors do so because they cannot read the sign and there is no-one to enforce the notice anyway. The convent library has important documents and manuscripts, but these are not available for public perusal. Saladin's sister was said to have visited the convent many times, making precious donations.

Lower down the hill immediately to the side of the road, look out for the distinctive Church of St Peter, originally a Roman temple built of finely crafted stone blocks, now kept closed and fenced off.

A further monastery, known as the Cherubim Monastery, can be visited 7km from the town of Seydnaya, reached by leaving the town on the road to Ma'loula, then forking left where signposted, climbing up onto the monastery site, 2,011m above sea level, overlooking the oasis of Damascus and the plain of Ba'albek. There was originally a spring nearby, which is why the site was chosen in the 3rd century, surviving as a working monastery till the 16th century when it fell into ruin. In 1982 however it was restored under the auspices of the Seydnaya community and is now a working monastery once more.

MA'LOULA معلولا

The 20-minute drive north from Seydnaya to Ma'loula, 42km north of Damascus and at an altitude of 1,720m, takes you through a landscape not utterly arid by Middle Eastern standards. The mountains rise up bare to the left but in the valley itself there is a fair bit of greenery with orchards and trees, mainly fig.

The entrance to Ma'loula village is heralded today by a large welcome archway over the road which then leads on into the cleft in the rocks where the village itself nestles. Seen en masse, the village today is ugly by any standards, with far too much unregulated building sprawling everywhere, and crowned incongruously by the Safir Hotel which has taken for itself the prime location overlooking the village, thereby ruining the skyline in the process. This reality has been recognised by the authorities and the Ma'loula Project has recently been launched to make a university here and to tidy up messy houses, to improve the unsightly pipe work and to re-engineer the sanitation generally, especially in the older houses. This work will be essential if Ma'loula is to retain its status as the bijou village where Aramaic, the language of Christ, also known as Syriac, is still spoken. Strictly speaking, Syriac is the branch of Aramaic spoken in Edessa (Urfa, southeast Turkey) and the neighbouring area from shortly before the beginning of the Christian era. It has remained the language of the liturgy in the Nestorian Church and in the Syrian Orthodox or Jacobite Church. It was the dominant language in the Near East from the 4th century BC right through to the 6th century AD, and was the most important language of the eastern Roman Empire after Greek. It started to decline after the Islamic conquest of the area in the 7th century AD, when it gave way to Arabic. Aramaic was originally written in the Hebrew alphabet, and the first Syriac alphabet developed from a later form of Aramaic used at Palmyra. Today there are three Syriac scripts in use: Estrangelo, Jacobite and Nestorian. Efforts are being made to keep the language alive among the young as well as among the village elders and to use it for more than just the liturgy in church and for reciting the Lord's Prayer.

Follow the road that leads right to the top beside the Safir Hotel to reach St Sergius, a Greek Catholic monastery, whose clean white limestone blocks belie its Byzantine origins. Sergius was a Roman officer who, along with Bacchus, was martyred at Resafe at the end of the 3rd century for refusing to carry out a sacrifice to the sun. The pair are highly venerated in Syria and there are numerous churches dedicated to them. Greek Catholics owe their allegiance to Rome but retain their liturgical language of Greek, practice baptism by immersion and believe in the marriage of clergy. They belong to the Uniat Churches who reaffirmed their allegiance to Rome and the Pope, along with the Melkites, the Maronites, the Copts and the Armenian Catholics.

In the car park are clean WC facilities charging a small fee, with a fine panoramic viewing point built above. Also worth a visit is the excellent shop where local

4

Many Westerners are surprised to discover that not all Arabs are Muslims. Syria's population is 10% Christian and there is no apparent discrimination against them throughout society. The Syrian constitution even stipulates that three government ministers must be Christian and there are Christians at all levels of government. One of the notable aspects of the Ba'ath Party philosophy is that it is totally secular: religion is irrelevant, a personal matter.

When the Arabs arrived having swarmed out of the Arabian Peninsula in the 7th century they found the countries to the north ruled by the Christian Byzantine Empire and the language to be Aramaic/Syriac. In most places for many centuries Christians continued to form the majority of the population and to account for a large proportion of the educated and professional classes. Gradually however increasing numbers of the population became Muslim, and Arabic began to take over from the local languages, the complete opposite of what happened in Anglo-Saxon England, where the Norman elite gradually adopted the Anglo-Saxon language and dropped their own.

The reasons for the fact that the majority of the population gradually became absorbed into Islam are complex, but one of the major factors was the special status given to Christians in a Muslim society. The new Muslim masters viewed both the Christians and the Jews leniently, as the Koran described them as 'People of the Book', recognising them as believers in the same God that they believed in and therefore quite different to the polytheists who believed in multiple gods. They were given status as protected minorities in return for payment of special taxes. Christians were allowed to worship freely and often given important financial, clerical and professional positions. One Christian poet in Umayyad times, called Al-Akhtal (meaning 'one whose ears are flabby and hang down'), was urged to convert to Islam by his caliph, 'Abd Al-Malik. He replied: 'I consent, if I am allowed to drink wine and exempted from fasting in Ramadan.'

The technical term given to non-Muslims under Muslim protection was *dhimmis*, but although they were protected they were in effect second-class citizens, denied many of the social and legal privileges afforded to Muslims. Conversion to Islam, a simple process achieved by the declaration of the Shahada, removed all these restrictions, whereas conversion of a Muslim to Christianity would result in death for the convert and the converter. Cumulatively therefore, the net effect was that the Christian population diminished gradually over the centuries, with most Christians adopting Arabic, and retaining their original languages only as the language of worship.

The remarkable thing in many ways, after nearly one and half millennia of the realities of such a situation, is that Christianity still exists in any form at all in the Middle East.

honey is sold and the local sweet wine is often available for tasting. Stamps, postcards and souvenirs are all for sale and attractively displayed.

The monastery itself is known locally as Mar Sarkis and has one of the oldest churches in Syria, dating to the 4th century, with some beautiful 16th–18th-century icons. Carbon dating of the wooden beams inside has shown them to be Lebanese cedar over 2,000 years old. The entrance is through a very low doorway and there are further low doorways inside to watch out for. The triple-nave church has 4th-century pagan rock-hewn altars and the fact that they have complete stone rims with no outlet for draining blood is held as proof that no blood sacrifices were conducted here. Among the icons the most notable are the smiling laid-back John the Baptist, relaxed now that his mission of the Baptism of Christ has been accomplished, and the Last Supper with Christ in the centre, very unusually combined with the Crucifixion in the same icon.

ST THEKLA MONASTERY (*Good WC facilities on the first major landing inside the complex; no refreshments; no fee, but donations welcomed*) From St Sergius you should now do the 15-minute walk to St Thekla, along the road past the Safir Hotel, probably the best and cleanest place to eat in Ma'loula. On the hilltop to the left are the weekend or holiday houses of many wealthy Damascenes, often still under construction. The new trend among the nouveaux riches is to have weekend houses outside the city, and Ma'loula, with its cooler elevation and relative calm, is one of the favoured locations.

The road leads down towards the St Thekla Restaurant, pleasantly set among a group of poplar trees, but a little scruffy and run-down these days. From the restaurant you follow a path under the bridge and into the gorge, following the stream as it winds through the rocky narrow defile, a separate water irrigation channel cut into the rock beside.

This defile, some 800m long, was said to have opened miraculously to allow Thekla to escape her pursuers. She was the daughter of the Roman governor of Iconium (modern Konya in Turkey) who, aged 18, heard St Paul preaching and converted to Christianity. It caused a scandal in high Roman society as she left the man to whom she had been promised in marriage to follow Paul as his disciple and remain a virgin all her life, despite her great beauty. For her disobedience she was sentenced to be burnt at the stake, but a huge storm blew up and drenched the flames. She was released and later in Antioch she was put in an arena with wild beasts for refusing the attentions of a nobleman. Once more she was saved as the wild beasts would not harm her. She returned to Turkey where she found Paul and asked him to give his blessing to her life as an ascetic and virgin. He granted her wish and she later travelled to Syria and went up into the mountains for a life of prayer and solitude. Even here, a young pagan found her and resolved to take her virginity, but she was saved by the defile opening up to allow her escape. She spent the rest of her years living here in the cave and was buried there aged 90, and has subsequently become one of the most popular saints of the Christian Orient, associated with miraculous escapes from difficult situations.

The defile emerges behind the monastery right at the upper end of the village, and from the main square full of stalls selling souvenirs, steps lead up into the Greek Orthodox monastery. Inside, everything is exceptionally clean. You can visit the church and the cave, involving a fair bit of step-climbing throughout the complex. At the time of the author's visit there was a christening in progress, curious for the mixed dress of the generations, from the grandmas in black in headscarves, to the young teenage girls in tight jeans and tops taking photos of each other and of the presiding priest, while the congregation and visitors came and went throughout. Notices in all the courtyards forbid smoking in a very unusual turn of rhyming Arabic, saying: 'Your visit pleases us, but your smoking harms us.'

From the church courtyard steps lead up the side of the cliff into the cave grotto where Thekla lived: ferns hanging down, a pleasant cool spot with a long bench for resting. This too, like Seydnaya, is known as a place of miracles where the sick can be cured, and in the little grotto shrine at the back, you can take off your shoes to enter and view the silver offerings of gratitude that hang all round the walls, then light a candle. An elderly lady here told of her grandchild who had been very late talking. After drinking some of the sacred water, he immediately began to speak, so she now comes regularly to give thanks.

MAR MOUSA MONASTERY دير مار موسى

This extraordinary and extremely remote monastery, whose name means Saint Moses, is located 94km north of Damascus and is reached via Yabroud. This Moses is not he of the bulrushes but the son of a king of Ethiopia who is said to have founded the monastery, and whose feast day is 28 August. It is now a thriving community thanks to the enthusiasm and devotion of Father Paolo, an Italian Jesuit who discovered the place in ruins in 1988 and spent three years with the local community restoring it and bringing it back to life. It now boasts five monks and five nuns, mainly European, a fact which has caused some raised eyebrows, and is ecumenical, mixing Catholics and Orthodox.

Well signposted from the main square at Nabek, 9km beyond Yabroud, the route then continues for 3km till you reach a track off to the monastery. Follow this for some 10km to the point where the track is no longer drivable. The final 20 minutes must be done on foot, along a wadi bed, then up 350 steps to the monastery's terrace. Take the path to the left that leads into the ravine about 300m from the entrance of the wadi. This is undoubtedly the most beautiful spot in the area, at the mouth of the gorge, the monastery dominating the steppe, almost reminiscent of Tibet. The monks will offer you wine on the terrace and then take you on a little tour of the museum where items found during the restoration are displayed, a library and above all the chapel and its frescoes. The first monks are thought to have installed themselves here in the 6th century, living in caves in the ravine. The actual church dates to the 11th century and the whole monastery was enlarged up till the 15th century. Inside the church the oldest paintings, dating to the second half of the 11th century, are either side of the choir. In the chapel to the left of the choir are more frescoes including one of St Simeon wearing a black hat on top of his pillar. The most remarkable fresco is on the western wall opposite the choir, representing the Last Judgement with Peter and Paul above, the throne and cross surrounded by other apostles, feet resting on soft cushions oriental style. Below the altar are Adam and Eve, while the judgement scales are held by two angels, framed by David and Solomon. To the left, the chosen ones are led by the first martyrs, while to the right are the damned, and on the first rung are the bishops of the other side, judged to be heretics.

Simple accommodation with solar-heated showers is available and three meals are served a day, but guests are expected to take an active part in the running of the monastery. Sundays and Christian holidays are reserved for religiously motivated visitors, while Fridays and public holidays are full of local visitors so you are best advised to visit on Mondays to Thursdays, or on Saturdays.

QARA قارا

Heading back to Nabek and the main Damascus–Aleppo highway you can make a detour to Qara, 16km from Nabek, another ancient Christian centre with the Greek Orthodox church of St Sergius and Bacchus complete with lovely frescoes painted c1000. The church is 50m up a side street off the main road through the centre of town. To visit you have to ask for the key from the shop on the corner of the street. The frescoes are protected by a curtain and represent St Sergius on a fine horse, the Virgin suckling the Infant Jesus, and John the Baptist. Other frescoes from this church are on display in the Damascus National Museum. On the edge of town there is also the Convent of St Jacques, considered by some experts to be the oldest in the region, built on the foundations of a Roman fort. It was restored in 1995, with the aim of installing a community of sisters. To reach the convent, go back into the main road from the church, cross the square to the right and continue straight on. At the first junction take the road to the right and the monastery stands on this road about 1km out of town.

The third major site in the town is now the Great Mosque, but was originally the Cathedral of St Nicholas, with a beautiful Byzantine façade. Two *mihrabs* were installed in the south wall when it was converted to a mosque in 1266, still decorated with ancient capitals. To reach it you retrace your steps to the main road in town, continue 300m beyond the turn-off to the Church of St Sergius and Bacchus, then turn right to find the mosque 100m further on. Allow about an hour to visit all three sites.

Jasmine

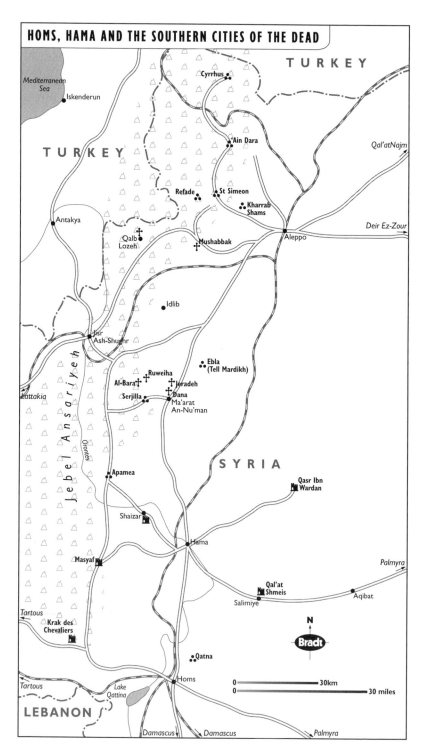

HOMS, HAMA AND THE SOUTHERN CITIES OF THE DEAD

Mediterranean Sea

TURKEY

Iskenderun

Cyrrhus

TURKEY

Qal'atNajm

'Ain Dara

Refade • St Simeon

Kharrab Shams

Antakya

Deir Ez-Zour

Qalb Lozeh

Mushabbak

Aleppo

Idlib

Jisr Ash-Shughr

Ebla (Tell Mardikh)

Ruweiha

Al-Bara

Jeradeh

Lattakia

Serjilla

Dana Ma'arat An-Nu'man

Jebel Ansariyeh

Orontes

SYRIA

Apamea

Qasr Ibn Wardan

Shaizar

Palmyra

Hama

Masyaf

Qal'at Shmeis

Aqibat

Salimiye

N

Tartous

Krak des Chevaliers

Bradt

Qatna

Tartous

Lake Qattina

0   30km
0   30 miles

Homs

LEBANON

Damascus   Damascus   Palmyra

5

Homs, Hama and the Southern Cities of the Dead

حمص حماه والمدن الميتة

We traded in shrouds; people stopped dying.

This part of Syria tends to come as the biggest surprise to most visitors, because it is so unlike anything they will have known about before, and so uniquely Syrian. The waterwheels of Hama cannot fail to impress and charm, and the romantic Cities of the Dead, whole hillsides of Byzantine ghost towns, will be hauntingly memorable.

GETTING THERE

PALMYRA TO HAMA From Palmyra you can take a scenically more interesting and virtually empty road to Hama, and if you have the time, incorporate a short diversion to Qal'at Shmeis, a 13th-century Ayyubid castle perched dramatically on an extinct volcano cone.

Follow first the main road to Homs for 34km from the petrol station outside the town, where you reach a fork to the left towards Ar-Raml ('The Sand'). This fork would take you to reach the scant remains of Qasr Al-Hayr Al-Gharbi, the western desert Umayyad Palace whose façade graces the entrance to the National Museum in Damascus. Shortly after to the right is a signposted tarmac road to Hama, 150km. The road surface is fine, though the road itself is quite wiggly in parts, making it difficult to drive faster than 80km/h. Along the way you pass a few tented nomad camps with attendant flocks of camels and sheep. Traffic on this road is extremely light with just the occasional truck. At the first junction after c20km you fork right, and at the second junction after a further 15km, you fork left. It is generally signposted in English though sometimes it is only in Arabic. The landscape is quite hilly with valleys and even patches of grass and *snober* trees from time to time.

From Aqibat, the first major town you will have passed so far, Hama is signposted 75km, and from here it is 42km to Salimiye, the next major town. In Salimiye as you begin to exit the town on the road to Hama, you will see a large blue sign in English and Arabic to Qal'at Shmeis, pointing off to the right. This turning heads north through a section of bad road between houses to reach within 1km a good tarmac road that then heads you straight to the foot of Qal'at Shmeis, unmistakably dominating the landscape. A normal car cannot get beyond the large metal sign announcing the castle, so you have to walk up the steep path for the last few minutes to the rim of the crater which served as the defensive moat. Straight ahead you will notice a cave in the rocky outcrop which looks as if it might be the entrance, but the entrance in fact lies just a few metres to the right. Scramble down inside the crater for a few steps, then up the partial steps that climb up into the castle itself. Though not particularly difficult, this does require a bit of clambering for the final section and good footwear is necessary. Once up inside, the most impressive thing is the rock rainwater cistern cut right down into the outcrop. Otherwise just a few walls and arches remain within the castle outer defences. Views are also impressive in all directions. A good shady picnic spot can be found under the trees to the edge of the planted young forest, a vantage point which also allows you time to enjoy the remarkable setting of the castle. From here it is a further 30km to reach Hama.

PALMYRA TO HAMA (VIA HOMS) The faster though less scenic way of getting from Palmyra to Hama is via Homs. The road is faster, taking just one hour 40 minutes to Homs, then just 30 minutes north on to Hama up the motorway. The road from Palmyra is totally featureless and uneventful, flat desert of the dullest sort, with no restaurant/café to stop at en route, so make sure you have what you need with you and have filled up with petrol at the petrol station just outside Palmyra before setting off. The occasional beehive house can be seen in villages to the right of the road, and you will also pass an oil gathering station run by a Croatian oil company. There is a huge military camp with hideous new housing 85km before Homs, with all its plastic rubbish cluttering the desert for miles on either side. Then, just 40km or so before Homs, the landscape undergoes a transformation and suddenly the bleak bare desert gives way to endless hillsides of almond trees covered in white blossom in late February/early March, as far as the eye can see on both sides of the road. The soil becomes red and fertile and even vineyards can be spotted, along with olive groves. If you have saved your picnic till now, you can enjoy sitting on grass under the shade of the trees, in total contrast to where you would have had to picnic in the desert terrain a little earlier.

As you come now to the edges of Homs, you will start to see signs of the heavy factories and refineries which have made Homs into Syria's industrial capital. Follow signs to the centre of town till you see signs to Tartous, if you are now continuing to Krak des Chevaliers, or to Aleppo if you are continuing north to Hama. If you are ready for a stop, Homs can boast a four-star hotel, the Safir, but otherwise will not detain you long.

HOMS حمص *Telephone code 031*

(130km west of Palmyra, 160km north of Damascus, 185km south of Aleppo, 47km south of Hama; population 700,000) Strategically located at the intersection of Syria's road and rail networks, Homs also controls what is known as the Homs Gap, the access route from the Syrian desert through the break in the coastal mountains to the sea. Homs is the third-largest city in Syria after Damascus and Aleppo, and most of the country's factories, oil refineries and sugar refineries are concentrated here.

As ancient Emessa, Homs had considerable historical importance. It was an Arab emirate in the 2nd century BC like Palmyra and Petra and was the third station on the Silk Road after Doura Europos and Palmyra. It was celebrated too as the birthplace of Julia Dumna, daughter of the high priest, who married the Roman emperor Sepimius Severus in AD175 and gave birth to three sons who all went on to become emperor in their turn.

The original citadel is still visible as an outcrop near the centre of town, and is currently the subject of excavations funded by the Council for British Research, one of the few involvements of the British in Syria in this field, where the French, Germans and Italians have tended to dominate. The excavations are headed by Dr Geoffrey King of SOAS, London. A few fragments of city wall remain here and there in the modern town. Emessa was an important early Christian centre and there are two early churches that can still be visited: the Church of Al-Zunnar (the Girdle of the Virgin), whose unlikely name is taken from the relic, a textile belt, said to have been discovered here in 1953 under the church's altar, and the Church of St Elian. Both are in the Christian quarter west of the Great Mosque and *souks*, and while the first's buildings date mainly to 1852 and it serves now as the Orthodox Syrian Archbishopric, the second is much older, with a series of murals dating to the 12th century discovered behind the choir, and some mural fragments even dating to the 6th century, making them possibly the oldest church murals in Syria.

Close to the Church of the Girdle is a recently restored 13th-century Mameluke residence called Azze Hrawe (*open 09.00–4.00 except Fri*) destined to be Homs' Folklore Museum. Set round a courtyard with fountain in the traditional manner, it has a fine *iwan*.

There are also two mosques of note, the Khaled Ibn Al-Walid, an Ottoman building from c1910 with two fine tall minarets set by itself in its own gardens a little outside the city centre, and the much older An-Nuri Mosque, also called the Great Mosque (Al-Jaami' Al-Kabeer), right in the centre of town beside the old *souks* of the city. This 12th-century church was built on the site of a pagan temple, later the Church of St John, following the pattern of evolution of the Great Umayyad Mosque in Damascus. The Homs *souks* have been recently restored with new roofs and floors.

Northeast of Homs, 15km in the direction of Salamiye, is the village of Mishrifiye, site of the Bronze Age city of Qatna, whose excavated finds have now been so impressively displayed in the upstairs Qatna Hall of the Damascus National Museum. On the site itself there is little to see beyond the impressive ramparts and the foundations of a temple and a palace, all dating to the 14th century BC.

WHERE TO STAY

⌂ **Safir Hotel** (175 rooms) Ragheb Al-Jamali St; PO Box 17465; ☏ 412400; f 433420; e safir@net.sy; www.safirhotels.com. 5-star luxury hotel on 5 floors, 2km southwest of the city centre. 2 restaurants, coffee bar, nightclub, swimming pool, tennis courts, bookshop. *US$120/135 sgl/dbl.*

✖ WHERE TO EAT

✖ **Mamma Mia** Good Italian restaurant in the Safir Hotel, open noon to midnight.

✖ **Mersia**, also in the Safir Hotel, offering Arabic and international cuisine. Both are licensed.

The cheap eateries are clustered near Shoukri Al-Quwatli St but are best avoided unless lack of funds dictates.

OTHER PRACTICALITIES

Deluxe bus station Called the 'Garagat Pullman', the intercity coach station is 2.5km north of the centre on the Hama road. Qadmous and Al-Ahlia plus others operate from here with frequent services to Damascus (S£70, 2 hours), Aleppo (S£80, 2½ hours) and Tartous (S£40, 1 hour). There is no need to book ahead.

Post office The main post office is 150m north of the Clock Tower roundabout (*open 06.00–17.30 except Fri*).

Internet A very swish internet café is Compuserv on Hafez Ibrahim St (*open 10.00–23.00, S£50 per 30mins*). Others are opening all the time.

Banks The Commercial Bank of Syria in the centre of town changes cash and travellers' cheques, but it is easier and much faster in your hotel. The Safir has money-changing facilities all day.

HAMA OLD CITY AND WATERWHEELS (*Altitude 308m; population 340,000; 209km north of Damascus, 146km south of Aleppo, 147km southeast of Lattakia, 47km north of Homs; allow ¹/₂ day*) The attractive river town of Hama makes an excellent base for exploration of the Cities of the Dead (see pages 130–7) to the south, for Krak des Chevaliers to the west and makes the best stopover point between Damascus and Aleppo and between Palmyra and Aleppo.

Famous for its extraordinary and enormous moaning waterwheels, it is these and the river frontage that make Hama a unique place. The wide Orontes (Arabic 'Al-'Assi') flows right through the centre and all Hama's sights are concentrated along or within easy walking distance of the river, so it is essential to stay in a hotel with river views.

Known as a highly traditional and conservative town, Hama nonetheless has its trendy youth these days. Though almost all are headscarved (and no photographs should be taken of veiled women without express permission), young fashion-conscious teenage girls can be seen here dressed in tight figure-hugging full-length denim coats with belts. On motorbikes of course women have to ride side-saddle, sitting astride pillion-style being out of the question for modesty and *jellaba* reasons. Health and safety remain unknown concepts in Syria, and it is still a common sight to see a white-bearded grandad driving his open pick-up truck with 20 of his extended family from young children to old women, all on their way to or from the fields to work for the day, all still living together in one house. Over 80% of Hama's population is engaged in agriculture, with many ponds for fish-breeding and dairy cow farms. It is also known as the capital of sheep, famous for its yoghurt and butter.

WATERWHEELS

Of the 100 or so waterwheels ('*norias*') that once existed along the banks of the Orontes, only 17 of them remain today. This ingenious irrigation system was abandoned in the middle of the 20th century in favour of the far less poetic modern petrol pumps, but the government funds the continued maintenance of the waterwheels by skilled carpenters and artisans who pass on the techniques from generation to generation to ensure that the cultural heritage does not die. Because the banks of the Orontes were lower than the fields to be irrigated, the waterwheel system, driven by the current of the river, scooped up the water in its wooden box devices fixed round the edge of the wheel, and let it fall out at the top into an aqueduct which then conducted it to the fields or indeed to houses or buildings within the town, each user being allocated a portion of flow per day. As a technique we know it must have existed as early as the 5th century because of a mosaic dated AD469 found at Apamea showing a *noria* on the banks of the Orontes. Of the ones that exist today, the earliest date to the 14th and 15th centuries. Their diameters range from 7m to 21m, and the largest, Al-Mamouriye, was equipped with 120 wooden scooping boxes. To ensure the wheel turned constantly the river's flow was channelled by a little dam into a sluice where the speed could be controlled by a series of little sluice gates. The ideal spacing of the blades was found to be 50cm apart. The wheels can be stopped anytime by blocking off the flow to the channel completely with the sluice gates. The distinctive moaning of the *norias* is caused by the friction of the wooden central pin against the two wooden pads that support it. Each *noria* has its own 'voice' and an expert can diagnose the exact health and condition of the waterwheel from its particular sound, like a doctor.

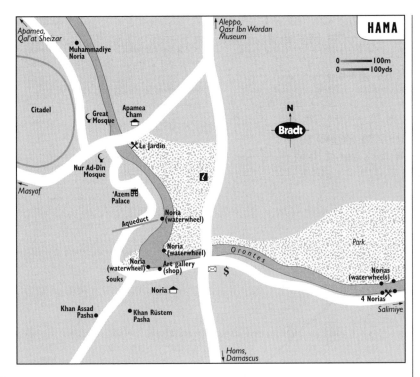

Apamea,
Qal'at Sheizar

Muhammadiye
Noria

Aleppo,
Qasr Ibn Wardan
Museum

HAMA

0 ═══ 100m
0 ═══ 100yds

Citadel

Great
Mosque

Apamea
Cham

N

Bradt

✕ Le Jardin

Nur Ad-Din
Mosque

Masyaf

'Azem
Palace

Aqueduct

Noria
(waterwheel)

Orontes

Park

Noria
(waterwheel)

Noria
(waterwheel)

Art gallery
(shop)

Norias
(waterwheels)

Souks

✉ $

Noria

4 Norias ✕✕

Khan Assad
Pasha

Khan Rüstem
Pasha

Salimiye

Homs,
Damascus

 WHERE TO STAY

🏠 **Hotel Apamea Cham** (173 rooms) PO Box 111, Hama; ☎ 525335; f 511626; www.chamhotels.com. The only luxury-class hotel in the city, superbly located overlooking the River Orontes with excellent views of the waterwheels, the Nur Ad-Din Mosque and the 'Azem Palace frontage. The 11-storey building has attractively terraced gardens, a large swimming pool and a tennis court. The dining room is on the lower floor with views of its own garden, not the river or the waterwheels. The rooms have all the usual extras except a hairdryer. The hotel is often quite empty and if there are no groups staying there is no breakfast buffet laid on, which means breakfast is reduced to basic Continental style

unless you are happy to wait an age after requesting eggs or other extras. US$115/135 sgl/dbl.

🏠 **Noria Hotel** (43 rooms) Sharia Shoukri Al-Quwatli, Hama; PO Box 970; ☎ 512414; f 511715; e bader@mail.sy. The next best after the Cham, friendly and well run, 3-star, spacious rooms with en suites, satellite TV and fridge. US$20/30 sgl/dbl.

🏠 **Apamea** At the point where the main road joins the fork off to Qal'at Al-Mudiq, just past the museum, is the recently opened Taj Apamea Hotel/Restaurant, trying hard to catch tourist custom from visitors to the site. At the time of writing the WC facilities there were not that clean, however.

✕ **WHERE TO EAT**

✕ **Le Jardin** In a superb location on the river opposite the Nur Ad-Din Mosque with views of several waterwheels, this is unquestionably the best location and value restaurant in Hama. It is actually linked to the Apamea Cham Hotel by a tunnel leading under the road from the bottom of the Cham's gardens, but its prices are much lower than that would imply because it is also open to the general public with a normal entrance from the

street. Service is good and the range of mezze on offer is quite extensive. Beer and spirits are served but not wine. Nargilehs here are popular with local people. Clean WC facilities.

✕ **Family Club Restaurant** In the Christian part of town near the Roman Orthodox church. Friendly and relaxed atmosphere. Pleasant 1st-floor outdoor terrace. Arab food, good mezze. Alcohol on offer. Open daily 18.00–midnight.

✕ Dream House ✎ 411687. Near the Roman Orthodox church. More international range of food with pizzas and burgers as well as Arab cuisine. *Open daily 12.00–midnight.*
✕ Al-Nil and Al-Mandil On the main Damascus–Aleppo highway near the Ma'arat An-Nu'man exit there are two large restaurants which make very good lunch stops. Both are on the left as you drive northwards. No alcohol is served. WCs are adequate. *Lunch for around S£600.*
✕ 4 Norias Restaurant A little way out of town by a cluster of 4 waterwheels. Excellent location on the river. Mezzes and *nargilehs* are what most people have, arriving after 21.00 and staying till late. Alcohol on offer.

WHAT TO SEE AND DO

Walking tour of Hama (*Allow about an hour*) From the Apamea Cham Hotel walk first across the bridge towards the black-and-white striped Nur Ad-Din Mosque built in 1172. This design was used since Mameluke times and is reminiscent of the same black-and-white striped building design used to represent the Black Sheep and the White Sheep clans of southeastern Turkey, found especially in Diyarbakir where black basalt was heavily used. It was badly damaged in the 1982 uprisings, but has now been restored. If you do manage to find it open make sure you are soberly dressed, women in headscarves, and remove shoes at the threshold as usual. Inside, note the remarkable 12th-century wooden sculpted *minbar.*

Take the covered passage immediately left between the mosque and the river to follow now the alleyway that runs along the river, bordered by old houses, many of them with overhanging Ottoman wooden balconies. This stretch towards the 'Azem Palace and beyond to the waterwheels in the centre of town is just about the only area of old Hama that remains (see box opposite). Silent and traffic free, this walk is especially atmospheric at night, with the old-style lighting and then the shock of looking into a lit window to see naked figures washing, only to realise it is the mannequin reconstruction of the *hammam* in the 'Azem Palace which rather oddly remains lit up at night.

'Azem Palace قصر العزم (*Open 08.00–14.00 daily except Tue; S£75 entry fee*) An absolute jewel of a place that in many ways outshines its namesake in Damascus, the 'Azem Palace is on an easily digestible small scale, and indeed did serve as a private family residence till 1920 when it became a school in order to avoid being confiscated by the French Mandate powers. It was given to the Syrian Antiquities Department in 1956 and used to be the Hama Museum till 2000 when the museum was moved to a new purpose-built museum in the northern part of town. Built originally in 1740 by a Syrian dignitary in the service of the Ottoman sultan, a dark corridor leads to the right to reach the courtyard of the haramlik where the women and children would have slept, eaten and spent their day, sheltered from the prying eyes of the street. The courtyard is exquisitely decorated with a magnificent giant magnolia tree dominating the space and a beautiful central fountain. In the evenings the master of the house would come and sit in the monumental north-facing *iwan.* Steps from the courtyard lead up to the first floor, another exquisitely decorated space, where the soft colours of the stonework and flooring, yellows and reds contrasting with the black basalt and purple porphyry from Egypt, are quite stunning. The floors are washed down with water every morning to enhance the colours and keep it all immaculate. Signs of recent restoration are evident in the woodwork of some of the overhanging balcony areas.

Returning to the ticket office and passing through the other little corridor you reach the palace's private *hammam* complete with mannequins washing. This in turn leads on to the smaller courtyard of the salamlik, the public reception area with steps leading to an upper loggia almost Italianate in design. At the time of writing access to these upper rooms was closed off, presumably for restoration, as they were badly charred from the 1982 uprising. These upper rooms face the river

By population Syria's fourth-largest city after Damascus, Aleppo and Homs, Hama has long had a reputation for religious conservatism and traditionalism. This made it fertile ground for the Muslim Brotherhood, an Islamic extremist fundamentalist movement, who in 1982 organised a revolt against the Assad regime from here, wanting to replace Assad's secular Ba'athist regime and its modernist ideology with strict Islamic rule and Shari'a (Islamic) law.

There had been a number of assassinations and bombings of members of Assad's government over several years, but this call for a general uprising against the authorities in Hama provoked a swift and effective response from Assad. He sent in the army, under his brother Rif'at, to crush the rebellion. In the fierce three-week battle that ensued Amnesty International estimated that between 10,000 and 25,000 were killed. Whole areas of the city centre were flattened, heavily bombarded by the army's tanks. The area where the Apamea Cham Hotel now stands for example was once densely populated with narrow streets and *souks*. According to rumour, the hotel was built on the graveyard of those killed in the uprising. The small area around the 'Azem Palace is all that remains today of pre-1982 Hama. Rif'at, noted for his love of armoury, was the right choice for such a mission, and though many critics felt he went too far in the sheer brutality with which he obliterated the uprising, others felt that if he had responded in a more conciliatory fashion and allowed the Brotherhood to continue, it would have remained a thorn in the side of the regime and represented an extremist ideology that is not what Syria's younger generation aspires to.

The December 2005 surprise election results in Cairo, where the Muslim Brotherhood (Al-Ikhwan Al-Muslimoun) took 20% of the seats with a policy based on little more than their slogan 'Islam is the solution', are a reminder of how quickly religion can come back into politics from nowhere. Some commentators say Syria too could be ripe for an Islamist revival but it is very hard to gauge how many ordinary Syrians really would want to see Islam play a role in political life. Local people in Hama tend not to speak much about such matters, and you should remain sensitive to people's wish to keep their counsel.

with beautiful views, but were the most heavily damaged in the fighting as they took most of the crossfire bombardment from the other side of the river.

Continuing your walk, turn left out of the 'Azem Palace following the same alleyway as before, towards the centre of town. Shortly after passing a public baths to your right, you come to a fenced area of two waterwheels which is where maintenance takes place. If the guardian worker is here, he will let you in for a small consideration to inspect at close quarters the wheels in action. Be careful of the very slippery stone floor. From these waterwheels one of the very few surviving aqueducts leads off into the town, impressively high. You re-emerge into traffic here and pass a group of popular café restaurants facing onto the river, to then walk down onto the beginning of a bridge where two more waterwheels are in action. Down a few steps here take a moment or two to look round an artists' gallery with paintings, some of which are of a surprisingly high standard. You can now cross the bridge into a municipal park area where another fine aqueduct stands.

From here you have to cross back over the next bridge to follow the opposite riverbank if you want to walk as far as the group of four *norias*, about 1km away. Not all of it is that pleasant as there is no riverside walk at the beginning, so you may be better off to take a taxi there just for a drink at one of the riverside restaurants, which, though attractively located, are not that clean for eating a meal.

If you are a keen devotee of Ottoman *khans* there are two you can visit by returning to the centre of town by the artists' gallery on the bridge, and then heading up the main street away from the river for some 200m to reach the 16th-century Rüstem Pasha Khan on the left (currently being converted into a handicrafts market), then about 200m further on to the right is the 18th-century As'ad Pasha Khan with an impressive doorway, recently in use as the Ba'ath Party headquarters.

The oldest and largest waterwheel, Al-Muhammadiye, is set apart by itself a little further west out of the town centre, about 1km away from the Apamea Cham or the Nur Ad-Din Mosque. It is the best *noria* for photos, as you can walk across to it on a low wall and pose in front while being photographed from the footbridge. There is no river walkway here that might link up with the more central waterwheels, so you have to come out here by taxi or car. On the way you could cast a glance at the Grand Mosque, a totally new but faithful reconstruction of the original Grand Mosque that was flattened in 1982. You will also notice the grassy mound of the Hama citadel on this route, not worth a visit as nothing remains today. The excavated finds are on display in the Hama Museum, and the tell has now been made into a landscaped garden popular as a picnic site with residents on Fridays, especially in summer to catch the breeze.

Hama Museum (*Open 09.00–14.00 daily except Tue; S£75 entry fee*) This newly built and very well-presented museum is set in its own pretty landscaped gardens with scattered mosaics and carved blocks and basalt grave doors among the jasmine. It is located on the north side of the river on the road that leads out of town towards Qasr Ibn Wardan and is worth a 30-minute stop mainly for the mosaics, above all for the famous mosaic of the Female Musicians, found originally on the dining-room floor of a Roman villa west of Hama. The tiny tesserae used give great detail to the ensemble. The six women are each playing a different instrument which is remarkable both for the insight it offers into the fact that women were clearly skilled in this art and for the instruments themselves. Dated to the end of the 4th century the serious expressions and big eyes are precursors of the Byzantine style. The instruments are the organ, the flute, the lyre (or zither), the castanets and six metal bowls on a table. The organ chest is concealed under a heavily embroidered cloth and two small boys disguised as angels are pumping the bellows which is providing the air to the 19 pipes. The woman on the far left holding the cymbals seems to be conducting the ensemble.

The other notable, albeit far more fragmentary mosaic here is the Mosaic of the Noria, wrongly placed in a different room, the last hall, which is for Islamic exhibits. Dated to AD469 it was found at Apamea and proves how early this irrigation method was in existence. Dominating the Iron Age Hall is a giant black basalt lion which was found on Hama's citadel mound guarding the gates of the 9th-century BC neo-Hittite Royal Palace, very like the lion which was found guarding the entrance to 'Ain Dara, the neo-Hittite site north of St Simeon's Basilica, northwest of Aleppo.

Qasr Ibn Wardan قصر ابن وردان (*58km northeast of Hama; unfenced site but buildings locked; open 09.00–16.00 winter, 09.00–18.00 summer; guardian and S£75 entry fee; allow at least 2 hours for the total detour from Hama*) From Hama Museum a 40-minute drive continuing out of town on the same road will bring you to this remarkable fortified Byzantine palace and church complex, the only one of its type in Syria. Built in the last year of the reign of Emperor Justinian (527–65), its purpose was as a defensive palace, partly to control the Arab nomadic population and partly to guard against the strategic threat from Persia. From afar its distinctive stripes of black basalt and yellow brick rise up in elegant shapes silhouetted against the flat desert landscape.

The guardian will observe your arrival from the nearby village and materialise to unlock the doors in due course. The largest part of the complex is the palace, where the military governor would have lived. Still standing to its full two-storey height, you can climb the steps to the roof. Badly crumbling in places, it is a struggle to maintain the roof against the winter rains and even occasional snow. The palace courtyard is very extensive and has kitchen areas with basalt grinding blocks, olive presses and lots of wells. In places there are mosaic fragments in the ground. There is also an animal stabling area.

The more interesting building, however, is the church, to the left (west) of the palace. It too has steps leading to the second storey, from where you can enjoy a magnificent view and can appreciate well the architectural style of the building with its elegant white limestone columns and heavily weathered capitals, thought to have been recycled from Apamea. This upper gallery may have been where the women sat, in the Byzantine tradition, and it is rare to find it as intact as this. The original church brick dome would have been 20m high, the only baked-brick dome to be found in Syria. The glittery gypsum is reminiscent of Resafe and would also have been brought from elsewhere. Nothing remains of the military barracks beyond a few crumbling foundations.

On the return journey to Hama, if you have time stop off at the village of As-Srouj, 7km back along the road, where you will see clusters of the traditional beehive mud and straw houses, as lived in by Abraham in biblical times, and only relatively recently abandoned in favour of modern breeze-block. Each dome was a room, and sometimes clusters of four or more are joined together to give remarkably spacious accommodation. Nowadays very few are still lived in, but tend instead to have been given over to stabling or storage. The stones left sticking out of the outside on the dome were to allow easy climbing up for repairs. The building technique is now all but lost. Other beehive houses can be seen on the main road from Aleppo east to Raqqa, and on the road between Palmyra and Homs.

TOWARDS ALEPPO

VIA QAL'AT SHEIZAR, APAMEA AND MA'ARAT AN-NU'MAN Finding your way out of Hama, as indeed out of many of the main towns and cities of Syria, on the right road to your destination can be a bit challenging. Signposts, if there are any at all in the centre, tend often to be in Arabic only, so be prepared to stop and ask a lot. Once beyond the town the major junctions are normally signposted in both English and Arabic.

After about 20 minutes' drive (c25km) you reach the small town of Shaizar with the castle fortifications clearly visible on the rocky outcrop immediately to your right behind the huddle of houses. Just about any of the roads off through the houses will bring you shortly to the foot of the castle with its fine rather proud gateway. Newly restored, it is well worth a 30-minute stop to climb up through the gateway into the castle precincts from where you get an unexpected view down into the magnificent Orontes gorge, something that is not at all apparent from the front. The whole scene here is in fact deeply rural with the outlying village houses boasting little plots of land with cows, turkeys, chickens and vegetable gardens haphazardly scattered.

The lowest blocks of the castle wall date from Alexander's time, though most of the castle was built by Nur Ad-Din, then restored in the 13th century by the Mameluke Sultan Baibars, who started his career being sold in the Damascus slave market. The site was abandoned in the 12th century and never again occupied. Continuing on the road to Apamea as you exit Shaizar and cross the

Shaizar Castle was also the home of the old Arab warrior prince Usama Bin Munqidh, who, at the age of 90, wrote his memoirs of an Arab-Syrian gentleman, a hilarious and illuminating critique of the Frankish Crusader knights he observed throughout his lifetime. A delightfully frank and down to earth book, (its Arabic title is Kitab Al-I'tibar, the Book of Consideration/Reflection), this is the first autobiography to be found in Arabic literature. He was born four years after the fall of Jerusalem to the Crusaders and died one year after the famous Crusader defeat at the hands of Saladin at the Battle of Hittin in 1187. His writings reveal a very low opinion of the Christians with their strange customs. He marvelled at their lack of honour in taking their women to the *hammam* to have all their body hair removed by a man. He was particularly scathing about their lack of culture and knowledge, telling clever anecdotes about their medical ignorance and poking fun at their judicial procedure with its trial by duel and by water. Now translated into English and available in paperback, the book makes very amusing reading. See *Appendix 3* for details.

Orontes, notice the 11-arched Roman bridge to your right, while to your left is a fine waterwheel and attached aqueduct to water the fields. The rich dark soil of the Orontes valley is very apparent here and cattle are plentiful with abundant grazing and lush crops in the fields. Potatoes are sold at the roadsides, and known as the best in Syria. There are also lots of fields of cotton, the white bolls glinting in the sun.

Apamea أفاميا (*60km northwest of Hama; no fence, so no opening hours; S£150 entry fee; allow 2 hours for the site visit; simple cafeteria selling drinks only; basic WC facilities*) From Shaizar it is a further 45-minute drive to reach Apamea (Arabic 'Afaamia'). The approach to this, Syria's largest classical site, is blighted by the scruffy town through which you have to pass first, but once up amongst the ruins the setting improves dramatically, especially in spring when the grass is green and the site is full of red flowers. The site is also signposted 'Qal'at Al-Mudiq', the modern name for the citadel beside the classical ruins, which is still inhabited by the poorer people of the town, though rarely visited because of its accompanying medieval smells and dirt levels. Originally the acropolis of the ancient city, it was destroyed by the Roman General Pompey (Arabic 'Bombeh') in 64BC. Only some of the lower levels of the Hellenistic stones are visible, and the remainder of what you see today is an Arab fort built in the 12th century by the Zengid leader Nur Ad-Din. The Crusaders occupied it before that in AD1106 but made no changes.

The track to the ruins leads off at the foot of the Qal'at Al-Mudiq Citadel and then forks to the left to follow the line of the impressive rampart walls rebuilt by Justinian in Byzantine times, originally 6.3km in length, now excavated to show their full 10m height in places. The lowest courses are Seleucid from the original city, and the middle courses are Roman. Their original total perimeter was 16km, with 100 towers. Outside the walls there were three distinct necropolis areas with many tombs. You then arrive at the far end of the colonnaded street at the north gate, where there is a small car park and ticket kiosk, often unmanned. If you have your own transport, this would be the preferred starting point for an exploration of the ruins because you can then walk down the street to end at the cafeteria for refreshments and it is also the correct chronological order of construction.

Visited by Mark Antony and Cleopatra, the city of Apamea, set on a natural elevation overlooking the Ghab depression, owes its special atmosphere today to

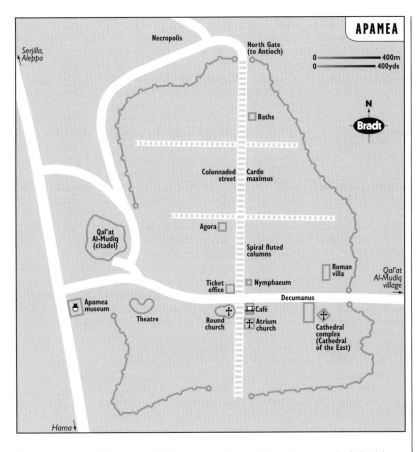

APAMEA

Necropolis

Serjilla, Aleppo

North Gate (to Antioch)

0 ———— 400m
0 ———— 400yds

N

Bradt

Baths

Colonnaded street | Cardo maximus

Qal'at Al-Mudiq (citadel)

Agora

Spiral fluted columns

Roman villa

Qal'at Al-Mudiq village

Ticket office | Nymphaeum

Decumanus

Apamea museum

Theatre

Round church | Café

Atrium church

Cathedral complex (Cathedral of the East)

Hama

the re-erection of the Grand Colonnade of over 400 columns, which had been tumbled by earthquakes over the centuries, one of the most beautiful avenues of the ancient world. Starting in 1930, Belgian excavators have conducted a thorough programme of excavations over a period of half a century, the main results of which have been published by Janine Balty, lead archaeologist in the 1970s and 1980s. There is still more to be excavated in future. The classical city of Apamea has been recognised as one of Syria's most major Roman sites, even rivalling Palmyra. It boasted Syria's largest Roman theatre and the site covers 200ha, compared with Palmyra's 50. Tragically many of the site's most beautiful finds were transferred to a museum in Brussels which was bombed in World War II destroying everything except the famous hunting mosaic which was protected by the debris. Fortunately many of the site's other mosaics survive in the Ottoman caravanserai museum by the entrance, described later.

Archaeological discoveries have proved that Apamea was inhabited from the early Bronze Age but it reached its peak cAD3000 under the reign of Seleucus Nicador, with the historian Strabo telling us that the city boasted 40,000 horses and 500 fighting elephants. Apamea was known as a centre for elephant taming, a skill originally brought from India. Apamean coins often depicted elephants. They were all slaughtered in 162BC as part of the Apamea peace agreement. The rich pasture provided excellent breeding ground for the army's cavalry. The city's population in its heyday was estimated at 500,000 of whom 380,000 were thought to be slaves.

Seleucus Nicador founded the city in the beginning of the 3rd century BC (along with Lattakia and Antioch), naming it Apamea after his Bactrian wife. Its agricultural wealth, based on the fertility of the Ghab plain, enabled Apamea's rich traders to expand their markets for trees, vines and sheep all over the Roman and Hellenistic world. In addition to the nearby Orontes River feeding the irrigation, the city also got its drinking water from excellently built water channels which conducted water in from Salimiye. There were also three lakes which irrigated the city, but they gradually dried up into swamps and in the 1950s the government had them drained and converted to agricultural land. The Greek and Roman eras still overlap here, but all buildings that were originally Greek were destroyed by earthquakes and then rebuilt in the Roman style. During its heyday the city was home to the school of thought known as Neo-Platonism, a philosophy that combined Platonism with oriental elements, one of the many examples of the fusion of Hellenistic, Roman and oriental ideas that took place in this part of the world. In Byzantine times, especially under Justinian, further building work was completed, notably two churches and a cathedral described later. Apamea was a centre for Jacobite Christians, followers of the Monophysite 'heresy', (see *Early divisions of the Church* box on page 170) and was the seat of a bishop.

The town was built in the standard grid pattern, its main street, the cardo maximus, running north–south with about 15 minor streets crossing it east–west. Starting from the often closed ticket office at the northern end of the colonnaded street, you will be following the chronologically correct sequence of building. This oldest section was the first to be built, after the devastating earthquake of AD115, with the remainder of the street built throughout the 2nd century. This end is also where most of the archaeological work has taken place today, so there is more to see in this first section. Some of the blocks are numbered like a jigsaw for reconstruction purposes. As you enter the street, first go back a little towards the north gate, where you will see a precarious arch and a pile of tumbled stones. This area was originally the Antioch Gate but seems to have been adapted later to become a fortified keep. Terracotta pipework that must have been installed later has been uncovered by the excavators above the level of the original paving.

The main street, the most phenomenal feature of Apamea, runs for a dead straight 2km (Palmyra's is 1.2km with a crooked angle), lined originally by a staggering total of 1,200 columns, 400 of which have been re-erected, as mentioned above, thanks to funding from the wealthy philanthropist and entrepreneur Osmane Aidi, owner of the Cham chain of hotels and tour group. Successive earthquakes had tumbled the columns. Like a kind of grand Champs-Elyssées, it was lined with porticoes which would have had upmarket shops installed, reflecting the wealth of the city. The columns are 10m high with a diameter of c120cm, each one spaced 3m from its neighbour. In style they range from conventional circular, to square, to the unusual and distinctive spiral design not seen elsewhere in the Roman world, always crowned with Corinthian capitals.

Continuing along the colonnaded street which, unlike Palmyra's, is paved and even bears the rut markings of wheels, you come after c50m to a reconstructed votive column in the middle of the street at an intersection. Just before this to the left is what remains of the baths complex, lavish in its scale, but still requiring considerable reconstruction work to convey this today. In the next section of the street, just past the recently restored and beautiful portico on the left, look out also on the left for three large stone slabs on the ground, two of which are finely carved with magnificent reliefs where you can see elaborate leaf and floral designs, with vines and motifs showing worship of Bacchus, god of wine, and Pan with a flock of goats.

At any point from about now, if you arrive at the site alone, you can expect to be caught up with by villagers from Qal'at Al-Mudiq furtively trying to sell you 'antiques' supposedly found on the site. If you like them, you can buy them as souvenirs to help support the local enterprise, but do not imagine for a moment they are genuine.

After the Bacchus and Pan blocks the next landmark is the excavated base of a large star-shaped votive column in the middle of the street. Beyond this, is a section of street with first plain columns, then the distinctive spiral-fluted columns unique to Apamea. Opposite these is a pile of stones marking the collapsed monumental entrance façade to the long rectangular agora, 300m by 45m, running parallel to the cardo. Note the two rows of column bases at its southern end: all that remains of the short approach way to the agora from the main street, a most unusual feature. Some Byzantine mosaic flooring has recently been revealed *in situ*. Further away from the main street beyond the agora a low grassy mound is all that remains of the Temple of Zeus, destroyed on the orders of a bishop in the 4th century.

Back in the main street the last building to be seen before reaching the tarmac road by the café is the *nymphaeum*, heavily ruined, to the left.

The final parts of the site dated to the 5th century can now be reached by following the tarmac road east (to the left). This road follows the course of the original decumanus, and after some 400m on the right, you come to the heavily ruined cathedral complex, the most important Christian ruin in Apamea, dated to the 5th century. Known as the Cathedral of the East, the huge complex is approached by steps from the decumanus. It covers 12,000 square metres and is today a confusing jumble of successive constructions, destroyed by earthquakes and rebuilt in the 6th century in basilica style, along with an archbishop's palace and dependent buildings. The original layout however, with its extra chapel to the east, is always associated with the presence of a relic, thought to be the True Cross which the Christians of Apamea were proud to possess. The 6th-century basilica was built on top of the original martyrium. Many of Apamea's most famous mosaics were found here, which have now been variously removed to the Brussels Museum, the Damascus Museum or the local Apamea Museum.

On the other side of the road are the remains of a Roman villa complex, thought to be the Ruler's Palace, where the 'Amazons' and hunting mosaics were found, with ordinary rural houses on the street opposite. Excavated since 1973, its entrance is impressive, heavily restored with a decorated lintel and porch to the right as you enter from the street. Inside, the large courtyard has 26 re-erected columns and then a smaller courtyard surrounded with rooms. There would have been a central fountain in each courtyard and marble paving.

Returning now to just past the cafeteria you can continue for the final stretch of the cardo maximus, much more ruined than the northern stretch, but along which you can find the remains of two churches, one to the right and one to the left of the road. The first one is after some 50m on the right, a 6th-century building known as the round church, built in the reign of Justinian (527–65). The circular chamber, now just foundations, was 25m in diameter, with a semicircular apse to the east.

Just a few metres further south on the other side of the cardo are the foundations of a large church of the 6th century, known as the Atrium Church. It was built on the foundations of an earlier 5th-century building, which was in turn built on the site of a 4th-century synagogue, whose geometric mosaic floor, dated to 391, is now in the Brussels Museum. The relics of the two saints Cosmas and Damien were originally contained in two large stone reliquaries found empty in the northeast chapel in 1934. One of these reliquaries is now in the garden of the National Museum in Damascus.

To reach the enormous but heavily ruined theatre, you need to follow the main tarmac road to the west, back towards the town for about 500m. Set in a natural hollow to the left of the road, and slightly obscured by a row of houses, it is the largest in Syria, possibly even in the Roman world, with a diameter of 139m (compared with Bosra's 90m for example) and a façade of 145m. It looks more impressive from the citadel above rather than from close up. As it has never been excavated, it is difficult to distinguish the masonry, not least because a lot of the stones have been carted off and reused in the town over the centuries and to build the Ottoman caravanserai. It is thought to date to the late 2nd century AD.

Apamea Museum (*Open 08.00–14.00 daily except Tue; S£75 entry fee*) Opened in 1976 inside an attractive 16th-century Ottoman caravanserai, the Apamea Museum is back down on the main road through the town. It is well worth a 30-minute stop, especially for the mosaics which are quite unlike the typical ones in that they do not represent scenes from Greek and Roman mythology, but instead depict nature. The scenes of animals running free are remarkable for their innocence, natural movement and grace.

The caravanserai is an impressive building in its own right, 80m square, built largely from stones recycled from the Roman theatre over the hill, as a stopover point on the road to Mecca for the pilgrimage from Istanbul. Inside, note the metal rings where the horses would have been tied up and the individual chimneys where pilgrims would have cooked.

Of the most famous mosaics here is the Socrates mosaic, dated 363, taken from the cathedral altar, which shows Socrates raising his right hand almost Christ-like at the Last Supper, surrounded by six philosophy students. The subject matter confirms the strong Neoplatonic philosophy that was prevalent in Apamea in the late 4th century. The chief site archaeologist Janine Balty observes it may represent Christ 'repaganised', in the process of rediscovering the Hellenism of the past that was given impetus by the decrees of Julian the Apostate (361–63) at the time. The other famous one is the Amazons mosaic, depicting female warriors on horseback, hunting tigers, found in the palace beside the cathedral, and dated to the end of the 5th century. The museum is well lit, but naturally very dark if there is a power cut, so your torch may come in handy.

Apart from the mosaics the museum has a collection of sarcophagi, statuary and inscriptions, all from the local area. In the centre of the courtyard steps lead down into what was once the reservoir.

Ma'arat An-Nu'man معرة النعمان You return now to the main Damascus–Aleppo highway and continue for c25km to reach the Ma'arat An-Nu'man exit. On the highway the Arabic road signs saying 'Reduce speed' are mistranslated into English as 'Make light speed', the Arabic root for 'to reduce' also meaning 'to lighten', resulting in the rather confusing instruction that suggests either 'Go at the speed of light' or 'Make light of speed'.

The town of Ma'arat An-Nu'man is an ugly sprawling dusty place, yet surprisingly, in the centre of town stands the largest caravanserai in Syria, 7,000m2, a very solid 16th-century construction that has a rather ominous appearance. In 1987 however it was converted to serve as a museum for exhibiting the many finds from the villages and towns all around, and most notably it houses an excellent collection of Byzantine mosaics, well preserved by the dry climate, and which were moved here from the villas of rich local Romans. The small building in the centre of the courtyard was an oratory, at the back of which was a place for serving food to the needy.

Ma'arat An-Nu'man Museum (*Open 09.00–16.00 daily except Tue; S£75 entry fee; basic WC facilities*) The mosaics reveal the incredibly rich animal life that clearly once

This blind poet-philosopher, whose *Treatise on Forgiveness* is thought to have directly influenced Dante's *Divine Comedy*, lived and died in Ma'arat An-Nu'man (hence his surname) 973–1057. He was orphaned and at the age of four smallpox cost him his sight, but he compensated for his blindness by an extraordinary memory. His poems and works expressed the scepticism and pessimism of the times, where political anarchy and social decay were prevalent. He adopted a vegetarian diet and a life of comparative seclusion. Parallels have repeatedly been drawn with the Persian 'Umar Al-Khayyam who died about 60 years later. Here is some sample verse translated by Ameen Rihani:

Tread lightly, for a thousand hearts unseen
Might now be beating in this misty green;
Here are the herbs that once were pretty cheeks,
Here the remains of those that once have been.

Afearing whom I trust I gain my end,
But trusting, without fear, I lose, my friend;
Much better is the Doubt that gives me peace,
Than all the Faiths which in hell-fire may end.

Among us some are great and some are small,
Albeit in wickedness, we're masters all;
Or, if my fellow men are like myself,
The human race shall always rise and fall.

The air of sin I breathe without restraint;
With selfishness my few good deeds I taint;
I come as I was moulded and I go,
But near the vacant shrine of Truth I faint.

A church, a temple, or a Ka'ba stone,
Koran or Bible or a martyr's bone –
All these and more my heart can tolerate
Since my religion now is Love alone.

thrived here, with bears, lions, elephants, ostriches, ducks, gazelles, tigers, leopards, bulls and many different types of bird. One mosaic conveys incredible movement in a lion chasing a stag. A 3rd-century mosaic shows the baby Hercules wrestling with snakes, while a 6th-century one represents Romulus and Remus set in a fine geometric frame. The lighting of the mosaics in the rooms round the courtyard unfortunately leaves a lot to be desired, as it is either too yellow, thereby destroying the natural colours of the mosaics, or else too dark and obscuring them.

Apart from the mosaics, the museum also has in its courtyard an amazing collection of black basalt doors taken from early Roman tombs nearby, and also an unusual collection of early clay toys, such as a cow towing a cart, all of which look fun to play with. Notice too the sheer scale of the huge and powerful entrance doors.

Ma'arat An-Nu'man is also famous as the place where the ghastly three-week siege took place by the Crusaders in 1098 on their way to Jerusalem, culminating in the massacre of some 20,000 Muslims including women and children, many of whom were then eaten by the hungry Crusaders. Raymond of Fulchre, the Crusader leader, described the scene:

> Our people suffered a severe famine. I shudder to speak of it; our people were so frenzied by hunger that they tore flesh from the buttocks of the Saracens who had died there, which they cooked and chewed and devoured with savage mouths, even when it had been roasted insufficiently on the fire.

And so the besiegers were more harmed than the besieged.

CITIES OF THE DEAD المدن الميتة

From Ma'arat An-Nu'man northwards you are now entering the area of the Cities of the Dead. The existence of these extraordinarily intact ruins in the hills to the south and west of Aleppo comes as a shock to most visitors. Although they are largely unknown to the outside world it is their sheer scale which is the most astonishing aspect: nearly 800 of them in total, with over 2,000 churches, spread over a hilly, in places mountainous area, about 30km by 140km. Most are at an altitude of 400–500m, but there are some on outcrops of up to 800m. The process is currently under way of having the whole area declared a UNESCO World Heritage Site, which would make it Syria's sixth after the old cities of Damascus and Aleppo, Bosra Theatre, Palmyra and Krak des Chevaliers, the last also being in the process of an application.

What were these places? And why were they abandoned so abruptly? Answers to these questions in the past have been largely fanciful and random, including such explanations as Muslim invasion, Christian persecution and nomad incursions. In the 1950s, however, Georges Tchalenko, a French archaeologist, produced an exhaustive study of the Cities of the Dead under the auspices of the French Institute for Near Eastern Archaeology in Beirut, in which he concluded that they had been early Christian communities dating from the 4th to the 6th centuries, based on the export of wine and olive oil to the Mediterranean via the port of Antioch. He speculates that the first olive presses were probably set up in the 2nd century AD under the auspices of the temples, but were later expanded considerably under private ownership when the price of olive oil boomed in the 5th century. Those trade routes were disrupted by wars between the Arabs and the Byzantines, thereby destroying the villagers' livelihoods and forcing them to move out of the hills and to resettle closer to the coast.

The abandoned villages sprawled in the hills for over ten centuries, uninterfered with by human hand, suffering only the occasional earthquake and the effects of the passage of time. The scarcity of wood in the hills meant that most permanent buildings were of stone, or fine masonry to be more exact, a white limestone covered with a grey or gilt patina. The architectural methods used were rather rustic, with irregular polygonal stones, reflecting the fact that the builders were local peasants of Syriac-speaking stock. No cement was used to bind the stones, and, reflecting the lack of wood, stone was used for just about everything – steps, balconies, porticoes, benches, cupboards, ceilings and roofs, made of stone slabs supported on arches. Whilst the architecture and building techniques in the villages were essentially simple and stolid, in the more ambitious public buildings, especially the basilica complex of St Simeon for example, the skill and splendour of the stone craftsmanship reveal an original and powerful talent for decoration, apparent everywhere in details such as door lintels, arches and uprights, mouldings and cornices of façades, even mosaics, all reminiscent of and, some scholars have even said, heralding the sculptured ornamentation of Byzantium.

Scholars have identified a theoretical total of 780 different settlements, of which over 100 are sizeable, though around 30 are generally regarded as the core of those

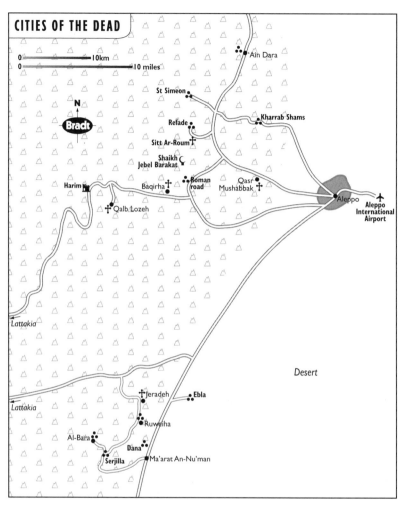

most worth visiting. It would take well over a month to visit all of them properly, something obviously only academics and specialists will be in a position to do. The ones described in this book are however enough to provide us with a unique insight into early Christian rural life and together they are probably the richest area of standing remains anywhere in the Mediterranean, most of them barely touched by tourism of any kind. Elsewhere around the Mediterranean basin most early Byzantine settlements were adapted or built over, but here their abandonment has ensured their preservation as a permanent record of that era.

Many of the ruins still have wonderfully isolated locations, standing eerily on the crests of the limestone hills. Others are now close to modern settlements, somewhat marring their atmosphere, while yet others have actually been settled in, dismantled and reassembled into modern villages, where suddenly an exquisitely carved piece of masonry protrudes incongruously from a cattle shelter or sheep pen.

Scholars have identified separate styles and periods among the settlements but on the whole the general plans of the towns and their buildings have a certain consistency. The settlement is usually surrounded by an enclosure wall with several watchtowers. There are paved streets which intersect at right angles to run between market places, inns, monasteries, churches, public meeting halls and private homes. The market stalls are recognisable in the shallow extended galleries lining the streets. The private houses are often two-storeyed with colonnades and loggias on the inner façade and blank windowless façades onto the street to give privacy as is the custom in Arab houses. The necropolis is on the outskirts of the settlement with tombs of various types, some hewn out of the rock, some like vaults built in the design of a temple, a pyramid or a mausoleum with a stone dome, while some are massive sarcophagi placed either on the bare earth or on a plinth with two columns rising up. Many of the buildings have inscriptions which give the date of construction, the name of the owner or the deceased, and some carry invocations or even personal wishes, all of which offer insights into the preoccupations of the builders of these monuments 14 centuries ago.

The first Westerner to 'discover' the Cities of the Dead was the Marquis de Vogué who saw them in 1860. He was followed by American expeditions in 1899, 1901, 1904 and 1905, and these were followed in turn by the archaeologists of the 20th-century, M M Butler, Lassus and Tchalenko, Ecochard and Krencker.

Geographically the Cities of the Dead fall into three groups on their three separate massifs. The whole area is usually referred to as the Belus Massif (or the French 'Le Massif Calcaire', ie: Limestone Massif), but within that the first grouping is the Jebel Riha (sometimes known as the Jebel Zawiye), the southernmost and largest group closest to Apamea and Hama. This grouping is about a century earlier than the other two groups and is more closely linked to classical art. Moving northwards the next grouping is in the twin massifs of the Jebel Al-'Ala and Jebel Barisha, separated by the Plain of Self. Then finally the northernmost group is the Jebel Semaan which, partly because of its closeness to Aleppo and partly because it boasts St Simeon, the single best preserved monastery complex anywhere among the Cities of the Dead, is the most visited and hence the most touched by tourism. The northernmost group with St Simeon is covered in *Chapter 7, Aleppo to the Coast,* on pages 163–8.

SERJILLA سيرجيلة *(60km from Aleppo via Ariha; allow 1hr; open site, S£75 entry fee during guardian hours)*

Getting there To reach Serjilla from Ma'arat An-Nu'man head west out of the town towards Kafr Nabel, 10km away. At the crossroads in the centre of Kafr Nabel, turn right for Serjilla and Al-Bara, then 8km later turn right to Serjilla. The site lies 3.5km from the junction at the end of the road, passing en route at about 2.5km the ruins of Bauda on the right, of which little remains among the rocks and trees except a pyramid tomb, several stone sarcophagi and a heavily ruined church.

What to see and do Undoubtedly the most hauntingly desolate of any of the Cities of the Dead, the eerie attraction of Serjilla lies in its location at the end of a dead-end road in a slight hollow between two wild and barren hillsides. Thanks to this setting the site is usually wonderfully silent, especially if you visit late in the day after the ticket office has shut up shop. In addition to its setting Serjilla is remarkable for the exceptional state of preservation of the buildings, and indeed the type of buildings.

The little path leading down to the centre of the village passes a cluster of ancient stone sarcophagi, scattered, as was the habit in all the Cities of the Dead, round the edges of the settlements.

Most unusually the path ends in a little square, the heart of the settlement, one of the rare examples of such a public amenity among the Cities of the Dead, off which are two further public buildings of exceptional if austere beauty. The first is a baths dated to 473 by the mosaic found on its floor by the first American archaeologists from Princeton University who arrived here in 1899 to document their findings. The mosaics have since disappeared as have the traces of murals. The small apses off the central 8m by 15m space were the caldarium and frigidarium, and the baths were fed by a cistern whose flagstoned floor is still apparent. A stream once flowed through the town providing the cistern with water. These baths are the best preserved of any in the Dead Cities and are especially interesting as an example of early Christian as opposed to early Roman baths.

The second public building off the little square is known as an *andron*, a men's meeting room or tavern, unique in any of the Dead Cities. Its plan is virtually square and its two storeys and double-portico façade of three columns on each storey, make it one of the best-preserved Roman buildings to be found anywhere. The existence of these two rare public buildings suggest that Serjilla was once very prosperous.

Fifty metres east of the *andron* stands a triple-nave ruined church tucked into the side of the valley, with three stone sarcophagi still in one of its side chapels. It has been dated from an inscription to 372, making it one of the oldest churches in the region.

Several two-storey fine detached buildings survive in a remarkably intact state of preservation, the stone arches that would have supported the wooden first floor still in place. There are no signs of stairs so scholars presume they were built of wood and set on the outside, so that they have obviously disintegrated over the centuries. Niches in the walls would probably have held oil lamps. Some of the largest villas would have had up to 16 rooms, perhaps four families sharing the villa (probably all one extended family), one on each side of the colonnaded front facing into a communal courtyard, similar to the Arab habit in a courtyard house where several generations live together.

Wandering round the rest of the settlement, you will notice there are no proper streets, just narrow grassy lanes passing between the high walls of houses with their immaculately carved windows and doors. The larger houses often have their own stone olive presses with carefully carved channels for the olive oil to drain off and be collected in jars. Grapes were cultivated here as well as olives.

No evidence of latrines of any sort has been found at Serjilla, a fact which has led scholars to conclude that the inhabitants must have originally been simple peasants who were not accustomed to using latrines.

Driving out to the north 17km via Ariha, the drive on to Aleppo takes about an hour.

AL-BARA البارة (*Allow 2–3 hours; open site; no entry fee*) The largest and most extensive of any of the Dead Cities, the ruins of Al-Bara sprawl over heavily treed hillsides and valleys covering an area 3km by 2km. You should allow two to three hours for a visit, as a lot of walking is involved. Its original population was estimated at 5,000 and it had five churches, three monasteries and many, many villas. The Crusader knights lived here from 1098 to 1123, and the Arab fort of Abu Soufyian, just north of the modern village of Al-Bara, was built here by the Ayyubids who drove the Crusaders out. An earthquake in 1157 left it uninhabitable.

Gertrude Bell (see box on page 134) spent two days in Al-Bara in the early 1900s and was entranced:

> It is like the dream city which children create for themselves to dwell in between
> bedtime and sleeping, building palace after palace down the shining ways of the
> imagination, and no words can give the charm of it, nor the magic of the Syrian spring.

A tarmac road now runs from the modern village down into the valley and over to the ruins, then meanders about linking the main parts of the ruins. As a result,

Born into a non-aristocratic family of great affluence, Gertrude Bell played a major and largely unrecognised role in supporting the Arab Revolt, along with her contemporary T E Lawrence who received most of the credit. At the end of the war she drew up the borders of the former Mesopotamia to create the modern state of Iraq.

Extremely clever, she got a first at Oxford in History in only two years, and went on to study archaeology and languages, acquiring passable fluency in Arabic, French, German, Italian, Persian and Turkish. She travelled extensively in the Middle East, dressed as a male Bedouin, studying local ruins and staying with the Druze and many local sheikhs. Her book *The Desert and the Sown* brings together her accounts of these travels and her descriptions of the desert were the first to reach a Western audience. Through her archaeological interests she met T E Lawrence who was working at the Hittite site of Carchemish on the Turkish–Syrian border.

When World War I broke out she requested to be posted in the Middle East, was initially refused, then later summoned in 1915 to Cairo to work in the Arab Bureau. Here she helped collect intelligence and again worked with Lawrence. In 1916 she went to Basra to work as adviser to Chief Political Officer Percy Cox, becoming the only female political officer in the British forces. She was awarded the CBE for her work in the war. She persuaded Churchill to endorse Faisal, recently deposed King of Syria, as first King of Iraq, and herself advised Faisal on matters of tribal geography and local business. Due to her influence she earned the nickname the Uncrowned Queen of Iraq. She went on to establish what would become the Baghdad Archaeological Museum, supervising excavations and examining finds herself. She committed suicide with an overdose of sleeping pills in Baghdad soon after the Baghdad Museum opened in 1926. She never married or had children, but wrote four books and has been the subject of several biographies.

what used to be quite an exhausting visit clambering about among the undergrowth and olive groves, has been greatly facilitated, and the best thing if you do not have a guide is to call first at the guardian's office on the main street of modern Bara to pick up either the guardian himself or his young son, who has the keys to the various main buildings such as the pyramid tombs and the olive press.

The first port of call is generally known as Deir Sobat, thought to be a 6th-century monastery. A very beautiful two-story building, evocatively set among groves of trees and covered in flowers and grassy mounds, it is an excellent picnic spot. Recent speculation, based on an elaborate reconstruction produced by the Marquis de Vogüé, is that it was more likely to have been a rich villa with balconies, courtyards and a garden. If so, it certainly conveys well the wealth of the Hellenised Antiochene upper classes who were the landlords here.

As indeed does the next monument along the tarmac road some 300m further on, the huge pyramid tomb, kept locked, decorated with flourishes of acanthus leaf round a frieze. The stone from which it is built is the same attractive yellow colour as Deir Sobat. Inside are five massive richly decorated sarcophagi, each one a family vault that would have held several family members. Again, the sheer scale of the tomb conveys the fabulous wealth of its inhabitants.

Walking across the road into the field opposite the pyramid tomb, you will see after 150m one of the reasons for the wealth, the massive wine press. On the way you come across a simple Muslim graveyard, where the graves could easily be overlooked by an untrained eye, consisting merely of simple stones marking the head and the foot.

The wine press building is quite ruinous, but still clearly visible at the side is the shaft into which grapes were pushed, above which is still an inscription in Greek to Bacchus, god of wine: 'This nectar that you see – gift of Bacchus – is the fruit of the vines fed by the warm sunshine.'

Across in the next field your guide will show you Al-Bara's second reason for wealth, the town's olive press, carved down into the rock, semi-underground like a massive vault. It is kept locked, but once inside you can see the stone for grinding, so big that two donkeys had to be tied up to it to turn it round and round. During the busy harvest season in September/October, people had to wait three weeks for their olives to be processed into oil, and this explains the nearby inns where they had to stay.

A further walk across the fields takes you to the church known as Al-Husn, the Fort, with its fine black-veined marble pillars and underground arches. Nearby, a second pyramid tomb, set in an olive grove, is smaller and undecorated. The stone of the roof goes grey from the rain and weathering, while the reddish/yellow colour of the walls stays this colour because it is less weathered and exposed.

RUWEIHA رويحة (*Allow 1 hour; open site, no entry fee*) Located 25km from Al-Bara on the western slopes of the Jebel Zawiye, Ruweiha is a very extensive Dead City of the 5th and 6th centuries on the edge of a modern village. The setting is prettily rural, overlooking a wide open plain, heavily treed and agricultural, especially attractive in spring with cherry trees in blossom.

The ruins themselves have been absorbed by the villagers into their everyday lives and serve now as animal pens, stables and chicken coops, not to mention washing lines and carpet airers. As a result it is not that easy to gain access to the church and temple tomb and agora set to the right of the dirt track, as the entrances have been carefully blocked up with stones to make their use as pens more effective. The spacious agora in the centre of the cluster of ruins had a two-storey portico. The tall building with pillars dated by an inscription to 384, is controversial, claimed by some authorities to be a dwelling for a St Simeon-style recluse, but the local people say there is a tomb underneath, and this seems far more likely from its general design.

A five-minute walk away along the agricultural dirt track you will reach the remarkably intact Church of Bissos, said to be the second largest in northern Syria

MUSLIM VIEW OF DEATH

No ceremony is attached to death in Islam. The value system is different. Life is just a passage, a preparation for the next life, where you will be rewarded in heaven. The only important thing is a person's deeds, not their material wealth. A life is judged by what is left behind of lasting value – a good son, a good book, charitable works. Grief is not prolonged – there is just a three-day mourning period on the whole. The body is wrapped in a plain cloth and put straight into the ground within 24 hours in a simple grave. Cremation is not permitted in Islam. The Archbishop of Canterbury, Rowan Williams, would approve – a thoroughly 'green' funeral, just as he advocates for the Church of England.

The Koran promises a second life after death:

The enjoyment of this life is a trifle and the Hereafter is better for those who are mindful of their duty to Allah. (4:28)

Every one shall suffer death, and you shall be paid your full recompense on the Day of Judgement. He who is kept away from the Fire and is admitted to Paradise, has indeed attained felicity. The life of this world is but an illusory enjoyment. (3:186)

The hither life is nothing but sport and pastime, and the Home of the Hereafter is the only true life, if they but knew. (29:65)

and certainly the largest in the Jebel Riha/Zawiye. Very much integrated into the villagers' lives as a gigantic animal pen, exploring the church involves encountering goats, chickens and cows, but everyone is friendly and welcoming and as long as you are respectful and polite, you are not treated as an intruder but rather as a valued guest and invited for tea. If tea is offered it is impolite to refuse, but on these occasions it makes all the difference if someone in your entourage can speak Arabic to help get the full benefit of such an invitation.

The architectural feature of note in the Church of Bissos is the pair of high transverse arches spanning the central nave, a feature that was not found in Europe till several centuries later. Also remarkable and unique is the stone cut dome of the tomb of St Bissos attached to the church. We do not know who Bissos was, possibly a local priest or bishop, but the inscription left of the door on the west façade reads: 'Bizzos son of Pardos. I lived worthily, died worthily and rest worthily. Pray for me.' This is the only example in Syria of a domed saint's tomb, and is a precursor of the common Muslim domed saints' tombs found all over the Middle East and Turkey.

The villagers do not mind if you clamber up on the roof of their dwelling and across onto the roof by the dome to take a closer look. Views from up here also combine the immediate rural aspects of the setting with the 5th- and 6th-century architecture to create a curiously charming picture. Steps lead down from the other side which enable you to get a closer look at the tomb itself.

JERADEH جيرادة (*Allow 30–40mins; open site; no entry fee*) The main reason to visit Jeradeh, an attractive and compact Dead City 2km from Ruweiha, set slightly apart from a small modern village, is for its remarkable six-storey tower complete with overhanging latrines on the top floor. This is the best example of such a structure in the area. The surrounding landscape is enlivened by pistachio trees which blossom pink in April and the crop is ready at the end of August. The exact purpose of this extraordinary tower is not known – another of the mysteries surrounding the Dead Cities. Were they dwellings for St Simeon-style recluses, complete with penthouse WC facilities, or were they watchtowers with the latrine-like structures used as machicolation boxes for pouring hot oil or whatever down on the enemy once he was inside the walls anyway? The town itself did have outer walls, part of which can still be walked round, an unusual feature for Dead Cities of this period. Maybe its location on the edge of the mountain range made it more open to Bedouin incursions from the desert. The other notable buildings of the town are its unusual church with five columns, very well preserved, and its elegant and attractively bucolic villa and courtyard in which village boys now play football.

DANA دانة (*Allow 30mins; open site; no entry fee*) From the main Ma'arat An-Nu'man–Aleppo highway the road to Dana turns off left (east) opposite Al-Ahram Restaurant. Not to be confused with the Dana to the north near Aleppo where the Roman road is still in good condition, the remains of Dana date to the 3rd or 4th century. There are really only two monuments to visit, but both are extremely well preserved. The first is an impressive and elaborately carved pyramid tomb of the type found at Al-Bara, but though it can be spotted from afar by its distinctive pyramid shape and mellow yellow stone to the north of the village centre, it is surprisingly hard to locate from closer to, when it is obscured by the buildings of the modern village. Lots of old recycled stones from ancient Dana can be seen in the lower courses of the stonework of the modern houses. The tomb itself also serves as home to hundreds of sparrows who nest in its roof.

Outside the village to the north, the tarmac road leads to Dana's second monument of note, Qasr Al-Banat, meaning Palace of the Maidens, presumably implying a nunnery, though it might in fact be an inn. Its layout is reminiscent of

Deir Sobat at Al-Bara, and it still stands three stories tall, surprisingly intact. Its setting by itself in the countryside is pleasantly rural and sheep are often to be found grazing among the pastures within it.

EBLA تل مرديخ (*Allow 1hr min; open site; S£150 entry fee during guardian's hours; Portakabin WCs beside ticket kiosk*) The vast 56ha site of Ebla, also known as Tell Mardikh, is well signposted just east of the main Damascus–Aleppo highway, a 3km drive on a tarmac road to reach the hill or series of hills which make up this, Syria's most important Bronze Age city. Only by visiting can you appreciate the sheer scale of the original settlement, with its extensive earthwork defence walls, a massive 40m thick at their base and up to 22m high, and its acropolis citadel in the centre. The non-specialist must use strong powers of imagination to conjure up the original grandeur, as only relatively small sections on the acropolis, lower town and rampart walls have been excavated, a project of colossal proportions that will take many decades to complete. It was the discovery of a major archive of clay tablets written in the Ebla language, an Akkadian cuneiform writing, that first revealed the importance of Ebla as a major trading hub. On a par with Sumer and Akkad in Iraq, Ebla's peak of prosperity was 2400–2250BC, when its population was estimated at 30,000. It fell into decline from 1600BC onwards, after a Hittite incursion and was finally abandoned c8th century BC.

The word 'Ebla' means 'white rock', a reference to the natural limestone of the acropolis. The city of Ebla was known as an important political and trading centre long before it was finally discovered, because of ample documentation about the city and its culture that came to light in the Mari archives and also in Hittite texts from Anatolia and on the walls of Karnak in ancient Egypt. Its exact location however was not known till the Italian archaeological expedition of the University of 'La Sapienza' of Rome under Professor Paolo Matthiae first discovered it during soundings taken in 1964. In 1968 a statue from around 2000BC was unearthed with an Akkadian inscription giving the name of a king of Ebla, Igrish-Khep, the first concrete evidence this might indeed be Ebla. Painstaking excavation work has been ongoing ever since.

Professor Paolo is now 68 and has built his considerable reputation on the good fortune of his finds at Ebla. Last year alone 22kg of lapis lazuli was found, thought to have been for jewellery and votive offerings. The red domed brick building just before the site entrance is where the excavators live during the excavation season. Their many finds, which include decorative items of gold, lapis lazuli and ivory, cylinder seals, statuettes of soldiers or priests, deities and deified animals, especially the leopard erect on his hind legs and the anthropomorphic Euphrates ox with beard, are on display in the museums of Idlib, 20km away, Hama, Aleppo and Damascus.

The real breakthrough came in 1975, when a major archive of over 17,000 clay tablets written in the Ebla language was discovered in a room of the Royal Palace. They are administrative documents which, in their entirety, give a clear picture of a thriving trading centre, dealing with taxes on the traded goods of metals, textiles and agricultural goods, supplies for the royal family, procedures for visitors, the raising of sheep and the production of woollen textiles for which Ebla was renowned. These tablets confirmed beyond doubt this was indeed the site of Ebla. Much controversy has surrounded the translation of the tablets, with Hebrew so-called 'biblical archaeologists' claiming the tablets provided evidence that the people of Ebla were early ancestors of the Hebrews. All these claims have since been rejected as the dates do not tally by a thousand years, leaving aside any disputes about the actual translation of words. The whole business however led the Syrian authorities to accuse Israel of a Zionist plot to hijack the findings, perhaps

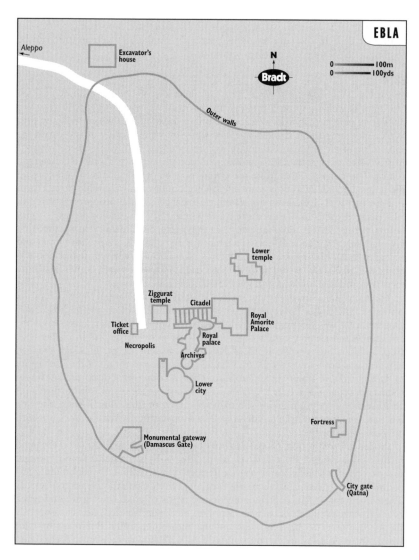

Aleppo

Excavator's house

N

Bradt

0 ——— 100m
0 ——— 100yds

Outer walls

Lower temple

Ziggurat temple

Citadel

Ticket office

Royal Amorite Palace

Necropolis

Royal palace

Archives

Lower city

Fortress

Monumental gateway (Damascus Gate)

City gate (Qatna)

with a view to making territorial claims on Syria. The fact that the pace of translation has been painstakingly slow also fuelled speculation that the Syrians were suppressing the contents.

Your best bet is first to climb to the top of the acropolis to get some feel for the overview and scale, passing on the way the remarkable reconstructed monumental staircase that led originally to the summit. The original shape of the city was an impressively regular oval, one of the most difficult shapes to make accurately, defined by its outer perimeter ramparts, the north–south axis measuring nearly 1,000m and the east–west axis 700m. In the centre stands the acropolis hill with the lower town ringed round its foot. The Royal Palace covered a large part, if not all of the acropolis, and in addition to the royal residence it contained kitchens, stores and workshops. Some of the less pretentious rooms in the northern lower town have been identified as for food preparation, or as workshops for shell and stone inlays, maybe related to the nearby sacred area of Ishtar. The acropolis itself measures 150m by 150m and covers almost 3ha. At the western edge of the acropolis the Temple of Ishtar has been uncovered, with its sacred area and part of the access ramp and monumental stone terrace. The various areas of the site are labelled on the ground, but it remains quite challenging to visualise the city as it would once have been.

In the excavations of the rampart walls, a moat was discovered, and the structure of the ramparts was shown to be layers of earth laid over a core of mud brick and ground limestone, then covered in white plaster which must have made them look very impressive from the outside, and reinforced by a low stone wall on the outer edge. Along the ramparts four gates have been identified: the Damascus Gate in the southwest, the Aleppo Gate in the northwest, the Qatna Gate in the southeast (the worst preserved and least fortified) and the Euphrates Gate in the northeast. Several fortresses of mud brick have been identified, their size regularly about 13m by 27m, built 300m apart from each other. The fortress walls would have protruded about 6m above the ramparts. Just inside the walls the remains of private houses have been found, as well as many tombs, for it appears the inner ramparts were used as a burial area. The entire city is thought to have been built over a relatively short period of time, a few decades maybe, using a large labour force. It was built as a monumental centre, planned at one time, not as a progressive adaptation to sporadic needs. The level of planning sophistication is remarkable. All the buildings would have been invisible from the outside, and even on entering the gates it would have been impossible to appreciate the city clearly till fully on the inside, as all the gates are built with a dog-leg, another impressive defensive tactic.

The lower town consisted of a grouping of important public and religious buildings, with at least two sacred areas, one in the north, to the cult of Ishtar, one in the west to the cult of the dead royal ancestors. There were also many princely residences and temples.

The acropolis was the seat of royal power, with the royal residence and the dynastic temple. Ishtar was the dynastic goddess, powerful patron deity of the city, guarantor of fertility and abundance. It has been speculated that her priestess might have been the king's eldest daughter.

As you stand beside the Royal Palace looking back down towards the car park area, the huge foundations of a temple with limestone blocks at its base lie just to the right of the ascent path. Basalt lions were found at the centre of this structure and it is thought to have been a kind of ziggurat temple with steps of mud brick which have long since been washed away.

The people who settled Ebla were clearly not nomads or semi-nomads of the steppe. They had an advanced urban culture, with the capacity to mobilise huge labour forces and their king had absolute power.

IDLIB إدلب All the major exhibits from Ebla have now been moved to the museum in Idlib (*09.00–18.00 summer, 09.00–16.00 winter, S£75 entry fee, closed Tue; the WCs are barely adequate*) about 20km away and a 50-minute drive from Aleppo. A purpose-built rather unattractive place, the museum houses downstairs a folklore collection, stuffed birds, Roman and Byzantine coins and some paintings, while the Ebla collection is upstairs. Well illustrated and explained in English the museum helps to make sense of the Ebla site and even boasts a reconstruction of the royal archive room. Photos of the site at the time of excavation also help to clarify the course of the excavations.

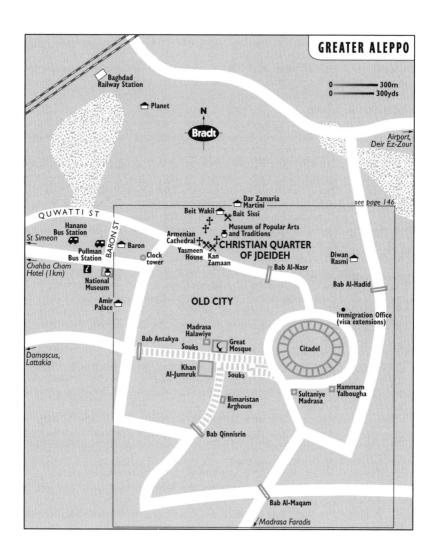

GREATER ALEPPO

Baghdad
Railway Station

Planet

N

Bradt

0 ———— 300m
0 ———— 300yds

Airport,
Deir Ez-Zour

Dar Zamaria
Martini
Beit Wakil   Bait Sissi
Museum of Popular Arts
and Traditions

see page 146

QUWATTI ST

Hanano
Bus Station

St Simeon

BARON ST

Pullman
Bus Station

Baron

Armenian
Cathedral   CHRISTIAN QUARTER
Yasmeen   OF JDEIDEH
House   Kan
Clock   Zamaan
tower

Diwan
Rasmi

Chahba Cham
Hotel (1km)

National
Museum

Bab Al-Nasr

Bab Al-Hadid

Amir
Palace

OLD CITY

Immigration Office
(visa extensions)

Damascus,
Lattakia

Bab Antakya

Madrasa
Halawiye

Souks

Great
Mosque

Citadel

Khan
Al-Jumruk

Souks

Bimaristan
Arghoun

Sultaniye
Madrasa

Hammam
Yalbougha

Bab Qinnisrin

Bab Al-Maqam

Madrasa Faradis

6

Aleppo حلب

It is better to endure the wind of a camel than the prayers of a fish.

Telephone code 021
(350km north of Damascus; altitude 390m; population 4 million. Allow 1½ days)

SETTING AND HISTORY

The feel of Aleppo as a city is different to that of Damascus. Aleppo is busier, less tidy, more oriental. Traffic always seems heavier, crowds denser. The population of Aleppo according to some sources is even larger than that of Damascus, but throughout the centuries the two cities have been rivals, always vying with each other for dominance. Both claim (along with several other cities in the region such as Babylon, Jericho and Byblos) to be the oldest continuously inhabited city in the world. It is said that in Aleppo 80% of its old monuments inside the walls have survived while in Damascus it is only 20% in the Old City. Like Damascus, its Old City has been designated a UNESCO World Heritage Site (in 1986), and in the winding lanes of the *souk* you will come closer to experiencing a medieval city centre than anywhere else in the Arab world. Only 8% of the current population still lives in the Old City. A 15-year, US$10 million effort is under way to kick-start the Old City's return to its former glory, but the focus is not on turning it into a museum. The new mayor has a PhD in urban planning from France and believes that the challenge is in striking a balance between preservation and development, encouraging more people to live and work there. The German government (through the German Agency for Technical Cooperation) is also closely involved, providing expertise, training and additional funding.

The reason for Aleppo's exact location today, on a large and featureless plain, is far from clear. Geographically, however, it is the point where the valley of the Quweiq River (ancient River Chalus) enters the plain, and the city's ancient name was Beroia. Trade has always been the raison d'être of Aleppo, and it has thrived over the centuries as a stopping place for trade routes from the Mediterranean inland to Mesopotamia and all the way to China along the so-called Silk Road. Today the city remains Syria's business hub, and it is that driving force of commerce that you feel as you wander the streets, making it a generally less relaxed place than Damascus, less dreamy and more down to earth. The modern areas north of the museum and Old City have benefited from French landscaping under the Mandate, when they were graced with tree-lined avenues and a pleasantly leafy city park, now slightly neglected and rubbish-strewn. In the late afternoons in summer the park fills up with strolling families, dressed up for the occasion, Italian *passagiata*-style, then reinvigorating themselves at the many ice-cream parlours. When the French gave Iskenderun, Aleppo's natural seaport, to Turkey in 1939 (see

THE POET AL-MUTANABBI

Al-Mutanabbi (915–65) was the poet laureate of the Hamdanid court of Sayf Ad-Dawla, and is the most popular and widely quoted poet of the Muslim world. His ornate and flowery style, full of rhetoric and metaphor, is particularly difficult to translate and sounds to the English ear rather over the top. His total command and mastery of the Arabic language is extremely difficult to convey in translation, especially in English which thrives on understatement rather than Arabic's natural exaggeration. An early authority calls his poetry 'the height of perfection'. Son of a water carrier, his name means 'prophecy claimant' because in his youth he claimed the gift of prophecy among the Bedouins of Syria. The following is a sample passage translated by R A Nicholson:

> That which souls desire is too small a thing for them
> To fight about and perish by each other's hands,
> Howbeit a true man will face grim Fate ere he suffer contumely.
> If the life of aught that lives were lasting, we should reckon
> The brave the most misguided of us,
> But if there is no escape from death, 'tis but weakness to be a coward.
> All that the soul finds hard before it has come to pass
> Is easy when it comes.

page 181), much of its trade declined, but the city has always retained its commercially active ethnic minorities, notably the Armenians, the Jews and the Kurds, as well as a sizeable Christian community.

With a history of continuous settlement for the last eight millennia, Aleppo's sheer complexity as a web of interwoven layers virtually defies unravelling. Whereas Damascus' connections were mainly to the south with Palestine and Egypt beyond, Aleppo's were generally to the north with Turkey and to the east with Mesopotamia. Earliest records from the stone tablets of Mari mention Aleppo c2000BC. It prospered under a succession of rulers, from the Amorites, the Hittites, the Assyrians, the Persians, and the Seleucids after Alexander the Great's conquest in 333BC. Buried under subsequent settlements, hardly anything can be seen of this chain of habitation, and even Roman and Byzantine relics are hard to find in modern Aleppo.

Its heyday came under the Arabs, when the Umayyads built the Great Mosque. In the 10th century it was the capital of the dynamic Hamdanid dynasty, an autonomous power separate from its rivals Baghdad and Damascus, founded by refugees from Iraq. Their most colourful leader was Sultan Saif Ad-Dawla ('Sword of the State') whose court was patron to many artists and saw a cultural revival and flowering that included Al-Mutanabbi, Syria's greatest poet, considered by some to be the greatest Arab poet of all time.

By 1800 Aleppo was Syria's largest city and prospered especially in Ottoman times again from the 16th to the 18th century. This is the period when the great *khans* and caravanserais were built in the city to house and trade the fabrics, spices, precious metals and gems carried by the camel caravans from the Silk Road to the east, which were re-loaded onto mules here and carried over the mountains to the Mediterranean. The *souks* date to this Ottoman heyday when Aleppo was the chief entrepôt of the Levant. A massive earthquake unfortunately destroyed two-thirds of Aleppo's residential buildings in 1822 which is why there are relatively few Ottoman houses left. Much of the Armenian population came as refugees from Turkey after World War I.

GETTING THERE AND AWAY

BY AIR Aleppo airport is located 10km east of the city, there are direct international flights to Amsterdam, Athens, London, Paris, Prague, Rome, Berlin, Munich, Frankfurt, Madrid, Stockholm and Vienna, as well as lots of domestic flights and flights to other Arab countries. A taxi into the centre of town takes about 20 minutes and costs S£500.

BY BUS The deluxe intercity buses run from a station about 500m west of the National Museum on Shari' Ibrahim Hanano. All the usual companies such as Qadmous and Al-Ahlia have their offices here round the bus bays, where you can buy tickets. There is no need to book in advance as departures are so frequent. There are seven daily buses to Beirut, taking six hours and costing S£300. Damascus takes five hours and costs S£150; Deir Ez-Zour takes five hours and costs S£135. For Palmyra you must go to Deir Ez-Zour and change. Lattakia takes three and a half hours and costs S£100, while Hama takes two-and-a-half hours and costs S£65.

The International/Karnak bus station runs deluxe buses to Turkey, Jordan and even Cairo and Riyadh. It looks like a huge parking lot and is situated just behind Baron Street. Karnak also runs services from here to Damascus and other Syrian cities, for much the same price as the other companies from the other bus station west of the National Museum.

BY TRAIN There is still a limited weekly service running between Aleppo and Istanbul, taking about 36 hours, but it is nothing like the old Orient Express. The railway station is about 1.5km north of the city centre and main public gardens, a 25-minute walk from the Baron Hotel. The only train journey that might be worth considering is the scenic route through the mountains to Lattakia, which takes about three hours. There are four departures a day, at 06.00, 07.00, 15.30 and 16.45; tickets costs S£70 first class and S£40 second class.

GETTING AROUND

CAR HIRE

Europcar based at Pullman Shahba Hotel; \ 2667200; f 2667213

Chamcar/Hertz at Chahba Cham Hotel; \ 2661600; f 2270150

TAXIS As in Damascus the yellow taxis are plentiful and cheap, with no ride in town costing more than S£50, though from the Cham Palace Hotel something like S£100 is more realistic since it is located a little way out of town.

WHERE TO STAY

There are currently about 90 registered hotels in the city with 4,500 beds, but this is not enough in peak season.

Chahba Cham (250 rooms) Shari' Al-Qudsi; PO Box 992; \ 2270100; fax; 2270150; e chamchah@net.sy; www.chamhotels.com. Massive 22-storey hotel that used to be the Meridien, Aleppo's major plush hotel for businessmen and upmarket tourists. Inconveniently located well out of the city centre in a residential/business suburb, but good views over the city. Attractive outdoor pool and terrace (not open till 10.00 though, so swims before breakfast are out), tennis courts. The health centre is rather seedy with a Turkish bath and fetid-looking pool, altogether not very inviting. The business centre is small and often unmanned, far less impressive than its Damascus counterpart. 2 restaurants, one with pleasant views towards the pool and the citadel, 2 bars, disco. The bookshop is the best English-language bookshop in town. US$190/160 dbl/sgl.

🏠 **Amir Palace** (131 rooms) Hanano St; PO Box 419; ☎ 2214800; f 2215700; e amir@net.sy. The best located of any of the hotels outside the Old City in that it is in easy walking distance of the National Museum, Baron St and the Old City itself. It is the cheapest of the luxury hotels, an unprepossessing purpose-built high-rise block but with all mod cons. Business centre. Sauna. Pleasant bar, disco. 2 restaurants, excellent food. Good bookshop. US$120/100 dbl/sgl.

🏠 **Mansouriye Palace** (9 suites) Located in the Old City near the Bimaristan Arghoun; ☎ 144180180; f 144180237; e benedicte@mansouriya.com; www.mansouriya.com. An astonishingly lavish and expensive 16th-century palace that has to be booked en bloc by a group for a minimum of 3 nights. Each suite is furnished according to a theme, so there is the Hittite suite with basalt lions in its bathroom, the Iznik suite with exotic tilework, the Byzantine, the Ottoman and so on. Each one is exquisite. Communal facilities include a library, Turkish bath and jacuzzi. Each room has satellite TV and internet connection. Restaurant by arrangement. *Prices on application.*

🏠 **Dar Zamaria Martini** (22 rooms) Located in the Christian Jdeideh Quarter; ☎ 3636100; f 3632333; e razahtl@net.sy. An attractively restored old courtyard house, all rooms with en suite bathrooms and traditionally furnished. The restaurant is open to the public and is very classy, frequented by local residents of all sorts from family groups with women in headscarves to expensive-looking prostitutes complete with fake nails and eyelashes. Cellar bar. US$115/85 dbl/sgl. Dinner for 2 with wine US$27.

🏠 **Beit Wakil** (16 rooms, inc 2 triple) Opposite Bait Sissi in the Christian Jdeideh quarter; ☎ 2217169; f 2247082; www.baitwakil.com. Opened in 1997. Attractive rooms arranged round a 2-storey courtyard. Showers only. Bathrooms a bit small and smelling of drains. Attractive restaurant in second courtyard but no fountain. US$100/80 dbl/sgl.

🏠 **Pullman Shahba** (c100 rooms) Shari' Al-Jama'a; PO Box 1350; ☎ 2667200; f 2667213. Well out of the centre, this businessman's purpose-built block is unexciting, but everything works. US$100/80 dbl/sgl.

🏠 **Diwan Rasmi** (32 rooms) Isolated location 10 minutes' walk from the citadel; ☎ 3312222. Strict Muslim management so no alcohol. Converted from 2 Ottoman houses with courtyard. Lovely views of the citadel from the terrace restaurant. Food has been disappointing on occasion and served luke warm. Big variation in room size and some are not suitable for older guests as access can be tricky. US$65/50 dbl/sgl.

🏠 **Baron Hotel** (c30 rooms) PO Box 130; 8 Baron St; ☎ 2110880; f 2110883; e hotelbaron@mail.sy. A magnificent building of the early 1900s, the Baron stands looking somewhat lost and forlorn in the street that still bears its name yet is now dominated by the usual ugly modern city buildings. When it was built in 1909 the location was chosen because it lay in the chic European part of town, near the Orient Express station, and with a terrace that overlooked a marsh from which game was shot for dinner. Among the famous visitors who passed through were T E Lawrence, Theodore Roosevelt and Agatha Christie, who wrote part of *Murder on the Orient Express* while staying. Run by the Armenian Mazloumian family, the hotel is gradually being refurbished. The rooms are quite spacious but still far from luxurious. The best part of the hotel is undoubtedly the atmospheric bar lobby area, full of memorabilia from Orient Express days, and comfortable old leather arm chairs. US$45/35 dbl/sgl.

🏠 **Planet Hotel** (48 rooms) Al-Talal St in the Aziziah Christian quarter north of the Baron Hotel; ☎ 4658934. Modern 5-storey, 3-star hotel. Neon lighting in the bedrooms but clean and decent. Good buffet breakfast and dinner with hot vegetarian dish. Two restaurants, bar and café. Minibar and satellite TV. US$117/94 dbl/sgl.

🏠 **Dar Halabia** (12 rooms) 100m from Bab Antakia, in the heart of the Old City; ☎ 3323344; f 3338836; email:halabiatour@net.sy; www.halabia-tours.com. A much more modest place than the Mansouriye Palace, the only other accommodation on offer in the Old City at the time of writing, the Halabia is set round an 18th-century courtyard on 2 storeys, and simply furnished in traditional style. B&B only. Very quiet at night, as the Old City is deadly empty after the shops close around 19.00, unlike Damascus where the city stays alive because of the large and ever increasing numbers of restaurants. US$35/25 dbl/sgl.

✖ WHERE TO EAT AND DRINK

Aleppo is renowned for its cuisine, probably the best in Syria, all made from wonderfully fresh (and organic) ingredients. Aleppo beer is called Al-Chark, 3–3.5% and is more bitter than Damascus' Barada beer.

✕ Bait Sissi In the heart of the Christian Jdeideh quarter, just off Jdeideh Square; ☎ 2219411. The best restaurant in Aleppo and indeed probably in Syria, and the first of its type when it opened in 1995. Beautifully restored and decorated, it is set in an 18th-century courtyard house. Piano bar and cellar bar. *Open noon till midnight. Full mezze costs S£375, local wine S£400, Lebanese wine S£600–700.*

✕ Dar Zamaria Martini See under *Where to stay,* opposite.

✕ Kan Zamaan In the Jdeideh Christian quarter in a restored Ottoman house; ☎ 3630299. A little less expensive than Beit Wakil and Bait Sissi. There is a lift to the eating area on the upper terrace which is very attractive and light but always under cover even in summer.

✕ Yasmeen House Opposite Kan Zamaan; ☎ 2224462. In an 18th-century house with outdoor eating in the courtyard. Photographic menu which can be quite helpful for the uninitiated. *Local wine S£400, Lebanese wine S£800.*

✕ Khan Al-Harir ☎ 3317756. Close to the entrance of the Great Mosque, the best place to eat in the Old City. Ultra-modern inside with very clean WCs. It offers good chicken dishes and salads, which can be washed down with mint tea. No alcohol. *Open daily except Fri 08.30–22.00. Low prices.*

NIGHTLIFE

Most nightlife in Aleppo is on the sleazy side, and takes place along Baron and Quwatly streets, heralded by red neon lights with alcohol and prostitutes in abundance. If you are in search of somewhere to go after dinner, your best bets are either the nightclubs attached to the five-star hotels, or the cellar bars of the new and expensive restaurants like Bait Wakil and Kan Zamaan in the Jdeideh district, where live music, either Arabic or European, is sometimes on offer as well. Cinemas are also an experience, owing to the extraordinary degree of audience participation. Attendance is almost exclusively male and you would feel very uncomfortable as a female alone or in a pair at the cinema, as all the men would simply assume you were there to be picked up rather than to watch the film. Original soundtracks are kept, with Arabic or French subtitles, so most films are in English. The Chahba Cham Hotel has the most Westernised cinema, reachable from the hotel foyer, but the preference in most of the local cinemas that can be found along Baron Street, is for kung fu-style movies, as the posters outside displaying violence and screaming girls testify.

SHOPPING

Opposite the entrance to the citadel and behind the row of cafés facing it, is the Souk Ash-Shouna, the handicrafts market which is Aleppo's equivalent of the Tekkiye Suleymaniye handicrafts market in Damascus. Here the prices in the shops are more or less fixed (though bargaining is always possible especially if you are buying more than one item) for a very good selection of cloths and textiles for which Aleppo is famous, in the form of scarves and pashminas. Better prices can be obtained in the heart of the Aleppo *souk* itself, but this is a good place to start. There are also several good carpet shops in this area of the *souk* around the citadel, many of them geared to tourists and with knowledgeable shop owners who speak good English.

Inside the Aleppo *souk* itself shops and stalls are less directed at tourists than in Damascus, but the practice of grouping stalls selling the same products together in the same street is still followed. Do not miss the soap stalls, where the famous Aleppo olive soap is packaged in all sorts of shapes and sizes, making very good and useful gifts.

In the Christian quarter outside the Old City there are also some good shops selling antiques, especially metal and brass ware. Most are clustered round the square by Bait Sissi, where there are also lots of jewellery shops selling gold items.

POST OFFICE The main post office (*open daily 08.00–17.00*) is downtown on the southwest corner of Quwatli Street.

TOURIST OFFICE The tourist office (*notionally open 09.00–14.00 except Fri*) is in the gardens opposite the National Museum .

HOSPITAL The best for foreigners is the Aleppo University Hospital (✆ *2236120*), opposite the Pullman Shahba Hotel, with a good standard of treatment and facilities. If you do fall ill and need a doctor, your best bet is always to go through your hotel in the first instance.

PHARMACIES Opposite the Chahba Cham Hotel is the Central Pharmacy, and the downtown area is full of pharmacies.

BANKS Changing money in the Commercial Bank of Syria is always a chaotic process, especially for travellers' cheques, best avoided if at all possible by carrying dollars in cash. The bigger hotels will usually change money albeit at a slightly

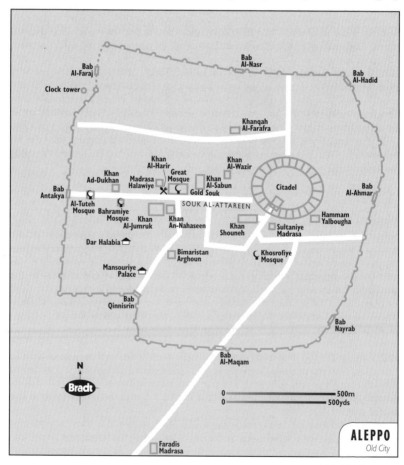

lower rate, but not enough to worry about when you are changing amounts of US$100 or less. The branch in the modern town tucked in a hard-to-find first-floor office building will change travellers' cheques.

INTERNET There are fewer internet cafés than in Damascus, but the number is growing all the time. The big hotels have business centres with internet access, costing around S£100 per hour.

UNIVERSITY Aleppo University has 60,000 students. It and Damascus University are the top universities in the country.

CULTURAL CENTRES Both the French Cultural Centre (✆ *2274460*) and the British Council (✆ *2680502*) have small offices in Aleppo, which sometimes organise cultural events.

LOCAL TOUR OPERATORS The local tour operators are mainly Damascus based but most have branch offices in Aleppo that are linked in to the big hotels. It is therefore very easy to fix up tours from your hotel reception desk, which will be only too happy to put you in touch with whichever local tour operator is best suited to your needs and budget.

AIRLINE OFFICES British Airways, Air France, Alitalia, Lufthansa, KLM, Aeroflot, Egypt Air, Saudi Arabian and Syrian Air are all represented here and most have offices either on Baron Street or Quwatli Street.

VISA EXTENSIONS The immigration office where visa extensions can be obtained is on the first floor of a building just north of the citadel in Shari' Al-Qala'a. (*The office is open 08.00–13.30 Sat–Thu.*) You will need four passport photos which can be obtained at the shacks opposite the immigration office. Forms have to be filled out in quadruplicate. There is a fee of S£25 and the processing takes 60–90 minutes.

WHAT TO SEE AND DO

ALEPPO OLD CITY
Aleppo Citadel قلعة حلب (*Open daily except Tue 09.00–16.00 winter, 09.00–18.00 summer, 09.00–15.00 Ramadan; S£150 entry fee; allow 1½hrs*) By far the most dramatic sight in Aleppo is the mighty citadel, a magnificent testament to Arab military architecture rising on its almost volcano-like mound. Today of course the full impact of its power is harder to gauge amid the modern sprawl and traffic, but in the 13th century when it rose untrammelled and dominated the landscape from miles around, it must have been truly overwhelming. The small hill on which it sits was a natural defence site used as far back as the Amorites in the 16th century BC. The moat was originally full of water.

The imposing entrance gateway with its ramp leading up is by far the most impressive aspect of the citadel, gracing many tourist brochures and book covers. The moat, 48°-steep glacis, entrance ramp and monumental gateway all date from the 12th-century Ayyubid period, in the reign of Saladin's son, Al-Zaher Ghazi, when it served as an impregnable base in northern Syria against the Crusaders. The whole citadel was later heavily damaged in 1260 and 1440 by the Mongol incursions and needed extensive repairs. The 20m-high outer defensive tower at the start of the ramp now houses the ticket office. It too dates from the 12th century but was restored by the Mamelukes in the 16th century. It was originally approached by a drawbridge. Eight huge arches support the entrance ramp as it spans the moat. Just below the machicolation boxes is a long Arabic inscription commemorating the repairs carried out by the Mamelukes after the first 1260 Mongol invasion. The tower bastions that flank the gateway house the Mameluke Royal Palace, notably the magnificently restored throne room on the upper floor, but otherwise just consisting of a series of empty rooms linked by stairs and passageways. Once inside and out onto the open summit the remains are fairly unexciting, so savour to the full the glory of this Ayyubid gateway as you approach up the ramp.

There is no door directly in front of you as you enter, only a false door, the real doors being to the right, splendid iron doors of massive proportions, decorated with horseshoe and arrowhead motifs, and because they are tucked around the corner, they could not be stormed at speed. In the archway above the entrance is a pair of intertwined serpent dragons to frighten the enemy. There now begins a series of zigzags designed to slow charging horses right down, while above are several holes both for surveillance and for pouring down deterrents of various sorts on the attackers, from excrement to stones. You pass through the fifth and final door at the last zigzag, past carved smiling lions and sad lions, seen as having magical powers and protecting against evil.

An alleyway off to the right leads downstairs into a Byzantine brickwork area with a vaulted roof and arches, thought to have been built originally as a cistern, not a church as once thought. It was later called the Prison of Blood when it was used as a dungeon. Various Crusader knights ended their days in this dungeon including Jocelin, Count of Edessa, and Renald de Chatillon, Prince of Al-Kerak. In punishment for raiding Muslim pilgrim caravans during the agreed truce period, he spent 16 years in this prison before being killed by Saladin. The French used it as a prison during the Mandate as well. The rooms were also thought to have been used for stabling and barracks at various times. At the end of the corridor, before entering the citadel proper, is the cenotaph of St George, venerated by Muslims under the name of Al-Khidr (see box page 204).

Once emerging into daylight, the open space on the summit is very large and you will notice the extensive excavations being carried out to the side of the path. Under the direction of Professor Kay Kohlmeyer (Berlin) the Syro-German team here began work in 1996 and has discovered two large temples, one of the Late Bronze Age, the other of the Iron Age. At the end of the season sandbags are used to protect fragile, partly excavated artefacts or remains until the next season. The excavated buildings are similar to others dug at Ras Shamra (Ugarit) and 'Ain Dara. Relief sculptures have also been found from the neo-Hittite period and two black basalt carved lions dating to the 10th century BC have been unearthed.

The citadel was used in Seleucid Hellenistic times for defensive purposes, but little is known about its history after that until the Byzantine era when Emperor Julian the Apostate is known to have come to offer sacrifices to Zeus at the temple in the 4th century, abjuring the link that Constantine established between Christianity and the empire.

The first set of buildings to the right of the path is the Ayyubid Palace, originally consisting of 40 rooms, now heavily ruined, grouped round a series of small courtyards. The entrance is still very fine with a striped black basalt and white limestone façade and stalactite vaulting above the doorway. Built on at the back of the palace is a 14th-century Mameluke baths complex, recently restored but often kept locked to avoid courting couples being able to get into dark private places. In the first cold room the niches down below were for shoes, the niches higher up for clothes.

The small simple little mosque to the left of the path is dated to 1167 and is linked to Abraham who is said to have stopped here. Legend has it that on one of

The Aleppo Citadel is one of the beneficiaries of the Historic Cities Support Programme financed by the Aga Khan. Other recent beneficiaries include Tunis, Samarkand and Mostar, and within Syria the Assassins Castle at Masyaf and Saladin's Castle are also the subject of renovation and support programmes requested by the Directorate of Antiquities. Not to be confused with his flamboyant grandfather or playboy father, the Aga Khan is an enormously polite man devoid of arrogance, who is deeply committed to the meticulous and scholarly restoration of a select number of landmark historic buildings and gardens in Muslim communities. Projects include the creation of a public park on a Cairo rubbish tip and the restoration of the grand verandahed Dispensary in Zanzibar.

In order to promote creative architecture in the Muslim world, the Aga Khan has an annual series of Awards for Architecture worth a total of US$500,000. Any project that benefits a Muslim community is eligible and recent awards include the Old City of Jerusalem where a courageous programme of more than 160 renovations has created an amazing complex of winding alleys and sunken courtyards with vaulted chambers transformed into attractive places to work and live. Huge logistical problems were overcome by the Palestinians in bringing building materials into the Old City. Another award, that of Iconic Landmark, was presented to the new library at Alexandria, built to replace the last ancient wonder of the world, and designed by Norwegian architects in the form of a giant tilting disc with four storeys sunk into the ground.

his many journeys from his home in Harran to the north (now southeast Turkey), he stopped here and milked his cow: in Arabic 'halab ash-shahba', meaning he milked the greyish cow. Aleppo ('Halab') is thought to be derived from this, and the Chahba Cham Hotel has named itself after the cow, also seen as a reference to the greyish limestone. The mosque was built on the site of an earlier church, and local legend claims the church as one of the numerous resting places of the head of John the Baptist. In the courtyard are three cisterns for collecting rainwater. The big mosque with three Aleppo pines in its courtyard and a tiny fountain is dated to 1214 and has a sombre pure architectural style with simple decorations and a lovely *mihrab* built by Saladin's son. The square minaret is 20m high and has 78 steps leading to the top. As well as the call to prayer it was also used as a watchtower and for communication by light signals. To the right of the mosque are the Turkish barracks, a long rectangular building dating to 1834 built by the son of Muhammad 'Ali. Today it is a small café with panoramic terrace and simple museum displaying a limited range of artefacts that barely warrants the extra entry fee. Next to the barracks is a deep well with a spiral staircase of 225 steps that led down to three tunnels leading outside the citadel.

The modern amphitheatre built in the 1970s holds 3,000 spectators and is a complete anachronism, built to enable singing and dancing festivals to be held here. It is in fact due to be removed as excavations will begin underneath it, a shame in many ways as the setting was superb and memorable.

At the back of the entrance gateway to the citadel a black and white paved courtyard leads into the grand Mameluke Throne Room housed within the tower bastions, lavishly restored in the 1980s by Syrian benefactor Osmane Aidi, with notably the ornately decorated wooden ceiling painted in geometric patterns. The original roof of the throne room had nine domes, but these proved too difficult to restore, so the current ceiling was rebuilt flat with concrete, but with a central elevated dome to allow light through the windows. The ceiling is partly 18th-century woodwork brought from the Al-Aidi House in Damascus, and the rest is modern, painted by the Khayat family of Damascus. The magnificent marble floor too is a wonderfully patterned riot of geometric shapes. Back in the 1970s the museum used to be housed here. A flight of steps leads back down to the final gateway of the entrance and out again down the ramp. Directly opposite the citadel ramp is a cluster of cafés which have now become very popular and which make good places to linger after a walk through the *souk* or after a hot and dusty visit to the citadel. The handicrafts market, known as Khan Shouneh, runs directly behind these cafés and is excellent for souvenirs, with prices that may be slightly higher than the main *souk* alleyways but are still government controlled, though there is always room for a bit of bargaining. The choice for foreigners is better here too and it will take less long to find what you want. It is also more spacious which can be a relief after hunting round the rather claustrophobic alleyways of the *souk* proper.

Hammam Yalbougha حمام يلبوغة (*Open daily 10.00–02.00 for men, reserved for women 10.00–17.00 on Mon, Thu and Sat; allow 2 hrs; cost S£400 for the full experience with massage*) The grandest baths in Syria, these 14th-century baths, also known as Hammam An-Nasri, were rescued and restored in 1985 by the tourist authorities from their use at that time as a felt factory. A visit to these baths should be seen as essential for all but the prudish and faint-hearted. If you coincide with a busy time (there were well over 100 women inside at the time of the author's last visit, only four of whom were foreign), entering the bath is like entering a rowdy hubbub of chaos and chatter. In the large changing area where you emerge after paying (so you are committed at this stage), you are confronted by an abandoned scene of everyone in various states of undress, with young children of both sexes running all over the place. As a foreigner it can be rather bewildering as there appears to be no system: you are simply handed a small cotton towel, and a bar of soap on a bed of rough pale palm fronds, to be used like a loofah. The soap is the famous Aleppo dark green soap made from olive oil and wonderfully soft even on the hair. See *Aleppo soap* box, page 152. Aleppo has been famous since Ayyubid times for its soap, and still today over six tonnes are produced daily, ie: 25,000 bars. Standards of hygiene are far from pristine though and as families often spend several hours inside, food, orange peel and Coke cans are liberally scattered about wherever they happened to be consumed. The actual toilets are extremely smelly and best avoided if possible.

You now exit the changing area wrapped in your little towel, having left all your clothes wherever you could find a space on a raised bench, and enter the first steam room which is off to the right. It has basins of flowing water in the four corners, and here you can soap yourself and rub yourself down with the loofah, then splash water over yourself to rinse off, till one of the female bath attendants (female during women's hours, male during men's hours) dressed in towel and underwear, appears and is ready to conduct the full head-to-toe wash followed by the massage. At this point you shed your towel, sit on the marble floor with your head cradled between her legs, while she rubs the soap all over your hair and body, then rinses you off with scooped-up bowls full of warm water. Next you are laid flat on the marble floor totally naked and rubbed and scrubbed with soap and the rough coir vigorously from neck to toe, first face down on your stomach, then rolled over and face up on your back. After more rinsing with scooped bowls, you are now treated to the massage in the same pattern, face down first, then face up. Everything is very quickly and skilfully performed, the whole process taking maybe 15-20 minutes per person. In order to enjoy it fully you have to abandon yourself to the experience, forgetting about prudery and what diseases might be carried on the floor of the bath. It is at bottom a very basic, earthy experience, devoid of sophistication, but at the end you certainly emerge feeling refreshed, invigorated, and in spite of the dubious hygiene conditions, remarkably clean. A free drink of tea or Coke (water costs extra) is included at the end as part of the unwinding process when back in the changing hall area on your raised bench, reunited with your clothes.

Souks and khans (*Open daily 09.00–19.00 except Fri; allow 2 hrs minimum*) Aleppo's *souks* are justly held up as the most authentic of any major city in the Middle East, the least touched by modern commercialism. In their heyday they grew to become the largest in the region, and even today they cover an area of 12ha and employ over 35,000 people. The *souks* with their 12km of narrow winding alleys, too narrow for anything other than people, mopeds and donkeys, have been unchanged since the 16th century, some even dating back to the 13th century, making them far older for example than the bazaars of Istanbul, and are still the place where every Aleppo citizen chooses to go and shop. In total there are 6,000 shops, so it beats any shopping mall. In the mid 18th century there were 68 flourishing *khans* and sayings ran such as 'What was sold in the *souks* of Cairo in a month, was sold in Aleppo in a day' and 'The lame of Aleppo reached as far as India'. In places the *souks* can be quite graphic, and the freshly butchered meat areas are positively stomach-churning with every conceivable part of the carcass on display within inches of your nose as you walk by. A hygiene inspector would doubtless have heart failure but the quality of the fruit and vegetables is unquestionably superb, bursting with freshness, all naturally organic. No-one here has heard of a supermarket or ready meals. On being asked whether such things existed in Aleppo one resident replied: 'Oh you mean those places where people push metal carts round – I've seen them on American TV. No there are none here. There are one or two in Damascus but there're rubbish and the food is horrible.' No mission for Jamie Oliver here – freshly cooked and prepared food is all anyone ever eats anyway.

Ideally you should set out to enter the old *souk* area through Bab Antakya on the western side of the Old City, where you also get a real feel of entering the walls between the two huge hexagonal Ayyubid 13th-century bastions. After the first few wiggles you then enter the main thoroughfare of Souk Al-'Attareen (Perfume-Sellers' Souk) which runs all the way past the back of the Great Mosque and emerges eventually 1,200m later, at the foot of the citadel – it was the original Roman decumanus, the main east–west thoroughfare. As a foreigner you should be aware that there have been a few pickpocketing incidents in the heart of the *souk*, though the perpetrators are thought to be visiting ex-Soviet nationals rather than locals. Keep your valuables safely, so temptation is not on offer.

The first specific building of interest you come to stands in the centre of a fork and is an old mosque which you can enter called Al-Tuteh (the Mulberry Tree). It has a quaint collection of old stones thought to be bits of the old Roman triumphal archway which marked the start of the decumanus. The original mosque built here was said to be the first mosque in Aleppo, to commemorate the taking of the city by the Muslims in the 7th century. The current one is dated by the fine Kufic inscription to 1150, when it was restored by Nur Ad-Din. Further on to your left the first huge *khan* or warehouse courtyard you come to is called Khan Ad-Dukhan (Tobacco), very attractive and still with some shops on its upper storey. On your right is the Ottoman-style Bahramiye Mosque founded in 1583 by the governor of Aleppo, Bahram Pasha. From here onwards the *souk* is roofed in its original stone-blocked vaulting with periodic holes for skylights. Having nothing like the height of Souk Al-Hamadiye in Damascus, this *souk*'s narrow alleys and crowds can get quite claustrophobic, trapping in the smells and fragrances.

Generally dark green as its natural colour, the soap is wonderfully soft and moisturising, and is even used on the hair especially in all the *hammams*. Many of the stalls sell it attractively packaged in various shapes and sizes. What sets it apart from other soaps is the use of *ghar,* laurel as well as olive oil. Laurel makes the soap milder, more fragrant, keeps moths away, heals minor skin conditions, helps rheumatism, is thought to protect from the evil eye, and is 100% natural. Due to the ever increasing interest in natural products, Aleppo's soap industry is set to expand. Around 60% of the 20,000 tonnes produced annually is sold domestically, even though it is expensive by local standards at about US$2 a bar. Traditionally Aleppans would buy it in bulk, 200–300kg at a time, to keep the price down, then store it in their cellars along with their pickled foods. The remaining 40% is sold mainly to Japan and Korea, and increasingly to eco-friendly, health-conscious Westerners who are willing to pay anywhere from US$6 to US$15 for a bar of *ghar*.

Originally made exclusively in the Bab Qinnisrin area of the Old City, there are now around 50 large-scale factories in the suburbs and about another 100-odd small-scale producers. Most of the factories are owned by a few families like the Fansas and the Zenabilis, while the actual soap manufacturing process is in the hands of other families, notably the Sabanas and the Sabounehs (from the Arabic 'saboun' for soap), who guard the secrets of their production process jealously. Ambient temperature is very important and the soap will only set properly in the cooler months of the year, so can only be made from November till early May. The olive oil is cooked in cauldrons over a high heat with caustic soda to turn it into soap: 'saponification', a process which in very cold spells may take only two hours, while by May it may take a whole day of stirring. The skill is in knowing when the right point is reached. The laurel oil is added towards the end of the cooking. When ready, the green goo is poured out into wooden frames on a smooth concrete floor and allowed to harden and set. Then it is cut into blocks and stamped with the manufacturer's name and the percentage of laurel it contains. The higher the laurel content the more expensive the bar: the bottom end may contain as little as 2% laurel, while the top end can have as much as 60%. The bars are stacked in 2m-high ziggurats to dry for eight to ten months, after which they are hard enough to put into raffia sacks and be taken to a cool dry room where they are left to mature for a further two years, just like cheese or wine.

Coming as a welcome change from the raw carcasses of the butchers' areas you now come to the area dominated by soap sellers. Like all Middle Eastern *souks* the stalls selling the same commodity are all grouped together in healthy and respectful rivalry, so the purchaser really does have maximum choice and bargaining potential. The famous Aleppo soap is made by hand using the same method since ancient times and is based on olive oil and laurel.

One curiosity of *souks* in Syria is the women's underwear, bras and pants of eyebrow-raising sizes, so openly displayed for men to buy. Local women certainly would not buy their underwear in such public view, and even in the West underwear sections in department stores tend to be tucked discreetly into corners.

The next major building to look out for is on the right, the massive Khan Al-Jumruk (Customs) dated to 1574, Aleppo's biggest *khan* with a small mosque in the centre of its open courtyard, 50 warehouses on the ground floor and 77 upstairs. In the 19th century the *khan* housed the French, Dutch and British consulates which operated out of here, representing their countrymen's business interests.

At this point you are at the back wall of the Great Mosque and the open alleyway to the left runs along its western wall. Follow this, passing the Khan Al-Harir converted into a very modern and clean fast-food restaurant, the best place by far for lunch in the Old City, to reach the Madrasa Halawiye on your left, opposite the tourist entrance to the Great Mosque. Steps lead down into the rather squalid forecourt of the *madrasa*, surrounded by gently decaying buildings, but it is worth visiting the prayer hall because it is interesting to see how it has incorporated the remains of the once very large 6th-century Byzantine Cathedral of St Helena, mother of Constantine, the first emperor to adopt Christianity as the state religion of Rome. Helena too zealously supported the Christian cause, and visited the Holy Land where she founded basilicas on the Mount of Olives and at Bethlehem. Later tradition holds that she found the Cross on which Christ was crucified. Shoes must be removed at the entrance to the prayer hall, and compulsory gowns are available for female visitors for which a token payment is expected. The guardian has a table just inside laid out with postcards, books and pamphlets. The current prayer hall, to the left as you enter, is dominated by six huge pink marble columns of the original cathedral, each complete with its beautifully carved Corinthian capital, whose acanthus leaves appear to be blowing in the wind. This is all that remains of the original central section of the cathedral which was surrounded by a deambulatory in the same style as the cathedral at Bosra. The apse of the church stood where the current courtyard of the *madrasa* now is, originally the Roman *forum* of the city. The cathedral was in use by Christians until 1124, worshipping freely here while the Great Mosque was built for Muslim worship alongside Christian worship in the cathedral gardens and cemetery. In that year, however, the governor of Aleppo requisitioned it along with five other churches, in retaliation for the atrocities committed here by the Crusaders.

Great Mosque الجامع الكبير (*No specific opening times or entry fees, just baksheesh for the guardian for the gowns and guarding of shoes. Fridays are best avoided as the mosque gets very crowded; allow 20mins.*) Built in the grounds of the 6th-century Cathedral of St Helena, Aleppo's Great Mosque was founded in the early 8th century, ten years after the Damascus Great Umayyad Mosque. The most architecturally significant aspect of the mosque is in fact the 50m-tall minaret, a Seljuk masterpiece of elegance and grace built in 1095, that has a noticeable lean, a relic of a past earthquake. It had 174 steps to the top and still bears its fine Kufic inscription. The rest of the mosque burnt down in a fire in 1169 and was then rebuilt by Nur Ad-Din, with further modifications added by the Mamelukes in the 15th century. Taken as a whole, this Aleppo Great Mosque completely lacks the atmosphere of its Damascus counterpart. In its Umayyad days the mosque had been decorated with beautiful stonework taken from the Cathedral of Cyrrhus (Qorosh), but the 'Abbasids later removed it all to the Anbar Mosque in Baghdad. The prayer hall has been recently renovated at great expense and the only structure of any age inside is the 14th-century Mameluke *minbar*, its fine carving patterned with ivory and mother-of-pearl. The renovation work was essential as part of the mosque had suffered serious subsidence. At the time of writing the renovation of the dome was in its final stages, with huge cement bags, weighing one and a half tonnes according to the engineer, hanging from the central chandelier to test its strength. Throughout the years of renovation work the mosque has remained open to visitors, with all sorts of safety hazards exposed, including gaping holes in the floor when the foundations were being shored up. In the Islamic mentality, what Allah wills will be, and such risks are a normal part of life. The mosque is sometimes called Al-Zakariye, after Zachariah father of John the Baptist, whose head is said to be buried here in the room to the left of the *minbar*.

The Christian Crusaders first came to the Holy Land convinced that they were themselves far superior to the local Muslim population, whom they imagined to be idolators worshipping Muhammad as a god. They were also hostile towards the local Christian sects, especially the Greek Orthodox, and towards the local Jewish communities. The Muslims on the other hand saw the Frankish Crusaders as infidels, worshipping three gods in the form of God, Jesus and the Holy Ghost. Neither realised it was the same god they were worshipping and the gulf of ignorance was huge. Usama Bin Munqidh (see box on page 124), in his chronicle of his encounters with the Crusaders, marvelled at their lack of refinement, describing them as 'animals possessing the virtues of courage and fighting, but nothing else', a reputation earned by their barbaric treatment of Muslim prisoners. To Arab nostrils the Crusaders were also very smelly as they did not wash. Washing and bathing are religious requirements for Muslims which is perhaps why they perfected the recipe for soap (see *Aleppo soap* box, page 152) still used today in the West. The Crusaders' religious pretext for invading the region was never viewed by the ruling Muslims as either credible or legitimate, since the indigenous Christians were not being persecuted, and Christians arriving peacefully on pilgrimage from Europe were allowed free passage to the Holy Land without interference.

At times of peace, however, which were after all much longer than times of war over the 200-year period that the Crusades spanned, good Muslim–Crusader relations did sometimes evolve. Safe conducts for travellers and traders were usually honoured, local Muslim workmen and farmers were often employed by the Frankish knights and good neighbourly practices gradually developed. The Franks also began to adapt their clothing and eating habits to their local environment, discarding their European dress in favour of the looser local clothing, and enjoying the generous use of sugar and spices that was normal local practice. They chose to build in the Arab style, so well adapted to the climate, with central courtyards and running water. There was occasional intermarriage with local women and their mixed-blood offspring were called 'poulains', meaning 'young ones', Latinised from 'pullani'. The great division that theoretically existed between the Muslim and Christian worlds was thus more blurred than is sometimes presented.

On the opposite side of the Great Mosque to the Madrasa Halawiye are the gold, silk and rug markets and just north of these the Souk Al-Manadil (Handkerchief) and the Souk As-Saboun (Soap). In the Souk Al-Manadil look out for the medieval public toilets, unique in any *souk* (though mercifully no longer in use), entered through a beautiful gateway into a courtyard with a high cupola. These 12th-century latrines are all round the courtyard and are a rare example of integrated planning of water, sewerage, lighting and ventilation.

Bimaristan Arghoun بيمارستان أرغون (*Open daily 09.00–16.00 winter, 09.00–18.00 summer except Tue; S£75 entry fee; allow 1hr*) Returning to the Souk Al-'Attareen behind the Great Mosque be sure to take the short detour to this remarkable mental hospital founded in the 14th century by the Mameluke governor of Aleppo. A revolutionary and advanced treatment centre, the best preserved Muslim hospital in Syria, it was geared to total rehabilitation of patients in the community and to which no-one had repeat admissions. In Europe by contrast the mentally ill were imprisoned and abused.

Follow the Souk Al-Nahasseen (Coppersmiths) south for some 400m till you exit the main covered *souk* area and reach the hospital on your left. Opposite is the

Al-Joubaili Soap Factory which can sometimes be visited if the door happens to be open, and is still in use, with soap stacked high in the gloomy back rooms (see *Aleppo soap* box on page 152). The hospital entrance has the typical Mameluke stalactite *muqarnas* above the door, and the Arabic sign outside calls it the hospital for 'nervous' illnesses rather than mental, which is in itself an interesting take on their view of such problems. They believed the three aspects of treatment were the calming influences of music, water and nature. Diet was also known to be important, and patients were fed a simple vegetarian diet and given calming herbal teas to drink. The first open courtyard, the largest, was for patients who were close to full recovery. They could sit in the *iwan* listening to music being played on the other side of the water pool. Notice too the wooden planks set across the tops of the courtyard columns, designed to help absorb the shocks of earthquakes. Aleppo was hit by two severe earthquakes in 1139 and 1157 which demolished many buildings. Nur Ad-Din and Saladin's son Al-Zaher Ghazi were the main rulers responsible for the reconstruction of the city in the 12th century.

The adjacent small courtyard with five to six cells was reserved for the most severely disturbed and even potentially dangerous patients. The cells had little natural light as it was believed that darkness kept them calmer. They were given opium as a tranquilliser. The pool in the centre contained serenely indifferent fish.

The next courtyard with 12 cells is lighter with fewer restrictions for the inmates. They were given fewer sedatives and were allowed to come out and sit by the fountain. The final courtyard with its central oval skylight and six cells was reserved for women. At the end of their stay before being released back into the outside world, they were given money to buy clothes and food to survive at the beginning in recognition that they would not be able to go straight into paid employment. The Islamic world's approach to the mentally ill was far more advanced than that of the Christian world at that time. The asylum was still in use until the beginning of the 20th century.

If you follow the street from the hospital away from the centre of the mosque for some 400m southwards, you will reach Bab Qinnesrin, the best preserved of Aleppo's old gates. Originally a 10th-century construction it was rebuilt in 1256, then restored by the Mamelukes in 1501. Of Aleppo's original 12 gates only seven are still in evidence. The original walled city covers an area roughly 1,250m by 1,250m, though the areas to the north of the citadel are generally less well preserved and with fewer monuments. One building worth seeking out because it is a rare example of a Sufi fraternity is the Khanqah Al-Farafra on Al-Sijn Street, behind a row of shops. Built in 1237, it has a fine honeycombed entrance, large *iwan* and cells round the courtyard for the Sufi adherents. In the mosque is a splendid marble *mihrab*.

JDEIDEH QUARTER الجديدة (*Allow* ¹/₂ *day*) Further north from Khanqah Al-Farafra, crossing the main road east–west called As-Sijn (the Prison), you can visit in the northwest corner just inside Bab An-Nasr, the northernmost gate of the Old City, the splendid 17th-century Bait Jumblatt, one of Aleppo's most beautiful palaces built for the city governor. The superb tall *iwan* is decorated entirely with blue geometric tiles. Much of the palace has disappeared over the years, and what remains is used as a school. You can visit by ringing the bell during class times before 13.00 except Fridays.

Beyond Bait Jumblatt the Jewish quarter of the Old City begins and you can still see here what remains of the Grand Synagogue of Aleppo, abandoned and closed to visitors. In the 19th century it was one of the most imposing buildings in the city.

The name Jdeideh is Syrian dialect for classical Arabic 'jadida' meaning new; new here meaning outside the old walled city, but in fact dating to the 17th century. That was when the first Christians moved out of the Old City into this suburb

Sufism is the name given to Islamic mysticism, and for the first five centuries of Islam Sufism was an almost entirely individual form of religious worship, not so much a set of doctrines but a mode of religious thinking and feeling. Partly as a reaction against the formalism of Islam and the Koran that followed the Prophet's death, Sufism strove for a personal and more intense experience of God. Muhammad himself had a mystical relationship with God, experiencing the divine presence in his revelations, and the Sufis came to consider themselves as the true interpreters of the esoteric teachings of the Prophet as recorded in the Hadith (Sayings of the Prophet during his lifetime). The word Sufism first appeared in the mid 9th century and comes from the Arabic *souf* (wool) which was worn by the early, ascetic, contemplative and solitary mystics. Nothing exists but God is the mystic principle. God is eternal beauty and the path leading to him is divine love.

One of the earliest Sufis was Ibrahim Ibn Adham (died 777), king of Balkh (in Afghanistan), who according to legend was converted when he saw from his palace window a beggar contentedly eating stale bread soaked in water, seasoned with salt. Assured by the beggar that he was fully satisfied Ibrahim put on a woollen robe and took to a wandering life. After his conversion Ibrahim migrated from Balkh to Syria, where Sufism had its earliest forms of organisation. Small clusters of disciples would gather round an inspirational mystic teacher like Ibrahim, and by the end of the 12th century self-perpetuating fraternities began to appear. The founder of the fraternity usually himself became the centre of a cult, invested with divine or semi-divine powers, therefore becoming a saint after death. Veneration of saints is not sanctioned by the Koran. It arose, as in the Christian practice, to meet the need of bridging the gap between humans and God.

The cults were predominantly, though not exclusively, male. A mystic woman from Basra for example, Rabi'ah Al-'Adawiye (717-801), was placed first on the list of saints. When young she was sold as a slave but was later freed by her master. She refused to marry and lived a life of extreme asceticism, voluntary poverty and total dependence on God. Asked whether she hated Satan she replied: 'My love for God leaves no room for hating Satan.'

The members of the cult were called dervishes and lived in special fraternities called *khanqhahs*, *tekkiyes* or *ribats* which also served as social centres. Many different fraternities developed over the centuries, the best known of which in the West are the Mevlevis (originally Turkish from Konya), commonly referred to as the Whirling Dervishes.

some 800m northwest of the citadel, and its feel today is markedly different to the rest of Aleppo. The traditional 17th-, 18th- and 19th-century houses line narrow alleyways, many of which had gates (like the one beside Bait Sissi Restaurant) which were locked and guarded at night. From the outside the high forbidding walls of the houses made them look like fortresses, yet inside they were gentle retreats arranged round courtyards in the traditional style. The streets are cleaner and somehow whiter than elsewhere with limestone flagstones and the signposting is very efficient in highlighting all the monuments/buildings worth viewing. From the 17th to the early 20th century 25% of Aleppo's population was said to be Christian. Of particular interest is Bait Ajiqbash, now the Museum of Popular Arts and Traditions set in a traditional Arab courtyard house, and then also the various Christian cathedrals. You should also spend your evenings here, as this is where Aleppo's upmarket nightlife and finest restaurants are to be found, like the Sissi House and Beit Wakil, all set in magnificent restored Arab houses.

Museum of Popular Arts and Traditions (*Open 08.00–14.00 except Tue; S£75 entry fee; allow 1hr*) Like all these houses, from the street it looks like nothing at all, just a doorway giving straight onto the alley, like any other doorway. But once you cross the threshold, you enter a different world. Known as Bait Ajiqbash, the name of the last Christian family to live there, it was built in 1757. The splashing fountain in the centre of the courtyard and the trees evoke an immediate atmosphere of calm and tranquillity, often likened to an earthly paradise. The deeply recessed *iwan* is, as always, on the north-facing shadiest side of the courtyard so that residents could sit outside during the heat of the day in the coolest spot. The intricate stone carvings above the windows are an especially lovely feature. All the rooms round the courtyard both upstairs and downstairs have been restored and furnished in mid-18th-century style with mannequins dressed in traditional costume going about their daily life. Of special interest is the underground area where the family spent time in the hottest periods and from which stairs lead down into an underground tunnel, said to be a secret passage to the citadel for refuge in times of danger, now blocked up.

Nearby are two other splendid houses, Bait Ghazzaleh, a large 17th-century house in the process of restoration, and Bait Ad-Dallal, an 18th-century house now used as an elementary school. Bait Ghazzaleh is on Qastal Ibshir Pasha Street by the goldsmiths' market near the Yasmin Restaurant and has a kiosk overlooking the street. Once said to be home to 45 people, it even has a *hammam* with eight alcoves and basins. It is now under the control of the city council. Bait Ad-Dallal is on Sissi Street and is also very large, even having stages for musicians both on the verandah for the women and down below in the courtyard.

Armenian cathedral (*Generally open, no fixed hours; allow 15mins*) Turning right as you leave Bait Ajiqbash and walking a few steps along the same street through the old wool bazaar, you pass first the 1852 Syrian Catholic church, Lady of the Assumption (Sayyidat Al-Intiqal), then the 1861 Greek Orthodox church, the Virgin Mary, both usually locked except on Sunday mornings, and then the 15th-century Armenian Orthodox Cathedral of the Forty Martyrs, renovated in 1869. To judge from the crowded pews, attendance at church is active. The shrines are heavily covered in glitz and glitter as in all Catholic and Eastern churches. Most interesting is the huge icon of the Day of Judgement, a highly graphic scene in which souls are weighed in the centre, then taken off either to the left if they were good, to enter heaven with the angels, or to the right if they were bad, to be pulled down into hellfire by the little black-winged devils.

It was painted in 1708 by the priest Ni'mat Allah, the best painter of icons of the Aleppo School. The 40 martyrs of the church's name refers to the gruesome tale of the 40 young soldiers who, in 320, were persecuted for their faith by the Romans. They were driven into a freezing lake in midwinter in Sebaste, their home town, with their mothers watching. From the shore, the Roman guards tempted them with warm baths. One of the soldiers renounced his faith, came out of the freezing lake into the warm bath and died. The other 39 remained steadfast, and 40 fiery crowns descended from heaven over the lake, and 39 of them landed on the heads of the steadfast ones. One of the guards then grabbed the 40th for himself and converted. The lake miraculously warmed and the soldiers stayed alive till morning, whereupon the Roman commander pulled them out to have their legs broken, then had them thrown back in to drown.

Next door to the cathedral, looking out into the same courtyard, is the Armenian Orthodox Virgin Mary Church, now a small museum for clergy cups, archbishops' maces, robes and old religious books and inscriptions.

Walk now along the paved white alleyways between the high stone walls of the streets till you come at the corner of the main Jdeideh square to Beit Sissi, probably the finest restaurant in Aleppo in a superbly restored house, and with an antique shop attached. A few steps further along the alleyway through a fine archway is Beit Wakil, formerly the Greek Orthodox bishop's house, a similar establishment to Bait Sissi except that it also offers rooms restored to a high standard and traditionally furnished with en-suite bathrooms. Notice too the splendid stone carvings above the gates that used to be closed at night to protect the residents from unwelcome visitors. Also nearby are the Maronite Cathedral of St Elias (1873-1923) and the Greek Catholic Church of the Holy Mary (As-Sayyida) (1849).

Other old courtyard houses can sometimes be visited if a doorkeeper happens to be around, such as Bait Sayegh, now an Armenian school; Bait Basil, now a Roman Catholic orphanage; and Bait Balit with a lovely 18th-century painted ceiling in the room off the *iwan*.

SOUTH QUARTER Directly opposite the rampway up into the citadel the attractive domed building standing by itself in a patch of greenery and isolated now by roads, is the Madrasa Sultaniye, an early 13th-century religious school. It also houses the tomb of the Sultan Az-Zaher Ghazi (died 1216), son of Saladin and governor of the city, who was responsible for most of the fortification work on the Aleppo Citadel. If you can get to peep inside there is a very lovely *mihrab*.

Crossing the street and heading west back towards the *souks* you will see just 50m away the Khosrofiye Mosque, Aleppo's oldest Ottoman mosque, built in 1537 by the famous architect Sinan at the start of his career, and whose work now dominates Istanbul. The style is unmistakable with its tall graceful minaret and the elegant domes above the portico that leads into a spacious courtyard shielded from the bustle of the *souk* by high walls. Named after Khosrow Pasha, an Ottoman governor of Aleppo, the construction of the mosque complex which includes a *madrasa* and a lodge, was completed in 1546 by his servant. Inside the *madrasa* is noted for its beautiful *mihrab* of coloured marble. It was reopened to students of religious law in the last century and is now known as the Madrasa Shari'a, the Al-Azhar of Aleppo.

If you want to stroll a little outside the *souk* areas to get a feel of the walls, you can walk south from Madrasa Sultaniye for ten minutes or so to reach Bab Al-Maqam, one of the original gates into the Old City on its eastern side, dating to the 15th century, a solid stone construction whose shaded arches are usually clustered with animals and merchants.

Faradis Madrasa مدرسة الفردوس Unless you are especially keen on the intricacies of Muslim architecture, you can frankly omit this 13th-century Koranic school from your itinerary. The name means 'School of Paradise' and the building is given rave reviews in many books. It lies well south of the citadel in the backstreets of an extremely scruffy quarter known as Bab Al-Maqam and is difficult to find. Now in use as a mosque it is nevertheless very run-down and verging on the squalid, despite a restoration programme in the 1990s which was said to be poorly managed. The guardian requires *baksheesh* for gowns to cover up Western women visitors. The actual rooms for the school are all now closed up or used as store rooms, so all that can be visited is the large rectangular courtyard and the prayer hall itself. The pure use of line and the restrained simplicity contrasting with complex forms are the features to note.

The inscription above the highly elaborate portal has a verse of the Koran and records that the *madrasa* was built in 1235 by Dayfa Khatun, niece and daughter-in-law of Saladin. Its dimensions of 44m by 55m make it the biggest school in Aleppo, and the rooms are thought to have been the cells of a Sufi fraternity. All round the inner walls of the courtyard, including the *iwan*, are Koranic verses in exquisite calligraphy, all exhorting the Sufi philosophy of prayer and contemplation. The *mihrab*, delicately interwoven in shades of cream, yellow, white and grey marble, has been considered by scholars to be the second finest in the world after that of Córdoba in Spain.

Further south of the Faradis Madrasa there is a curious cube-shaped mausoleum, reminiscent of the Ka'aba, originally part of a *madrasa*, the tomb of the historian and traveller Al-Harawi who died in 1207. He covered his tomb and walls with inscriptions about the virtues of being alone and having no baggage at all:

> Safety is in being alone, and rest is in solitude; Oh man … do not cheat, for things will not remain as they are forever; Do not resist your fate; Do not seek to collect money for it will move from you to someone else, whose thanks and blessings will not be of use to you … Solitude is the ship of safety; Forget trivial matters and prepare yourself for great things.

The area around the tomb is known as the Harawi quarter. Al-Harawi wrote a book on the prophets, saints and 'ulema (learned men of religion) whose tombs are scattered over Bilad Ash-Sham (Greater Syria), the Maghreb (Morocco, Tunisia, Algeria and Libya) and the northern Roman provinces, having travelled all over these regions.

National Aleppo Museum المتحف الوطني (*Open 09.00–18.00 daily except Tue; S£150 entry fee; allow 1¹/₂hrs; there are adequate WC facilities*) The museum houses an impressive collection of exhibits, notably from the early Iron Age Syrian sites, and though not as large or varied as the Damascus National Museum is still well worth a visit. The museum gardens also have some fine architectural fragments and statues dotted about, but alas, unlike in Damascus, there is no café in which to sit and enjoy them. Located by itself about 150m south of the Baron Hotel this purpose-built two-storey block is laid out quite well round a courtyard. It will mean more to you if you have already visited the major sites featured here, such as Ebla, Mari and Ugarit. The western entrance is guarded by black basalt lions and figures with white eyes popping out almost cartoon-like. These are replicas of those found at the entrance to the 1st millennium BC Aramaic temple at Tell Halaf, near the Turkish border in the north of the country, by the German excavators of the 1920s, and the museum was originally built in 1931 to house these Tell Halaf finds.

Starting to the right of the entrance it makes most sense chronologically to conduct your visit anticlockwise round the courtyard, then progress upstairs in the same way. The first area displays finds from the sites of Tell Brak excavated by Max Mallowan, husband of Agatha Christie, and from Mari, excavated by the Frenchman André Parrot, a contemporary of Mallowan's.

Look out for the remarkably sophisticated bread moulds in the shape of stags and fish, and naked terracotta women holding their own breasts. There are also the distinctive basalt statues of the Mari bearded men in what appear to be frilly skirts, made of sheep's wool and called *kaunakes*. These were the standard Sumerian dress for men. Also from Mari is the fine bronze lion head, with eyes of lapis lazuli and alabaster, an excellent example of Sumerian/Babylonian art, and the striking necklaces found in the tombs, worn by both men and women, and made of lapis, agate, crystal, ivory and gold. Very revealing and surprisingly topical are the tablets of clay covered in instructions from the king to the queen about the women priestesses: 'Make sure they don't overeat so they don't ruin their figures. Be careful with their ration so their looks won't change.' He also instructs her to be careful with their hygiene so that infections don't get passed on. Another exhibit from Mari, the statue of the goddess of water/fertility dated to 1800BC pouring water from her vase, is considered one of the most beautiful pieces of sculpture in

Max Mallowan was Agatha Christie's second husband, 14 years her junior. The breakdown of her first marriage coincided with the death of her mother, leaving her in a vulnerable state. It was on a trip with friends after this to the Middle East that she first met Max Mallowan while he was working on a dig. He was a thin, dark young man, very quiet, while she, according to her own description, was in the 'outsize' category and quite a chatterer. It was however a 'true marriage of minds' and they were extremely happy together. Already well known in her own right as a crime writer by this time, she took a great interest in his work, becoming especially skilled at the jigsaw work of reconstructing pots. 'An archaeologist', she wrote, 'is the best husband any woman can have. The older she gets, the more interested he is in her.'

His interest was in the Hittite period and the Mitanni dynasty of warriors. 'Max is eating tea in the present,' she would say, 'but his mind is roughly about 4000BC.' The Romans were regarded as hopelessly modern – 'children of yesterday'. She never enjoyed or appreciated alcohol or tobacco, though she wanted to desperately and tried for months to force herself to smoke after lunch and to savour a good wine.

She describes amusingly in her book *Come Tell Me How You Live* the archaeological digs they went on together in the 1930s, travelling out to Aleppo on the Orient Express with enormous quantities of luggage (books in Max's trunks, shoes and clothing in hers), then on by car to the northeast region round Hasake, painting entertaining pictures of the other members of their team and their infuriating servants. She used her time on the digs profitably: *Murder in Mesopotamia* was based on her experiences, as was *Murder on the Orient Express*.

Max Mallowan excavated a number of early tell sites in northeastern Syria and rose to the top of his profession as a distinguished archaeologist with a fine reputation. He was knighted in 1968, after 25 years of Mesopotamian excavations, and died in 1978, two years after Agatha.

ancient Syrian art. The wavy lines and fish chiselled into her long flowing robe symbolise over-flowing water. More astonishingly detailed finds are the little figures made from ivory and mother-of-pearl, rather like silhouette puppets. In them the king seems to be taking prisoners who are all tied up with rope. The ivory would have been imported from Africa via Egypt.

Moving on now to the Ugarit room, look out for the gold dish decorated with a hunting scene and a chariot. The original is at the Louvre. There are also fine bronze figurines of the god Baal, equivalent of the Egyptian god Horus, thought to have been gifts from a pharaoh to the King of Ugarit. Then there are attractive weights in stone and bronze in the shape of reclining cows, birds or olives, and an ivory duck container used for kohl and a tiny hair comb. There are diorite moulds for gold jewellery, so exquisitely elaborate they are almost like a crown.

The Tell Halaf room is dominated by more giant statues similar to the ones guarding the museum entrance, all examples of the neo-Hittite art which developed in Syria following the collapse of the Hittite Empire. Many of the originals were taken to Berlin by the German excavators, only to be pulverised by a bombing raid on the German museum in 1945. Notice the monumental statue of the scorpion man with a man's face, lion's chest, winged body like a bird, two legs and a scorpion's tail. This sculpture decorated the base of a doorframe, the upright section of which rested on the animal's back. Then there are the delicate ivories such as the suckling cow and other sphinx-like creatures which were found in the bed decoration of the king. These ivories, thought to be of Phoenician workmanship, reveal an Egyptian influence, particularly in the themes treated, such as the birth of Horus, and the woman at her window is wearing an Egyptian headdress.

From Ebla the notable exhibits are basalt slab altars for sacrificial animals with channels for the blood run-off dating 1800–1600BC, and a giant animal's foot with claws and long toenails, very finely worked.

Moving now upstairs there are explanations about the German, French, American, Syro-Italian, Dutch, Belgian, Spanish and British missions of archaeologists, most of which were 'rescue' excavations carried out before the sites were flooded by the creation of Lake Asad when the dam was built on the Euphrates at Ath-Thawra. Then there are some fine coins from Roman times, and some unusual green-painted Byzantine sarcophagi from Raqqa. Also from Raqqa are the giant turquoise bowls from the 12th and 13th centuries and other attractive pottery bowls in green, blue and turquoise, dated to 'Abbasid and Ayyubid times. Finally there is the Arab weaponry from Crusader times, with finely decorated swords, elaborate helmets and shields with chain-mail face protection and chain-mail tunics. The scale model of Aleppo's citadel and surrounding areas is also worth a look.

In the central open courtyard is a mosaic of running animals including bears, stags, leopards and gazelles, fast losing its colour in the bright sunlight. The modern art area is often locked for unexplained reasons.

MASHAD AL-HUSSEIN مشهد الحسين On the western outskirts of the city stands an unusual Shi'a monument, the Memorial to the Martyrdom of Hussein, grandson of the Prophet Muhammad. This, together with the shrine of Zainab, brother of Hussein, in Damascus are the most important Shi'a shrines in Syria. Dating to the 12th and early 13th centuries it was built here around the stone where a drop of blood from Hussein's head was said to have fallen, after the bloody Battle of Karbala on the 10th of Muharram 680, the date that marks the most important festival in the Shi'ite calendar (see *Sunni/Shi'ite Split* box, page 80). The building is quite large, with an outer courtyard, honeycombed entrance gateway and inner courtyard with *iwan* and prayer hall. The most notable architectural feature is the gigantic *mihrab* nearly 4m tall built in superbly carved wood with imitations of ancient columns, which remarkably survived an explosion in 1920 in which half the building was blown up by accident, its use at that time being an ammunition store. Thirty people were killed in the incident. During World War I all religious ceremonies were forbidden and so the Young Turks had turned it into a munitions store because of its proximity to the Sham railway terminal.

You will have to ask several times to reach it, but in general direction it is off the old Damascus road, past the old stadium and under a railway viaduct, then take the first street on the left to reach it some 600m later on the right.

EXCURSION TO QAL'AT NAJM قلعة نجم

This is a rarely made excursion because most people do not have time and it is difficult to incorporate with anything else, about 90km to the northeast of Aleppo, on the banks of the Euphrates. The 12th-century Arab castle, whose name means 'Castle of the Star', stands in spectacular scenery overlooking the river. It has been well restored and has dungeons which you will need a torch to explore, as well as a *hammam* and a central palace. There are no facilities and you will need to bring your own food and water. It is best to allow a full half day for the excursion.

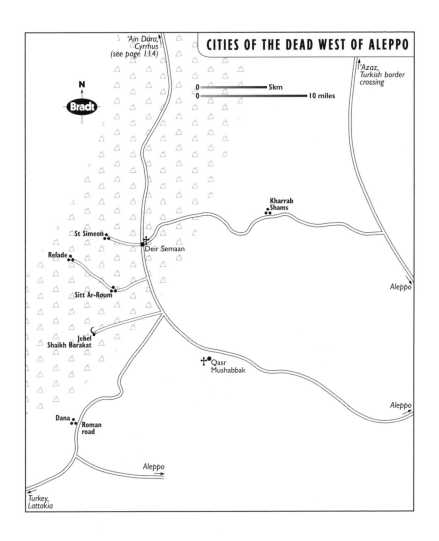

CITIES OF THE DEAD WEST OF ALEPPO

'Ain Dara,
Cyrrhus
(see page 114)

N

Bradt

0   5km
0   10 miles

'Azaz,
Turkish border
crossing

Kharrab
Shams

St Simeon
Deir Semaan

Refade

Aleppo

Sitt Ar-Roum

Jebel
Shaikh Barakat

Qasr
Mushabbak

Aleppo

Dana
Roman
road

Aleppo

Turkey,
Lattakia

7

Aleppo to the Coast

He who takes a donkey up a minaret must take it down again.

NORTHWEST FROM ALEPPO

A full and exciting day trip can be taken from Aleppo by first heading northwest towards the superb St Simeon Monastery complex, the most splendid of all the Dead City sites (see pages 130–2 for Dead Cities background), built to commemorate the popular ascetic known as Simeon Stylites. From here you can continue north to the neo-Hittite temple of 'Ain Dara, and finally up to Cyrrhus, a Roman city right up on the edge of the Turkish border. Go prepared with a picnic, as the hilly fertile scenery abounds with good picnic spots, and there is nowhere suitable to buy lunch en route. If you have only half a day to spend, just stick to St Simeon, to which you can take a private taxi from Aleppo for about US$25. The journey takes around an hour each way. If there is only one excursion you have time for from Aleppo, it should be St Simeon.

Setting off from Aleppo on the St Simeon road, you will come after 25km to Qasr Mushabbak, a worthwhile brief detour, signposted off to the left on a good dirt track climbing up about 1km to the striking and well-preserved late 5th-century basilica on the hill with a little well beside it. It follows the standard basilica plan of a central nave and two side aisles separated from the nave by two rows of columns. The nine-arched windows add a great sense of height and the whole creates a wonderful sense of elegant space. It was probably used as a staging post en route to St Simeon by pilgrims. To the west of the basilica is a little quarry where the stone was cut, and about 100m to the east are the remains of what seems to be a monastery complex, now lived in by local farmers. To the other side of the main road is an extensive fenced-in ex-military zone, all now derelict and rather eerie.

ST SIMEON (QAL'AT SAM'AAN) قلعة سمعان (*42km northwest of Aleppo, 45mins' drive from Aleppo; open 09.00–18.00 summer, 09.00–16.00 winter; S£150 entry fee; allow 1¹/₂hrs*) The ticket kiosk sells cards, books and CD-ROMs. Note the picture on the wall of the reconstructed complex as it was thought to have originally looked. There is an adequate WC block beside the ticket kiosk and a pleasant outdoor terrace café under the pine trees just inside offering titbits like packets of crisps and nuts, and drinks, even beer and *nargilehs*. Avoid Friday and public holidays if possible as it is a popular place for outings with local people.

From afar the hillock of St Simeon is distinctive by its pine-covered slopes, the only heavily treed eminence in an otherwise relatively bare landscape. Its setting alone, free from modern building incursion, together with the beauty of the trees and the wind moaning in the branches, combine to give this, the most famous church and basilica complex of the Dead Cities, the feeling of a sacred, holy place, elevated beyond everyday life. As the most famous it is inevitably also the most popular and the only thing that can mar a visit today is the sheer numbers, should you happen to coincide with several tour groups or with various school outings. Out of season though, or early or late in the day in season, the place has a wonderful peaceful atmosphere and it is sufficiently extensive to absorb large

ST SIMEON STYLITES

Simeon, son of a local farmer, was clearly not a conventional young man and, aged around 20, he had a revelation which prompted him to join the monastic community at Telanissos (now Deir Semaan), the village at the foot of the current St Simeon complex. He found the monastic lifestyle too undemanding, and moved instead into a cave on a hill (where the basilica now stands), imposing a regime of severe austerity on himself. His behaviour seemed designed to test himself and his faith, and his reputation spread as stories grew of how he would bury himself up to the chin in summer, wear spikes which drew blood, and chain himself to a rock on a nearby hilltop. People began to come from miles around to see for themselves, to ask him questions and to seek miracles from him. Their attentions were not welcomed by Simeon, who then took to standing up on a pillar, about 3m above the ground, to stop the people touching and poking at him. Later, as his reputation grew and he sought greater privacy from the increasing numbers of visitors, the pillar height extended to 6m, then 11m and finally 18m, with a railing round the top to stop him falling off in his sleep: hence his name Simeon Stylites, Simeon of the Pillar, from *stylos*, Greek for pillar. His disciples brought him food once a week on a ladder, though quite how his hygiene arrangements worked is not clear from the first-hand account of his life written by Theodoret, Bishop of Cyrrhus.

Although he did not relish the intrusion to his contemplations, Simeon nevertheless took to preaching twice a day to the assembled pilgrims, warning against the dangers of earthly vices and describing the heavenly rewards that awaited the virtuous. As more and more important visitors came to see him, they would ask his advice on questions that troubled them, and on one occasion it is recorded that the Byzantine emperor even consulted him on a matter of doctrine. He always refused to speak to women or even to allow them into his sight, not even greeting his own mother. He also had a peculiar method of praying, whereby he stretched out his arms, then bent from the hips to make his head touch his toes, and then straightened himself up again repeatedly. As he spent 36 years on top of the pillar, this was probably very sensible to keep his flexibility and as a form of exercise, for he would straighten himself over 100 times, as pilgrims below kept count. This is reminiscent of the Muslim prayer style where the genuflexions of the five daily prayers serve as a form of exercise, the sheer regularity of it ensuring strong and flexible joints for the faithful. When he was not praying, he stood erect.

Simeon died in 459 aged 69, having spent some 36 years on his pillar, and his body was carried off to Antioch by 600 troops sent by the emperor, though it was later transferred to Constantinople. The Simeon pillar-living lifestyle was copied by many other aspiring ascetics, even as far afield as in central Europe where the colder climate made it even more of an ascetic experience, but none achieved the same renown as he did, and their pillars, some of which can still be seen in other smaller Cities of the Dead, were shorter. The last recorded stylite was at Mt Athos in the 16th century. Today, Simeon's actual pillar has itself been so chipped away at over the centuries by memento-seeking visitors, that only a stubby misshapen stump now remains, set in the centre of the octagonal courtyard from which arches lead into four original basilicas, north, south, east and west. His feast day is 1 September in the Eastern Orthodox Church, 27 July among the Syrian Orthodox and 5 January in the West.

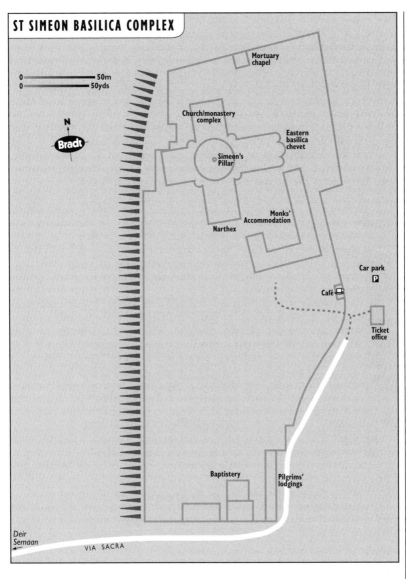

ST SIMEON BASILICA COMPLEX

0 ━━━━ 50m
0 ━━━━ 50yds

Bradt

N

Mortuary chapel

Church/monastery complex

Eastern basilica chevet

Simeon's Pillar

Monks' Accommodation

Narthex

Car park
P

Café

Ticket office

Baptistery

Pilgrims' lodgings

Deir Semaan

VIA SACRA

numbers on the whole. Photography is best in the evening sunset light, when the stones take on a reddish glow and the lines of the ruins are set in sharp relief.

If at all possible, to get the best appreciation of the setting, you should aim to approach St Simeon for the first time from the Pilgrims' Path which snakes up the hill to the baptistery on the summit from the opposite side to the conventional ticket office approach. The start of this path is marked by an impressive gateway near the foot of the hill, just off the main road that winds through the village of Deir Semaan (ancient Telanissos) in the valley below, and off northwards towards 'Ain Dara. If the gateway is locked you can still enter by simply walking uphill following the line of the wall to the summit and then round the other side of the hill to reach the main ticket office entrance. Once on top, the trees, the grass, the little paths, the hilltop setting and the beautifully crafted mellow stonework all combine to give the place its special charm. A group of boisterous philosophy students from Aleppo University enlivened the author's last visit with their happy and earnest chatter about Descartes, the philosophy of hedonism and theories of the meaning of life. It is a place that encourages philosophical thoughts, for you have to ask yourself here why on earth Simeon, son of a shepherd born near Antioch (modern Antakya, now in Turkey) c390, decided to spend most of his adult life sitting on top of a pillar.

From the conventional approach via the ticket office and car park, the path winds up past the pleasantly shaded café to bring you onto the summit, from which you have the church/monastery complex to your right, and the baptistery 200m away to your left, the two distinct areas separated by a long wide open courtyard. Your first sight of the Romanesque church narthex (its triple-arched entrance) is likely to be one of your enduring memories of Syria. Apart from the scale, the sheer beauty of the conception, the delicacy of the proportions, it is the setting, framed by swaying pine trees on the hilltop and echoed by the acanthus leaves of the carved stone decoration, that make the visual impact so striking.

This magnificent 5th-century church complex took 14 years to build, and on completion in 490 it was the largest and most important church in the world, later surpassed only by Haghia Sophia in Constantinople. In Europe it was not equalled till the 11th and 12th centuries.

The construction of the St Simeon complex was an imperial project undertaken on a huge scale, and architects and skilled artisans from the two Byzantine centres of Constantinople and Antioch were employed. Before construction work could begin the top of the hill had to be flattened to create an immense esplanade. The reasons were essentially political because the Eastern Church was at that time in a state of turmoil over the internal disputes about the nature of Christ and the Monophysite schism (see *Early divisions of the Church* box on page 170), and Emperor Zenon hoped, by taking over responsibility for building the church after the death of the enormously popular St Simeon, to reinforce Byzantine orthodoxy and power in this region, against their rival Monophysites in Antioch.

In 526 and 528 violent earthquakes rocked the area, though the damage to the complex was not too great. The Muslims in the 7th century allowed worship to continue there, but later on when relations deteriorated between Muslims and Christians in the 10th century the Byzantines fortified the whole complex, from which time its Arabic name became Qal'at Sam'aan, the Fortress of Simeon.

The Hamdanids of Aleppo under Saif Ad-Dawla captured it in 985 and it was then sacked by Fatimid armies from Egypt in 1017. It nevertheless survived as a pilgrimage centre till the late 12th century, after which it was abandoned and left largely as we see it today.

Sitting in the central courtyard, surrounded by four separate basilicas, is Simeon's mutilated stumpy pillar. This courtyard was originally covered by a wooden dome which collapsed in 528 as a result of an earthquake, and was never replaced. The eastern basilica (to the right as you face the church) was the largest of the four and was the one most used for religious ceremonies and has lovely floral decoration on its apse. The four basilicas together make the shape of a cross. Aerial photos show that not all four arms of the cross are at right angles to the central building, due to the constraints of the topography. The other three were assembly halls for the pilgrims to gather in. At the far end of the western basilica an artificial terrace was built out, to accommodate the need for the whole complex to be centred on St Simeon's pillar. The views from this terrace out over the Afrine valley towards Deir Semaan and the Kurd Dağ and Amanus mountains across the Turkish border are very impressive.

To the north, following a little path slightly uphill through the trees, you come to a small mortuary chapel carved from the rock, a good vantage point from which to gaze back over the whole complex. From here notice how the curve of the apse extends beyond the basin rectangle of the eastern basilica. This design was later to become typical of Syrian Christian architecture, but the only precedent at this time was the church at Qalb Lozeh. In the area between the south and east basilicas are the ruins of a chapel and monastery complex, mainly just a collapsed heap of stones but with the odd wall still standing. The resident monks and important visitors to the complex would have stayed here, most visitors staying down below in the inns at Deir Semaan.

At the other end of the hilltop, walk now across to the domed baptistery, which was used for mass baptisms of pilgrim converts.

DEIR SEMAAN دير سمعان This is the modern Arab name for the ancient pilgrim town of Telanissos which grew up in the 5th and 6th centuries at the foot of the monastery complex to provide accommodation and commercial services for visiting pilgrims. As such it is unusual among the Dead Cities in providing examples of such buildings as inns, hostelries and bazaars. One such inn rising up to two storeys is clearly visible just to the right of the road as you skirt the foot of St Simeon's hill. The village continued to thrive on the pilgrim trade till the 12th century, when the cult died out. Today much of the ruined town is muddled in with the modern village, making it difficult to appreciate amongst the animal pens and fences.

An interesting complex of buildings remains though, and more easily visible because they lie on the edge of the modern village, opposite the monumental arch of the Via Sacra. Take the track on the opposite side of the tarmac road and follow it some 200m to reach the ruins of a law court, a pilgrims' hostel, a monastery and a cluster of 11 market stalls. On the western edge of the village is a curious building, a little stone cabin built of roughly dressed blocks, still with three of the four pillars standing that supported the roof. It is thought maybe to have been the hut of a recluse. No excavation work has taken place here so the ruins are fairly tumbled and overgrown, but attractive nevertheless.

JEBEL SHAIKH BARAKAT جبل شيخ بركات On a hilltop near St Simeon you can make a 4km detour from Deir Azza up to the summit of Jebel Shaikh Barakat (Arabic 'Mountain of the Shaikh of Blessings') now reached by a good tarmac road. On the windy summit are the foundation remains of a massive temple of Zeus and also a shrine of the local saint Sheikh Barakat. The views are extensive and it is a popular picnicking spot with local people especially on Fridays and in the summer to catch the breeze.

SITT AR-ROUM AND REFADE ست الروم ورفادة Back on the main road and heading north towards St Simeon, a good lunch picnic spot can be found by turning left (west) after 3km to the village of Qatoura, beyond which lie the two Dead Cities of Sitt Ar-Roum and Refade.

Sitt Ar-Roum is located 1km beyond Qatoura to the west and is reached by forking to the right outside the village. The name itself means Lady of the Greeks in Arabic, and refers to the 5th-century convent and church here, of which only the well-preserved rectangular nave still stands, bare of decoration.

Less than 1km further on the same track you will come to Refade, immediately recognisable by its 9m-tall square watchtower. This tower, complete to virtually its full height, has latrines on the first floor, showing it was inhabited. It casts good shade for a picnic and the spot is usually deserted, being set a little way from the village. Besides the tower, Refade is remarkable for its memorable and distinctive domestic architecture, a cluster of grand houses behind the tower. The grandest of all has a tower at each end with a double colonnaded loggia linking them. No church has been discovered on the site.

Kharrab Shams خراب شمس Set in a beautifully isolated location the Dead City of Kharrab Shams has a charming bucolic atmosphere. There is no village in the immediate environs, a fairly rare phenomenon, and the church in particular is a wonderfully elegant structure. The side aisles collapsed long ago, leaving the central nave with its five graceful arches topped by ten windows in an almost perfect state of preservation, and this, together with its remote and wild location, combine to make the site one of the most atmospheric and romantic of all the Dead Cities. The church has been dated to 372, by analogy with other churches in the area, making it the oldest in the area. In later Arab times a wall was built across the nave, thereby accidentally preserving the carved chancel rail behind it, the only such example to survive in Syria today. The eastern half of the apse has collapsed because of the oak tree that is still growing in the middle of the altar. Further up the hill are clusters of houses, mostly in a poor state of preservation, and another smaller, later 6th-century church with outbuildings, probably part of a monastery complex. Its capitals have some interesting carving and the church also has a *bema* (raised area where the altar and bishop's throne were situated and from where the sermons were delivered).

'AIN DARA عين دارة (*17km north of St Simeon, 10km south of 'Afrin; open daily 09.00–18.00; S£75 entry fee; allow 45mins; no refreshments but you can picnic under the trees; single WC for use by visitors; the guardian usually has booklets for sale from his kiosk beside the excavators' house*) Driving north from St Simeon towards 'Afrin, you pass through a very attractive fertile and heavily treed landscape with the 'Afrin River gorge, where it is worth making a stop at the newly excavated neo-Hittite temple dated to 10th–9th century BC, the only site in Syria with visible remains from this period. It was under construction when the region was invaded by the Assyrian armies of Salmanazar III. The uncompleted temple was abandoned but the rest of the site was occupied without interruption till the Middle Ages. These small neo-Hittite kingdoms established themselves in northern Syria and southeast Turkey in the wake of the destruction of the Hittite Empire. The neo-Hittites, Indo-European in origin, are the people mentioned in the Old Testament, whom the Israelites knew. It seems doubtful that the Israelites knew of the mountain Hittites of Anatolia, for when King David married Bathsheba, the widow of Uriah the Hittite in about 1000BC, the Hittites had long been driven out of their mountain homeland. Forced southwards from the cities and pastures of the Anatolian plateau towards the plains of northern Syria, they founded a series of small and disunited city states on the fringes of the Assyrian Empire. The artistic style and quality of these cities of the Hittite diaspora, like Karatepe, Carchemish and 'Ain Dara, are generally inferior to that of the earlier Hittite kingdom. Part of the difficulty may also lie in the hard black basalt so plentiful in the northern Syrian plain, but coarse and much more difficult to carve than the fine white limestone used for the reliefs of the old kingdom.

A sign points off left onto a small tarmac road, just past Al-Basoota Restaurant (which often looks very closed), to the tell of 'Ain Dara 2km further on where the road ends at the ticket office building. The site is unfenced so in practice you can visit any time, by climbing the wide path that leads up to the summit in about five minutes. Here a lone 3m-tall black basalt lion guards the outer approach to the temple. The setting of the site is quite lovely overlooking the lush river valley, with cypress trees dotted amongst the fruit and nut trees adding something haunting and even magical to the landscape.

Walking on past the outer guardian lion you come now to the temple itself, thought to be dedicated to Ishtar, Semitic goddess of fertility, represented by a lion. Ishtar was of Babylonian/Assyrian origin and was equated with Astarte, Phoenician goddess of love and fertility. She in turn was identified with the Egyptian Isis and then later with the Greek Aphrodite and the Roman Venus. The steps leading up to the south entrance of the temple are flanked by two carved lions. Before entering, notice the stone basin which must have been for cult libations, next to a pit. Although the remains are in some ways unspectacular, being quite low, the sheer scale of the massive basalt blocks is undeniably impressive. Notice too the carved scenes on the basalt blocks flanking the entrance with winged lions and sphinxes representing the Hittite gods of the sun, the moon, water and fertility. On the stone entry threshold look out for the two gigantic footprints, 1m long, thought to belong to the god Hadad, a Jupiter-like figure, then on each of the following two thresholds is a single footprint, right, then left, representing his massive steps as he entered the temple. This feature is unique to this site and is not found in any other Hittite temple (most of them are to be found in what is today eastern Turkey, notably Karatepe and Kultepe), though the lions are a recurrent theme in all Hittite sites. Even the pottery of 'Ain Dara bears this footprint motif so it seems to be a local peculiarity. Inside the middle entrance notice the carved-out hollows as if for water, which were in fact the huge swivel points for the massive basalt doors that originally closed the temple.

The site was excavated recently by a Syro-Japanese mission, and many of the major finds were moved to the Aleppo Museum. One of their efforts was to erect a hideous concrete structure at great expense to protect the temple after their excavations, but it was dismantled as unsafe, having been left uncompleted when the sponsoring company went bankrupt.

CYRRHUS النبي هوري (*76km north of Aleppo open unfenced site; allow 1hr; no facilities of any sort; no guardian or entry fee*) Continuing north you should allow about an hour just to reach the interesting Roman site of Cyrrhus, in a wild and romantic setting right on the Turkish border. It has become quite tricky to reach now, because a newly constructed dam has created a large lake thereby flooding the original direct approach road near the Midanki Falls. These waterfalls too are a casualty of the dam, but it is quite interesting to drive into Midanki village and see where the road now disappears straight into the lake.

The site of Cyrrhus is known locally as An-Nebi Houri and this is what you should ask for en route. From Midanki it is 20km to An-Nebi Houri and the heavily pot-holed road is slow going, though the fertile landscape with its rich red soil is very attractive, with rolling valleys and hills. The area is famous for its olives, the best in Syria. No snakes or scorpions are said to live in this red soil. On the way you pass through a series of villages in this order: Al-Muhabbabeh, Karkeen, 'Atiyeh, Dorakly, Saaer and finally Seem. All the villages are Kurdish and many of the villagers barely speak Arabic. The older men are dressed in baggy black *sirwaal* trousers, Kurdish style, like the Druze, the other mountain people.

Just a kilometre or so before the site you come to the extraordinary pair of very well-preserved Roman bridges, both of which you will have to drive across as they are part of the road and the only way to cross the rivers. The fact that they have no side walls and are only 5m wide makes the crossing a bit of an act of faith, though their actual strength is not in question. The first bridge has three arches, the second has six, and both are 2nd century AD, with repairs in Byzantine and Arab times. Repairs were actually ongoing at the time of writing too.

The early development of Christianity was accompanied by several centuries of serious divisions. In 325 the Christian Emperor Constantine called the Council of Nicaea with the purpose of resolving the dispute between the Arian and Orthodox Christians on the divine status of Christ. The Orthodox held that the three elements that together made up God – the Father, the Son and the Holy Ghost – were equal, and the Arians claimed that the Father came before the Son and Holy Ghost. In the 5th century the arguments continued, with the Nestorians, following Nestorius of Constantinople (died 451), insisting on the importance of Christ's human nature, but being condemned as heretics in 431 at Ephesus by the Third Ecumenical Council. The Monophysites on the other hand put the emphasis on Christ's divine nature, and were in their turn condemned as heretics by the Council of Chalcedon in 451, but remained numerous, especially in the Antioch region. The Orthodox view was that Christ had a dual nature, at once both human and divine. From the start of Justinian's reign in 518, violent persecutions of the non-Orthodox Christians began, particularly of the Monophysites. Sometimes the fights took the form of civil war, where Orthodox pilgrims for example coming from Byzantium to the sanctuary of St Simeon near Aleppo, were massacred en route by Monophysite monks. Finally, under the leadership of the monk Jacob Baradeus, a dissident Monophysite Syrian church was founded, known as the Jacobite Church, which still has numerous adherents in Syria and Lebanon.

The existence of such schisms in the Christian church helped pave the way for the extraordinarily rapid spread of Islam across the lands of Egypt, Syria and Iraq. The conquering Muslim armies met a series of weakened and incohesive series of Christian communities, who readily accepted Muslim administrative control since they were allowed to practice their faith freely. The Arabs knew no Greek, so had to depend in the early days on translations made by Nestorian Christians, who thus became the link between Hellenism and Islam, with all material having to first pass through a Syriac translation.

You know you have arrived at the site when the pyramid-shaped roof of a Roman hexagonal tomb hoves into view just to the right of the road. The name An-Nabi Houri comes from this tomb, an impressively built construction of the 2nd century AD in lovely reddish stone blocks and decorated with carved acanthus leaves. Its lower part houses the tomb of the Muslim saint Houri, Nebi meaning 'prophet', and has a mosque attached. The tomb is thought originally to have been that of a local Roman soldier. Cyrrhus was made into an administrative centre and headquarters of a legion in the mid 1st century AD. For the Romans it served both as a military base to conduct their campaigns against the Armenian Empire to the north, and as a commercial centre on the trade route from Antioch to the Euphrates river crossing at Zeugma (now in Turkey). In the 3rd century it suffered a number of raids by the Persians, but recovered in the 4th century to become an important centre of Christianity. The remains of St Cosmas and St Damien were buried here, making it a popular pilgrimage site, and Theodoret, author of the biography of St Simeon, was bishop here from 423 to 450. The Emperor Justinian fortified the town in the mid 6th century against the Persian threat. It remained an important Christian centre even after the Muslim conquest of 637, and the Crusaders in the early 11th century placed it under the control of the Count of Edessa. It was abandoned sometime late in the 12th century after it lost its strategic role.

From the tomb the site of Cyrrhus with the theatre dramatically set into the hillside is clearly visible and a drivable track leads over to it and enters by the south gate. From the theatre the track continues along the old cardo maximus. Never excavated and heavily jumbled by earthquakes over the centuries, the theatre is nonetheless impressive for its size, slightly larger even than Bosra, and its location set into the hillside overlooking the distant valleys, with no village or habitation in sight. A fine fig tree grows in the stage area of the theatre, well endowed with fruit if you are lucky, to give you the strength for the 15–20 minute clamber up the dishevelled seats and on up to the citadel on the summit of the hill.

From here the views are extensive and you can return back down along the city walls, examining the defensive structures and the occasional tower base. Much of this stonework dates from Emperor Justinian's refortification of the site in the 6th century.

WEST OF ALEPPO

TOWARDS LATTAKIA VIA QALB LOZEH AND SALADIN'S CASTLE Making an early start from Aleppo you can enjoy an exciting and varied day that crosses the mountains and ends up on the coast in Lattakia in the evening. On the way you can incorporate the stunning Byzantine church of Qalb Lozeh and Saladin's Castle, together with several other sites of interest. There is nowhere recommended for eating en route, so it is best to take your own picnic and be independent, stopping whenever the fancy takes you.

Setting out from Aleppo on the main road west towards the Bab Al-Hawa crossing into Turkey, you will come after c40km to a fine stretch of Roman road in the village called Dana, on the left just as the main road through the village turns right. The Roman road leads downhill for a stretch of 1,200m and is about 6m wide, a highly impressive piece of Roman construction with fine limestone paving above a rubble base. Some of the limestone blocks are 2m long. It dates probably to the 2nd century AD and was restored under the French Mandate. At this time the whole of Syria was crisscrossed with a network of Roman roads, and this one originally led from the port of Antioch inland to Mesopotamia via Chalcis (Qinnesrin). Little has survived of these roads because the blocks were generally reused over the centuries as convenient quarries for other buildings by local residents. This stretch seems to have survived partly because it was more sturdily built to climb the hill and partly because the area was always lightly populated.

Follow the signs on towards Harim, then Sarmada. After a further 6km look out on your right for the Monastery of St Daniel, set back about 450m from the road, also known as Breij, cut into a rocky outcrop of the hillside. It is well camouflaged against the rock, but definitely worth a quick detour on the tarmac road that leads off to the right and stops directly below it. The three-storey façade dates from the late 6th century and is thought to have been a Monophysite monastery and therefore heretical in the eyes of the central Byzantine orthodoxy. The Monophysites broke away to form the separate Syrian or Jacobite Church based at Antioch. This whole region of the Dana plain was largely Monophysite.

A newly resurfaced road now winds on up the hill towards Harem and at the summit a rusty little sign points off right to Baqirha. After about 1.5km as the road winds along the ridge you come suddenly upon the striking four-column portico of the Temple of Zeus, dated by an inscription to AD161. The whole landscape here, wild and rocky, has a quiet power, and it is easy to spend a long time here, gradually exploring the many Cities of the Dead, such as Dar Qita with its extensive churches and houses, with the elegant curving patterns following the arch of the church windows, so inelegantly described by one observer as reminiscent of 'drooping spaghetti'. The main façade of the church here is virtually intact still and is dated by its inscription to AD546. The stonework decoration inside is also very attractive with a free style unconstrained by classical dictates.

Khirbet Al-Khateeb is another ruined settlement nearby, lost in the rocky landscape, difficult to spot at first as it is so well camouflaged.

Returning to the main road, a fork soon after is signed off left to Qalb Lozeh, and the road then passes through a pretty, heavily treed valley, before forking left to climb up 13km to the summit, a detour from the road to Harem, but well worth it.

On the drive up you pass through the Druze village of Bnabel, once a Byzantine Dead City, whose ruins have now been incorporated into the modern village, with only a solitary column to the right of the road. There has been a small isolated Druze community here on the Jebel Al-'Ala since the 10th century, and that has survived despite being so far removed from the two main Druze communities of the Jebel Druze south of Damascus and the Golan Heights near Mt Hermon.

Near the summit to the left of the road are the remains of Kirkbezeh, with a group of house churches dating from the 3rd to the 6th century and a recluse's tower, 3.65m high, with just two narrow openings on the upper level. This may well have been built for the daughter of a villager who had decided to devote herself to God, whilst still living near her family, a practice which texts of the time indicate was quite common. A tarmac road forks off to it just before the main road turns to the right into the village of Qalb Lozeh.

Qalb Lozeh قلب لوزة (*Open daily 09.00–16.00. S£75 entry fee; allow 1hr; no facilities of any sort*) Rightly praised as one of the best examples of Syrian ecclesiastical architecture, a magnificently proportioned broad-aisled basilica still very well-preserved in parts, the Church of Qalb Lozeh has to Western eyes an appearance of familiarity. This is because it was the forerunner of what in Europe came to be known as the Romanesque period, with the characteristic flamboyant entrance arch flanked by twin square towers. It was rediscovered in 1862 by the French Marquis de Vogüé, then studied in detail by the French Dead City specialist Georges Tchalenko in 1935. The church is thought by him to have been built during the lifetime of St Simeon (died 459) or immediately after, and many of its innovative architectural features were refined and enhanced in the great basilica of St Simeon, built just a few decades later. The fact that no other buildings have survived here and that the church was surrounded by a walled compound, suggests Qalb Lozeh was a stopping place for pilgrims on their way to the already famous St Simeon Monastery, where they would stay in the pilgrim inns at Deir Semaan, at the foot of the hermit's pillar. It was always far too big to serve just the local village population.

Today the setting of the church, just on the edge of the Druze village of Qalb Lozeh (Arabic 'heart of the almond') rather mars the atmosphere, for the inevitable village squalor is in evidence and it is hard to enjoy and fully appreciate the aesthetic qualities of the church while village children are staring from all directions, or even climbing the railings round the three-storey towers like mountain goats in some huge adventure playground. A guardian will unlock the gates and charge you for a ticket.

The huge arch between the three-storey towers has largely collapsed and parts of the north wall have been lost to the villagers' building projects, but on the whole the basilica is remarkably well-preserved for its age. Once inside you are struck by the two rows of massive pillars which divide the church into three, with a central nave. These echoes of the Holy Trinity are everywhere in the design, in the three aisles, the three pillars on each side of the nave, the three apse windows, the three façade windows, and the three arches dividing the nave from the side aisles. This is the first ever example of a church using pillars instead of columns, which had the effect of reinforcing the structure and making it more resistant to earthquake damage. Other examples of later churches using such powerful pillars are the Basilica of St Sergius at Resafe (480-500) and the Church of Bissos at Ruweiha. The giant capitals of the pillars are heavily carved, with one solid block of stone at least 2m wide, whose weight must be amazing. In the side aisles some of the stone roofing slabs are still in place, showing how the roof was flat here. The upper floor of the central nave has windows to both sides, called clerestory windows, with small elegant columns separating the windows, and the church would have been extremely well-lit by these. The nave would originally have had a wooden roof. The vaulted dome over the semi-circular apse still survives and the classical decorative elements of the cornice and framing are especially striking. Another innovative feature is the apse protruding from beyond the rectangle of the main groundplan, a feature known as a chevet, used again to great effect in the later St Simeon Basilica.

Harim to Saladin's Castle Returning to the main road you now continue on to the town of Harim, a scruffy rambling town dominated by a 12th-century Ayyubid castle built on a conical artificial mound that was originally paved with smooth stone to prevent it being scaled. Only a small section of this remains, the blocks having been carried off and re-used elsewhere in other building projects over the centuries. The castle as a whole is in a poor condition. It controlled the trade route between Antioch and Aleppo and was an important defence against Crusader incursions in the Antioch area.

After Harim the road continues to Salqin and Kafr Takharim, from where you can either follow the road towards Idlib, or fork off right on a more major road towards Jisr Ash-Shughur. This road, rather pot-holed and winding, is nevertheless interesting for the agricultural villages it takes you through, with pleasant rural scenery, fertile soil, and lots of sheep, goats and cows.

At Jisr Ash-Shughur look out for the old bridges over the river, then you can make a detour to see the dramatic Castle of Bakas, probably the most breathtakingly situated Crusader castle in Syria, though its state of preservation is poor. To reach it you continue for 6.6km on the main road to Lattakia, then turn right onto a little tarmac road that leads after 5km to the village of Shugur Qadim. Perching precariously on a promontory, the castle is almost within arm's reach across a deep ravine, but cannot be reached except by hiking down into the ravine and up the other side, which takes at least half an hour if you are fit. The wild mountainous scenery and river gorge make it an enjoyable excursion if you have the time.

Instead of continuing direct to Lattakia on the busy main Aleppo–Lattakia highway, you are now advised to continue south towards Hama, driving down into the Ghab valley, flat, lush and fertile, till you reach Qal'at Burzey, a small village named after the dramatically situated 12th-century Crusader castle visible perched up on its own outcrop high in the Jebel Ansariye hills to the right, dominating and controlling access to the Ghab.

Be warned that there is no road up to it and you can therefore only reach it by a 45-minute stiff climb. Your reward will be the challenge of the climb itself plus the views, rather than the castle remains themselves, as within the walls it is mainly rubble. The castle was taken by Saladin in 1188 in a raid from the western ridge above. You can see how this was done, as you fork right up into the mountains at the next junction, winding up, with fine glimpses back down onto the castle outcrop from above. The good road winds on up the mountains passing a few viewpoint restaurants on the way, to reach after about 15 minutes the town of Slunfeh which, together with Al-Haffeh, are the two popular summer hill resorts where Gulf Arabs come in the summer to spend the hot July and August months in cool forested hills, distantly overlooking the sea.

Saladin's Castle قلعة صلاح الدين (Arabic 'Sahyoun', Frankish 'Saône') *(43km northeast from Lattakia; altitude 410m; closed Tue; open 09.00–16.00 winter, 09.00–18.00 summer; S£150 entry fee; allow 1¹/₂hrs; simple refreshments available; basic WC facilities)*

The original Byzantine fortress was taken over by an early Crusader knight around 1108, called Robert de Saône, and it was he and later his son who built the present castle, which stayed in the family till Saladin captured it in 1188. Hence the three different names by which the place is known. Unlike both Krak and Marqab castles, Sahyoun never became the property of the military orders such as the Knights Templar and the Knights Hospitaller.

From the bottom edge of the town of Al-Haffeh as it sprawls down the hillside, a signpost points left to Saladin's Castle. From Al-Haffeh it is about 4km to the castle, a gruelling walk if you do not have your own transport, with steep ups and downs. It is therefore advisable to take a local taxi from the microbus stop where they lurk, haggling to get a price around S£100. The approach is memorable, leading off down into the ravine on a steeply winding road that coaches find extremely difficult to negotiate. In between negotiating the road yourself you can catch glimpses of the dramatic construction on the hill above. To the left side as you look, stands the fortified citadel and main buildings where the rulers and his knights would have lived, while to the right is the lower courtyard where the soldiers would have lived along with the livestock and workmen, on a much lower level its buildings largely in ruins and covered in scrub and thick undergrowth. This area slopes gently downwards and, as the weakest point of the castle defences, was the natural point for Saladin to choose for his successful assault. He laid siege to it for two days, and while his son bombarded the northern walls of the lower court with stones hurled by catapults, Saladin himself led a simultaneous attack from the Byzantine village to the east on the cliff immediately opposite the drawbridge of the keep. The Crusader soldiers inside were not sufficiently numerous to defend both places and concentrated their forces on what they thought was the major offensive on the keep. Meanwhile the walls in the lower court were breached by his son's forces, whereupon they swarmed easily into the upper court by crossing the uncompleted ditch between them. The Crusaders were forced to surrender and were allowed to depart freely.

Like most of the castles of northern Syria the fortress at Sahyoun, as it is known in Arabic, from its Crusader name of Saône, is largely Byzantine in origin, but added to very distinctively by the Crusaders. It was renamed Saladin's Castle only in 1957, because Saladin conquered it, but the castle itself is entirely Crusader in design and construction. In terms of its setting, it is the most dramatic of any of the Crusader castles, built on the summit of a narrow spur running 700m east–west, with sheer drops all round plunging into deep ravines. The whole landscape is heavily wooded, mainly with green oaks, adding still further to the picturesqueness of the site. The outer walls of the castle enclose an area of 5ha, making it twice the area of Krak and easily the largest in surface area of all the Crusader castles anywhere. Its location was chosen to guard and control the main route between Lattakia and through the mountains. The origins of the fortress go right back to the 1st millennium BC when the Phoenicians fortified it, and they were still in possession of it in 333BC when Alexander the Great passed through on his way to Egypt. In the late 10th century the Byzantines re-established the Duchy of Antioch and seized the city from the Hamdanid Dynasty of Aleppo. The remnants of this Byzantine castle are still visible in the old citadel on a hillock in the centre of the eastern half, and in traces of defensive walls built of small stones, in contrast to the more substantial Crusader stonework. After its fall it remained in Muslim hands, passing from its Ayyubid conquerors to the Mamelukes. From the 13th century its strategic importance declined and it fell into obscurity, housing a small village for a time which was then in turn abandoned.

The road, having reached the bottom of the ravine now crosses the stream below and begins to climb up on the castle spur itself, arriving after a couple more hairpin bends, at the extraordinary defensive gully, cut out of the rock, leaving just the solitary obelisk-like pinnacle of rock, 28m tall, to support the drawbridge. It is not known for certain but this extraordinary achievement is thought to be the work of the earlier Byzantines, the Crusaders at best deepening and widening it. The sheer scale of labour involved in this feat of stonework defies belief, especially given the relatively primitive tools at their disposal and the lack of dynamite. This was the point at which the spur on which the castle sits had originally been joined to the mountain, so by separating it with this vast gully, 156m long, 28m deep and 15m wide, the constructors ensured total security from attack by a higher vantage point. Some 50,000 cubic metres of rock must have been cut out in total, then used for the construction of the fortification walls. In times of peace horses were kept in this gully ditch, and their shelters can be seen cut into the rock.

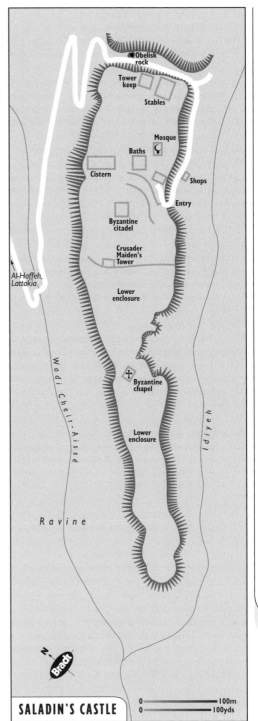

SALADIN'S CASTLE

Aleppo to the Coast   WEST OF ALEPPO

7

The large number of Crusader castles spread over the landscapes of the Levant represent a relentless energy, a building frenzy that lasted nearly 200 years. There seem to be three main reasons why the Crusaders devoted so much time and effort to castle building. Firstly the unusual shape of the Latin kingdom, secondly the lack of manpower, and thirdly the need for a feudal administration.

The shape of the land, a long thin coastal strip backed by the Muslim cities of Aleppo, Hama and Damascus, which were never taken, meant there was a constant threat of attack. The lack of manpower was an ongoing chronic problem. Although the armies that set out for Jerusalem on the First Crusade in 1097 were huge, losses were heavy, and by the time they reached Jerusalem, no more than 1,500 knights and 13,000 soldiers remained, many of whom then returned home after Jerusalem was taken. A mere 5,000 or so stayed and were prepared to defend their conquest of the Holy Land. Out of necessity therefore they had to build the most impregnable castles they could to defend themselves, with stronger taller walls and round towers along curtain walls to withstand bombardment better than the traditional square towers, and to permit wider firing angles. Machicolations – projecting boxes at the tops of walls for dropping stones or hot oil on attackers – were adopted and improved, and the entrances were made as impregnable as possible. Robin Fedden, author of *Crusader Castles*, wrote: 'The desperate shortage of manpower encouraged every device by which stones might do the work of men.' Even a castle like the mighty Krak des Chevaliers had a normal garrison of just 200 men, and yet was never taken except by trickery.

Finally, the Frankish barons required a secure centre from which to administer their fiefs. They were not short of money and could afford to pay thousands of workers to labour in the fields and vineyards around their castles. In times of peace the architects and builders who had come with the knights also had plentiful opportunities to observe how local Muslims designed and built their fortifications, and from this exchange the Crusaders learnt many military techniques which enhanced the defensive capability of their castles. Saladin's round towers for example, impressed them as being easier to defend, and it was here at Saône in 1120 that we have the first recorded example of the square being abandoned in favour of the round tower. Arrow slits were popularised by Muslims in 8th-century Iraq, but their first recorded use in England was in 1130. Machicolations were first seen in 729 at Qasr Al-Hayr near Palmyra, and did not appear in Europe till the 12th century at Chateau Gaillard near Rouen built by Richard the Lionheart after his return from the crusade. The idea of battlements to give cover to wall defenders also came back to Europe with returning Crusaders.

The approach road to the castle now passes through the dramatic gully, itself like a mini gorge, before winding round to the right to the car park below the massive and superbly crafted stone walls towering above. A handful of shops offering simple refreshments are clustered among the trees at the foot of the splendid long ramp-like stairway that leads up into the castle gateway, originally protected by a portcullis. There are basic WC facilities here.

At the top of the long flight of steps, you pass through a large hall area where books and souvenirs are sold, laid out with seating for the guardian and visitors. You buy your ticket here and head out into the castle compound. Immediately in front of you are the recently restored baths and palace complex together with a small mosque and minaret. The baths in particular are very elaborate with four *iwans* and a courtyard, and the palace doorway has beautifully carved stalactite decorations. All these Muslim additions date from the late 12th century and were probably completed under Saladin's successor, the Mameluke Sultan Qalaun. They have been the subject of extensive restoration funding from the Aga Khan in recent years, along with the Aleppo Citadel and the Assassins' Castle at Masyaf.

Returning to the tower opposite the mosque you can climb the stairway to admire the views. Further east along the walls behind a second square bastion tower, is a large long cistern and beside this is a pillared room which once served as the castle stables. Some people still claim to smell horses here. Next, in the centre of the eastern wall, situated in the deep gully, is the massive square-built *donjon* (keep) with 5m-thick walls. Inside there are two storeys, the first one dark with the only light from slit holes for arrows with a massive central pillar supporting the vaulting, while the other has three windows. The first one dark with the only natural light from narrow arrow slits and from the doorway itself. A torch can be useful for the darker recesses. The second storey is a little lighter with three windows. A massive central pillar supports the ceiling in both storeys. Further stairs lead up onto the roof for excellent views in all directions. In all of these square towers note the Crusader building style using neatly jointed square blocks of stone, prominently bossed. The semicircular towers along the eastern defences were originally built by the Byzantines, then strengthened by the Crusaders.

Back outside you can see in the next group of buildings as you work your way round anticlockwise the gateway where the drawbridge would originally have been laid down across the pinnacle in the gully, now of course just a sheer drop below. Moving on round the walls, note the cruder Byzantine stonework compared with the larger finer Crusader blocks. You come next to another enormous barrel-vaulted cistern 32m long by 10m wide, with steps leading into it. All the cisterns within the castle were built by the Crusaders and would have held enough water to withstand a long siege. Beyond the cistern in the centre of the enclosure are the remains of the heavily ruined Byzantine citadel, its stonework again greatly inferior to the later Crusader fortifications.

Further on, at the juncture between the upper and lower courts, a little café has been installed (though it is not always functioning) in the Crusader Maiden's Tower building. Only those with scratch-proof legs should venture into this lower enclosure as the undergrowth is thick and prickly. The little Byzantine chapel is the only attractive building that will reward your efforts. From the café follow the path that loops back towards the entrance, passing on the way the heavily ruined Crusader church beside a small Byzantine chapel.

Returning to Al-Haffeh, it is now an easy half-hour drive down the foothills to reach the coast at Lattakia.

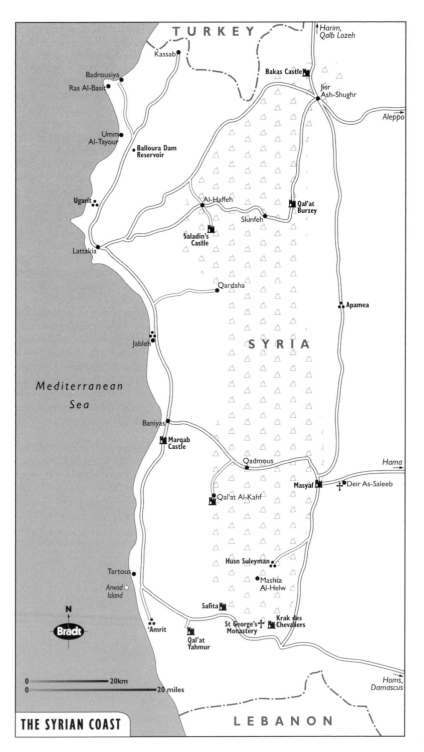

THE SYRIAN COAST

8

The Syrian Coast

Fight for honour, for dishonour is easily won.

Syria's coast on the Mediterranean has great potential with extensive sandy beaches. So far however the only area developed for tourists is the so-called 'Côte d'Azur' north of Lattakia which has just three five-star hotels. There are plans for another further south near 'Amrit. The coast has Syria's two working ports of Lattakia and Tartous. Stretching for 180km from the Turkish border in the north to the Lebanese border in the south, the fertile plain is intensively farmed, with the focus on fruit and vegetables. The coastal mountains behind the narrow plain used to be much more thickly wooded in ancient times. Even so, they offer what is probably Syria's most beautiful scenery with gently undulating terraced hills of olive groves, tobacco and fruit orchards, rising to heights of over 1,500m with steep rugged peaks still densely forested in places. Known as the Jebel Ansariye, these mountains provide in summer a welcome retreat from the intense heat and humidity of the coast, and many of the tiny villages on the high slopes swell in size in the summer months to accommodate escaping visitors. The best time to visit however is the spring when the mountains are covered in wild flowers, or in the autumn with changing leaf colours and the scent of freshly pressed olives in the air.

The Ansariye mountains have always formed throughout history a barrier between the coast and the interior, and as a result the coast has always been culturally different to the Fertile Crescent and the desert. It was here on the coast that the Phoenicians established a series of important city states based on maritime trade from the 2nd to the 1st millennium BC. The Crusaders too established their foothold here in medieval times, building immensely strong castles in the mountains to protect the coastal plain and permit Christian passage along the coast to Jerusalem further south. The other function these mountains have historically performed is to serve as refuge from persecution for religious minorities, notably the 'Alawis discussed later in the box on page 188 and the Assassins (see box page 205) who built a series of castles here in the 10th century in much the same way as the Crusaders, to consolidate their military strength.

The major Crusader castles which perch on the peaks of these mountains are all readily visitable on good roads but the smaller, more minor, Isma'ili Assassins castles are difficult to reach or even find among the myriad of tiny roads that crisscross the mountains. The best map is actually the free Ministry of Tourism map called 'Syria: the Coast', which gives more detail than any of the foreign whole country maps available.

LATTAKIA اللاذقية *Telephone code 01*

(*186km southwest of Aleppo, 90km north of Tartous*) Syria's main port and largest Mediterranean town, Lattakia is a pleasant cosmopolitan place with a lively student population and an active cultural and sporting life. Its wide palm-treed boulevards, busy shops and street cafés lend it a prosperous, even sophisticated air, and it has the most French feel of any Syrian town, and not surprisingly, since the French were responsible for its modern revival under their mandate. The town also benefited from massive Lebanese investment during the recent Lebanese civil war, when businessmen were seeking an alternative to Beirut.

Settled since 1000BC, Lattakia's heyday was as a Seleucid city when Alexander's general Seleucus Nicador named it after his mother Laodicea. Its port thrived and it was known as the main supplier of wine to the Hellenistic Empire. Under the Romans it was even briefly declared capital of the Province of Syria, a role then taken over by Antioch (modern Antakya in the Turkish Hatay, see box opposite).

It then fell in succession to the Arabs, Crusaders, even Venetians from 1229 till 1436, gradually dwindled to a small fishing village by the end of the 19th century, and in Baedeker's 1876 Guide was described as 'squalid and poverty-striken'. It was the French Mandate after World War I that brought Lattakia back to prominence. The creation of modern Lebanon and the handing back of the Hatay province to Turkey meant that Syria had to expand and develop Lattakia as its major port.

Today the only relic of Lattakia's illustrious past is the tetrapylon, squatting impressively if incongruously down at Roman street level among modern buildings, its four-arched tower marking the crossroads of the old Roman city. The museum is worth a brief look, of interest more for its location, attractively laid out in an Ottoman *khan* surrounded by lush flowering gardens, close to the docks. The exhibits themselves are well labelled with interesting finds from Ugarit.

Lattakia has no actual corniche, unlike Tartous, so you never get any sense of being by the sea. Though there are a couple of adequate hotels, such as the Riviera, the Zenobia and the Palace, there is no reason to stay here as a foreigner as there are no beaches. Almost all visitors therefore will head north c10km from the city, following the signs to Côte d'Azur, where the two major hotels the Cham Côte d'Azur and the Meridien are located on what is known as Syria's Blue Beach, its Mediterranean Riviera, with good clean sandy beaches.

GETTING THERE AND AWAY

By air Lattakia's Al-Basil airport is 25km southeast of the town, with one weekly flight to Damascus (Fridays), and one to Cairo (also Fridays). Taxis into town cost S£250.

By train Lattakia's railway station, on Al-Yaman Square east of the town centre, is one of the very few in the country that has the air of being used, and indeed the scenic train journey from Aleppo to Lattakia through the mountains is probably the only train ride in Syria worth considering. There are two trains a day to Aleppo. Before boarding the train your ticket must be stamped and your details registered at the counter opposite the ticket guichets.

By coach The Garagat Pullman deluxe coach station is just behind the railway station, east of the town centre. There is no need to book ahead as there are at least 12 private companies offering regular departures. Aleppo for example has departures every 30 minutes.

Ferry services to Alexandria and to Izmir were not operating at the time of writing.

TOURIST INFORMATION There is a tourist office (☏ *416926; open 08.00–20.00 daily*) offering the standard free maps and leaflets on 14 Ramadan St in the centre of town.

After the end of World War I the French were given control of Syria and Lebanon, while the British were given control of Palestine, Jordan and Iraq. This French Mandate was a period of traumatic dismemberment for Syria. First 'Le Grand Liban' was carved out, with a protected Maronite enclave of Mt Lebanon in the south. Two mini-states were then created centred on Damascus and Aleppo, as well as two separate enclaves, the 'Alawi in the mountains around Lattakia, and the Druze in the Hawran south of Damascus. Finally parts of the old Ottoman province of Aleppo were given to Turkey. By the time the French finally withdrew in 1946, Syria covered an area of c185,000km^2, compared with the former Ottoman province of Syria which covered nearly 300,000km^2.

The administration of these mandates fell short of the ideal laid out in the League of Nations, that the well-being of the mandated peoples formed 'a sacred trust of civilization' and that the chief concern of the mandatory power was to provide any advice and assistance necessary to achieve full independence. The Syrians however accused the French of using the same colonial methods as in north Africa, using the native government as a façade, discouraging the use of Arabic with heavy censorship and printing presses confiscated. They failed to recognise the rising national spirit, depreciating the native currency by tying it to the franc, playing off the various sects against each other and using oppressive measures against resistance such as imprisonment, exile and espionage.

They divided the country into several administrative états and ceded controversially the Sanjaq of Alexandretta to Turkey in the face of German aggression on the eve of World War II in an attempt to ensure Turkish neutrality in any future war. Now known as the Hatay Province of Turkey, with a population of over a million, the Sanjaq of Alexandretta – which included the cities of Antioch (now Antakya) and Alexandretta (now Iskenderun) – was awarded to Syria in 1920, but in 1936 was the subject of a complaint by Turkey to the League of Nations claiming the privileges of the Turkish minority in the Sanjaq were being infringed. It was given autonomous status in 1937, riots broke out there in 1938 between the Turks and the Arabs, and joint French and Turkish military control was imposed. In 1939 France transferred the Sanjaq to Turkey and it became the Hatay Province. Aleppo was thereby effectively severed from the port of Iskenderun (Alexandretta), its natural outlet to the Mediterranean.

Any benefits that may have come from improved communications, widening areas of cultivation, improving and extending education and setting up the framework for modern government were not enough to contain the rising discontent. Rebellion broke out in Jebel Druze in 1925 and spread to Damascus, leading the French to shell the capital several times in 1925 and 1926. Around 3,000 people were killed and the Hamadiye Souk was damaged, the bullet holes in the roof still testimony to the rebellion. Opposition continued sporadically across the country, often in the form of strikes, till the last French troops were expelled in 1945. Lebanon had succeeded in expelling them two years earlier and declaring itself a republic.

The Hatay is still predominantly Arab and Armenian, and maps published in Syria to this day show the Hatay as part of Syria. Although the Syrian economy stagnated under the French Mandate the good legacies were a better road network and state education system and the University of Damascus. Mains water and electricity were installed in all major towns and the land under cultivation increased by 50% while the population grew from 2 million to 3.5 million. Also the Department of Antiquities was created to preserve and administer the country's architectural heritage, doing its most notable work at Palmyra, Ugarit, Krak and Apamea.

The Syrian Coast **LATTAKIA** 8

🏠 WHERE TO STAY AND EAT

🏠 **Cham Côte d'Azur** (100 suites with kitchenettes) PO Box 1097; ☎ 041 428700; f 428285; e chamreasa@net.sy; www.chamhotels.com. All rooms have good-sized balconies half with lovely views overlooking the sea and the beach gardens, and the other half looking inland to the mountains. Tennis courts, mini golf, nightclub. No pool. Chamcar/Hertz car hire. *US$120/80 dbl/sgl.*

🏠 **Meridien** (215 rooms, 28 suites, 26 chalets) PO Box 473; ☎ 428736; f 428732; e merlatco@net.sy; www.lattakia.lemeridien.com. Lots of shops, internet café, business centre, bank. Pool, watersports, tennis courts, nightclub, 4 restaurants, 1 bar. *US$150/120 dbl/sgl (out of season reduced to US$88).*

🏠 **Sofitel Afamia Tourist Resort** (246 rooms, 42 chalet apartments) ☎ 41 317405; f 41 317406;

www.sofitel.com. Situated 2km north of the city centre. 3 restaurants, bar, disco, business centre, health club, tennis court. Pool 24m by 10m. Poolside snacks, bridge to hotel across sea-channel. Marina, jetty, windsurfing, pedaloes, water scooters, kayaks.

✗ **City Café** Lattakia. Tucked just off the cornice up a side street just north of the museum grounds. Trendy air-conditioned place with varied international cuisine, pastas and pizzas. No alcohol. Photos of Claudia Schiffer and Marilyn Monroe on the walls. *Open 10.00 till late.*

✗ **Plaza Restaurant** Lattakia. On the corniche about 100m north of the museum. Upmarket Arabic and international cuisine. Alcohol served. Balcony overlooking corniche. *Open evenings only, 20.00 onwards.*

NIGHTLIFE Both the Côte d'Azur Cham Hotel and the Meridien along the Côte d'Azur north of Lattakia have nightclubs which are the only places worth considering. The area around the Côte d'Azur Cham is also very lively at night with many stalls lining the streets selling beach kit, inflatables, souvenirs and with snack bars and simple restaurants as well as amusement arcades. In high season these areas are thronged with Syrian and Gulfi families strolling about, eating and drinking.

OTHER PRACTICALITIES

Hospital Lattakia's best hospital is Al-Assad University hospital (☎ 478782) in the town centre at 8 Azar Street.

Pharmacies There are many pharmacies downtown on Al-Mutannabi St and 8 Azar Street, always well-stocked and offering the usual range of prescription drugs over the counter.

Post office The main post office (*open 08.00–19.00 except Friday*) is 200m north of Al-Yaman square roundabout.

Internet Internet cafes downtown are starting to open up, offering cheap connection rates. The Meridien Hotel has its own internet café.

SYRIA'S CÔTE D'AZUR الشاطىء الأزرق

This part of Syria has a very different feel to it, the most cosmopolitan and Westernised stretch of coastline in the country, though it never quite feels like the Mediterranean of Europe. There is a definite holiday atmosphere with shops selling colourful inflatables and bikinis of all shapes and sizes. In the hot summer months from June to the end of August it tends to be full of Gulf Arabs, escaping the heat of their own countries (Syria is after all the most northerly of the Arab countries), and the hotels are therefore geared for long-stay visitors. The Cham for example has mini suites with small kitchen areas and fridges and a supermarket shop within the hotel selling food supplies. Out of the summer months from March to May and from September to November, Europeans come as it is hotter than at home and the sea is fine for swimming as late as November. Mosquitoes can be problematic in the summer, so come equipped with repellent and electric vape mat plus tablets. In the winter months from November to February very few visitors come at all and the hotels are largely empty.

These contrasts in visitors are also apparent in signs on the beaches, for example at the Cham, where large signs on the way out to the beach from inside the hotel announce (in Arabic): 'It is forbidden to go onto the beach in clothes.' Any Westerner for whom this is translated will assume this means you have to go naked, whereas of course what the Arabic means is that Arab women, most of whom, especially the older ones and Gulf women, would go onto the beach fully dressed in long robes and also swim fully clothed, are not allowed to do so here as it would lower the tone. They must be in proper swimwear.

Non-hotel guests can pay to use the hotel beaches and watersports facilities such as waterskiing or windsurfing, and the beaches themselves are excellent for swimming in the clear blue water; the Cham even has a kind of bay with mock-Roman statuary and buoys delineating the outer perimeter of the recommended swimming area. Palm trees provide ample shade, but sun loungers and shades are also available. Pedalos and day pleasure boats with shades can be hired. The beaches at the Meridien, out along the promontory, tend to be a little less crowded than at the Cham.

It is also possible to use the stretch of beach a little before (south of) the two big hotels, paying S£50 to enter one of the turnstiles. This stretch of about 2km has groups of holiday complexes and apartments used by less well-off Gulf Arabs in the summer and tends to get much busier (and consequently dirtier) than the hotel beaches. The area is not recommended for European women, who are definitely better off using the hotel beaches out of season, ie: April–May, and September–October. Sand flies can sometimes be a nuisance.

UGARIT رأس الشمرة ('Ras Shamra', literally 'Fennel Headland')

(*15km northeast of Lattakia; open 09.00–16.00 winter, 09.00–18.00 summer daily; S£150 entry fee; allow 1½hrs; simple refreshment cafés beside the entrance with WC facilities; no shade, so come prepared with sunhat etc*) Famous today as the place where the world's first alphabet was discovered on clay tablets in the palace archives, the site of Ugarit requires quite a feat of imagination on the part of the visitor to conjure up the original grandeur of its setting on the sea, now invisible about 1km away across the fields.

The existence of the site was discovered by a local farmer in 1928 when his plough hit a large piece of stone which turned out to be a manmade flagstone, covering a tomb below. The whole area round Ugarit is still heavily farmed due to its fertile soil. A river originally led past the city out into the harbour, but over the centuries it gradually silted up, leaving the rich alluvial soil.

By far the most striking aspect of Ugarit today for the visitor, is its extraordinarily advanced water system. Everywhere there are wells, water channels and basins ingeniously devised by the inhabitants 14 centuries BC. In such a well-endowed location, with river water and wells, they clearly enjoyed what would have been, in other locations and cities of the era, an almost extravagant use of water, even having it flowing freely in channels round the banqueting room, presumably so that hands could be washed frequently. Water was also very important in funeral rites and the inhabitants believed that the dead had to have water close by, which is thought to be why the royal tombs are within the city walls.

The site today is set at the edge of an unsightly sprawling village and there is a cluster of cafés selling souvenirs directly opposite the entrance. Try to rise above this and focus instead on the massive and well-preserved stone-slab postern gateway, reminiscent of

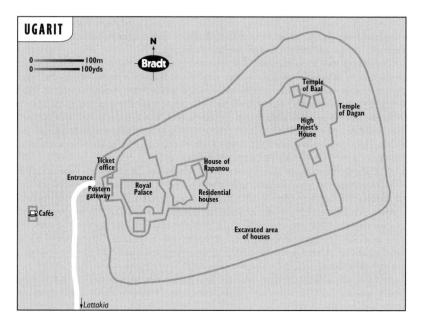

UGARIT

0 ———— 100m
0 ———— 100yds

N

Bradt

Temple of Baal

Temple of Dagan

High Priest's House

Ticket office

House of Rapanou

Entrance

Postern gateway

Royal Palace

Residential houses

Cafés

Excavated area of houses

↓Lattakia

Mycenaean design, thought to have been the original entrance to the Royal Palace, located below and to the right of the current modern entrance by the guardian's ticket office. The ceiling height of the inside passageway reaches 5m in places and shallow steps lead up to the level of the Royal Palace. In the forecourt where it enters is a guardroom with triangular stones at eye height which could be pushed out to create peep-holes for observing the route up to the palace from the harbour.

The poor presentation, labelling and signposting of this site belies its enormous importance as one of the most major Bronze Age sites in the Middle East. Excavations began as long ago as 1929 under the French, which explains why the main finds are now in the Louvre, Paris. The remainder are on display in the national museums of Aleppo and Damascus, and to a lesser extent, Lattakia. In 2000 the excavation project officially became a joint Syrian–French enterprise.

The earliest occupation of the site has been shown from the excavations to go back to the 7th millennium BC, but the city's golden age was in the 2nd millennium BC when the population seemed to have been of Canaanite origins. The city's harbour (Minet Al-Beida, meaning White Harbour) 1.5km away to the northwest was the key point for the importation of copper technology to the region. The name Ugarit appears in records from this time as a separate city state, yet clearly had links with the ancient Egyptians and the Mitannite Dynasty of Mesopotamia, as well as the Minoans of Crete. Ugarit traded with Egypt, Mesopotamia, Anatolia and the Aegean region, as evidenced by the tablets found on the site where such trade was recorded. The Royal Palace of King Niqmadou II (ruled 1360–30BC) belongs to this golden age and tablets found elsewhere refer to it as the most magnificent palace of its time. The Hittites to the north posed a considerable threat to Ugarit's independence and it is clear from documentation found on the site that the Hittites regarded Ugarit as part of their extended empire.

The city's demise seems to have come quickly with the invasion of the Sea Peoples (famously the Philistines) in c1200BC, after which it went into decline. It has been speculated that the city suffered an earthquake and tidal wave, followed by rampant fires. Its end coincided with the start of the Iron Age, and it was never able to adapt to the new technology, and declined, lying largely forgotten till the 20th century.

As you climb up onto the mound itself and look out for the first time over the ruined city proper, it appears at first glance to be a random jumble of low walls and pathways. In fact this area closest to you immediately in front is the gigantic Royal Palace, consisting of over 90 rooms including reception rooms, audience halls, throne rooms, five courtyards and an internal garden. The famous clay tablets were found in the secretariat room, one of the five separate archive rooms, close to the throne room. As you wander round, look out for traces of the water system and imagine the fountains in the courtyards to help recreate this, the largest and most lavish palace of its day (late 14th, early 13th century) in the whole region. Look out for the large courtyard labelled Reception Hall with a sunken pool in the centre. Following the water channel east from the Reception Hall you come to what has been identified as the palace's large interior garden, with a well and bucket beside a small structure thought to have been the gardener's hut. Stairs in many places show how the palace was originally on two floors. The upstairs rooms, where the royal apartments would have been, have collapsed over the centuries as their wooden rafters crumbled away, originally a feature used to help the houses withstand earthquakes by giving an element of movement in the house which stone would not. In the southwest corner a small oven was found, used for baking the tablets on which the letters, treaties, inventories and texts were written. Watch out next for the signpost to the Royal Tombs, right in the far north of the Royal Palace, a series of three sepulchral vaults under the paved floor. These tombs yielded rich finds of effigies, votive offerings, jewellery, golden bowls, figurines, vases of faience and alabaster, cylinder seals, bronze weapons and even furnishings. Heading east you come next to two buildings, the first labelled Stone Vessel Building, because of the huge stone urn discovered intact inside, and then the House of Rapanou, a spacious 34-room villa with its own excellently preserved underground mausoleum belonging to Monsieur Rapanou himself.

Beyond the Royal Palace is an area of houses, some of which have their own personal bathrooms and systems. Many were also on two floors, and the families used to live upstairs, while downstairs was used for shops, storage and commercial activities. The citizens of Ugarit were known from the tablets to include gold and silver smiths, scribes, soldiers, priests, cartwrights, bowmakers, shipbuilders, farmers and herders. Beyond the area of houses on its own little mound, are the remnants of the Temple of Baal, a temple that was famous all over the Middle East and used to receive offerings from as far away as Egypt, and conduct many bloody animal sacrifices of bulls, donkeys, sheep, doves and so on, according to the tablets found in the house of the high priest. Raised up on its hillock it used to signal to passing ships. The god Baal as mentioned in the texts of the city is described as son of El, creator of the universe, source of all wisdom and god of storms, rains and hills. One of the tablets describes the great god El becoming drunk and having to be carried home by his sons. There then follows a recipe for restoration after alcoholic collapse, that states that the hairs of a dog are to be put on the drunken person's forehead, along with the head of a specific plant, while he is made to drink the plant shoot mixed with fresh olive oil. El also foretells in the tablets the decline of Ugarit and the destruction that was to come from the sea.

Beside the Temple of Baal is the Temple of Dagan, slightly better preserved. Dagan, associated with rain and grains, was a fertility god but lord of death and the underworld as well. Interestingly he was also the principal deity of the Philistines, who subsequently invaded from the sea. Look out near the two temples for a black basalt stone in a triangle shape with three holes, which was an anchor used for tying up ships. Ugarit's gigantic anchors were celebrated. They weighed up to half a

Before the 14th century BC the two forms of writing that existed in the region were Egyptian hieroglyphs and Mesopotamian cuneiform, both of which used hundreds of symbols to represent whole words or syllables. Here at Ugarit however the clay tablets used in the archive room are written in a highly simplified form with just 30 signs or letters. They are based on a phonetic system of one sound, one sign, with no vowels or accents, the same as modern Arabic. Even the pronunciation and alphabetical order is similar to modern Arabic, and it is evident that this alphabet, devised between 1400BC and 1300BC was the origin of Arabic and one of the earliest alphabets developed in the world. The Ugaritic language has been identified as Semitic, an ancient form of Hebrew.

The majority of the tablets were religious writings, among which names familiar to us from the Old Testament occur, and give us the first known insights into the religion of these Canaanite peoples before the invasion of Joshua. They therefore provide us with the first ever body of Canaanite literature and set the scene for the surroundings in which the religion of Jehovah grew up and developed, showing the analogies that existed between the beliefs and rites of the Canaanites and those of the Hebrews.

Most of the remainder of the tablets are administrative records of trade, listing for example the cargoes of ships, with items such as milk, fish, dried fruits, wool, clothing (fine woollen garments from Ugarit were famous, often dyed purple from the coastal murex shell), slaves, animals for husbandry and consumption, olive oil from the Orontes valley, cedarwood from Lebanon, and grains from Carchemish in the heart of the Fertile Crescent.

Also among the tablets are some other curiosities like the first known musical text with rhythm and short notes, deciphered and played in the 1970s, and declared to sound very like our music of today. Other tablets have such pieces of advice as: 'Do not tell your wife where you hide your money', and even a will, in which the husband leaves all his money to his wife and two sons, as long as the sons treat her 'with respect and consideration'. The documents were written in both Ugaritic and Akkadian languages, a fact which helped enormously in the speedy decipherment of the new alphabet.

tonne each, giving an idea of the size of the ocean-going vessels. There used to be lots of these stones, but most have now been stolen. The whole site has been newly fenced to prevent theft which had become something of a problem. Look out for a black basalt stone in a triangle with three holes, which was an anchor used for tying up ships. There used to be lots of these stones, but most have now been stolen.

NORTH TO RAS AL-BASIT رأس البسيط

Heading north from Ugarit towards the beach at Ras Al-Basit you pass through the fertile orchards of the coastal plain protected from wind behind the tall cypress trees. This whole northeast corner of Syria is unlike anything most Westerners will associate with the Middle East. Not a desert in sight, the landscape is hilly, even mountainous in the extreme north, and covered in forests of mainly pine.

First of all though, in the sprawling development of the outlying towns, you can see the signs of new wealth. A lot of new and often large houses have been built in the last 20 years or so, many of them by newly rich families of the 'Alawi sect, Syria's largest religious minority (see box on *Alawis* on page 188). Under Hafez Al-Assad, the first 'Alawi to rise through the military ranks, many 'Alawis were for the first time given powerful jobs and gained positions of influence. As a result the minority which used to be rather looked down on by the mainstream as inferior mountain people, scarcely within the bounds of Islam, have become acceptable and everyone wants to know them. Hafez Al-Assad had to become a Sunni when he became president because the constitution states that the president must be Muslim. His son Bashar Al-Assad has married a Sunni. Today people are discouraged from talking about 'Alawi versus Sunni, and are encouraged to think of everyone as just Muslims.

As the road climbs north you pass the turn-off to Umm Al-Tayour, where there are lots of hotels popular with Syrians from Aleppo and Damascus for their summer holidays. Further up is the Balloura Dam, a large reservoir of collected rainwater and snowmelt. In winter these roads are closed by snowfalls. There are a couple of simple restaurants with terraces overlooking the lake where people swim in summer. The area is known as heavily snake infested. You come next to a fork where Ras Al-Basit forks left 13km while Kassab is straight on.

Ras Al-Basit with its black sandy beaches is an impressive spit, dominated by the mountain headland to the north that gives the bay its name. Known as Mt Casius in Western languages, its summit was held sacred by the Greeks and Phoenicians with a cult site to Zeus. Beyond the headland lies Turkey. The little resort itself however is distinctly scruffy and even a bit fetid by European standards, with uncleaned beaches and rubbish liberally strewn about the place. There is a certain run-down charm though and in the summer it pullulates with holidaying Syrians staying in the many beach apartments or even camping, something that sometimes results in forest fires when barbecues rage out of control.

Further north still is the village of Badrousiya, an 'Alawi village, now with many houses abandoned, presumably by families who preferred to move to the cities or build new houses elsewhere. There is a spring here beside the mosque where a restaurant in season sets up under the shady vines and trees. Out of season it is all just a jumbled heap of broken furniture with bar football and pool tables lying at drunken angles in the mud.

Kassab itself is an Armenian village with street signs in Arabic, English and Armenian. The Armenian church is in the centre, but what was once an attractive mountain village hut has been overdeveloped in recent years. North of Kassab and Ras Al-Basit the influx of Kuwaiti and Gulf Arabs has led to a rash of new apartments being built all over the hillsides with tempting signs erected saying: 'deluxe apartments for rent'. In August the population surges from some 5,000 to over 30,000. The largest church is the Armenian Evangelical church. A big new mosque stands 50m further on. There is no obvious old centre to the town any more, and a handful of older houses remain, the typical style having red-tiled roofs and red wooden shutters.

SOUTH ALONG THE COAST

QARDAHA القرداحة If on your itinerary southwards along the coast you have an hour to spare it is well worth making the short detour from the coast road up into the 'Alawi village of Qardaha, birthplace and final resting place of Hafez Al-Assad, creator of modern Syria, its leader from 1971 till his death in 2000. There is nothing to see in the village apart from Assad's mausoleum, but the dignified, solemn yet elegant tomb has its own extraordinary power, and a visit will help you get a little closer to understanding the influence this man of humble origins had over his proud but beleaguered country.

The turn-off from the main coastal highway is clearly signposted and is the same exit as the airport. A wide four-lane highway was specially built to lead up to the village and mausoleum, and at the time of the funeral, the walls, doors, even trees,

Before the French Mandate, the 'Alawis, Syria's largest religious minority numbering about 1,350,000, an offshoot of Shi'ism, were known as the Nusayris after the name of the mountains, the Jebel Nusayriye or Ansariye in northern Syria, where they settled. The Assad family were all 'Alawis and today 'Alawis make up about two-thirds of the population of Lattakia where they are concentrated. They appear to be the descendants of the people who lived in this region at the time of Alexander the Great, and when Christianity flourished here the 'Alawis, isolated in their little mountain communities, clung to their own pre-Islamic religion. After hundreds of years of Isma'ili influence, they moved closer to Islam, but contacts with the Byzantines and Crusaders added Christian elements to their creeds and practices. Unlike Isma'ilis they consider 'Ali the incarnation of the deity in the divine triad, hence the name 'Alawi. As such, 'Ali is the 'Meaning', Muhammad, whom 'Ali created of his own light, is the 'Name', and Salman the Persian is the 'Gate'. The 'Alawi catechesis is expressed in the following formula: 'I turn to the Gate; I bow before the Name; I adore the Meaning.' 'Alawis believe all people were at first stars in the world of light, but fell from the firmament through disobedience. Faithful 'Alawis believe they must be transformed seven times before returning to take a place among the stars, where 'Ali is prince. If they fail they may be reborn as Christians. Infidels are reborn as animals. Their religion is practised with even greater secrecy than the Druze and they incorporate Christian festivals such as Christmas, Easter and Epiphany, and believe in the symbolic significance of bread and wine, as well as many rites and rituals thought to be traceable to the Phoenicians, with elements of Zoroastrianism. Only a select few learn the religion after a lengthy process of initiation, and the young are initiated into the secrets of the faith in stages. Their prayer book, the source of religious instruction, is the Kitab Al-Majmu' (Book of the Totality), believed to derive from Isma'ili writings. 'Alawis study the Koran and recognise the Five Pillars of Islam, interpreting them in an allegorical way. They do not use a specific building for worship, and when in the past the Sunni government authorities used to force them to build mosques, they were not used but simply left standing empty. Only the men participate in worship.

They were autonomous till the mid 19th century when the Ottomans, regarding them as infidels, persecuted them and imposed heavy taxes. 'Alawis were at that stage mainly servants or tenant farmers working for Sunni landowners. During the French Mandate a separate mini-state enclave was created for them round Lattakia, the French hoping to court them as allies, as they did the Maronites in Lebanon, and after Hafez Al-Assad came to power rising up through military ranks, the 'Alawis, after centuries of persecution as heretics, came to the fore and found favour, prompting considerable jealous resentment from the rest of the population. After the Iranian Revolution in 1979 which first mobilised Shi'a identity and emboldened the Shi'a, after years of oppression and marginalisation by ruling Sunni regimes, to actively seek power in other countries of the region, Ayatollah Khomeini issued a fatwa (religious edict) declaring the ruling 'Alawi sect in Syria to be within the pale of Islam. This gave Assad legitimacy at a time when he was under pressure from the Sunni Muslim Brotherhood, and Tehran did not condemn the massacres at Hama in 1982 (see box page 121). Political observers are now watching with interest, following the Shi'a revival in Iraq. Regime change there disenfranchised the Sunni minority leadership that had ruled Iraq since its independence in 1932, and there will inevitably be reverberations of Shi'a empowerment in Iraq that will extend well beyond its borders. The 'Alawi area around Lattakia is noticeably prosperous these days, but so far there is no sign of the predicted 'Alawi backlash.

along the approach road were all painted black, though only traces of this remain today.

The mausoleum is not that easy to find, but if you keep following the black railings on the side of the street, this will lead you up to the large gold-domed tomb. The first surprise is that there is no military presence here at all and no security checks. There are just a few dark-suited guards who smile courteously, show you the way and keep a gentle eye on you. Most days the tomb is quiet and you will be one of a handful of visitors, but on Fridays, busloads descend on the place and it can become positively rowdy with children rushing round playing and yelling happily.

A series of huge photos line the approach from the car park in the last one of which, taken shortly before he died aged 69 from a heart attack, he looks like a French resistance fighter in a beret, and there are usually some fine huge wreaths outside the entrance. Inside the mausoleum is simple but very dignified. Assad's tomb lies in the centre beneath the dome, draped in dark green like a low bed, green always being the preferred colour in Islam.

In a side annex is the tomb of Basel, Assad's eldest son, tragically killed in a car crash in 1994. Basel, a popular and dashing figure, had been the natural successor to his father, and when he died the whole nation mourned. He was a talented equestrian and had a collection of beautiful horses, and was known for fast driving and fast living. He was killed while trying out one of his new cars on the airport road to Damascus in the early hours of the morning in thick fog. He was driving himself and wore no seat belt, as is normal in this part of the world. People used even to joke: 'Watch out, the road is clear, Basel is coming in one of his new cars.' Since Basel's death his mother has never appeared in public again, though she is still alive.

The mausoleum and its atmosphere and presentation is a kind of reflection of the country and the way it conducts itself: surprisingly dignified, simple, a relaxed atmosphere with no apparent tension, and no violence or petty crime. A bit of hooting of horns goes on but far less than in Egypt or Lebanon.

JABLEH جبلة On the coast between Lattakia and Baniyas the town of Jableh was once an important Phoenician, Roman and Byzantine port. Little remains today beyond a Roman theatre with a capacity for 8,000 spectators, currently under restoration, with its first 11 rows of seating well preserved. The town still has its two original fishing harbours and some attractive clifftop cafés with sea views.

MARQAB CASTLE قلعة المرقب (*Open 09.00–16.00 winter, 09.00–18.00 summer daily except Tue; S£150 entry fee; allow 1hr minimum; simple refreshments, café at entrance*) Moving on southwards down the coast the next site worth a detour is the Crusader Castle of Marqab. From afar the castle looks much less significant, so it comes as a pleasant surprise once you are up close and go inside, just how much still remains. It was in fact the largest in area of all Syria's Crusader castles, and second in power only to the mighty Krak des Chevaliers. Its vast cellars were stocked with enough provisions to last 1,000 men for a five-year siege. The best approach is from the main Tartous–Baniyas highway, taking the exit just south of Baniyas, beside a lone basalt tower on a headland. From this exit the castle is clearly signposted, taking the underpass under the motorway. The road which leads up the 4km to the castle is too small and winding for coaches, so the castle has but few visitors. There is a pleasant terraced café for refreshments by the entrance with fine views out to sea.

Along with Krak des Chevaliers, Marqab, whose name means 'Place of watching', is the other great Hospitaller castle of Syria, and dates likewise to the 13th century, serving as the Hospitallers' headquarters. Its huge round towers, 14

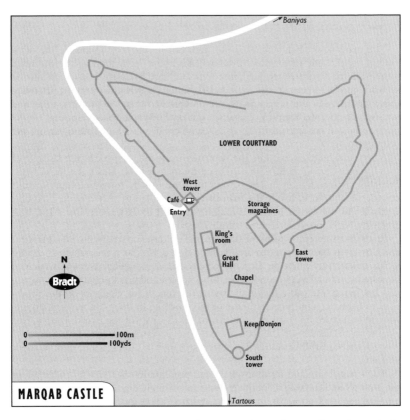

Baniyas

LOWER COURTYARD

West
tower

Café

Entry

Storage
magazines

King's
room

Great
Hall

East
tower

Chapel

N

Bradt

Keep/Donjon

0 —————— 100m
0 —————— 100yds

South
tower

MARQAB CASTLE

↓Tartous

in total, are unmistakably Christian. Of the Crusader castles it is the only one built of black basalt, quarried from the extinct volcano cone on which it sits, brooding, overlooking the coastal plain and the Mediterranean. The blackness lends it an atmosphere of power and mystery.

Originally an Arab stronghold fortified by the Muslims to protect Baniyas in 1062, then captured by the Byzantines in 1104, Marqab was sold to the Knights Hospitallers in 1186, who went on to build the castle much as we see it now between 1186 and 1203, with its superb strong battlements. It was bypassed by Saladin in 1188, who considered it too strong, and it withstood attacks from other Muslim emirs, but by the late 13th century the Crusader manpower had dwindled to the point where it succumbed after a five-week siege that culminated in the undermining of the south tower by the Mameluke Sultan Qalaun and his forces in 1285. It was the last of the three great Crusader castles of Syria to fall, Krak having fallen 14 years earlier.

The entrance is very impressive, climbing up to the gateway in shallow steps to allow horses easy access, then into the double-arched gateway through to the vaulted entrance that forks with two ways out. From the huge lower courtyard to your left you can begin a lengthy and rather overgrown circuit of the battlements along the walkway, past an Ottoman *khan*, an Arab cemetery and ruined village.

The most interesting parts of the castle however are all to the right of the entrance, where you come first to the King's Room, then to the Great Hall of the Hospitallers, then to the chapel in the centre, an austere early Gothic jewel with beautiful doorways and elegant vaulting in lovely and simple proportions. Note the handsome engaged capitals of the chapel interior and its side entrance. In the small room to the left of the choir traces of fresco of the 12 apostles at the Last Supper in red, black and yellow can be seen in the roof. From the room beyond the church, a flight of dark narrow steps leads up into rooms above the chapel, then up a further flight to the top level of the tower. The views from the roof are stunning, both over the surrounding landscape and over the astonishing defences of the castle. The *donjon* was in a circular tower with a 22m diameter and two square rooms one above the other. The south tower was repaired by Sultan Qalaun, successor to Baibars, after the siege and the typical Mameluke band of white stones running round in the upper section was added then, and carries a long Arabic inscription describing the exact repairs done. There are still lots of wells, most of them working, within the castle enclosure.

TARTOUS طرطوس (*Telephone code 043*) Syria's second port after Lattakia, Tartous today is a busy, rather scruffy conurbation whose modern sprawl is extending annually and whose harbour front has a cluster of unexciting fish restaurants. A

TIM SEVERIN'S 'CRUSADER'

The explorer Tim Severin, generally associated with sea voyages and recreating the journey of Sindbad the Sailor to India from Oman, stayed overnight within the walls of Marqab, watering his horses from the castle wells, en route to Jerusalem in a re-enactment of the journey on horseback that the Crusader knights would have made. His adventure was recorded in his entertaining book *Crusader* (1989) in which he describes how he, who had never ridden before and knew nothing about horses, and a sole companion, who had ridden before and did know about horses, set off from France on the 2,000-mile journey.

Their starting point was the Chateau de Bouillon, seat of Godfrey de Bouillon, a 'perfect knight' of unsullied reputation, great physical strength, piety and selflessness, who was chosen by the other European noblemen to be their Prince of Jerusalem. Godfrey never married and the main influence in his life was his mother, Ida, a lady of celebrated piety. He mortgaged his chateau to pay the cost of raising a small army and set off on the First Crusade to the Holy Land in 1096. Far from being an enriching venture for the warlords as was sometimes imagined, they had to sell valuables, dispose of lands and raise loans. For Godfrey the costs would have been at least three years of ducal income. He sold the county of Verdun and the family chateau of Bouillon to raise the massive sum of 1,300 marks of silver. He had inherited his castle at 27 and could have ruled one of the greatest feudal estates on the Continent. Instead he abandoned everything for a cause that promised only penury and death. It took three years for Jerusalem to get firmly in their hands. Godfrey then died only one year later and his body was buried within what is now the holy sepulchre, close to the spot where Jesus was buried, the holiest place in Christendom.

Severin chose to ride the closest thing to a medieval warhorse that exists today, an Ardennes Heavy Horse, weighing 800kg and nicknamed Carty. Severin actually rode the horse, though it was very uncomfortable because of the sheer width of its back, and no saddle could be found wide enough, thus leaving nasty sores both on the horse and Severin. In the Crusades these Belgian horses as they were known, were the most devastating mobile weapon of war. Ownership of such a horse was strictly controlled by royal edict as kings knew that a small army of Heavy Horses in the hands of a rebel could cost them their throne. Godfrey's army covered an average of eight miles a day. Very few of the Heavy Horses made it beyond Turkey, as the heat and change in grazing was more than they could adapt to.

new development is under way on the corniche, a joint venture with a local and a UK-registered company, to build a massive complex, to include a 200-bed four-star hotel, a 150-bed three-star hotel, tourist apartments, a commercial centre, a marina and sports park. Boats run from the harbour to the island of Arwad just 3km opposite; not recommended as an excursion. The litter-strewn beach has scant appeal for Westerners and only local youth venture into the sea here. The modern docks lie north of the centre.

In Roman times the town was known in Latin as Antaradus (Anti-Aradus, the town facing Arwad) and as Tortosa by the Crusaders. The city was favoured by Constantine for its devotion to the cult of the Virgin Mary and a chapel was said to be built here as early as the 3rd century dedicated to the Virgin. Two centuries later a huge earthquake destroyed the town and chapel but the altar, with its icon of the Virgin believed to have been painted by St Luke (like the one in Seydnaya, see page 107) was miraculously spared. The Crusaders built the Cathedral of Our Lady of Tortosa on the site of this miracle in 1123, and the cathedral still houses this altar.

In medieval times Tartous was a Crusader stronghold of considerable importance for the Knights Templar, and tucked away in its old centre are a very fine Crusader cathedral, now Tartous' museum, and the old citadel, densely inhabited with Tartous' poorer families and now distinctly squalid. Those on a tight itinerary should therefore simply bypass the city on the main coastal highway, but the dedicated, if they want to venture into the centre, should allow at least two hours for the total diversion.

If you aim for the corniche you will eventually reach the centre where the Crusader cathedral and citadel lie about 200m from each other. The honey-coloured walls of the citadel are quite distinctive and easy to spot with their well-crafted stone blocks topped now with modern slum-like dwellings. You can park nearby and walk in through any one of the roads to explore the hotchpotch of relics mixed with the current modernity. In the northeast corner is a chapel and in the centre in a small square is the keep. This is where the Templar soldiers were forced to blockade themselves in 1188 when Saladin's army raided the town. They survived, though much of the town outside was destroyed, then retreated onto Arwad Island, where they maintained a garrison for another 11 years, but were irrelevant to events on the mainland. By 1303 the last of the knights had withdrawn to Cyprus, abandoning the Levant for good. Today children play barefoot in the filth, their modern squalor contrasting oddly with the still unmistakable grace of the Crusader remnants.

A 200m walk to the south and slightly inland brings you to the attractive cathedral set among colourful gardens. Strolling round the back of the cathedral there are three extraordinary *neem* trees with cafés, making a very pleasant shady spot popular with the city's teenagers.

Where to stay and eat

🏠 **Shahin Tower Hotel** (156 rooms) On the corniche; ☎ 329100; f 312529; www.shahinhotels.com. 4-star hotel. Balconies with views towards Arwad Island.

✗ **Sea Whispers Restaurant** The best of the group of fish restaurants along the seafront. Fish is still expensive though because only small boats are allowed to catch fish.

Mashta Al-Helu Telephone code 043

🏠 **Mashta Al-Helu Resort Hotel** (185 rooms) ☎ 584000; f 584060. 4-star Alpine-style comfortable hotel up in this popular hill resort, excellent as a walking base in the mountains. Very crowded high season (mid-Jul–mid-Aug). Rooms have satellite TV,

minibar and balcony or you can stay in chalets sleeping up to 6 complete with kitchen and lounge. Restaurants, bars, swimming pool, tennis, sports hall. US$75/110 sgl/dbl.

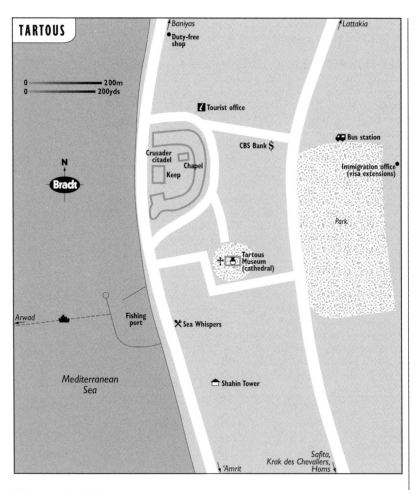

TARTOUS

Baniyas
Duty-free shop

Lattakia

0 ———— 200m
0 ———— 200yds

N

Bradt

i Tourist office

CBS Bank $

Bus station

Crusader citadel
Chapel
Keep

Immigration office
(visa extensions)

Park

† 📷 Tartous Museum (cathedral)

Arwad

Fishing port

✕ Sea Whispers

Mediterranean Sea

🏛 Shahin Tower

'Amrit

Safita,
Krak des Chevaliers,
Homs

Other practicalities
Hospital There is a good private hospital south of the railway station just off Tishreen Avenue, called the New Medical Centre (☏ *317319*).

What to see
Tartous Museum (*Open 09.00–16.00 winter, 09.00–18.00 summer; open daily except Tue; S£150 entry fee; allow 15mins; very basic WC facilities*) On the outside the fine west wall of the cathedral has impressive buttresses to protect against earthquakes. Inside, apart from the architectural interest of the building itself, with its early Gothic three-aisle interior, the exhibits are scattered illogically round. Just inside the door to the left in a frame about 1m by 2m, is a fragment of a fresco taken from Krak des Chevaliers, still quite colourful with yellow, blue, red, black, white and grey. Then there are lovely Arab turquoise pottery items from the 13th and 14th centuries and some Roman and Byzantine glass. Probably the most striking are the recently discovered Phoenician marble sarcophagi from 'Amrit dating to the 5th and 4th century BC, carved in the shape of human figures, each with different faces of great serenity. There are then other 4th- and 5th-century BC fragments from 'Amrit such as sacrificial statues, house utensils, bronze weights and jewellery.

Excavations by the American University of Beirut have been ongoing locally since 1985 at Tell Kazel (Simyra) 18km south of Tartous.

ARWAD ISLAND جزيرة أرواد The children on Arwad swim like fish, even swim to school. The whole crowded community on the tiny island (which measures only 800m by 500m) is very poor with inadequate sanitary conditions. There are no beaches, hotels or decent restaurants and whilst it is true that the traffic-free winding streets leading up to the Crusader fort on the highest point have a certain charm, the whole place is horribly polluted. The journey over takes about 20 minutes and boats run frequently, packed to bursting at holiday times, and can be seasickness-inducing because the boats are so small and bob around so much. The nominal fare of S£20 is payable on return. Needless to say, there are no lifejackets on the boats.

Arwad's original settlers are mentioned in the Bible as descendants of Canaan, one of Noah's grandsons. DNA testing in Lebanon has revealed that both Muslims and Christians today share common Phoenician ancestors going back more than 5,000 years. St Paul is said to have visited on his way to Asia Minor and Rome. The fort can be entered 09.00–16.00 except Tuesdays but its only real interest is historical as the last Crusader foothold in the east before they retreated to Cyprus.

'AMRIT عمرت (*Unfenced site, no entry fee; allow 1hr*) Unique among the ruins that Syria can boast, 'Amrit is a rare example of a Phoenician city that was never tampered with by later Hellenistic or Roman settlers. As a result its feel is quite different to the usual classical remains of this part of the world, and its attractive rural setting in a heavily treed region with the sea glistening in the distance makes it a very enjoyable place to linger with a picnic.

At the time of writing there was no fence, no guardian or entry tickets, though there has been talk for some years of a five-star luxury hotel opening on the beach nearby. The site, lying 8km south of Tartous, is not easy to find, as it is not signposted. Ignore the new dual carriageway that runs inland, and continue south out of Tartous, staying on the road that hugs the coast as closely as possible. It eventually disintegrates into a sandy track, but is easily negotiable in a saloon car. You will probably need to ask any local people you encounter to help with directions.

In 2004 'Amrit was included on the World Monuments Watch list

'AMRIT

- ↑Tartous
- ↑Tartous
- (Phoenician) Stadium
- 'Amrit
- Melqart temple (Phoenician)
- Mediterranean Sea
- Meghazil tower tombs
- N
- **Bradt**
- Al-Qabli
- 0 — 500m
- 0 — 500yds
- Burj Al-Bezzaq tomb
- Tripoli (Lebanon)↓

of 100 Most Endangered Sites. The Syrian Directorate General of Antiquities and Museums recently carried out rescue excavations when road widening work on the Tripoli to Tartous highway in 2003 revealed 1st- and 2nd-century AD tombs decorated with wall paintings. Since listing, however, little has been done to protect the site. The earliest excavations here were carried out in the 1920s when the sculptured limestone statues showing Egyptian and Persian influence were discovered, some of which are now on display in the Tartous Cathedral Museum. The Ministry of Culture now holds an annual 'Amrit Festival for Culture and Arts during 28–31 August to raise awareness of 'Amrit's importance.

As you arrive the first thing you will see is the great central sandy-coloured, 3m-high stone block of the Phoenician temple of the 2nd millennium BC, sitting in the middle of a huge sunken courtyard 55m by 48m, cut directly into the rock to a depth of 5.5m. The scale and decorative style are impressive, all the more so when you realise that the sunken courtyard was originally a sacred pool fed by a local spring and the temple itself could therefore be reached only by boat. You can descend into this area by processional steps and find a sheltered and shaded spot for a picnic among the huge stone blocks of the colonnade round the sunken area. On the floor of the pool itself are the carved stone blocks of two lions' heads scattered among the other blocks, whose mouths were used as the gushing fountains for the pool, a feature still in use today in our modern garden centres, and it's quite sobering to realise this idea first developed as early as the 3rd millennium BC. The name of the god to whom the temple was dedicated has been discovered by excavators' finds on the site to be Melqart, thought to be similar to the Greek Hercules. There is also thought to be a link with Imhotep, the Egyptian god of healing. The whole site at 'Amrit is more of a religious centre than a city and was built to support the Phoenician settlement on Arwad Island. A dispute seems to have arisen in the 2nd century BC between the inhabitants of 'Amrit and Arwad that caused the Arwadians to destroy 'Amrit, and from that time it was abandoned and neglected.

From the temple if you follow the track 200m over towards the line of trees you will reach the remarkable and again unique rock-cut stadium 220m long by 30m wide, and dated to the 15th century BC. Thought to be the first ever place where competitive games took place as part of the religious rites, this place is therefore the origin of the Olympic Games concept which the Greeks have always claimed as their own, along with so many other things whose actual origin was further east than they cared to admit. The stadium has two tunnel entrances cut into the rock with steps and represents a remarkable feat of labour. It has been calculated to be able to hold 11,200 spectators. On the southeast side there are traces of adjoining structures, thought to be what the Greeks called the Gymnasium and the Palaestra, training areas for the sports. The stadium was clearly used for sports like running, jumping, throwing and wrestling, not as a hippodrome for chariot races as some have postulated; hippodromes were much larger and wider, typically 480m by 160m. The stadium at Olympia in Greece has almost identical dimensions to the stadium here, 214m long by 30m wide, far too narrow for chariot racing. Watersports such as swimming, rowing and diving are also thought to have been held here at the mouth of the River 'Amrit some 700m away, in an area observed in 1860 by a French traveller, but by the 1970s diggers and transporters were removing great areas of sand so it was no longer possible to investigate further.

Further off to the south of the temple, some 500m away and reached by a sandy drivable track, are an impressive pair of tall funerary monuments, known locally as the Spindles (Arabic 'Al-Maghazel'). One has four heavily weathered lion sculptures carved into its base and castellated patterns round its domed top. Impressive in their scale and very unusual in their style, they each have a flight of stone cut steps descending below them into the tomb chamber below the spindle.

Inside the vault are loculi for bodies cut into the walls. Visible still further south but not currently visitable because it lies within a military area (so no photography), is a massive two-storey tomb block known locally as Burj Al-Bezzaq (Snail Tower) containing two burial chambers which must have been for one of 'Amrit's most important families. It originally had a pyramid on top, showing the interesting blend of Egyptian, Persian and Greek styles to which these Phoenician sites were exposed by virtue of their extensive trading activities.

QAL'AT AL-KAHF قلعة الكهف **(CASTLE OF THE CAVE)** Some 30km southeast of Marqab set up in the mountains and reachable only with persistence and lots of stops to ask the way, lies the unusual and dramatically sited Isma'ili castle of Al-Kahf (The Cave) on a ridge between a pair of gorges. Built originally in the early 12th century by a local chieftain it was then sold to the Assassins (see box on page 205) who used it from their headquarters at Qadmous, as one of their ten mountain bases to escape persecution from the mainstream Sunnis. The Mameluke Sultan Baibars finally captured it in 1273 and it then remained in use till Ottoman times. The most remarkable thing about the castle today, apart from its wild setting, is the entrance passageway carved from the solid rock and which gives the castle its name, as it appears you are entering a cave, not a castle. It also carries an Arabic inscription.

The best approach is from the town of Shaikh Badr, then 4km north to 'Ain Breisin, then 7km to Al-Nmreije, the nearest village, from which a drivable track runs the last 2km to the castle. The drive is slow, along winding narrow tarmac roads, and should be attempted only if you are prepared to devote the whole day to the excursion from Tartous or Krak. It makes a wonderful picnic spot.

QAL'AT YAHMUR قلعة ياحمور (*10km southeast of Tartous; allow 30mins*) Between Tartous and Safita a brief but interesting diversion can be made to the charming miniature 12th-century Crusader castle keep of Yahmur, standing proudly in the village of Bait Shalluf. As you drive from Tartous on the main road, the name 'Yahmur' is marked off by a blue signpost in Arabic beside a green signpost in English to Qal'at Al-'Uraymah. Just 2km off the main road you will spot the honey-coloured unmistakable stone blocks of the keep rising above the modern houses and the road winds round in front of it.

Now lived in by the guardian and his family, they are only too delighted to receive you, even though you may feel, typical English fashion, that you are invading their privacy. They will proudly show you where they live on the ground floor, using a big curtain to divide the big room into living and sleeping quarters. The keep room directly above it is totally intact and has its central pillar supporting the roof. A flock of pigeons lives inside and objects more to the disturbance. External steps lead onto the roof of the castle, now complete with television aerial. From here too you can see the well-preserved outer wall, with two Arab watchtowers added later. In 1177 the Hospitallers carried out substantial modifications to the original Byzantine 10th-century fort, calling it Chastel Rouge. Saladin captured it briefly in 1188, but the Crusaders retook it, holding it till 1289 when it finally fell to the Mameluke Sultan Qalaun, who also took the great castles of Marqab and Krak.

SAFITA
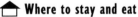
Where to stay and eat
🏠 **Safita Cham Hotel** (50 rooms) PO Box 25; ☎ 531131; f 525984; www.chamhotels.com. The smallest and least luxurious of the Cham chain this hotel on the lower slopes of the town is rather overpriced and has little to recommend it except its swimming pool and terrace. It tends to be packed at holiday times and empty otherwise. *US$100/80 dbl/sgl.*

There is now a good wide road up to Safita from the Tartous–Homs highway, reflecting the fact that, as an 'Alawi area, it has benefited from government money, and many 'Alawis from mountain villages around have converged to live in the big modern town.

What to see

Safita Castle قلعة صافيتا (*Allow 30mins*) Known as Chastel Blanc by the Crusaders, the White Castle, Safita's big square white keep stands today at the highest point, protruding from the modern town of Safita on the hillsides all around, virtually obscured by modern development. What would have been its dominant position controlling the valleys all around is thus difficult to appreciate now. As you enter the town your sight of the castle is lost, but you must keep heading upwards till a small sign points up to the summit, leading up a narrow cobbled street, through a stone arch, past the White Horse Restaurant and into the square directly in front of the *donjon*, now reincarnated as St Michael's Church. It is almost like a drive-in castle, and its sheer scale and the craftsmanship of its stonework cannot fail to impress now that you are right up next to it. The ground floor was originally the Crusader chapel, and never having been desecrated or turned into a mosque, it can still function as a church. This is all that remains of the castle which was dismantled by Nur Ad-Din to whom it fell in 1167.

The keep as it appears today is a Templar construction of the early 13th century. Its garrison was ordered to leave by the Templar Master based in Tartous when the Mameluke Sultan Baibars approached in 1271, and was thereby spared a siege and attack. There is no entry fee as the castle is a church serving the Greek Orthodox community of the town. The guardian can usually be found somewhere in the vicinity to open up if the church is locked and on the author's last visit simply emerged from behind the sacristy screen talking on his mobile phone. Donations are expected in the conspicuously placed collection box. The arrow slits provide the only natural lighting. Steps lead up to the big main room above the church and you can see the hole over the entrance through which deterrents would have been poured on attackers below. The stone steps then continue right up onto the crenellated roof, from where the castle's location can be appreciated for the first time. It had direct line of sight with Krak des Chevaliers to the southeast so they could communicate with a system of flares.

KRAK DES CHEVALIERS قلعة الحصن ('QAL'AT AL-HUSN) (*Altitude 750m; 51km west of Homs, 65km southeast of Tartous; open 09.00–16.00 winter, 09.00–18.00 summer daily; S£150 entry fee; allow at least 2hrs for the actual visit; simple café/restaurant inside offering good light lunches and snacks, with pleasant outdoor seating on the first floor terrace; adequate WC facilities within the castle just by the stables, manned and therefore a small tip of S£10–25 expected; bring a torch for the darker recesses*) Signposts from the Homs–Tartous highway clearly mark it as 'Husn Citadel', and it takes only about 15 minutes to reach from the turn-off, climbing steeply through a series of villages and orchards. Microbuses run regularly from Homs and take about an hour. The drive from Hama takes about one hour 45 minutes, and from Damascus around two hours. You can drive straight from Palmyra, skirting Homs, in two hours 30 minutes.

A visit to this, the most magnificent and perfectly preserved Crusader castle in the world, should be done either early or late in the day to avoid the large numbers of day trippers and school children in coaches from Hama, Lattakia or even Lebanon, who will pour in from 11.00 onwards, have lunch here, and be gone again by 15.00. Your best option therefore is to stay in a hotel as close as possible to the Krak, such as Al-Wadi in the valley directly below it. As to the season, Krak is at its busiest in April, partly because of the Easter holidays and the national

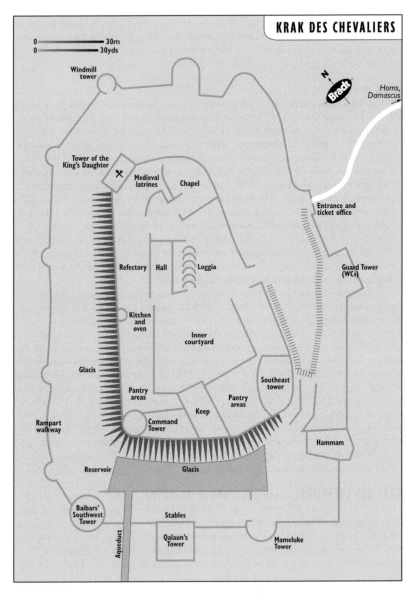

0 ⟍———⟍ 30m
0 ⟍———⟍ 30yds

Windmill
tower

N

Bradt

Homs,
Damascus

Tower of the
King's Daughter

Medieval
latrines

Chapel

Entrance and
ticket office

Refectory Hall Loggia

Guard Tower
(WCs)

Kitchen
and
oven

Inner
courtyard

Glacis

Southeast
tower

Pantry
areas

Pantry
areas

Keep

Rampart
walkway

Command
Tower

Hammam

Reservoir

Glacis

Baibars'
Southwest
Tower

Stables

Aqueduct

Qalaun's
Tower

Mameluke
Tower

holiday of 17 April, and partly because the climate is at its best then, with temperatures around 20–24°C with only an occasional rain shower. For this reason most Europeans choose to come in the March to May period, when the spring flowers and local greenery are at their most attractive, too. The name Krak is thought to be a medieval French corruption of the Syriac word for fortress. Another theory is that it derives from the castle's original name 'Husn Al-Akrad', Castle of the Kurds.

Your first sight of Krak des Chevaliers is important and can heavily colour your response. The village of Al-Husn has encroached badly, so that all views from below are marred by ugly modern building work directly underneath it. The entire castle used to be lived in by villagers, and the French excavators evacuated them before work began. Many of those displaced of course have since grown wealthy on the tourism the Krak brings, and have thus delighted in building their houses as close as possible to their old home. It is to be hoped that the Syrian authorities exert their control over this kind of unplanned development in future to prevent further visual pollution. Undoubtedly the best vantage point from which to admire the Krak is from above, something you can achieve from Al-Kala'a Restaurant built a little out of the village on a prominent hill to the west, or by approaching on the road along the crest of hills from the west, so that your first sight of it is crowning in all its perfection the summit of the hill with no other intrusions.

The castle you see today is essentially unchanged from the 12th –13th centuries, an amazing testament to its strength and durability. Its defences were never breached and it was never taken except by trickery. In its heyday Krak had a garrison of 2,000 men, but by the end of the 13th century it and Marqab (by then the only other important fortress in the area still in Crusader hands) could together muster only 300 knights.

In 1271 the Mameluke Sultan Baibars lead an Egyptian army and contingents from three local rulers and laid the last and final siege. After nearly a month of attacking Krak's defences, he still could not break through. Then a letter arrived from the Crusader commander at Tripoli (Lebanon) advising there were no more reinforcements, so the knights should negotiate a surrender. Defeated by their own meagre numbers, they did so, and gave up Krak to the Mamelukes under offer of safe conduct. On reaching Tripoli they learnt that the letter had been a forgery. After 160 years of resistance to force, the castle was taken by trickery.

From this vantage point you can best appreciate the two distinct lines of fortifications: the outer wall protected by round towers, and the inner ring wall which so tightly hugs the central keep that in the south it is actually joined to it. At the base of the inner wall is the massive reservoir, fed by the beautiful arched aqueduct that runs in through the upper walls from the western hills above. This smooth slanting base, known as a glacis or talus, was built to prevent scaling of its slippery surface and to expose attackers to fire while they attempted to climb it, but it also gave extra strength to the massive wall of the keep above it, an especially important aspect in this earthquake-prone area. Two severe earthquakes happened here in 1157 and 1170, and the glacis was added as a refinement in the late 12th and early 13th centuries by the independent military order of the Knights Hospitallers, also known as the Knights of St John, who occupied the castle from 1144 to 1271.

🏠 Where to stay

🏠 **Al-Wadi** (c50 rooms) ☏ 730456; ƒ 730399. Well located in the valley below Krak and close to St George's Monastery, this hotel is constantly being expanded and renovated. Rooms on the 4th and 5th floors are the best and most recently renovated, but all rooms are spacious with high ceilings, balconies, TV and bathrooms. It rates as a 4-star with a good restaurant, pool and spacious terrace areas. It is owned by a priest turned business magnate.

US$72/60 dbl/sgl.

🏠 **Francis** (c50 suites) ☏ 730946; www.francishotel.net. Catering for Saudis and Gulf Arabs who pack the place in July and August, this is a newly completed apartment hotel on a hillside a few kilometres from Krak, with no view of the castle itself, but a pleasant mountain outlook. There is a large pool, bar and restaurant. US$95/75 dbl/sgl.

✗ Where to eat

✗ **Al-Kala'a** Recently opened and in the best location outside the village, overlooking the Krak from above with panoramic views. Reached by following the road that runs immediately round the foot of the Krak walls, then climbing up past the aqueduct to the restaurant on the right. Coach tours have now discovered it, so go early or late to avoid congestion. Simple menu with chicken and mezze but clean.

The Hospitallers who, as the name suggests, founded their order in 1070 originally to shelter pilgrims arriving in Jerusalem in Christian hostels, gradually extended their role to the protection of all Crusader Christians in the East and became militarised. Krak des Chevaliers had been passed to them in 1144 by Raymond II, Count of Tripoli, in recognition of the fact that the Crusader presence was under threat and its resources needed bolstering to face the growing strength of the Muslim forces. There were 2,000 Hospitallers here at their peak, and no fewer than three local villages were taken over to provide food for them and their horses. They set about a massive programme of enhancements and expansions to the castle, the result of which is what we see today, what T E Lawrence described as: 'perhaps the best preserved and most wholly admirable castle in the world'. In its imaginative use of defences, making the best possible use of the natural lie of the land, the end result gives an initial impression of great symmetry, yet closer inspection shows there is no rigid ground plan underlying it. It was one of the very few castles to resist an onslaught from Saladin in 1183.

The other military Christian order of the east was the Knights Templar, founded in 1119, often bitter rivals of the Hospitallers, and certainly not as skilled in their castle building, but having a superb administrative ability in addition to their military discipline. Their name was derived from the Temple of Solomon, where the King of Jerusalem was thought to have given them special rooms. Their leanings towards obscure oriental practices and heresies have been revealed now through Dan Brown's *Da Vinci Code*, and at the time lent them enormous recruiting appeal. The Hospitallers were more conservative in their traditions. T E Lawrence comments on how these military orders were ideally suited to the work of protecting Crusader interests in the east:

> The members were celibate, and so, easy to control, and without private interests: they had no heirs to search after and no domain to preserve intact ... Most important of all, perhaps, the orders were very rich, not only in the precarious possession of one half of the most fertile land of Palestine, but in property in Europe.

In addition to this their military commanders were skilful and capable, and they were able to draw on endless supplies of 'the finest chivalry in Europe'. The Cistercian monks' ideal life of simplicity, purity and self-denial combined with aggressive military discipline resulted in the most potent Christian force of the age, and these military orders became the storm-troopers of the Church. The sworn allegiance of both orders was directly to the Pope.

Visiting the castle A modern bridge today replaces the original drawbridge which probably existed at the main entrance to the castle, in through a square Crusader tower. Notice the long Arabic inscription on the tower commemorating the restoration work carried out by Baibars in 1271. Though the castle did not fall to him by force, his attacks had nevertheless caused considerable damage to the walls, through use of catapult-like war engines called mangonels which could hurl stones weighing up to 270kg. The two large rectangular towers to the left of the entrance are of Mameluke construction. The ticket office is just inside the castle across the bridge and you have to first run the gauntlet of the irritatingly persistent touts selling postcards and booklets.

Once inside, the magnificent entry ramp zigzags up into the inner enceinte, its long dark vaulted passage climbing steadily in low steps to enable horses riding two abreast to grip better on the ascent. The contrast between the glaring sunlight outside and the darkness within must have been quite an adjustment for both horse and rider. There is only one opening in the roof which allowed in light, located at the halfway point, and this was also designed as a *machicoulis* for raining down upon any intruder such delights as hot oil and stones. The long chamber to the left on the way up was almost certainly used for stabling. It now has basic WC facilities built incongruously into the side walls.

By the bend of the zigzag, a passage leads out into the area between the two walls, which can be explored later. For now it is preferable to continue up the ramp to reach the main gateway with its portcullis and machicoulis, and you now enter the open space of the inner castle, which is rather confusingly irregular with large flights of steps leading up onto various terraces.

There is no particularly recommended order here in which to conduct your tour, so it is best simply to wander and explore at leisure. The first building that may catch your eye is the beautiful Gothic colonnaded hall opposite, fronted with a splendid arcaded cloister-like loggia of great elegance. Three tombs were discovered in this loggia with skeletons, swords, shields and other weapons. Carved in Latin on the window lintel to the extreme right is an inscription that reads: 'Grace, wisdom and beauty you may enjoy but beware pride which alone can tarnish all the rest.'

Behind the loggia is the rather gloomy great hall or refectory with a cradle-vaulted ceiling, and behind that again is an even darker room, thought to be the kitchen, with a well and bread oven. In the far right-hand corner of this dark area, where a torch will be helpful, is a gigantic olive press set in its own vast dedicated room the size of a two-storey house. Going further still through the pillared rooms which formed the castle's giant pantry, you will find remnants of colossal pottery jars for storage. The stocks here in Crusader times were said to be enough to last five years. Right at the very back of the storage area you can, with the aid of a torch, follow a hidden passageway running along the edge of the inner walls that finally emerges back at the massive oven. Inside the passageway is a water channel, part of the castle's elaborate water conservation system.

From the oven you can now head in the other direction into an enormous open-plan room that bends for 120m in a great loop round to the chapel on the other side of the castle. About halfway along this room are 12 latrines, elegantly laid out, euphemistically labelled 'restrooms' in Arabic. At the far end of this huge room you come now to the chapel, built in Romanesque 12th-century style, converted to a mosque by the Mamelukes under Baibars in 1271 through the addition of the *minbar* (pulpit) and the three *mihrab* niches to indicate the direction of prayer towards Mecca. It is now labelled 'Prayer Hall'.

A wide flight of steps from near the chapel leads up onto the upper court, where, a little to the left, the tower called the King's Daughter Tower, serves as an attractive little café/restaurant selling books, souvenirs and drinks, even Lebanese wine and 'arak. Tables and chairs are laid out on the wide terrace too, giving a wonderful setting from which to admire the inner defences of the keep. There are usable WCs here. Head over now to the southern area of the upper court, an area where the *donjon* is housed between two towers. T E Lawrence records at the time of his visit that the provincial governor, his harem and his *diwan* (administrative staff) were in residence here.

Over on the southwest corner, the third separate tower above the glacis ramp is labelled 'Command Tower' and is well worth the ascent by the stone spiral staircase to the most elegantly decorated room in the castle, clearly the castle commander's quarters, with a rosette frieze, fine vaulted ceiling and beautiful Gothic window seats. The stairs continue on to the top, the highest point of the castle. The views from here are stunning, over towards St George's Monastery and the Al-Wadi Hotel opposite. On clear days even the white keep of Safita Castle to the northwest and the sea to the west can be seen. From here too you can appreciate the reasons for the Krak's location, as it guarded and controlled the exit from the rich Beqaa valley in modern Lebanon, and the Homs Gap or route between the sea and the interior. As such it was also a defensive location against the threat from as far afield as Damascus and Aleppo, or even Cairo and Mosul. After the Mameluke conquest, with the Crusaders in decline and no longer a threat, the castle lost its strategic importance and simply degenerated into a shell to house the 500 'Alawis who lived here till the French excavators moved them out into the modern village below so that restoration work could begin.

Retrace your steps now back out through the vaulted entrance passage, and this time at the bend in the zigzag, walk out into the open space between the curtain walls. Here you are greeted by the massive reservoir, 72m long, fed by the aqueduct and a series of other ducts to channel in rainwater, and by the domes of the *hammams* built by the Mamelukes, set below ground level but reachable by precarious steps. The castle had an elaborate water conservation system, with rainwater collecting in 21 reservoirs, the deepest of which was 8m. The aqueduct was fed by a nearby spring. Look up from the reservoir at the colossal glacis or talus which supports the three towers of the inner walls and protects the residential quarters of the *donjon*, and also up at the pair of headless stone lions above the tower gateway from which you emerged, possible symbols of Richard the Lionheart.

Towards the outer walls you now enter an enormous dark hall, 60m long, the main stables of the castle, still with tethering irons in the walls. From the centre of the stables a huge central square tower juts out, known as Qalaun's Tower, with a massive central pillar and vaulted ceiling. The inscription and heraldic arms date it to 1285, when Qalaun restored it. Notice the extremely long arrow slits. A secret door was said to lead from here to the outside of the castle.

Emerging from the far end of the stables, be sure to climb up onto the crenulated rampart walkway which leads you now all along the entire magnificent circuit of the walls. The tower at the extreme northwest corner is called the Windmill Tower. Windmills were invented in 634 in the Middle East for a Persian caliph for grinding corn and drawing up water for irrigation. They had six or 12 sails covered in palm fronds or fabric. It was another 500 years before the first windmill was seen in Europe. You then pass a later mosque addition and complete the circuit back to the entry ramp from which you began. Notice as you walk round the ramparts the machicolation boxes overhanging the walls, which T E Lawrence comments resemble French latrines, and from which stones or other missiles could have been dropped onto the enemy below as he attempted to scale the walls. During its relatively brief history Krak survived two major Muslim challenges, the first by Nur Ad-Din, then the Emir of Aleppo, whose forces were defeated at the foot of the castle by strong Christian reinforcements sent from Antioch and Tripoli on the coast in 1163; the second by Saladin, who stopped just briefly for a trial one-day siege in 1188 soon after he defeated the kingdom of Jerusalem at the Battle of Hittin.

ST GEORGE'S MONASTERY دير مار جرجس (*Open 09.00–18.00 daily; no entry fee; 1km from Al-Wadi Hotel; basic WC facilities outside the entrance in the car park*) Sitting in the valley below Krak is the 6th-century Greek Orthodox Monastery of St George, well worth a short detour to see the different eras of the monastery building from the 6th century, to the working monastery of today with a handful of monks left, bearded and black-robed, and very friendly and welcoming.

The atmosphere is pleasantly peaceful and contemplative and the courtyards have been lovingly enhanced with potted trees and cacti. You will be shown round the various levels, all of which have been beautifully and carefully restored. The spacious so-called New Church dates to 1857 and is to the right as you enter the courtyard. The beautiful ebony iconostasis is 300 years old and was carved in Aleppo. Among the many icons are some depicting George slaying the dragon.

The donation box is prominently displayed in the New Church. You will then be led across the courtyard to the smaller Old Church, at a lower level and dating to the 13th century. It too has a beautiful iconostasis with more icons of St George. Note the fine huge tin font, still apparently in use. From here steps lead down to the lowest level of all, thought to be the remnants of the original 6th-century monastery, small and claustrophobic. These lower levels have been turned into a museum with hi-tech lighting and even recordings of chanting music. Notice the solid basalt stone door that still swivels on its hinges.

Look out for the beautiful 300-year-old ebony iconostasis carved in Aleppo, and the fine icon to the right of St George and the Dragon. In the oldest church of all, which will be unlocked for you, the solid basalt stone door is still in use and there is a deep well. The monks plan to turn these lower levels into a museum and the recorded chanting music is already in place.

HUSN SULEYMAN حصن سليمان (*Unfenced site, no entry fee; no facilities; bring a picnic; allow 90mins for the drive from Krak each way, and 1hr on site; if you do not have your own transport Husn Suleyman can also be reached by hiring a minibus or taxi from Safita, 25km away*) A 90-minute drive up into the hills north of Krak lies this unusual and gigantic temple enclosure, used for pagan rituals to the god Baal from 2000BC, then Zeus till the 4th century AD after which Christianity took hold. The name, which means Fortress of Suleyman, is very misleading, for it was always a temple, never a fortress, and had nothing to do with Suleyman.

From Krak the best way to reach Husn Suleyman is to head north towards Masyaf. The first village is called Al-Nasirah. The pretty rural road climbs up past an extraordinary thick clump of forest. The next village is Baidar Ar-Rafii'. You pass a large church all by itself called the Church of the Lady of the Mountain. The hillsides are heavily treed with apples and pomegranates. Follow the turn left to Masyaf and Hama. The drive is attractive with poplar trees and deciduous trees in valleys, very colourful in autumn, and passes lots of churches in villages. You come next to a major junction marked right 15km to Masyaf, and you take instead the left towards Tartous and Dreikish. The road climbs up through very beautiful thickly treed slopes to the village of Ar-Rasafe at the top. Your landmark is the three television masts on a hilltop in the distance, as the site of Husn Suleyman lies immediately below those to the right. It is signposted once you are virtually there anyway. The actual villages of Dreikish and Mashta Al-Helu, both famous for their mineral water, offer nothing special to the Western visitor, except a few restaurants and a four-star hotel, Mashta Al-Helu Resort, very much geared to wealthy Gulf Arabs spending the hot summer months here.

The colossal temple as it is today is largely early Roman (1st century AD), roughly contemporary with Baalbek in Lebanon of which it is reminiscent in its scale. There is nothing else like it in Syria. The reason for its remote location here high in the mountains, nestling in a natural rocky amphitheatre, is far from clear. It is the sheer scale of the site, the temple compound measuring 134m by 85m, that is most impressive, some of the massive blocks of grey stone over 10m long. In the centre of the compound is a small *cella*, its blocks jumbled and collapsed from earthquakes. The enclosure had four entrance gateways, the most impressive to the north. On the undersides of the monolithic lintel blocks of each entrance is a carved eagle with wings outstretched, and on the lintels of the east and west lintels

Most English people are more than a little surprised to learn that George, their patron saint, is buried in southern Syria, in a church at Ezraa near Bosra (see page 217). What on earth was St George doing slaying his dragon here? George himself would almost certainly never have heard of England. He was probably a soldier, and was martyred at Diospolis (now central Israel) CAD30, and after his death, myths and legends grew up around his deeds throughout Palestine and Syria and later in Europe. Muslims call him 'Our Lord Al-Khidr'. In England he was first mentioned by the Venerable Bede in the 8th century and Richard I placed himself and his Crusader knights under the protection of George in 1191. In Shakespeare's *Henry V*, at the Battle of Agincourt, Henry invokes George as the patron saint of the English army. He did not become patron saint of England until the 14th century when Edward III made him patron of the Order of the Garter, and the Pope ratified him as Protector of the Kingdom of England. The dragon myth came to England for the first time in the 15th century when it was translated and published by William Caxton, the English printer, in a book called *The Golden Legend*. In the story the citizens of a country were terrified of a fire-breathing dragon, and tried to appease it by offering the king's daughter as a sacrifice. George appeared and fought the dragon, telling the citizens he would kill it if they accepted Christianity. The king agreed and George baptised 15,000 men. He took no reward, but asked the king to maintain the churches in his country and to show mercy to the poor.

there are additionally a pair of winged victory figures. Eagles fit well in this landscape and the eagle has always been a symbol of power from above. The whole site has a very pagan feel to it. Archaeological work is due to start here soon.

Across the road, scattered among a ploughed orchard are the remains of a monastery, originally thought to have been another temple, later adapted for use as a Christian basilica and convent. The portico is well preserved with a winged eagle above the lintel. A bit of modern habitation, known as 'Ain Al-Dhahab, encroaches on the setting below the temple enclosure, but nothing intrudes into the internal space itself, which thus retains its special atmosphere. The altitude means it can be very cold and windy up here in the winter and spring months, and sheltered picnic spots are hard to find in the huge open space.

MASYAF CASTLE قلعة مصياف (*40km west of Hama, 45km east of Baniyas; erratic hours according to the guardian's movements, but in theory daily 09.00–16.00 winter, 09.00–18.00 summer, best chance of entry mornings before 13.00; S£75 entry fee; allow 30mins*) From Husn Suleyman it now takes 30 minutes to descend back to the main junction between Tartous to the left and Masyaf to the right, where this time you fork towards Masyaf. As you approach the town the sandy-coloured stone castle and its distinctive towers rise to the left of the road perched on a rocky crag, though the castle looks at its best as you approach from Hama, 40km to the west. Masyaf is the largest and best preserved of the castles of the Assassins, an esoteric Shi'a Isma'ili sect of Islam that thrived here in the 12th century, and about whom many rumours spread. The central tenet in the Isma'ili faith is their devotion to the 8th-century leader Isma'il, son of the sixth Shi'ite Imam, Ja'far As-Sadiq. Most of the 18,000 population of the village is still Isma'ili, and the castle has been since 2000 the beneficiary of an extensive restoration programme funded by the Aga Khan, himself an Isma'ili.

The Assassins quickly expanded from their stronghold at Alamut and captured the hill fort of Masyaf in 1140, followed by a string of others in the area such as Al-Kahf, Qadmous and Al-'Ullaqah. At their height there were ten, and Qadmous was the principal headquarters. All traces of Qadmous Castle were removed in the 19th century, and today apart from Masyaf and Al-Kahf, the only ones that survive, albeit in a heavily ruinous state, are Abu Qubeis and Maniqa. The castle stayed under the control of the Assassins till it surrendered in 1260 to the Mongols. In later centuries under the Ottomans it continued to play a military role, till in 1816 the eccentric English aristocrat Lady Hester Stanhope who was living in Lebanon at that time, persuaded the Ottoman governor of Tripoli to storm and destroy it with the aim of freeing a French captain who was being held there. The tomb of the Old Master here, Rashid Ad-Din Sinan, can be visited in a small whitewashed shrine among some trees on the summit of a ridge next to the castle.

THE ASSASSINS

Founded in 1090 at the stronghold of Alamut south of the Caspian Sea, the Assassins were controlled by a grand master, Hassan As-Sabah, known as the Old Man (Shaikh) of the Mountains. The name Assassins comes from a corruption of the Arabic 'Hashish', meaning grass, as the 'Hashashoun' were those who took hashish and the name was given to them because their adherents were said to be drugged with hashish and then sent to conduct murders of specific prominent opponents. Our word 'assassin' comes from this.

The group inspired terror out of all proportion to their small numbers and territory because they slayed their victims in public, often in mosques on a Friday. Typically they would approach in disguise, using a dagger rather than poison, bows or other weapons that would allow them to escape. They never committed suicide, preferring to be killed by their captors. Their aim with these assassinations was to destroy the power of the 'Abbasid caliphate which had been persecuting them as a Shi'ite minority, by murdering its most powerful members, most of whom were Sunni Muslims. Christians were never targets, and the first victim was the famous Seljuk vizir Nizam Al-Mulk in 1097. Saladin, who sought to promote Sunni orthodoxy by ridding the country of Shi'ite influence, had several threats made against him by them, in one of which the Old Man (Grand Master of the time) himself apparently crept into Saladin's tent at night in the heart of his camp, and left a poisoned cake on his chest as he slept, with a note saying 'You are now in our power.' In retaliation Saladin besieged their stronghold at Masyaf, but later relented and withdrew after negotiations and attempted to maintain good relations with the sect.

The power of the Assassins was destroyed by the Mongol warlord Hulagu in 1256 when the library at Alamut was burnt down. The only accounts of their practices therefore stem from chroniclers of the time. Marco Polo has given us a description from when he passed through the area in the 13th century, saying how the youths aged up to 20 would be brought into a beautiful garden by the grand master, having first drunk the potion of hashish. When they woke they thought themselves in paradise, so if he wanted a prince or ruler killed, he would instruct the youth to carry it out, promising him a return to such paradise afterwards, saying: 'Go thou and slay so and so; and when thou returnest my Angels shall bear thee to Paradise.'

Some political commentators today make comparisons between the Assassin movement and Al-Qa'ida, because of the similar tactics of terror, political assassination, and the cult-like mysticism around Osama Bin Laden. Al-Qa'ida is also a secret society, with its leaders supposedly concealed in mountain hideouts. Martyrdom is also a key element of Al-Qa'ida's tactics. Unlike Al-Qa'ida however, the Assassins targeted very specific individuals, never innocent bystanders.

The approach today by foot is along a rocky ledge below it, now with a simple local café spread out, tables placed overlooking the valley, with some tables even tucked into caves in the castle rock base, out of the wind. Continue past the café to reach the fine entrance doorway, with its impressive rock steps. Inside is a central keep protected by its high outer walls and square bastions. The mixed masonry of the construction, from Roman crafted stones to rubble-like infill, reflects the eclectic origins of the fortification which was in use since Hellenistic times as a defensive post. Restoration work is making more to see inside, out of the rubble that was left after Lady Hester's instructions were so thoroughly carried out, and torches are needed for the underground galleries.

DEIR AS-SALEEB دير الصليب (*Open site no entry fee; allow 30mins*) Leaving Masyaf en route to Hama, look out for the signpost off to the right in English and Arabic to Deir As-Saleeb, where an architecturally simple but impressive 6th-century Byzantine church warrants a brief detour. The approach road from the turn-off winds up 3–4km into the low hills, with good views towards the mountains beyond. The attractive church, basilica in plan but almost square in shape, sits just 20m off to the left of the road before the village of Deir As-Saleeb itself, so the setting is pleasantly rural and contemplative in its own undisturbed fig grove. The curve of the apse protrudes beyond the rear wall of the building, and the windows are larger and bolder than in earlier churches of northern Syria. The colour of the stone is very soft and honeyed especially at sunset, and the carved shapes of the arches are pleasingly aesthetic. The name means 'Monastery of the Cross', from the carved crosses which are the only decorative features in the stone work. A beautiful cruciform font cut out of one huge piece of white marble can be seen on the ground of the baptistery on the southern side of the narthex.

To the south of the church stands a fine stone mausoleum with three sarcophagi inside presumably of senior bishops, and carved crosses inside circle-like medallions. To the north is a deep well with a shaped slab of rock over it and two tiny hollowed-out basins and one large basin cut from the rock. Two kilometres off to the southeast, reachable only by foot, is another more ruined Byzantine church.

From here it is about 35km west to Hama (*see Chapter 5*).

Walnut

9

The Hawran and the Jebel Druze
حوران وجبل الدروز

When danger approaches, sing to it.

Though it is difficult to credit today, with the dry bleak landscapes that prevail south of Damascus, in Roman times this whole area, known loosely as the Hawran, was a major agricultural centre and one of the great granaries of the empire. Important trade routes also passed through from the Nabatean centres further south like Petra, and brought even more prosperity. Under the Romans irrigation schemes were developed and new crops introduced to develop the agricultural potential of the area.

When the Roman Empire adopted Christianity the area continued to flourish, with many important churches, cathedrals and bishoprics established. Under the Muslim Arab expansion northwards out of the Arabian Peninsula in the 7th century, however, instability and conflict began to set in and the region found itself caught in the crossfire between rival dynasties of the Shi'a Fatimids based in Cairo and the Sunni 'Abbasids in Baghdad, and then later between Muslims and Crusaders. Bosra, the main city of the Hawran, was attacked twice by the Crusader knights, both times unsuccessfully.

In the 18th and 19th centuries the area was overrun by large numbers of Druze (see box pages 218–19), an extreme offshoot of the Shi'ite Isma'ili sect regarded as heretical by both Sunni and Shi'ite sects, migrating out of Mt Lebanon after their bloody conflicts with the Christian Maronites. As a result the mountains in Syria's southeast corner became known as Jebel Druze (Druze Mountain), and the area is still largely populated by Druze today.

The Hawran and indeed much of western Syria has been highly volcanic in recent geological times, with plate movements deep in the earth causing volcanoes and earthquakes. The volcanic massif of the Jebel Druze rises to 1,800m and it is from here that the black basalt rock flowed for huge distances into the countryside all around, then to be used in the distinctive black buildings of Bosra and in the black stripes so favoured by the Mamelukes, alternating with the white limestone blocks, a style known as *ablaq*.

QUNEITRA القنيطرة (THE GOLAN HEIGHTS)

A visit to the highly sensitive border zone of Quneitra (*some 50km southwest of Damascus*) requires a special pass. Getting hold of the pass is a rather tedious process which will take at least an hour out of your day. First you have to a catch a taxi out of the centre of Damascus to the department of the Ministry of the Interior that deals with passes for foreigners, which lies in a northwest suburb of Damascus and looks from the outside just like a residential detached house. The taxi driver will help you pinpoint it exactly. Take your passport with you and hand it in at the little kiosk in front of the building. A soldier will then be dispatched with it into

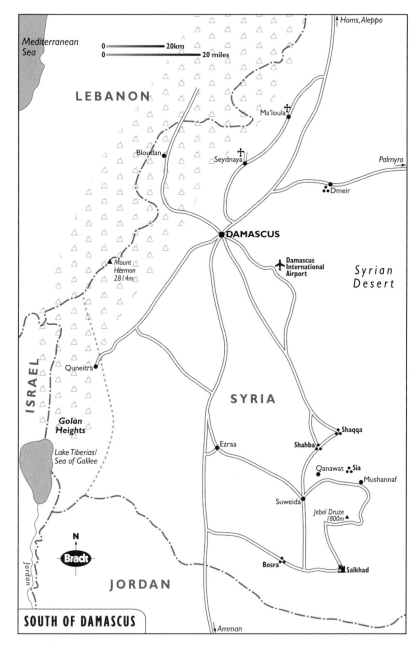

the building, while you wait outside on the pavement for about 15 minutes, till he returns. You have to specify in advance whether you want the permit to be valid for today or tomorrow. It is generally best to organise it for the next day, so that you can incorporate your visit into an itinerary that continues south via a stop at Ezraa (see page 217) to explore the Hawran region of Bosra and the Jebel Druze, by spending two nights at Bosra. Only those with a particular political interest will probably bother to go through the process, but if you have the time, it will certainly make an unforgettable impression.

The interest of visiting Quneitra lies in the fact that it is the only part of the Golan Heights that is still under Syrian control. The Golan, east and north of the Sea of Galilee (Lake Tiberias), is the part of Syria that was lost to Israel in the 1967 Six Day War. In 1973 Egypt and Syria launched an attack on Israel in an attempt to regain the territory they had lost in the 1967 war. Fighting continued sporadically in the Golan for months but with no decisive result and in the end a UN-brokered peace was reached under the auspices of Henry Kissinger, then US Secretary of State, and the current UN buffer zone was established. Before that deal was reached, however, Quneitra itself was razed to the ground by Israeli bulldozers in a gratuitous act of violence. The rest of the Golan is important to Israel as the melt waters from the snow-covered mountains here feed Israel's largest reservoir, Lake Tiberias. Also from the highest points Damascus itself is in view and Syria used to launch bomb attacks from here down onto northern Israel from 1948 to 1967. Israel lost no time in establishing Jewish settlements on the Heights, and today the Golan is largely forgotten by the international community.

Syria's position has remained unchanged since 1967, in insisting on Israeli withdrawal in line with Resolution 242 of the UN Security Council of the same year. It is the only neighbouring country that has not arrived at some sort of peace agreement with the Israelis. The Sinai peninsula and the Gaza Strip have been returned to Egypt and Palestine respectively, as they are of no use to Israel, being essentially barren waterless areas with no natural resources. The West Bank however has major underground aquifers and is therefore important, like the Golan, to Israel's considerable water needs, while east Jerusalem is important for its political significance. Israel will require massive international pressure especially from the USA ever to consider surrendering these areas which it took in the 1967 Six Day War.

Some 15,000 Syrians still live under Israeli occupation in the Golan, most of them Druze. Only 400 have been allowed to return to Syria. Many families were bisected by the new border, forced to communicate by megaphone across the wire fencing. Since the Druze faith expressly forbids intermarriage, very occasionally and in exceptional circumstances, the border is opened briefly to allow Druze brides to cross over and marry Druze grooms. Some 15,000 Israeli settlers now live here too, their numbers expanding faster than the Druze.

Hafez Al-Assad took the decision not to rebuild Quneitra, though this had been the original intention, but to leave it as a showpiece exactly as it was left by the Israeli army, a powerful testimony to Israeli aggression. Bashar's position on the Golan seems to be the same as his father's thus far. In recent years Israeli archaeologists have been engaged in trying to prove that the Golan was part of biblical Israel back in the Iron Age, in order to substantiate their inalienable right to be there and that Arab settlers only appeared in the Hellenistic age two thousand years later. Arab scholars, however, insist that the Israelis are tampering with the evidence and using it selectively, and claim in turn that Arabs of Semitic origin, the Amorites, lived here in the 3rd millennium BC. For a closer look at the opposing viewpoints see the following two websites: www.golan-syria.org and www.golan.org.il.

Heading out of Damascus on the Mezzeh road from Umawiyeen Square, the drive to Quneitra takes about 90 minutes. Take the underpass under the square towards Mezzeh and follow the signs from there all the way. There is a checkpoint some 30km before Quneitra where you have to be registered and show your Quneitra pass and passport. At this checkpoint itself there are UN personnel after the town of Khan Arbel, then at the final Quneitra checkpoint you show the pass and your passport again and a military escort soldier will join you in the car. You then drive round the network of roads all through the utterly flattened remains of

Quneitra. Recognisable among the rubble are an orthodox church tower, a mosque and a hospital, its black basalt stonework heavily pockmarked with gunfire. For a ghost town, it has a surprising number of military personnel around, mainly UN from Canada, Japan, Austria and Poland. The barbed-wire fence is the actual border and up on the hill beyond the fence sits an Israeli early warning station.

✖ **WHERE TO EAT** In the site itself there are good facilities with clean WCs in an unlikely but attractive cafeteria in the middle of the bulldozed rubble. It boasts an open fire in winter and is surprisingly welcoming. It seats about 50 people but is usually empty. Simple, cheap meals are served.

BOSRA بصرى الشام *Telephone code 015*

(140km south of Damascus; population 15,000; allow 2hrs minimum)
On an ideal itinerary two nights should be spent in Bosra, so that one full day can be spent pottering at leisure round the very extensive black basalt Roman city, the second most important Roman city in Syria after Palmyra. The colour of the stone makes a striking contrast with the pale honey-coloured limestone of Palmyra, Bosra's rival to the north. Try to avoid if at all possible visiting in a day trip from Damascus, as that will give you only a partial feel of the place and inevitably be concentrated on the Roman theatre, Bosra's major monument. Acknowledged by UNESCO in 1980 as a World Heritage Site, it is probably the most perfectly preserved and intact Roman theatre in the world, made all the more dramatic in some ways by the blackness of its volcanic basalt stonework, and by the fact that it is actually concealed inside a 13th-century Ayyubid fortress. The Swiss traveller Burckhardt on his way to Petra in 1810 passed through and did not even realise there was a theatre inside. At first sight therefore, you understandably wonder where this much-vaunted theatre actually is, since it is not until having entered the fortress by crossing the drawbridge over its moat, and having climbed up inside the vaulted passageways, that you suddenly emerge into the sunlight to see the magnificent huge semicircular theatre below you.

Sitting high on this vantage point it is now a good time to digest some history. Originally a Bronze Age settlement, Bosra appears under the name of 'Busrana' in Egyptian archives of the 18th dynasty. After Alexander's death it fell within the dynasty of Seleucus, one of Alexander's generals. Later, the Nabateans, whose original capital was at Petra in Jordan, made Bosra the capital of their newly created Provincia Arabia, and it is from this time that most of the extant ruins of the city date. Emperor Trajan built a network of roads at this time linking Bosra to Damascus, Amman and Aqaba, so Bosra found itself at the heart of the trading crossroads here, as well as east to west between the Mediterranean and Mesopotamia. Over 5,000 legionnaires were stationed in the city and the grid network of streets was considerably expanded to accommodate the new garrisons and their administrative buildings. It remained an important imperial city and was declared a metropolis in the 3rd century AD by Philip the Arab, the locally born emperor from Shahba.

In Roman times this region, known as the Awranitis, modern-day Hawran, was far more fertile and considered one of Rome's main granaries, along with Egypt. After Christianity was adopted throughout the region under the later Roman Empire, Bosra remained an important centre as is testified by the size of the cathedral here, one of the largest in the Middle East. The Prophet Muhammad is thought to have visited in the course of one of his trading journeys for his rich merchant wife Khadija, before he had his first revelation aged 40. He is said to have spoken to a resident Christian monk called Bahira and to have discussed religious

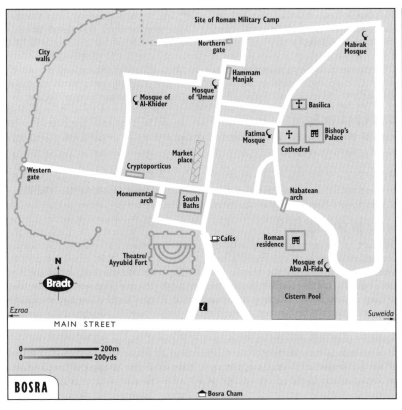

BOSRA

Scale: 0 — 200m / 0 — 200yds

Map labels: Site of Roman Military Camp; City walls; Northern gate; Mabrak Mosque; Hammam Manjak; Mosque of 'Umar; Mosque of Al-Khider; Basilica; Fatima Mosque; Cathedral; Bishop's Palace; Market place; Cryptoporticus; Western gate; Monumental arch; South Baths; Nabatean arch; Cafés; Roman residence; Theatre/Ayyubid Fort; Mosque of Abu Al-Fida; Cistern Pool; N; Bradt; Ezraa; Suweida; MAIN STREET; Bosra Cham

issues with him. The chief Arab Christian tribe in the Bosra region were the Ghassanids, who adopted the Monophysite version of Christianity, thus making them very unpopular with Constantinople (see box page 170 on *Early divisions of the Church*). These Arab Christians emigrated in 250 from Maarib in the Yemen to the Hawran. Their capital was at Jabiyah in the Golan Heights, and by the 6th century the Ghassanid kingdom covered much of Syria, Palestine, Jordan and the northern Hijaz as far as Medina. It remained a Byzantine vassal state till the Muslims overthrew it in the 7th century. Bosra's location on the major trade route into Syria from the Arabian Desert meaning it was the first Byzantine city the Arabs conquered in their surge outwards from the Arabian Peninsula in 632. Its fortunes declined after the 7th century, and, lying as it did on the fringes of Palestine, it was occasionally sucked into Crusader battles and was attacked twice in 1147 and 1151 by Frankish knights who attempted unsuccessfully to take control of the Hawran from Saladin's dynasty of the Ayyubids.

 WHERE TO STAY AND EAT Bosra offers the only suitable tourist accommodation in the region and neither Suweida nor Shahba have any suitable hotels or restaurants, so come prepared to picnic if you are not staying in Bosra.

Bosra Cham Hotel (c50 rooms) ↘ 790881; f 790996; www.chamhotels.com. An attractive and well-situated hotel about 10mins' walk from the site, the smallest in the Cham chain, with views and balconies over gardens towards the theatre. Swimming pool May–Oct. Restaurant serving alcohol. A few shops. No internet facilities for guests. *US$120/100 dbl/sgl.*

✖ La Citadelle Within the Bosra Cham Hotel is the most upmarket and cleanest restaurant and certainly the only one with alcohol.

🛏 Basic sleeping is also possible in the dormitory 'hostel' within the theatre, above the café on the top floor.

The square in front of the theatre has a number of simple restaurants, most with tables outside, most without alcohol. There is also a simple restaurant/café inside the theatre and basic WC facilities both inside and outside the fortress/theatre.

OTHER PRACTICALITIES

Tourist office There is a new tourist office (*open 09.00–14.30 except Fri*) on the only main road through town.

Bank There is a Commercial Bank of Syria booth for exchanging money near the entrance to Bosra theatre/fortress (*open 09.30–14.00 and 16.00–19.00*). The Bosra Cham Palace Hotel will also change money.

WHAT TO SEE AND DO

Theatre (*S£150 entry fee; only theatre building requires a ticket, the rest of the site is open to stroll round any time; theatre open 09.00–16.00 winter, 09.00–18.00 summer daily*) The open square in front of the theatre is alive with cafés and souvenir shops and you are generally rather pestered in the approach to the theatre entrance by young men selling postcards and wanting to be your guide. Once inside, having crossed the moat on the drawbridge and entered through the massively fortified gateway, an arrowed itinerary points you up the stone steps to emerge from the maze of stairs and corridors into the almost blinding sunlight at the top of the theatre.

The seating capacity was 15,000 spread over 37 rows with room for a further 2,000–3,000 spectators standing, putting it in the same size category as Leptis Magna in Libya which could accommodate 16,000. The Roman theatre at Aspendus in southern Turkey, with which it is also directly comparable, is slightly larger, designed to seat 20,000, though of course at festival times, double that number manage to squeeze in, making it 40,000 at Aspendus and 30,000 at Bosra. The amazing state of preservation is partly accounted for by the fact that the theatre's interior was largely filled with sand blown in by the wind over the centuries. It took some 20 years to clear, most of the work taking place between 1947 and 1970. The theatre also owes its exceptional condition to the fact that it was converted into an Ayyubid fort and thus maintained and repaired. The stage and top rows of seats have been the subject of major restoration work, and several of the columns of the stage building, known as *scenae frons,* are copies of the original ones, easily recognisable by their perfect condition compared with the rather worn and rough surfaces of the marble originals. This *scenae frons* would once have been decorated with statues and sculptured friezes, and from the stylistic details the theatre has been dated to the late 2nd century AD. Behind the stage are dressing rooms for the actors and passages where the actors waited for their turns. The original stage roof would have been wooden and the rest of the theatre would have had silk awnings pulled across to shield against the harsh sun. During the performances perfumed water used to be sprayed into the air to waft down over the audience and keep them refreshed.

The massive entry and exit passages on either side of the stage are rather graphically called *vomitoria,* as the audience spewed out of them. The acoustics, as in all Roman theatres, are superb, and actors did not even have to raise their voices to be heard on the top rows.

Behind the stage building are the Ayyubid rooms which served as the citadel's headquarters, including some elegant ground-floor rooms with pools which were thought to be the ruler and his wife's private quarters.

Festival Every two years in early September a large festival is held in Bosra which is well worth visiting. It lasts around 15 days and includes dancing, drama, music and singing.

Ayyubid Fort The Ayyubid fortification built round the original Roman theatre was constructed piecemeal between 1202 and 1251, but this was still not enough to withstand the Mongol onslaught in 1260. The Mamelukes then defeated the Mongols at the Battle of 'Ain Jalud, and although Baibars in 1261 repaired the damage inflicted by the Mongols, Bosra gradually lost importance as the caravan routes and with them the pilgrimage route to Mecca moved further west via Deraa into less troubled areas where their security was more assured. With the ensuing depopulation, the local agriculture was neglected and the entire region sank into oblivion.

There are two high towers and five subsidiary towers in total. From the highest point of the towers you can also look out over the extensive Roman town and see how much of it is still lived in by simple folk whose houses are often semi-incorporated into the ruins. At one point these inhabitants were mainly Druze but now they are mainly Sunni. A great deal of the modern housing has in fact been cleared in recent years, and as more and more is cleared, other aspects of the ancient town will no doubt emerge from underneath. Some of the reconstruction work on the site, following the clearing, has been a bit comic in places, with randomly matched columns re-erected at strange angles. A Syro-Italian archaeological mission has recently been conducting excavations in the northeast of the town, in the area of the Mosque of Mabrak, the Mosque of Fatima and the 'complex' of Bahira.

The earliest of the towers were Seljuk constructions of around 1089, but the majority were Ayyubid, built as a response to the Crusader threat. On the upper ramparts of the Ayyubid addition on a wide open roof area, an imaginative café has been established offering simple refreshments, and the whole roof area has been used as an open-air museum to display statues and carved blocks from the site, many of them rather crudely worked, an indication more of the difficulties of fine carving on the tough basalt rock than any inherently inferior artistic ability.

Folklore Museum Also in this part of the fortress in the southwest tower is a small folklore museum, under restoration in 2005, once housing a rather grotesque collection of stuffed birds – a particular favourite among Arabs – and mannequins dressed in traditional costumes doing traditional things with traditional utensils.

The Roman town To explore the rest of the Roman town you now need to take the alleyway running north from the theatre (to the right as you face the theatre entrance). In the 19th century thousands of Druze settled here after being forced to flee Lebanon during the 1840–60 Druze/Christian sectarian strife. The town also retains a considerable Greek Orthodox community, whose bishopric is now in nearby Suweida.

South baths The first complex you come to is the Roman baths with a T-shaped ground plan. Dated to the late 2nd or early 3rd century AD, the baths were recently renovated and you now enter into the huge domed octagonal changing room, *apodyterium*, then pass through into the cold room, *frigidarium*, from which you then pass into the hot areas, first the warm room, *tepidarium*, then the two hot steam rooms, *caldarium*, on either side. These facilities, which we associate with five-star hotels and health spas, were free and open to all, and most inhabitants would have used them on a daily basis.

Main Street Immediately north of the baths you come to the main street, decumanus, running east–west for nearly a full kilometre. Originally some 8m wide it would have had a grand colonnaded pavement, of which just a few columns, crowned with Ionic capitals, now survive. Looking to the west (left) you can see along it some 600m to the western gateway of the town, whereas to the east the view is shorter, just 200m or so, to where the so-called Nabatean archway stands, marking the entrance to the pre-Roman town.

Over the crossroads immediately to the left is the long thin Roman marketplace (20m by 70m), which makes an excellent football pitch much used by the local youth. It is known locally as Khan Ad-Dib, Caravanserai of Molasses.

Monumental arch Continuing west (left) along the decumanus you will come after c100m to a 13m-tall triple monumental arch, dating to the 3rd century and built to honour the III Cyrenaica Legion. A further 50m westwards just to the right of the decumanus, look out for the entrance down into an underground area (*cryptoporticus*), thought to have been used either for storage or for stabling, unearthed during excavations in 1968. The impressive construction is 106m long, 4.5m high and some 4m wide with 34 rectangular apertures in the south wall to allow light and air in, though today it is generally used as local rubbish tip, so not very fragrant or inviting.

Western gate Also known as Bab Al-Hawa (Gate of the Wind), the western gate of the Roman town and the walls either side of it have suffered heavily from reuse of their stones in other later buildings, but the simple style of the gateway is still apparent and quite unusual in Syria where the preference in Roman times was usually for more ornate decoration.

Mosque of Al-Khider and Mosque of 'Umar Take now the street running north from the *cryptoporticus* towards the Mosque of Al-Khider, a small building only 7m by 7m that is thought to date to 1133, making it one of Bosra's oldest constructions of the Islamic period. Al-Khider ('The Green One') was an Islamic hero who is said to have discovered the Fountain of Youth. He is closely linked to the Green Man of pre-Islamic and pre-Christian myth, and also associated with St George (see box on page 204). According to the Koran he was a companion of the prophet Moses. It has a large minaret, added in 1258, standing slightly apart. Continuing north some 50m to the next junction, turn right (east) to reach, after another 200m, the Mosque of 'Umar, much bigger than Al-Khidr Mosque. It was named after Caliph 'Umar, second caliph after Abu Bakr who succeeded the Prophet Muhammad. 'Umar conquered Syria in 636 and this is thought to be one of the oldest surviving mosques anywhere, though the current building is heavily reconstructed and dates mainly from the 12th–13th centuries under the Ayyubids.

Opposite the Mosque of 'Umar is a little souvenir shop and café very tastefully decorated and laid out. The mosque itself is still in use and is generally shut to visitors at prayer times. It should however be viewed if at all possible, as it is the only mosque in Islam to have survived from this time, just four years after the death of the Prophet. Built on the site of an earlier temple and heavily reconstructed by the Ayyubids, the internal layout of the mosque nevertheless conserves its original plan. Its courtyard is now roofed and has double arcades on its east and west sides, but would originally have housed a marketplace and sleeping areas, a good illustration of how closely early Islam was linked with commerce. Today the building still serves as Bosra's main mosque and as a religious school, *madrasa*, for children.

Hammam Manjak (*S£75 entry fee for the small ethnographic museum inside*) Directly opposite the Mosque of 'Umar is a Mameluke baths complex built in Damascus style in 1372. A wonderfully elaborate maze of 13 chambers, the baths are an impressive example of Muslim medieval engineering, and would have been heavily used by pilgrims stopping over in Bosra en route to Mecca on the annual pilgrimage or Hajj. Many stopped for as long as a week.

Basilica From the souvenir shop and café follow the little alleyway east away from the mosque for c200m to reach the basilica, just to your left as you emerge from the alley. A large rectangular building with a semicircular apse at the far end, this is where the local monk Bahira, was said to have been consulted by Muhammad (before the Koran was revealed to him) during his trading visit to Bosra. The story goes that Bahira predicted the young Muhammad would 'go beyond Christian precept to advance further a reconciliation between origin and destiny, between evil and suffering, giving a name and a sense to injustice, cruelty, arrogance and the ecstasy in faith, by means of a divinely revealed doctrine in which the simplest soul could find inner peace'.

The impressive façade of the basilica was probably originally a Roman civil building of some sort built in the 3rd century, converted to a church after the 4th century. As it appears today the building borrows the plan of a single-nave basilica. The interior is lit by eight windows high in the lateral walls. At the entrance there is a Greek inscription between two dovetails.

Mabrak Mosque If you want to be exhaustive in your tour you can now divert from the basilica 200m up into the northeast corner of the city, to the extensive Mabrak Mosque, jointly restored by the Syrians and Germans in 1986–89. The name means mosque of kneeling, derived from the legend that a camel carrying the first ever copy of the Koran to Syria, knelt here where the *mihrab* now is. An inscription above a window of the façade, to the right-hand side, gives the date of construction as AH530, ie: AD1135. The eastern larger part, with its courtyard and two *iwans*, dates to the 13th century. It housed a famous Koranic school and became an object of pilgrimage for Muslims.

Cathedral Retracing your steps to the alleyway, the large building in front of you just past the basilica but on the same side of the road, is Bosra's cathedral, widely thought to have been the inspiration for the first version of St Sophia Cathedral in Istanbul, with comparable dimensions for the dome, which promptly collapsed and was never rebuilt. The design is complicated, the first domed edifice on a rectangular plan, and measured 51m by 37.5m, the dome itself having a 36m diameter originally supported on eight columns. This ground plan of a large square delimited at the four corners by exedras (semicircular indentations) is called a quadrefoil.

In the centre of the large square were four L-shaped pillars and 18 columns creating a quadrilobe space of more circles and squares. Other buildings with this ground plan in Syria are the Cathedral of St Helena in Aleppo, the Cathedral of the East in Apamea, the church at Resafe and the Church of St George at Ezraa. (St Sophia in Istanbul has a different ground plan, being a basilica form with three aisles; only its dome was similar.) Heavily damaged today not least because much of its stonework has been carried off elsewhere in the last century for reuse, it is quite difficult to pick out the complex combination of square and circular shapes used in its architecture. Dated by its dedication in 512 to the three early Christian martyrs Sergius, Bacchus and Leontius, the cathedral had 50 windows round the rim of its dome, which must have made the interior unusually light.

The Koran is the greatest work of literature for Muslims. Marmaduke Pickthall wrote of it: 'That inimitable symphony, the very sands of which move men to tears and ecstasy', while Thomas Carlisle wrote: 'As tedious a piece of reading as I ever undertook, a wearisome, confused jumble, crude, incondite – nothing but a sense of duty could carry any European through the Koran.' Why did two intelligent men of similar academic backgrounds reach such different verdicts? Answer, because Pickthall read Arabic and Carlisle did not. Muhammad made no claim to be divine. He was simply 'the reciter' (Arabic 'qu'raan' means recitation), the mouthpiece. He was illiterate and could not write. It was not put into written form till well after his death. The 114 chapters, called 'suras', are arranged by length, with the longest first. Whilst the exact order of revelation remains uncertain, the longer ones were on the whole revealed to him later, while in Medina, and the subject matter was drier, legal text. The shorter ones were revealed earlier, while he was still in Mecca, and are altogether more dramatic and powerful. When reading the Koran as a book therefore, one is in fact reading it in the reverse order to how it was composed, a serious obstacle for any book to overcome. The best translations are by Pickthall and Arberry, and also Richard Bell's *Introduction to the Koran*. The original Arabic is a form of prose poetry called '*saj*' and is deemed untranslatable by Muslim scholars. Koranic teaching dissociates itself from Christianity which it sees as worshipping three gods, not one:

> Say: He is God – One!
> God – the eternally sought after!
> He did not have a son
> And was no-one's son.
> And there is no equal to Him. (112)

But of the other religions, Christianity was regarded the most warmly:

> You will discover that those who are most implacable in their hatred of the Muslims are the Jews and the pagans, while those nearest to them in affection are those who profess to be Christians. That is because there are priests and monks among them, and they are free of pride. (5:85)

Recent excavations have found many fragments of marble and mosaic tesserae in gold and silver, indicating how richly decorated the interior once was. There are also traces of frescoes painted in the absidal body of the wall and on the presbyterium walls. They are badly damaged, but are being worked on by restorers. Frescoes are rare in Syria, but important, as they show the extent of the peaceful coexistence of Islam and Christianity in the early days. Just beyond the cathedral are the heavily ruined remains of the Bishop's Palace.

Fatima Mosque Just opposite the cathedral on the other side of the road stands the Mosque of Fatima, named after the daughter of the Prophet. Its 19m-tall minaret dates from 1306, and the arched main building was constructed earlier in the 11th-century Fatimid period. The Shi'ite Fatimids, founded originally in Tunisia in 909 and then based in Cairo from 970, legitimised their claim to rule through claiming descent from the Prophet by way of his favourite daughter Fatima and her husband 'Ali, the first Shi'ite imam. Saladin put an end to their dynasty in 1169 when he seized Egypt and formed the Sunni Ayyubid dynasty in their place. The mosque is still in use.

Nabatean arch Continue south along the road now to return after c100m to the Nabatean arch you were able to view earlier from the decumanus by the South Baths.

Roman residence Continue straight on southwards beyond the Nabatean arch for 50m or so to reach this substantial villa thought to be the residence of the governor. A grand building 33m by 50m, it was arranged with colonnades round a courtyard, on two storeys.

Cistern Continuing south again you will soon come, after c50m, to the gigantic Roman cistern 120m by 150m, locally called Birket al-Hajj, Pool of the Pilgrimage. One of the largest such constructions in the Roman East, it was originally 8m deep, but is now half that, due to accumulated debris, and supplied all the town's water needs all the year round. Today it is a popular swimming pool with local youths in summer, who appear oblivious to its fetid staleness and the floating rubbish.

Mosque of Abu Al-Fida Beside the pool stands the Mosque of Abu Al-Fida, an Ayyubid construction of elegant and sober proportions. The interior is a vast bare rectangular room, its ceiling supported by six arches resting on antique recycled columns. Four *iwans* opening from this room give the traditional *madrasa* ground plan. Locally the mosque is known as Madrasa Ad-Dabbagha, School of Tanners, as the tanners here probably used the waters of the pool for their work.

EZRAA إزرع

(*80km south of Damascus*) In this unlikely village setting on the edge of southern Syria's volcanic wilderness, sits the Greek Orthodox church of St George, possibly one of the most exceptional buildings in Syria. Its extraordinariness rests on two counts: its architecture and its dedication.

The church (*no fixed opening hours, look around for the guardian who has the key*) lies c3km north of the town centre and is reached by turning left (north) off the roundabout in the centre of town near a black-and-white striped minaret, following a signpost marked 'Archaeological Area' and continuing for about 2km till the church appears straight in front of you. Architecturally it is most unusual and is one of the oldest churches still in use in Syria today. Dated to 515 from the inscription on the lintel above the triple-arch main entrance, the church stands on the site of an earlier ancient temple and also shows signs of defensive fortifications, testimony to the hostile environment it frequently had to survive in. The whole conveys considerable power and solidity as a result.

Its unusual design is an octagon built within a square, then topped by a dome. The shape of the large dome, 10m across, is reminiscent of a pointed ellipse of the mud-built beehive houses of northern Syria. Recently restored and recovered, the original dome may have been stone built. The sombre grey/black stone gives the interior a gloomy aspect, but the quality of the masonry is nevertheless very impressive, especially when you observe how the internal octagon shape metamorphoses itself into a circular shape before rising into the dome. There are eight windows in the drum, but they do not let in much light. The octagonal shape is formed by cutting off the corners of the squares, then filling out the angles with small semicircular chapels. St George's tomb is said to be behind the altar. Above the west entrance (left of the current entrance as you enter) an inscription in Greek reads: 'What was only a lodging place for demons has become a house of God; where idols once were sacrificed, there are now choirs of angels; where God was provoked to wrath, now He is propitiated', a text which clearly indicates the site used to be a pagan temple.

In Suweida, Shahba and Qanawat, the population is 100% Druze, and in Syria as a whole they account for a little under 3% of the population with about 430,000 followers. They outnumber the Druze of Lebanon who total about 200,000, though they represent closer to 5% of the Lebanese population. Lots of new building and fine houses are apparent in these areas, built with money the Druze have brought back from abroad, mainly the Spanish-speaking countries of South America, like Venezuela. In modern Syria they are well respected and get on well with other minorities.

As a people they are often very good looking, and many Druze women have jobs as newsreaders and presenters on TV. The dress of the older male generation, heavily moustachioed Druze is highly distinctive, the village elders always wearing tall white turbans, and the characteristic black baggy trousers called sarwaal, said to be designed to catch the next messiah safely in its folds when he is born to a man, belted at the waist with a white cummerbund; and a black jacket. This dress also signifies their status as 'Uqqal' ('Knowing' ones who have been initiated into the secrets of the faith). Women too can be 'Uqqal', at which point they wear white headscarves and participate in the council of elders. Most Druze are 'Juhhal' ('Ignorant' ones). The community is headed by an Emir.

Founded by an Iranian mystic and a Turkish preacher (whose name Ad-Darazi has given the sect its name) in the 10th century, the Druze are an esoteric offshoot of the Shi'a Isma'ili sect who believed that the Cairo-based enigmatic blue-eyed Fatimid Caliph Al-Hakim, was a divine representation of God. He 'disappeared' in 1021, which was taken by his followers as an act of divine concealment, though more likely a discreet assassination. Both Sunni and Shi'a sects regard them as heretical for accepting the divinity of Al-Hakim and the Druze practise their rites with great secrecy to avoid persecution. The religion itself is complex, involving Neoplatonism, Sufi mysticism and Iranian religious traditions. It calls itself the 'Tawhid' faith ('Unifying') because it aims to unite the best spiritual and social concepts of previous religions. God's fairness and justice are paramount. Everything is preordained and part of God's plan. They believe in reincarnation, in the sense that each soul comes back into a new body many times to keep improving itself. Verses of the Arabic ode *Al-Burdah*, the Prophet's Mantle, are

Nearby just 200–300m away is a second 6th-century church, the Church of St Elias. Reached by turning left as you leave St George to follow the edge of the line of black arches of a ruined Ayyubid mosque, the modern dome topped with a cross draws you in the right direction, visible above the rooftops of the village houses. It is unusual for being a cruciform shape oriented east–west with the apse projecting outwards to the east.

SUWEIDA السويداء

(*128km southeast of Damascus*) Suweida today is the modern capital of the province of the Hawran, a bustling centre with a population of some 25,000. Its Arabic name means 'the Black One' from the black basalt stone. Suweida's modern claim to fame is only as the birthplace of Farid Al-Atrache, the major Arab singer of his generation (1950s), a kind of Arab Frank Sinatra. He was also a talented lute player and composer. The Al-Atrache family were the most prominent Druze family of Syria, like the Jumblatts are of Lebanon, and the family still enjoys great prestige in the Druze community of Syria. By virtue of its continuous habitation most of its ancient remains have been buried or reused in some form or another, so that only a few Roman columns and arches remain to be seen scattered about today.

recited as charms and used at burials. Intermarriage is strictly forbidden and you cannot convert to Druzism, you can only be born a Druze. They do not pray in mosques, but in a plain building called a *khalwa* at the outskirts of the village. Thursday is their holy day and they reject all Five Pillars of Islam, banning fasting in Ramadan and the pilgrimage to Mecca. Instead they have seven pillars of their own: truthfulness; fellowship (treating others as you would wish to treated yourself); abandoning false beliefs; avoidance of confusion; monotheism and unitarianism; acceptance of your lot (be grateful for what you have and never complain); and finally submission to God's will while still working hard. A 'muwahid' (practiser of the Tawhid faith) knows that problems and obstacles are unavoidable lessons he has to learn from the world.

They regard Jethro, father-in-law of Moses, as their chief prophet and make annual pilgrimage to his tomb in lower Galilee. They also revere Moses, Jesus and Muhammad, Islam's three most important prophets. The only festivals they celebrate are the Feast of the Sacrifice (common to all Muslims) and 'Ashoura (the main Shi'a festival). They accept the Koran, the Bible and the Torah as sacred texts. The men drink alcohol, and the young of both sexes generally adopt quite a Western dress style.

Civil unrest between Druzes and Maronites which began in 1841, was fuelled by the Ottoman Turks under the divide and rule policy. This culminated in the massacre of 1860, in which 11,000 Christians, mainly Maronite, were killed by Druze, and up to 150 Christian villages are estimated to have been burnt. Europe intervened and French troops occupied Lebanon to restore order. This is when many retreated to the Hawran. Under the French Mandate the Druze were given their own autonomous state in the Jebel Druze, after their leadership played a crucial role in launching and sustaining the anti-French revolt of 1925–27. They agreed to surrender their autonomy in 1944. In Israel they are granted a 'nationality' status distinct from the Muslim population and are expected to serve in the Israeli army. Known to have a strong propensity to revolt against authority, they are fearless fighters. The Druze community worldwide is estimated at around 1,126,000 today, concentrated in Syria and Lebanon, Jordan and Israel. A few communities also exist in Europe, Australia, the Americas and the West Indies and some even have their own website, notably, www.druze.com and www.druze.net.

WHAT TO SEE

Suweida Museum (*Open 09.00–16.00 winter, 09.00–18.00 summer daily except Tue; S£150 entry fee*) The town does, however, boast a fine two-storey museum, that displays some spectacular mosaics from Roman Shahba (Philippopolis) and some fine sculptures.

The French helped arrange and set up the museum. The purpose-built black building lies 1km off the main thoroughfare that runs north–south from Damascus to Bosra. At one of the many roundabouts, follow the sign uphill (east) towards Qanawat and the museum lies a little off the road, on a palm-tree-lined avenue in a wealthy residential suburb. The upstairs is devoted to an interesting ethnographic and folkloric collection of costumes worn by Bedouin at various occasions and displays of simple tools used in the earliest forms of agriculture.

Three of the mosaics are generally singled out for special attention, namely:

- Artemis taking her bath, dated to the mid 3rd century AD; it depicts Artemis crouching naked beside a spring attended by four nymphs. She is wearing a diadem of pearls along with other jewels. A man's head, said to represent Actaeon, watches from the shrubbery. If it is indeed Actaeon, Artemis then

Many buildings throughout Europe today use architectural devices which were developed and perfected by Muslims. These innovations found their way to Europe a thousand years ago via Muslim Spain and Sicily and via Crusaders, pilgrims and scholars returning from the Holy Land and from cities like Cairo and Damascus.

With their advanced knowledge of geometry and the laws of statics Muslims developed new forms of arch like the horseshoe, the pointed and the Gothic. The horseshoe arch for example, known in Britain as the Moorish arch, was first used in the Great Ummayad Mosque in Damascus between 706 and 715, and gave more height than the classical semicircular arch. In Islam the horseshoe is a symbol of sainthood and holiness, not luck as in other cultures. It was popular in Victorian times and was used in large buildings like railway station entrances in Liverpool and Manchester. The pointed arch, forerunner of the Gothic arch, came to Europe from Cairo via Sicily. Amalfi merchants in 1000 had seen the powerful pointed arches of the Ibn Tulun Mosque in Cairo, and in Europe the first building to use them was the Abbey of Monte Cassino in 1071, financed by Amalfi merchants. It then moved north to the Church of Cluny which boasted 150 pointed arches in its aisles. The fashion quickly spread from these, the two most influential churches in Europe, and soon religious buildings all over Europe used it. This Gothic arch was much stronger than the rounded arch, employed by the Romans and the Normans, thereby allowing the construction of much bigger, taller, grander and more complex buildings like the great cathedrals of Europe.

Other borrowings from Muslim designs included ribbed vaulting, rose windows and dome-building techniques. Europe's castles were also adapted to copy those seen in the Islamic world, with arrow slits, machicolations, battlements, a barbican and parapets. Square towers and keeps evolved to the more easily defended round ones. Henry V's castle architect was known to be a Muslim. Sir Christopher Wren in the mid 17th century thoroughly studied and researched Ottoman and Moorish mosque architecture and became convinced of the Muslim roots of Gothic architecture. 'The Goths', he said, 'were rather destroyers than builders: I think it should with more reason be called the Saracen style.' This Muslim influence can be seen in St Paul's Cathedral, London, his greatest ever project, in the structure of the domes in the aisles and in the use of the combination of the dome and tower.

---

turned him into a stag, for no-one was permitted to see the gods without permission, and he was then torn to pieces by his own hounds. An incredibly elaborate frieze of intertwined fruit and foliage forms the border.

- Venus at her toilet. Again mid 3rd century AD; the goddess is shown naked but heavily bejewelled, adjusting her hair in a mirror, attended by two cupids and with a sea god on either side. Venus herself is found inside a shell.
- Banquet scene. A little later, early 4th century AD and the largest of the three mosaics; this scene shows a banquet set in a circle within a square frame.

The expressiveness of the faces makes these mosaics especially remarkable.

SALKHAD صلخد

(30km southeast of Suweida; open unfenced site; no entry fee; no facilities) From Bosra the drive east to this extraordinary volcanic cone that dominates the flat landscape from afar takes about half an hour. As it is no longer militarised, you can now drive right up to the original Ayyubid fortress that sits atop the cone, which is utterly

abandoned. From the village below a sign in Arabic which translates as 'the ruined castle' points left up to the top.

Leaving the car in the large open space at the end of the road you can climb up the dramatic steps to the fortifications above. They were built in the 13th century as part of the defences against the Crusaders in Jerusalem, along with the Bosra fortified theatre. The fortress itself was largely constructed within the cone, and quite a lot remains of steps, ramparts and towers.The Ayyubids, in their military architecture against the Crusaders, displayed much ingenuity, and the Crusaders absorbed and learnt from their enemy's craftsmanship, later taking back this knowledge to Europe, where they built many of the castles we now think of as British.

There is a lot of water at the site and the old reservoirs are still evident near the car park beside the abandoned military installations. Even as late as March patchy snow can still be found here. Looking down at the village, red is obviously the preferred colour of the company that has the monopoly on plastic water tanks. Their appearance is like a red rash that has spread all over the town.

In the main square of the town stands a solitary 13th-century minaret, hexagonal and rather striking in its style, built of black basalt, relieved by two bands of limestone inscribed with verses from the Koran. Salkhad has been identified with the biblical town of Salecah, mentioned in Deuteronomy 3:10 and Joshua 12:5 and 13:11, as lying within the territory captured by Moses from Og, King of Bashan.

MUSHANNAF مشنف

High in the remote hills of the Jebel Druze there stands in this small mountain village a remarkable jewel of a Roman temple built beside an artificial lake. As you enter the village from Salkhad in the south, look out for the pool and temple to the right of the road, just after crossing a bridge in the centre.

Today the pool is fetid with village rubbish and the temple and its walled enclosure have been taken over by a local family and their goats and chickens. Living in these incongruous surroundings the family nevertheless seems totally at ease in their 2nd-century AD home, and the Holy of Holies now serves as the laundry room, a giant washing cauldron taking centre stage where the altar would have been. Tea will be offered during your visit and it is utterly charming to sit among the goats and drying washing, gazing up at the elaborately carved façade of the temple with its rosette motifs and Corinthian capitals. The walls now tilt at precarious angles, their hotch-potch blocks the result of earlier rebuilding for defensive purposes, with jumbled masonry crookedly reassembled in an utterly random fashion over the centuries that nevertheless results in a very appealing if bizarre overall effect. An inscription dates the temple to AD171. If you look closely as you drive through the village, you will see much ancient stonework incorporated into modern village dwellings.

QANAWAT قنوات

(100km southeast of Damascus; open 09.00–16.00 winter, 09.00–18.00 summer daily; S£75 entry fee; town setting, no facilities but simple shops opposite the entrance, selling soft drinks and even beer and wine) The road to Qanawat runs either from the centre of Suweida, up past the Suweida Museum, if you are coming from Bosra, or, if you are coming from Damascus, it is signed off to the left before Suweida, and is reached some 6km later up in the hills. Near the entrance to the town of Qanawat look out for the seven columns of the Helios Temple, 75m to the left as you approach from Suweida. At the edge of the modern town, a sign announces

'Qanawat Ruins' to the right, and about 500m later, the road crosses into the walls of the old city, built of the now familiar black basalt, mixed in with the modern town. Shortly afterwards, the ticket booth comes into sight to your left, beside the large fenced-in complex of two basilicas from the 5th and 6th centuries AD, adapted from the original 2nd-century AD Roman temple on the site here.

Although located in the town, the setting of this complex, known locally as the *seraya* or palace, is still attractive because of the grove of oak trees it sits within. In its heyday when Christianity flourished here in the 4th and 5th centuries, Qanawat ('channels' from the water system) became the seat of a bishop, but when it fell to the Arabs in 637 it went into a long and gentle decline, and by the 19th century was totally abandoned. The original foundation here was probably in the 1st century BC, so it has been a holy spot for over 2,000 years. The buildings themselves as we see them now were originally 2nd-century AD Roman, then adapted to serve as basilicas in the 4th and 5th centuries. The quality of the classical stonework is high, ingeniously reworked into the Christian buildings.

Returning to the main square and heading up the first turning to the left, you will reach the jumbled remains of the Temple of Zeus dated to the 2nd century AD, mostly just at foundation level now, with gigantic stone slabs scattered randomly about by the destruction of earthquakes over the years. Within the town if you go down the steep hill into the river gorge to the east, you will find on the eastern bank of the green and grassy slope two unusual buildings: the first is a small *odeon* with nine rows of seats built into the hillside, then further towards the river, an unusual *nymphaeum* that still collects water and channels it into a pool.

SIA سياء

(*3km southeast of Qanawat; open site; no entry fee*) Difficult to find up in the hills beyond Qanawat are the fragmentary ruins of Sia, a sanctuary complex of three linked buildings dating from 50BC to AD200. It only remains in its lower courses today, most of the blocks having been removed and reused by Turkish Ottoman forces in the early 20th century, the same fate that befell the Nabatean temple at Suweida. It lies along the crest of a small ridge, but has to be reached through a farmyard at the entrance to the village. The drawings and records of early 19th-century travellers show how rich the decoration once was here, but today it requires a considerable degree of imagination to reconstruct the temple complex mentally. The bust of Baal-Shamin that once adorned the lintel of the main door is now in the Louvre.

SHAHBA شهبا

(*87km south of Damascus*) A rather odd little town, Shahba is heavily populated by Druze from Lebanon. It is dwarfed by its extinct volcano cone (Tell Shihan), on the top of which there is now a *mezaar*, a religious spot where Druze come to make sacrifices and to stay for a few days in the dormitory-like buildings on the summit. The bottom areas of the cone are mined for bitumen. There is no longer an actual crater to see inside.

A surprising number of Roman ruins remain to be seen in the middle of the town, well signposted from whichever direction you enter, and the sheer scale of them makes you realise how important this place clearly once was, a fact difficult to reconcile with how unimportant it appears now. The walls of the town are still discernible and show that the town covered a rough square of 800m, very small, yet with buildings on a disproportionately lavish scale inside. On each of the four walls was a monumental gateway, the north and south ones of which have been restored.

Founded by Philip the Arab, its Roman name was Philippopolis and it could well be that he endowed it with such grand buildings to honour his birthplace here. He was emperor from 244 to 249, the only Arab ever to become a Roman emperor. He joined the army and rose to the rank of Praetorian Prefect. He was hailed as emperor by his legions after the Emperor Gordian was killed in a battle against the Persians on the Euphrates, but then had to sue for a humiliating peace with the Persian Sassanids. His reign was brief, however, as he was murdered in a military mutiny after just five years. His early death meant his grand schemes for Philippopolis never achieved completion. Although he did not adopt Christianity openly, he allowed Christians to practise their faith and some 4th-century writers describe him as the first Christian emperor.

WHAT TO SEE

Shahba Museum (*Open 09.00–16.00 winter, 09.00–18.00 summer; S£75 entry fee; basic WC facilities; small shop opposite for stocking up with drinks and snacks*) The museum is tucked off the main road down a side street diagonally opposite the domes of the huge Roman Baths. Though small, it is extremely well laid out and is definitely worth a visit for the dramatic mosaics, probably Syria's best examples of this late Roman period. The museum was built directly over them as they were found *in situ* here in a private house.

The most noteworthy are:

- Orpheus and the animals. A square mosaic of Orpheus playing his lyre while sitting on a rock, with the entranced animals all around him listening. Dated to the 4th century the mosaic succeeds in conveying an atmosphere of harmony and sensitivity.
- The Wedding of Bacchus and Ariadne. Another square mosaic of the same date as Orpheus but rather more static and frozen in its atmosphere. The couple, both with halos, sit on a rock with Hymen behind with her flaming torch to represent desire. Hercules sprawls at their feet in a rather drunken pose and an old satyr-like being seems to be reaching for Ariadne's crown. Bacchus had found her abandoned on his home island of Naxos, by an ungrateful Theseus whom she had helped escape from the labyrinth and the minotaur. He married her and gave her a crown, and when she died he threw the crown into the sky where its jewels turned into stars as a constellation between the kneeling Hercules and the man who holds the serpent.
- Aphrodite and Ares. Again square and from the same period, this is a scene from the Odyssey. An almost naked but heavily jewelled Aphrodite stands with her lover Ares in front of an angry Hephaestos, her husband, and brother to Ares.
- The Sea Goddess Tetys. Another square mosaic with the goddess and her thick tresses bursting with fish and other signs of sea life.

Roman ruins The Roman Baths just opposite and back up towards the main road are colossal and built to a very high standard of construction, higher even than the Baths of Caracalla in Rome itself. There were originally six rooms for the different heat levels, and traces of the underfloor heating can still be seen. An aqueduct fed them from the southeast and the interior walls were evidently marble and alabaster lined, with high-quality plaster work lining the domes.

The main grouping of ruins lies directly uphill from the baths, after crossing the main street, and you come first of all to the theatre on your right after 150m. It was the last of the Roman theatres to be built in the East and is well preserved, if rather small at 42m in diameter, and stark in its decoration.

Continuing north past the side of the theatre, the path opens up just a few paces further on, into the huge paved *forum*, marketplace, around which are grouped Shahba's main Roman buildings. Immediately to your left is the small but very well-preserved temple, erected in honour of Philip's father, Julius Marinus, used as a school till the beginning of the 20th century, its horseshoe seating plan lending itself very well to that purpose. Stairs climb up from the back onto the roof, from where you have a fine view, not only over the Roman remains but also down into the charming house nearby complete with its satellite dish, television aerial and washing hanging out in the courtyard.

On the western higher end of the *forum* stands the former palace with its grand façade with a colossal 30m wide niche now empty, but originally designed to display statuary. As you walk back down the wide Roman street from the *forum* to rejoin the main road, note the house on the left that has incorporated itself into the façade of a hexastyle temple with columns.

SHAQQA شقا

(10km northeast of Shahba) Very rarely visited because it is a detour off the main circuit between Damascus and Bosra, this small Druze town sitting in the middle of a fertile plain is worth a visit if you can spare the time, to see three well-preserved buildings dating from its time as Roman Maximianopolis. To reach the town you head north out of Shahba on the Damascus road, then take the first road to the right, about 1km out of Shahba.

The most major building stands at the eastern edge of town and is the palace that probably served as the Roman governor's residence. Locally it is known as the 'Kaisariye'. Note especially the ceiling, carefully constructed from basalt slabs, supported by five closely spaced arches. Going out into the courtyard on the other side you can look up onto the façade of an adjacent building to see Byzantine crosses, suggesting it was once a basilica. From the entrance to the palace you can spot, some 400m away, a square stocky tower to the east, which is part of a 6th-century monastery, known locally as 'Ad-Deir'. It is lived in by a family of peasants who do not mind curious visitors at all. The final building to find is to the right off a side street on the way to the monastery, more difficult to spot, is a very well-preserved Roman tomb, whose cavity within an octagonal base serves today as a meeting place and prayer hall for the local people.

10

Palmyra and the Desert

تدمر

Trust in God, but tie your camel.

Telephone code 031
(245km northeast and 3hrs' drive from Damascus, 201km southwest and 2hrs' drive from Deir Ez-Zour)
Palmyra today, described variously as Bride of the Desert or Venice of the Desert, is Syria's most visited site, and with over 20 hotels, boasts more tourist accommodation than anywhere outside Damascus. And justifiably so, for Palmyra is one of the world's most evocative and complete classical cities, set at the edge of a massive desert oasis and crowned by a hauntingly omnipresent Arab fort that stands sentinel on its volcanic cone above the city. The small town of Tadmur (Palmyra) with some 40,000 inhabitants living off tourism, agriculture and trade, is a scruffy place that far from enhances the ruins, but is at least tucked to the side. The original Aramaic name 'Tadmur' was thought by the Greeks and Romans to be a reference to 'tamar', meaning 'date' in both Aramaic and Arabic, and hence they renamed it Palmyra from the Roman 'palma' meaning palm-tree. Scholars today think the Aramaic 'tadmur' is in fact more likely to have been derived from the Semitic root meaning 'to guard', and therefore meant 'guard post' instead.

By way of diversion and entertainment on the drive to Palmyra , this chapter is broken up with descriptions of three colourful British lady adventurers, all of whom visited this part of the world in the 19th and 20th centuries, all very different from each other. Despite the sometimes overlapping dates none of them knew each other. (See pages 228, 234 and 239)

HISTORY

Not surprisingly, Palmyra's fertile oasis and plentiful subterranean springs meant that it was already permanently inhabited as early as the 2nd millennium BC. It is mentioned as a settlement in clay tablets found in Cappadocia (now central Turkey), in Mari on the Euphrates and in Hittite texts as 'Tamar in the land of Amurru'. The inhabitants were Aramaic and the Palmyrene dialect as discovered in inscriptions is a dialect of Aramaic. From the 6th century BC to the 6th century AD Aramaic was a kind of lingua franca, the language of diplomacy throughout the Near East.

Most of the ruins you see before you today date from the 2nd and 3rd centuries AD when the city was in its heyday. Throughout its long history Palmyra's raison d'être was its oasis, but at that particular point the city shot to a prominence unknown before, thanks to its strategic location as the halfway mark on the trade routes from Antioch on the Mediterranean coast to Doura Europos on the Euphrates.

The natural and easier trade route between these two points up till the 1st century BC had been to the north, following the curve of the Fertile Crescent, but that region had become too dangerous with the hostile Parthians, who had ultimately undermined and destroyed the Seleucid kingdom post-Alexander the Great, seeking to expand their empire westwards from their base in Persia. Arch enemies of the Roman Empire in the east, the Parthians were superb horsemen, famous for the 'Parthian shot', an arrow fired at full gallop while facing backwards. Little is known of them as their literature has not survived.

The new route via Palmyra though more arduous across the desert, was now not only safer (because Palmyra had long been on good terms with the Parthians), but more direct. Rome's appetite for exotic substances from the East, where the price of traded goods might well have risen 100-fold between their place of origin and Rome, was growing in parallel with the power of the empire, and much of this trade from India and China was now carried by camel caravans through Palmyra to Antioch on the Mediterranean coast.

Coinciding with this to the south, Petra and its Nabatean kingdom fell in AD106, thereby losing control of all its long-distance trade routes, and leaving Palmyra more unchallenged than ever, and with the chance to become for the first time in its long history, more than just the seat of a minor chieftain. Palmyra's fortunes flourished in consequence of the heavy duties they levied over the next 200 years. Spices, silks, ebony, dried foods and slaves were among the 'goods' traded, and as the wealth of the merchants grew, they began to bestow upon the town a succession of flamboyant monuments, temples and grandiose archways, often embellished with themselves in statue form.

The privilege of this very sudden rise to prominence by the wealthy merchant class was in reality enjoyed by very small numbers of people, as control of the camel caravans was held in the hands of very few. So anxious were these nouveaux riches to gain fame and recognition that one of them, called Male Agrippa, paid personally for the Roman Emperor Hadrian to make a state visit to Palmyra, and for a while the city was renamed Palmyra Hadriana and declared a 'free city', i.e. able to set and collect its own taxes. The city had been nominally under Roman control since Pompey in 64BC annexed Syria as a Roman province.

DECLINE Roman conflict with the Parthians to the east of Syria during the reign of Marcus Aurelius (161–180), last of the Five Good Emperors, led to instability in the trade routes and a commercial decline. Under Septimius Severus there was another brief resurgence of trade and Palmyra became a Roman colony, freed from the burden of paying taxes to Rome. Then, in the second half of the 3rd century AD, the Zoroastrian Sassanids from Persia arrived, annexing Mesopotamia and thereby controlling the headwaters of the Tigris and Euphrates. This in turn took from Palmyra control of the sea routes over to the Indian Ocean. Rome faced a series of bloody conflicts during this time and the Sassanids even succeeded in capturing and murdering Emperor Valerian in AD260, a scene graphically depicted on the famous Sassanid rock reliefs at Bishapur and Naqshi Rustam in Iran. The Palmyrene Consul and Governor of Syria, a man named Udainat of Arab origin, fought valiantly against the Sassanids in many campaigns but when he was eventually murdered in AD268, his power-hungry wife Queen Zenobia took charge in the name of her young son.

In a highly ambitious bid for power that succeeded initially, she attacked Emesa (Homs), Antioch, Egypt and parts of Asia Minor (Turkey). On her success she had coins minted in Alexandria bearing likenesses of herself and her son, and declared her son emperor and the eastern half of the Roman Empire to be theirs. She claimed descent from Cleopatra, whom she equalled in beauty according to historians, and exceeded in chastity and valour.

The ruling Emperor Aurelian had had enough, and marched his armies to Palmyra in 273, forcing Zenobia to surrender. As a lesson in Roman authority, her garrison was sacked, the city plundered, with even the treasure of the Bel Temple confiscated. Zenobia was taken back for display on Aurelian's triumphal entry into Rome, and forced to live out her days in exile. It is not recorded what happened to her son.

Palmyra never fully recovered from this plundering. It became thereafter no more than a military stronghold to house the legions of Diocletian (284-305), when the wall was built to protect the Roman garrisons against the Sassanian threat and an aqueduct was built to supply the drinking water. All trade fell away.

Over subsequent centuries Christianity secured a strong foothold, the oasis becoming the seat of a bishopric, with the remains of two Byzantine churches still visible at foundation level.

In 634 the city was captured for the first time by Muslims, by one of the military leaders of the first caliph, Abu Bakr, after Muhammad's death. Bypassed by the main caravan routes, the city began its slide into oblivion, the last flourish coming in the 12th century, when, in pursuit of some minor defensive role, the Mamelukes converted the Bel Temple to a fortress and the fortress of Qal'at Ibn Ma'an was built on the volcano cone.

The Mongols lay waste to the town in the 13th century, and from then on throughout the Ottoman period, Palmyra lay consigned to oblivion in the desert.

ARCHAEOLOGICAL EXCAVATIONS It was 1929 when the first archaeologists arrived, the French unsurprisingly, since Syria was at that time under French Mandate, and a Frenchman Henri Seyrig was appointed director of antiquities. They found a village nestled within the conveniently sheltering walls of the massive Sanctuary of Bel. Their first task, before any excavation work could begin, was to persuade the villagers to evacuate to what is now the modern town of Tadmur. The 50 or so huts were neatly arranged in lanes and had been ingeniously constructed using the building materials that were to hand, namely ancient column bases and capitals, finely crafted Roman blocks, with roofs of corrugated iron or whatever scraps of wood or palm fronds had been scavenged from the oasis.

Since then, work on Palmyra has been ongoing by successive archaeological teams, mainly French, but also Swiss and Polish, and latterly since the country's independence in 1958, by the Syrian Directorate-General of Antiquities, and are still ongoing today. For six centuries the ruins lay largely forgotten, increasingly swallowed in sand, visited only by a handful of intrepid Europeans, among them two English architects called Wood and Dawkins who spent two weeks at Palmyra in 1751 drawing up plans of the ruins and sketching the main monuments. The series of engravings they published on their return, called *The Ruins of Palmyra*, chimed with the neoclassical architectural movement that was highly popular in Britain at the time and the engravings' designs were copied in Palmyra-style ceilings and cornices in several 18th-century stately homes, notably Blair Castle and Drayton House.

Many early travellers met with bandits and hostile tribes in their attempts to reach the legendary city and, robbed even of their clothes, fled back to Aleppo or Damascus. Such tales had a deterrent effect on later 19th-century romantic orientalists, but among those who did succeed was Lady Hester Stanhope (see box on page 228) the first Western woman to reach the 'Bride of the Desert'. She entered it in 1813 astride an Arab stallion, followed by her retinue, and directed the local Bedouin sheikh to charge a tax of 1,000 piastres to all future visitors. The large sum was clearly a considerable deterrent, as a traveller named John Carne wrote in *Letters from the East* in 1826: 'This enormous tax which it is impossible to escape causes several travellers to leave Syria without seeing the finest ruin in the world.'

Outspoken and headstrong, but well educated and presentable, Lady Hester was well known in English society as the niece of the unmarried British Prime Minister William Pitt, for whom she acted as hostess of his household. On his death in 1806 the nation awarded her a pension of £1,200 a year (worth a staggering £96,000 a year in today's money) which she enjoyed for the rest of her life.

With no relations left in England and a romantic disappointment to boot, she set off in 1810 with a small retinue on a long sea voyage, but was shipwrecked en route to Cairo. Having lost all her clothes she began to dress in local male costume and travelled from Cairo to Jerusalem and Damascus. By this stage she claimed to have heard from fortune tellers and prophets that she was destined to be the bride of a new Messiah. Dressed as a Bedouin and accompanied by a caravan of 22 camels she travelled to Palmyra, becoming the first ever Western woman to visit the desert city. Impressed by her courage and bearing, she was greeted like royalty and crowned Queen Hester by the local Bedouins.

She then settled in Lebanon for the rest of her life in a disused monastery near Sidon, establishing a large household of servants. She never married or had children but was rumoured to have a succession of lovers. Over the years she offered sanctuary to hundreds of Druze, and wielded great local power, no doubt through her large income, getting involved in inter-clan squabbles and even ordering whole villages to be massacred. She ended her days a bad-tempered recluse, her servants running off with her possessions, once she no longer had enough money to pay them. She wrote no books herself, but has been the subject of a couple of biographies.

GETTING THERE AND AWAY

BY CAR The journey from Damascus direct to Palmyra, a distance of 245km, is reckoned to take between two-and-a-half and three hours from downtown Damascus, depending on cruising speed. It is possible however, in one longish day, to drive from Damascus to Palmyra, incorporating en route the Christian sites of Seydnaya and Ma'loula, and then also to stop briefly at the remarkable Roman temple at Dmeir. The drive from Ma'loula to Dmeir takes nearly a full hour as the road is small and winding. The town of Dmeir itself, an ugly sprawl of a place, has nothing to recommend it beyond the temple which lies some 300m to the right of the main road and its massive blocks can be glimpsed through the modern buildings. Its setting today, surrounded by unappealing recent development, detracts greatly from the fine temple, whose state of preservation is truly astonishing. Dated to AD245 it is located here because of the junction of two major caravan routes, and the temple is all that remains of the stopover point. Sunken down some 5m below today's ground level, the temple is fenced in and locked, the guardian's telephone number written in Arabic numerals on a notice on the fence. Entry into the temple itself is by a metal door right at the bottom, and none of the inside is visible from above.

From Dmeir to Palmyra is a further 200km which takes a good hour and 45 minutes as the road is not dual carriageway but just normal two-way traffic. There are always plenty of buses and trucks travelling along it, for it is also the main road to Iraq, which forks off to the right after 61km by a petrol station. The road surface itself is pretty good, though there are no road markings, only cats' eyes in the middle to help with the tricky night driving. A lot of the trucks are pretty ancient, a good 30-40 years old with incredibly thick metalwork like tanks, weighing a tonne.

The scenery to the side of the road, apart from the bare mountains to the left, appears featureless and empty to the untrained eye unused to desert landscapes. Yet if you were to stop the car and walk a little off the road, you would be amazed at the amount of life – lizards, insects, little plants. To an Arab however every tree and plant is noticed, and once your eye becomes more trained, you too will notice birds, bushes and even entire flocks of sheep well camouflaged against the desert colours. The hills to the left are also quite impressive, with a biblical aspect to them, like the mountains around the Dead Sea in Israel and Jordan.

At one point after a further 50km a railway track appears from nowhere, a mining railway to Homs from a phosphate quarry here in the desert, complete with factory for processing the phosphate into soil fertiliser. Soon after, there is a major crossroads: left to Homs, right to the Iraqi border 125km away, and straight on to Palmyra.

A regular pit stop now for all travellers to Palmyra is the enterprising Baghdad Café which has set itself up at roughly the halfway point, 100km before Palmyra. In 2006 it developed a clone of itself, just a few hundred metres away, the first you reach on coming from Damascus, calling itself Baghdad Café 66. Both are simple cafés, offering a range of soft drinks (no alcohol) and simple food. They are decorated in traditional style and sell an interesting range of souvenirs including desert rocks and marine fossils, illustrating how this desert terrain was the sea bed geological eons ago. Both have clean toilets out the back. They have even built a cluster of beehive houses where tourists can overnight very simply or, if they prefer, they can stay in Bedouin tents, permanently erected for the purpose.

As you get closer to Palmyra you will start to spot the occasional Bedouin tent and encampment, relics of a lifestyle that is fast dying out now. The Ethnographic Museum at Palmyra is the best in Syria in giving you a flavour of what their lifestyle was like, their clothing, jewellery, food, music and mores, though sadly it is little visited. (See also box, *The end of the Bedouin lifestyle?* page 269.)

The oasis of Palmyra is visible from about 30km away, looking like a dark patch in the distance across the desert, the darker form of the greenery contrasting with the bare yellow desert. Try if at all possible to arrive at sunset (as early as 15.30 in winter months, and more like 18.00 in summer months). The caravan city of the desert owes its existence to the oasis, the ideal staging post between the Mediterranean coast and the Euphrates river valley.

Try if at all possible to arrive by sunset (as early as 15.30 in winter months, and more like 18.00 in summer months) when the colours are at their most dramatic. Only the Arab castle, the Sanctuary of Bel and the tombs have opening hours, so the majority of the site is unfenced and you are free to wander round even by moonlight if you wish.

BY BUS The state-owned Karnak coach company has its ticket office and bus station conveniently located opposite the Archaeological Museum. There are three departures to Damascus a day, costing S£100 and taking three hours. For Deir Ez-Zour there are six daily departures, costing S£75 and taking two hours. The private Kadmous coach company has its ticket office and bus stop a little to the north of the museum, but its main ticket office is way out of town 2km to the northeast in the Sahara Restaurant.

PLANNING

The site today covers an enormous area, 10km² (50ha), too large to be fenced in, which is why access to most of the site is free. However, entry tickets are required for certain parts, namely the Arab Fort, the Palmyra Museum, the Ethnographic

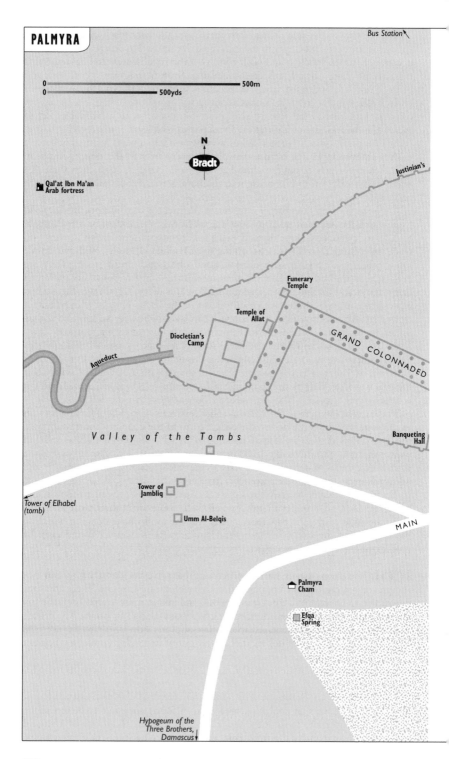

0 ——————————————————— 500m
0 ————————————— 500yds

Bus Station

N
Bradt

Qal'at Ibn Ma'an
Arab fortress

Justinian's

Funerary
Temple

Temple of
Allat

GRAND COLONNADED

Diocletian's
Camp

Aqueduct

Banqueting
Hall

Valley of the Tombs

Tower of
Jambliq

Tower of Elhabel
(tomb)

Umm Al-Belqis

MAIN

Palmyra
Cham

Efqa
Spring

Hypogeum of the
Three Brothers,
Damascus

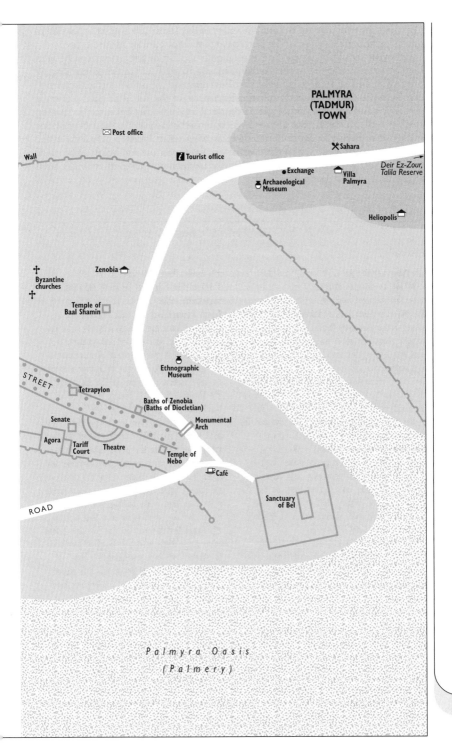

Post office

Wall

Tourist office

PALMYRA
(TADMUR)
TOWN

Sahara

Exchange

Archaeological
Museum

Villa
Palmyra

Deir Ez-Zour,
Talila Reserve

Heliopolis

Byzantine
churches

Zenobia

Temple of
Baal Shamin

STREET

Ethnographic
Museum

Tetrapylon

Baths of Zenobia
(Baths of Diocletian)

Senate

Monumental
Arch

Agora

Tariff
Court

Theatre

Temple of
Nebo

Café

ROAD

Sanctuary
of Bel

Palmyra Oasis
(Palmery)

Museum, the Sanctuary of Bel and the valley of the Tombs, all bought *in situ* except the last, whose tickets have to be purchased at the museum in advance.

Any visit should include at least one night's stay, so that the ruins can be seen both at sunrise and at sunset. Arriving ideally in mid–late afternoon your first priority should be to drive straight past the ruins and on up the tarmac road that climbs to the Arab fortress dominating all aspects of the site. The final section is very steep and coaches cannot get to the very top, not least because the turning space is very limited. Before the road was built in the early 1990s the ascent of this castle outcrop was a major undertaking requiring serious exertion especially in the summer months. But then in the days before the motor car and before the tarmac road from Damascus, the excursion to Palmyra, which now takes three hours, used to take five or six days on horseback.

WHERE TO STAY

High season is from April to September, when beds can be scarce and prices can be inflated.

 Palmyra Cham Hotel (250 rooms) ✆ 912231; f 912245; e champalm@net.sy; www.chamhotels.com. Formerly the Meridien, this is the only luxury-class hotel in Palmyra at the time of writing. Rather exclusively located on the edge of the palmery about 2km before the town. Very attractive pool with kiddies' area, open May–October only as it is considered too cold to swim in the winter months. Two dining rooms and a couple of shops. The best thing about the location is that it is well away from the scruffy town of Tadmur, well placed for a stroll in the palmery and also for walking straight into the Valley of the Tombs. *US$190 dbl, US$160 sgl.*

Heliopolis Hotel (c35 rooms) ✆ 913921; f 913923; e heliopolis-palmyra@usa.net. Built in 1998, a 5-storey 3-star hotel with clean rooms down a side street off the main Tadmur street on the very edge of the palmery. Most rooms have good views over the palmery towards the ruins. Top-floor restaurant. *US$65 dbl, US$45 sgl.*

Villa Palmyra Hotel (c40 rooms) ✆ 913600; f 912554. An adequate and comfortable hotel on the main street of Tadmur. Rooms are small but all have A/C and TV. Top-floor restaurant. US$65 dbl, US$45 sgl.

Zenobia Hotel (24 rooms) ✆ 912907; f 912407. The only hotel set inside the ruins, a single-storey rather charmless building built during the French Mandate. Once the most expensive and luxurious Palmyra had to offer, it is now a bit run-down and basic, with idle staff and standards of hygiene not that great, despite a recent renovation. The terrace is a pleasant spot for a drink overlooking the ruins, especially at sunset. *US$80 dbl, US$60 sgl.*

Semiramis Hotel (225 rooms), PO Box 30301, Damascus; ✆ 112233555; f 112216797; e semiramis@net.sy; www.semiramis-hotel.com. 5-star hotel, opening late 2006, right at the entrance to the Palmyra oasis, on the left as you approach from Damascus/Homs, just before the Bedouin Corner and about 1km before (ie: further out of the centre) than the Palmyra Cham Hotel. All the usual 5-star facilities, it has been years in the building, wth endless hiccups, but now seems to be on a final push.

Zaman Al-Majd Forced to shut just days before opening, this illegal hotel may be given permission to recreate itself in a new location. It was recognised as a work of genius, just that proper permission to build within the palmery was never obtained (see page 235).

WHERE TO EAT AND DRINK

Palmyra Cham Hotel Best and most expensive place to eat in Palmyra. Excellent views over the ruins, especially at night when the Arab castle is floodlit and appears to float in mid-air. Good selection of Lebanese and other wines.

Heliopolis Top, 5th-floor restaurant with good clean WC facilities. The food is good and there are excellent views over the palmery towards the Bel Sanctuary. Licensed. *Reasonable prices.*

Villa Palmyra Top, 4th-floor restaurant with views not quite as good as the Heliopolis as it is set further back from the palmery. *Similar food and prices to the Heliopolis.*

X Zenobia The only restaurant located within the ruins. Alcohol served. Slow service so don't attempt to be in a rush. *Average prices, average food.*

X The Bedouin Corner A newly opened place as you enter Palmyra from the Damascus road, to the left about 500m before the Palmyra Cham Hotel. Approached up a long unmade-up drive, the intention is that there will eventually be rooms on offer, but at the time of writing it offers food and entertainment only in large black Bedouin tents. Geared for groups, it is attractively laid out in rocky gardens with abundant palm trees. Same ownership as the Villa Palmyra Hotel. *Fair prices.*

X Sahara For a cheap quick lunch this is a good clean restaurant offering local food. Opposite Villa Palmyra Hotel in the main street.

NIGHTLIFE

The closest thing to nightlife in Palmyra is the hotel bars and the Villa Palmyra even has a basement pub. Not surprisingly the Cham Palace Hotel is the most expensive and also the most plush, while the most atmospheric is the outdoor terrace bar of the Zenobia Hotel, especially in summer at night, directly overlooking the ruins.

SHOPPING

All along Tadmur's main street numerous shops selling handicrafts and antiques have grown up, many of them selling Bedouin carpets, silver jewellery and traditional costumes. The entry kiosk to the Sanctuary of Bel has a very good selection of books on Palmyra, and postcards, including some very impressive large aerial pictures of the site. The two shops within the lobby of the Cham Palace Hotel also offer a surprisingly good range of souvenirs, from jewellery to clothing to books and leather ware. They also sell colour film and even disposable cameras for anyone who has had a disaster with their own. The hotel and plenty of other places in the town of Tadmur will change money at any time.

OTHER PRACTICALITIES

TOURIST INFORMATION Opposite the Museum and open from 08.00 to 14.00, this office has the usual selection of maps and pamphlets and can organise guides.

BANKS The Commercial Bank of Syria has an exchange booth open from 08.00 to 20.00 except Fridays in front of the Museum. The Cham Palace Hotel also changes money any time of day.

INTERNET At the time of writing none of the hotels offered internet facilities to guests and there were no internet cafés in town, but this is bound to change very soon.

WHAT TO SEE AND DO

ARAB FORTRESS QAL'AT IBN MA'AN (*Signposted 'Fakhr Ed-Din Citadel' on the ground. Open daily 09.00–18.00 summer, 09.00–16.00 or sunset in winter; S£75 entry fee*) The exact origin of the fort is under some dispute, with some scholars attributing it to the celebrated Druze emir Fahkr Ad-Din Ibn Ma'an (1590-1635), who declared himself master of Lebanon and part of Syria, building a network of forts to protect his new possessions against the Ottoman Turks. He failed and was captured and executed in Istanbul, after which the fort was abandoned. Pottery and architectural fragments dating to the 12th and 13th centuries have been discovered at the fort, leading to speculation that its original construction, with its seven towers placed at irregular intervals round its outer wall dated from then, the same time that the Sanctuary of Bel was fortified. Entry today is via a splendid newly constructed wooden bridge over the impressive moat which was dug from the bedrock. Six hundred soldiers are estimated to have been garrisoned up here in a complex series of rooms including a kitchen, oven, baths, 30m-deep well and a prison. Steps lead all round the ramparts with spectacular views in all directions. The walk down from the Arab castle, a descent which takes some 20 minutes and then brings you into the back of the site gives you a real sense of scale as you pass along the main street to the Sanctuary of Bel and regain your transport. Allow one hour 15 minutes for the total walk.

THE PALMERY AND EFQA SPRING A half-hour stroll through the palmery is a very pleasant way to get the feel of the oasis itself, and the paths are all very public and communal. The local owners often use ancient bicycles to commute from their homes in the village of Tadmur to their palm gardens.

The largest oasis in the country, fed by a number of underground springs, Palmyra still produces more dates than anywhere else in Syria. Harvest time is between September and December and during those summer months visitors will see stalls lining the road selling all the many different types of dates. Arabic has over 50 words for date, each for a different state of ripeness, sweetness, size, colour, etc. The cheapest are the small yellow ones and the most expensive are the black ones that melt in the mouth. There are also pomegranate and olive orchards.

Many of the springs have now dried up, including the famously sulphurous and smelly Efqa spring near the Cham Hotel, which used to produce 32 gallons a second at a constant 33° C as recently as 1960. It dried up in 1994 supposedly after a landslide. Now all that remains is the battered blue sign beside the sunken area which can be viewed from above, with a few column bases and the dried-up water channel. With the increase in the number of hotels, water reserves are being put under increasing strain and many of the hotels now have notices in the rooms exhorting guests to be frugal in their use of water. Palmyra's water is currently pumped in from underground aquifers about 30km away.

Begin your walk at the foot of the Cham Hotel, entering the palmery along its perimeter wall. Very soon you will come upon a spring where local families are often to be found doing their washing or rinsing out newly shorn sheep's wool.

A few minutes further on you will come to the controversial site of a new hotel called Zaman Al-Majd, Time of Glory, which got permission to build inside the palmery, normally forbidden, on the pretext of being a film set only. The hotel was an absolute delight of imaginative and traditional design, with lots of small buildings sympathetically constructed from the natural sandstone and with the minimum of trees lost. Water channels and waterfalls ran everywhere and coffee houses were perched in treetops with marvellous views of the ruins. In the event however the relevant authorities were informed just days before the hotel was due to open in March 2005, the governor of Homs was sacked and the bulldozers were ordered in to destroy it for having broken planning laws, an interesting example of an attempted corruption that did not work.

VALLEY OF THE TOMBS (*Visits daily 08.30, 10.00, 11.30. 14.00; S£75 entry fee with tickets bought at the museum in advance; buses run from the museum at these set times, when the guardian opens them up*) The necropolis of Palmyra, with over 150 tombs surveyed so far, is one of the most spectacular sets of graves in the Near East. The tower tombs are the oldest and range from 9BC to AD128. The Hypogeum of Yarhai has been dismantled and reassembled now in the Damascus Museum. Only two tombs are currently open to the public – one tower tomb, called Elahbel, and one underground (a hypogeum) called Tomb of the Three Brothers – but both are well worth a visit for the elaborate paintings and decoration inside.

SYRIA'S WATER RESOURCES

Syria's water resources are limited and are already being over-utilised. The average annual availability is estimated at 14.58 million cubic metres, of which 68% is surprisingly from rainfall (much of it meltwater from the mountains), 23% from rivers, 6% from springs and 3% from underground water. Since total annual water use is currently running at 19.16 million cubic metres, and this figure is likely to rise as industry and tourism expand, the government has recognised that the problem must be addressed. Agriculture uses 85–90% of all the country's water resources through wasteful and inefficient irrigation, and this is what has to change. Spearheading the research into how to achieve this is the International Centre for Agricultural Research in Dry Areas (ICARDA) with its headquarters 32km south of Aleppo. Through more effective water management, the use of drip and sprinkler irrigation instead of the old-fashioned flood or basin type, and the growing of more water-efficient crops, water productivity can be greatly improved. The Ministry of Irrigation has been working with German technical support to try to implement new policies and encourage new investment which will gradually correct the problems. Desalination plants are also an option off Syria's coastline.

If you are fortunate enough to be staying at the Cham Hotel you can set off on foot, onto the signposted path opposite the hotel and aim to reach the Tomb of Elahbel for the 08.30 visit. Otherwise you have to come by taxi or arranged bus or walk the 3km from the modern town. The first group of tower tombs that you reach, on the slopes of the hill called Umm Al-Belqis (Mother of Belqis, Arabic name for the Queen of Sheba), either have their entrances blocked up or have metal grilles or their entrances are too high up to climb into without help or someone's shoulders to stand on.

The second tallest, the Tower of Jambliq, dates from AD83, still has four of its five storeys, and has elaborate carving on its façade with a pair of winged caryatid-like figures. Through the metal grille you can peer in to see the square holes in the side walls where the bodies would have been put, stacked five high, and the ceilings still have traces of red, blue and yellow painting in triangular and diamond patterns.

Crossing to the other side of the valley, the tallest tower tomb can be entered but has no decoration. Round the other side of the tomb however you can clamber inside and then ascend the steps up to each level, the steps ending at roof level on the third floor. From this roof you have a good view across to the Tower of Elahbel where you will be heading next, a ten-minute walk away to the west from the main site along the valley bed.

This magnificent tower tomb, dated to AD103, is well worth the visit. The stairs to the roof are intact and the views from the top are exhilarating. There is room for 300 bodies spread over its four storeys. From the back of the ground floor steps lead down into an underground crypt, making this both a tower tomb and a hypogeum. The dry air of Palmyra meant that the bodies put individually in their openings did not smell as they dried out quickly. They were simply mummified and wrapped in strips of cloth, as can be seen from the examples in the Palmyra Museum. The hole was then sealed with a slab bearing a facial likeness of the deceased. The blue used as the background for the images of the dead was extremely important in that it represented the celestial blue of heaven. It was also difficult to obtain due to scarcity of the woad plant from which it was made. From the top you can also see traces of the 6th-century Byzantine aqueduct that came along the valley bringing water to Diocletian's Camp, an indication that the local water system must have failed by then.

The only other tomb currently open to the public is the Hypogeum of the Three Brothers, dated to AD140, restored by the Syrian Directorate of Antiquities in 1947. Located entirely separately in what is known as the southwest necropolis, you need separate transport to get here as it lies out of town about 350m beyond the Cham Hotel on the right (north) of the road. Nothing is visible from above ground, just a large flight of steps leading underground into a spacious T-shaped chamber. The central part is decorated with a complex mix of motifs painted colourfully onto the plaster walls. Though heavily damaged in places and covered in Arabic grafitti, there are compositions with birds, a serpent and a scorpion, thought to be for warding off the evil eye, hunting scenes, winged figures and portraits of men and women painted in medallion shapes. On the back wall the painting is thought to represent a scene from *The Iliad*, in which Achilles, at the court of King Lycomedes, is disguised as a woman, hiding among the daughters. He is found here by Ulysses and taken back to the mortal world. On the ceiling in a circular border of yellow is Zeus as an eagle abducting Ganymede to be his cup-bearer. Both frescoes therefore point to human mortality, yet also suggest a future role in the afterlife.

There was room in this tomb for 65 bays with six recesses for bodies, making a total capacity of 310 bodies. A long Aramaic inscription on the door lintel to the tomb makes it clear that this was in fact a commercial venture, the body space being sold on in later generations to other families, almost as if they were blocks of flats. The elaborately carved sarcophagi of the three brothers themselves, Male, Sadi and Nomai, lie in the chamber to the right of the entrance.

It is in the portraits and paintings that the originality of Palmyrene art again shows itself, notably in the representation of the women with generally enlarged eyes and small mouths, dressed in Parthian or Graeco-Roman robes and wearing elaborate jewellery (see box on page 245). Note too the elaborate stone door of the tomb, carved to represent wood, a symbol of wealth.

From this southwest necropolis, another cluster of underground tombs lies at the southeast necropolis (confusingly also signposted southwest necropolis by mistake at the time of writing). Following the little tarmac road you will reach after about 3km a group of stunted tombs to the left of the road on the southern edge of the palmery, and three underground ones, all of which are kept locked. The tombs were accidentally discovered in the 1950s when the Iraq petrol company was laying a pipeline in the area. A section of the pipeline can still be seen running across the steps down to the Arteban Tomb, which has two massive stone slabs as its doors, decorated with demon-like griffins and a Medusa holding the ring. They are not generally open to the public, but the museum guardian has the key. Inside, the Arteban Tomb is a similar T-shaped plan to the Three Brothers Hypogeum and interestingly many of the loculi (holes for the bodies) still have their funerary busts in place. There is a frieze of Arteban, head of his clan, at his funeral banquet, being attended by various figures in the arch at the end of the main gallery. The tomb has been dated to the second half of the 1st century AD.

The nearby Japanese Tomb was officially opened in 2000, after excavations started in 1994. It has been immaculately restored by Japanese archaeologists and gives an excellent idea of what the original would have looked like, with all its rich decoration intact. An inscription on the lintel dates the tomb to AD128. Nearby is a black tent where the local guardian lives, but he has no authority to open the tombs. There are still enough visitors to warrant little children running up to sell you cards.

MAIN PALMYRA SITE From the Valley of the Tombs you should now walk over towards the main ruins, passing a few other ruined tower tombs, and climb the hill at the back of Diocletian's Camp for an excellent overview of the city. The suggested visit starts from here, not only because it allows the climax of the visit to be the Sanctuary of Bel at the furthest end, but also because the street was developed from west to east, so your visit will follow its chronological order, after Diocletian's Camp.

Diocletian's Camp After Palmyra was plundered in AD273 this was the camp set up by the governor of Syria under Diocletian after the fall of the over-ambitious Queen Zenobia. The Roman garrison lived here, and the main structures remaining are the Praetorian Gateway, a huge triple-bayed structure, the Temple of the Emblems and the Sanctuary of Allat, a local goddess. The whole area was criss-crossed by two colonnaded avenues, and was excavated by a Polish team who began work in 1956. Further excavations have been carried out, the latest in 2003–04.

The most prominent of the buildings is the Temple of the Emblems (AD293–303), approached by a vast, heavily weathered flight of steps. Right at the back was the *cella* or shrine where the Roman legion's standards were housed, and from which a staircase can still be climbed to roof level for a good view over the city.

Zenobia's palace was thought to be located here, as the street layout and remains of a tetrapylon pre-dating Diocletian's occupation suggest a monumental complex of some sort, and this area is also thought to be the earliest settled part of the city. The street here ends in what has been identified as an oval piazza, the only one known in the Eastern world apart from that at the Roman site of Jerash, north of Amman, immediately before the collapsed remains of the Damascus Gate.

Temple of Allat Only the door frame, lintel and some ornate fluted columns remain of this temple, but the famous giant lion holding an antelope now sitting at the entrance to the Palmyra Museum, was found inside. Seen as a warrior goddess who protected the nomads, Allat was Arab in origin but was equated with Ishtar in Mesopotamia. A very fine statue of the goddess, with the features of Athena, was found here in 1975 and can be seen in the local museum. It dates to the 3rd century AD.

Funerary Temple Also known as the House Tomb, this fine building with its six-columned portico is very well preserved and has some fine vine and grape carving. It dates to the late 2nd century AD and still has steps down into a vault-like crypt. The portico was always standing, but reconstruction work was used to build up the back and outside walls, as can be seen by the extensive use of concrete where the stones were missing.

Colonnaded Street This end of the street, less marked by public buildings, was the first stretch of the axis to be developed and has been dated to the first half of the 2nd century AD. The further stretch, where most of the public buildings are concentrated, dates from the later 2nd century. A phenomenal 1.2km, this open-air main street of Palmyra was deliberately never paved, in order to allow easy use by camels. Its width was a massive 23m including the porticos on either side that would have been lined with shop stalls. Many of the Corinthian columns have been re-erected by the Syrian Department of Antiquities. They measure a full metre in diameter and stand 31ft tall including the base and capital. The moulded plinth known as a console halfway up each column would originally have carried a statue of the city's various dignitaries or wealthy citizens. Baedeker in his 1876 Guide tells that many of these were on sale to passing travellers, and he even advises that no more than 30-40 piastres should be paid for them as they were 'generally of rude execution'.

Byzantine churches To the left (north) as you walk along the colonnaded street towards the tetrapylon are the vestigial remains of two basilicas, set within what seems to be a residential area of grid-layout streets and housing, now all reduced to ground level. Traces of piping and drains can be seen in the residential area along with remains of the characteristic Byzantine small stone rubble jerry-building scattered about. This Byzantine infill can also be seen in the repairs done to Diocletian's city walls during the reign of Emperor Justinian.

Tetrapylon Reconstructed in 1963 by the Syrian Directorate of Antiquities, the groupings of four-pillared podia would originally each have held a statue standing on a plinth in the centre of the four columns. Only one of the original pink Aswan granite columns transported from Egypt has survived here, the remainder having been reconstructed from concrete substitutes. A 10° change in orientation of the colonnaded street is skilfully concealed by the placement of this tetrapylon. Meaning 'crossroads', it marks the crossing point of the two main roads of the city, to the north and to the south.

Continuing now along the colonnaded street look out on the right for a series of eight columns of interest for their inscriptions. On the sixth column is a dedication

When Lady Jane Dibgy, born into the English aristocracy in 1807, first arrived in Damascus in her late 40s, she had decided men brought her nothing but trouble and her love life was over. In the event it was here that she was to meet and marry the love of her life, a Bedouin sheikh 20 years her junior.

At the age of 17 she had married Lord Ellenborough, only to then be the subject of a divorce that so shocked English society that she was forced to leave the country. She spent her middle years in Europe with a succession of lovers, including an Austrian prince, a German baron, mad King Ludwig of Bavaria, a Greek count and an Albanian rebel leader. Stunningly beautiful with blue eyes and long golden hair, she had been well educated by her family, acquiring fluency in many languages and a knowledge of classical history. She was also a superb equestrian and retained her physical condition and athletic horsemanship well into her 70s. She had six children with various fathers, some of whom she was married to, some of whom she was not – in short she behaved like most aristocratic men of the age, but was condemned for so doing. Her family supported her throughout, sending her money, the latest London fashions and long, loving letters. The only child of her own for whom she had any real maternal feelings, son of the Greek count, died in a tragic accident aged six.

Contrary to all expectation and prediction, Jane remained married to Medjuel, younger brother to the head of the Mezrab tribe, till her death in 1881. They met when he was assigned as her safety escort to Palmyra, and when he proposed, she accepted only on condition that he divorce his other wives and never take another. They communicated initially in Turkish and she later learnt Arabic.

Thus began an unconventional marriage in which she built and maintained a beautiful Arab courtyard house north of the walled Old City with fine gardens, kept a menagerie of animals, and spent whole chunks of the year in the desert with the tribe. She attained great respect and status among the tribe, not only because of the money she was able to bring to them which enabled them to have the best mounts and weapons, but also because of her fine spirit, horsemanship and willingness to nurse them with European medicines. She is buried in the Evangelical cemetery near Bab Qinnisrin about 2km south of the Old City.

Through her time spent in the company of the Turkish harem women of Ottoman princes, Jane learnt a great deal about the intimate sexual practices of the Arabs and she was indeed the source of much of Richard Burton's information for his translation of the Arabian Nights, especially the terminal essay, and for his later book *The Perfumed Garden*, a manual of sexual instruction. Burton said she was out and out the cleverest woman he ever met. She spoke nine languages, could read and write in them all, painted, was musical, sculpted and gardened. She authored no books but wrote excellent letters throughout her life which formed much of the basis for several biographies including one by Mary S Lovell (see *Appendix 3*).

to 'Septimius Odainat, King of Kings, and Corrector of all the East' on the bracket of the column, but the bracket of the next column is missing, the dedication to his wife Queen Zenobia having been scratched off by the Romans, as she was considered a traitor. Next you pass, after about 50m, the remains on your left of the small *nymphaeum* with three columns of its four still standing, and then you come to the main collection of civic buildings, with the theatre on your right.

Theatre First cleared of sand in 1952, the theatre has been the subject of extensive restoration by the Directorate of Antiquities, and work was completed in the early 1990s. It has been dated to the 1st or 2nd century AD, with a very elaborate *scenae frons* (stage building), boasting five rather than the usual three doorways. Considering the size of the *scenae frons* it is surprising, given the prominence of the city, that the theatre capacity is so small, with only 13 rows of seats. It has been speculated that the upper seats may therefore never have been completed, since there are no further foundations. The theatres at Bosra, Apamea and even Cyrrhus were all considerably larger. It would have been used in Roman times for wrestling spectacles with wild animals. Nowadays it is in use during the Palmyra Festival which started in 1993, usually held 2-5 May, and during the Silk Road Festival, usually held at the end of September. Various folkloric dancing and singing performances take place, as well as horse and camel races in the recently built racecourse below the Arab fort, and even marathons for local youth. The local inhabitants take part with great gusto in these events, highlights of their year, making them exciting and exhilarating occasions for foreigners to be part of.

Senate, Tariff Court and Agora At the back of the theatre, away from the colonnaded street, walk now in a straight line towards the group of buildings which comprise the Senate, the Tariff Court and the agora. The first building, labelled the Senate, heavily ruined, is surprisingly small, with an entrance hall and peristyle courtyard. By AD60 the Roman Senate was the sole governing body of Palmyra, and the senate members are thought to have sat in tiered seats arranged in a semicircle in the chamber at the far end. This whole area of the city was the hub of commercial and administrative activity. The agora, a massive 71m by 84m and with 11 entrances to avoid congestion in coming and going, was found during excavations to have column bases holding some 200 statues of prominent citizens. The inscriptions that have been found from some of these statues have yielded much of the detail of civic life in the city at the time. We can deduce from them for instance that senators' statues were reserved for the eastern colonnade, officials of Rome and Palmyra to the north, soldiers to the west and caravan chiefs to the south. To the eastern side of the agora, through what is known as the Senator's Gate, is a smaller courtyard usually referred to as the 'Tariff Court' because it was here that the massive stone block was found, known as the Tariff of Palmyra, setting out in Greek and Aramaic, the two languages of the bilingual city (Latin being used only rarely) the rates of tax payments for goods being brought in or out of the city. Here it would have been where city officials would have stood demanding the various amounts from the traders and this was how Palmyra accumulated its wealth. The block was engraved with the date AD137. It was discovered in 1881 by a Russian aristocrat traveller, Prince Lazaref, and was carted off to the Hermitage Museum of St Petersburg in 1901. The tariffs carved on the stone showed that perfumes were heavily taxed, as were dried fish from Lake Tiberias, olive oil, cattle, water and prostitutes.

Over in the furthest (southwest) corner of the agora are the scanty remains of what has been identified as a small banqueting hall because of the benches for the diners who would have reclined on their sides to eat, Roman style. The walls are decorated with a geometric swastika motif, a symbol thought to have originated in India and widely regarded as a sign of peace and good luck.

Baths of Diocletian Signposted as the Baths of Zenobia, the entrance to these baths is marked by four massive Aswan granite columns 1.3m in diameter and 12.5m tall. How these gigantic blocks each weighing at least 20 tonnes were transported from Egypt remains a mystery. Not much remains of the rest of the baths, but the outline of the bathing pool frigidarium is still visible, partially surrounded by a colonnade of Corinthian columns, together with the paving stones of the octagonal dressing room with a drain in the centre.

Temple of Nebo Very little remains of this temple beyond the podium and the column bases of the portico. Nebo was a Mesopotamian god of oracles, wisdom and writing, often identified with Apollo, whose popularity in Palmyra illustrates again how the city was not conventionally Roman, preferring to worship Eastern deities. In the Babylonian pantheon he was son of Mardok, Lord of Heaven and scribe of the Table of Destinies, a role which gave him great power over the fortunes of mortals. The merchants of Palmyra clearly wanted to keep his favour, so when they built the colonnaded street, they were afraid of displeasing him through moving the temple, so decided instead that the pre-existing temple should stay where it was, and the colonnaded street be diverted round it, necessitating the triumphal arch device described below.

Monumental arch Very cleverly constructed in the triangular splayed-out shape of a fan, the monumental arch uses this device to disguise the 30° change of orientation of the colonnaded street. In effect there are two monumental arches, one facing the Bel Temple, the other facing the colonnaded street, each one aligned to its street and carefully joined together to make a V-shape. Inscriptions tell us that it was erected in the reign of Emperor Septimius Severus (AD193–211), the peak of Palmyra's prosperity, reflected in the richly and elaborately carved decoration of the arching and the pilasters, typically Syrian in their geometric and floral patterns, with acorns and palm trees.

Temple of Baal Shamin One of the most complete structures of Palmyra, this little temple was cleared in c1956 by a Swiss expedition, who then planted the tree which graces the interior. Originally part of an extensive precinct of three courtyards and built in cAD150, the temple was dedicated to Baal Shamin, a Canaanite deity associated with rain and therefore fertility. It is a beautiful and complex building, displaying a range of architectural influences, resulting in a pleasing mix of Roman and oriental. The architectural tradition in its proportions and column capitals is pure Roman, yet the crenellations above the architrave and the side windows show an oriental tradition, with the highly stylised acanthus leaves of the Corinthian capitals revealing an Egyptian influence. It was converted to a church in the 5th century when Palmyra was the seat of a bishop. An inscription tells us the temple was erected by Male Agrippa, the wealthy Palmyrene citizen who also paid for Hadrian's visit.

You can also break your tour here for a drink on the nearby terrace of the Zenobia Hotel, the only hotel actually set within the ruins, and very pleasant at sunset after a hard day's exploring and walking.

Ethnographic Museum (*Open 08.30-15.30 daily except Tue; entry fee S£75; basic WC facilities*) Set by itself near the Temple of Bel is this simple single-storey whitewashed building, originally built as the residence of the Ottoman governor of Palmyra. During the French Mandate it was converted to a rather notorious prison.

Inside are displays of the interiors of Bedouin tents and traditional Palmyrene houses, along with traditional Bedouin costumes, chunky silver Bedouin jewellery and local handicrafts such as baskets and sandals. There are also some colourful rugs, with displays to show spinning and weaving techniques. Captions are all in French only, but the displays have been attractively and sympathetically designed and do their best to explain the Bedouin lifestyle and the sheikh leadership system. His duties were to solve disputes at his *majlis* or open council usually held once a

10

Just here before the Bel Temple is the one place in Syria where you are certain to be offered a ride on a camel, as there is almost always a cluster of them lying in wait, their reluctance matched only by their owners' determination to persuade you to mount. If you decide to go for it, hang on tight for the sudden lurch forwards as the back legs are straightened, followed by the equally violent lurch backwards as the front legs are straightened to join them in an upright position. Compared with this getting up, and of course the getting down when the process happens in reverse order, the actual ride is child's play and rather fun as you hook your leg round the wooden pommel as an anchor.

The lifestyle of the traditional Bedouin (from the Arabic Bedu [singular] meaning 'desert dweller', [plural] Bedouin) was inextricably interwoven with the camel. His constant companion, his alter ego, he drank its milk instead of water, made his tent from its hair, ate its meat, used its dung as fuel and its urine as a hair tonic and medicine. Using a thick comb the Bedouin girls collected winter hair from the camel and used it for weaving. They span and dyed the wool themselves. Most things used to be computed in camels – the wealth of a sheikh, the dowry, the blood price in a feud, even gambling profit. The Bedu was the 'parasite of the camel', in the words of a 19th century German traveller. In times of emergency either an old camel was killed or a stick thrust down its throat to make it vomit water, which was drinkable as long as the camel had been watered within the last couple of days. Arabic is said to have over 1,000 names for the camel in its different stages and breeds – only the sword has a similar number of names. Enormous care was taken of the camels: ''ata Allah', the 'gift of God' is how they were often referred to. Riding camels are invariably female and are often adorned with charms round their necks. Camels live to be about 20 years old. They mate for life when they are two and camel calves are generally born in the autumn. They are very expensive to buy so the sacrifice involved in slaughtering them is great. Each family brands its yearling camels on the cheek and on the hind quarters, applying yoghurt to the burn to soothe it. 'Better than beauty is a camel', runs the saying.

Today camel herds are relatively rare in Syria and most Bedouin herd goats and sheep, often using Nissan or Toyota pick-up trucks to transport them within hours instead of days, to areas of new pasture, a fact which is altering forever the ecological balance as new pastures are devoured almost immediately they appear. (See box *The end of the Bedouin lifestyle?*, page 269.)

week, where all could approach him with their grievances; to declare war or peace; to distribute booty after warring raids on enemy tribes; to decide on marriages and divorces; to decide on where to move the tents next (his tent was always the first to be folded); to collect taxes for the government; to receive guests and offer hospitality.

Sanctuary of Bel (*Open 08.00–16.00 winter, 08.00–13.00, 16.00–18.00 summer daily; entry fee S£150; no WCs inside; basic WC facilities and refreshments at simple portakabin nearby with open-air seating and sunshades*) The degree of hassling to ride camels and buy headscarves etc in the vicinity of the Bel Temple is now becoming tiresome, and the Ministry of Tourism needs to curb this, as at present it acts only as a deterrent from buying anything. The ticket kiosk has a good collection of books and cards for sale.

Keep your visit to the Sanctuary of Bel, the most important and impressive monument of Palmyra, till last. From the ticket office on the outside you have little idea of what lies within. Once inside the temple enclosure, the sheer scale of the place cannot fail to impress.

Look back first of all at the west wall through which you have just entered. The massive blocks of this wall, built in the 2nd to 3rd century AD, are immense, but note that mixed in are much rougher rubble reconstructions following later 10th-century earthquake damage and the 12th-century Arab conversion to a fortress. Roman fragments like round column drums, pediments, pilasters and niches can be picked out jumbled up randomly in the walls, especially the north wall. The original sandy-coloured stone is in fact all limestone. This quarry was only rediscovered a few years ago, and still has unfinished column shafts, loading ramps and a sophisticated water system and channels to supply water for the workers, who lived in caves. So-called 'dragonhouses' built from broken or rejected blocks can also be seen, used for guards' shelters and for storing materials. With the building boom of the 2nd century AD new methods of quarrying developed to meet the demand, with larger blocks being cut faster and using better tools.

Take a moment now to consider the general layout and ground plan of the temple which represents the complex blending of Roman and oriental elements we have seen already elsewhere at Palmyra in many stylistic and architectural features. The striking feature of the layout here is the isolation of the temple *cella* within the huge 210m by 205m courtyard, a feature first developed in Syria and to be seen at the Phoenician temple of Amrit, the Roman temple compound of Husn Suleyman and then at the Temple of Jupiter at Baalbek which can be described as the climax of the Syro-Phoenician style. This layout confines the religious area with the gods' image and the priestly worship to a relatively small space, leaving the open area of the courtyard for big gatherings of worshippers and ritual processions. The whole complex was built in four stages: first, the original Hellenistic temple of which only fragments incorporated in later walls survive; second, the *cella* itself, completed in AD32; third, the peribolos or outer area of the sacred enclosure was enlarged between AD80 and AD120 and surrounded by a roofed double colonnaded portico of Corinthian columns on the north, east and south; and fourth, the portico and monumental pillared entrance (propylaeum) was added in the late 2nd century. The model reconstruction in the museum to be seen later helps give a very clear idea of the original layout and grandeur of the temple.

Turning back to face the centre of the enclosure, the next thing to notice to your left is a sunken passageway which is thought to be where sacrificial animals (camels, cattle, sheep, bulls and rams), were led along towards the altar in the main temple. The animals used were not sick or poorly, but top quality. Anything else would not be good enough for the gods. Lining the passageway are steps where the rich of Palmyra dressed in all their finery would have sat to watch the procession of sacrificial animals, led by the priests. The mural described later outside the *cella* depicts just such a scene.

As you now proceed towards the steps leading up into the *cella* or shrine of the temple, you will notice to the left of the stairs, the base of the sacrificial altar where the animal passage ends, and to the right of the steps the remains of the lustral basin, a ritual pool for knife-washing ablutions, with water channels still visible. The base itself measures 10m by 8m and below it is a tunnel which leads off into the oasis, into which the blood ran, mixed with water. The iron-rich solution was known even then to be very good at improving the fertility of the soil, a good example of early recycling. The meat of the sacrifices was eaten too, after cooking. It was never wasted. These elements of the altar and the lustral basin outside the *cella* are also typical of the Syro-Phoenician temple style, and are found too at the temple sanctuary of Husn Suleyman (see pages 203–4).

The *cella*, relatively small within the huge compound, is the undoubted centrepiece of the complex, yet curiously, is set off-centre, a little to the east, to create a larger space between it and the monumental entrance. Its 18m-tall columns look unfinished as they appear to have no decorative capitals. This is because they would have been plated in gold from Africa and silver, a mark of oriental opulence that would have contrasted with the relative simplicity and restraint of the single-chambered walls of the *cella*. None of the statues that would have adorned the consoles two thirds of the way up the columns has ever been found. An inscription suggests these statues were made of bronze, which would explain why, as they would have been melted down and sold or traded by later inhabitants.

The original roof would have been of Lebanese cedarwood. The rather precarious-looking reconstruction of the portal was carried out by a French team in 1932. Its amazingly elaborate and exuberantly carved decoration with rows of eggs symbolising birth and fertility, fruits and floral and geometric patterns, illustrates once again the Syrian version of the essentially Roman styles. The step pyramid battlements (called 'merlons') crowning the peristyle and a few of the outer walls show a Babylonian influence.

Once inside the *cella*, note it has two shrines, one at each end of the 30m by 10m chamber. This, another Semitic adaptation (used in the Temple of Jerusalem), is to reflect the fact that Bel was Palmyra's supreme deity, identified with the Mesopotamian Bel Mardok, equated with the Greek Zeus and Roman Jupiter. Note too that the *cella* entrance itself is off-centre, more to the right (south) as you enter, to allow better viewing and prominence to the main shrine of Bel to the left (north). The shrine niches today are heavily blackened by the smoke of open fires and barbecues which used to take place here, but it is still possible to make out on the domed ceiling in the northern one (to the left as you enter), the images of seven gods of the planets – Jupiter in the centre, surrounded by Helios, Selene, Ares, Hermes, Aphrodite and Cronos, surrounded in turn by 12 signs of the zodiac. Of these the Fish and Sagittarius are the most readily discernible. Astrology developed in this part of the world long before it came to the west. Bel himself is represented as an eagle controlling the heavens with wings spread out. The shrine niche, which would originally have contained an image of the Palmyrene trinity, has two concealed chambers from which a staircase leads up onto the roof (now grilled off), thought to have been where ritual sacrifices would also have taken place.

The southern, slightly smaller shrine niche (to the right as you enter) is remarkable too for its ceiling motif, cut out of one solid giant stone block, a massive stylised flower ringed by acanthus leaves and lotus leaves, with a border and rosettes of great detail and beauty. This motif is reproduced in one of the drawings by the English architects Wood and Dawkins, a motif which went on to influence directly the patterns used in the classical revival of the 18th century in England. On either side of the niche are two more staircases leading to the roof, now blocked off by a protective grill. The niche itself would have contained a movable idol which is why the steps were not so steep, to facilitate its removal.

In Byzantine times the *cella* was used as a church and traces of faint frescoes can still be made out on the western wall, of the archangels Gabriel and Michael and St George. In the 12th century it was converted to a mosque which remained in use till 1929 when the villagers who had taken up residence in the temple precincts were moved out by the French archaeological team. There are many grafitti on the *cella* walls, some of which go back to the first centuries of Islam, and in the southern *cella* niche a *mihrab* was added to indicate Mecca and the direction of prayer.

Outside the *cella* to the left as you exit, note the exceptionally beautiful carved blocks with bas reliefs that have fallen from the roof architrave of the temple peristyle. From left to right you can discern two worshippers wearing the Persian

The Palmyrenes were open to all influences and the blend of these can be seen in the decorative elements of the extraordinary blocks in front of the *cella* entrance. Islamic art is dominated by geometric shapes representing infinity, Assyrian art is dominated by lions representing power, Egyptian art is dominated by symbols of perpetuity. All in rows around the sides of the main *cella* portal are olives, grapes, opium, arrows (death) and eggs (birth). On the lintel are pineapples and figs. Also represented is Tainat the goddess of evil and of all catastrophes, represented as female on the top half and five snakes on the bottom half, with arrows and eggs in bands underneath. Their need to cover the surfaces in exuberant decoration was greater than was usual in Roman sculptural art and gives a strong contrast with the formalism of the plain classical walls, especially here at the Bel Temple.

In the museum too you will see examples in the statues and carved funerary scenes showing how the local styles differed from the conventional Roman with which they were contemporary. So distant from the influences of Rome it is perhaps not surprising that a unique style developed here, a kind of blend of Persian, Egyptian, Babylonian and Phoenician within a Hellenistic and Roman artistic and architectural framework. They used the oriental custom of showing figures full frontal, never in profile, with timeless rather than realistic facial expressions, though the later funerary sculptures, like those to be seen in the Palmyra Museum, did show individualised faces with lifelike expressions. Note too that the ladies' immaculate hairstyles, headdresses, clothing and jewellery are unique to Palmyra and have not been seen elsewhere.

Parthian large baggy trousers; the god of fertility Malakbel, recognisable by his attributes the pomegranate, the fir cone and the kid; and then the moon god Aglibol beside a tree with a diamond halo and dressed in Roman style. On a second huge slab is a further unusual bas relief showing a procession with a camel led by a cameleer and carrying on his back a red tent which would have held a statue of the god. This is a procession which would have taken place each year on 6 April. An unusual and surprisingly modern feature is the crowd, which is depicted as a series of faceless female figures draped in robes, possibly even veiled, which is interesting considering this is four centuries before the advent of Islam, and which some have taken as evidence that veiling was a pre-Islamic heritage of pagan times. Getting down on your knees to look at the underneath of the carved lintel block you can see the lavish grape design that would originally have been clearly visible under the lintel architrave.

In the far northeast corner of the precinct is the house of the French excavation team that started work here in the late 1920s. Walking round behind the *cella* you can see where further excavations were conducted in the 1990s by a French mission, looking at the original Hellenistic foundations of the temple. Simple house foundations were also uncovered, each house with its small hall, with six levels of occupation covering 500 years.

Beyond the precinct wall itself outside the east wall, a pair of 3rd-century AD patrician houses, each round a central courtyard, were also excavated, the mosaics from which, including one of the Cassiope myth, are now on display in the Palmyra room of the Damascus Museum.

Archaeological Museum (*Open 08.00–18.00 summer, 08.00–13.00, 14.00–16.00 winter, 08.00–15.00 Ramadan; S£150 entry fee, students S£10; allow 45mins; tickets for the tombs must be bought here, too; basic WCs*). At the museum entrance note the gigantic

1st-century BC statue of the lion apparently sheltering a gazelle beneath him. Found in the Temple of Allat within Diocletian's Camp, it is thought to represent the dual principles of bravery in the face of the enemy whilst showing mercy to the vulnerable.

Opened in 1961 the museum is less impressive than it might be, not least because a lot of Palmyra's more exciting finds have been transferred to the Damascus Museum or even to other museums around the world. It is best visited after seeing the site, as the exhibits will mean more.

Inside there are several exhibits of note. Room I shows examples of the ancient Palmyrene writing, related to Aramaic, and some altars discovered near the Efqa spring. In Room II is the striking model reconstruction of the Bel Temple, complete with roof which illustrates just how major this temple precinct was, one of the most important in the Middle East at this period, along with Baalbek in Lebanon. Beside it is a smaller-scale reconstruction of Diocletian's Camp.

In Room III look out for the carving of a Palmyrene sailing boat on one of the stelae, showing how maritime trade was also important to these desert people. Walking past some attractive displays of green pottery and glass found at the palace of Qasr Al-Hayr Ash-Sharqi, you will note next the exceptionally beautiful jewellery, with necklaces of coloured stones, dangly long earrings and finely worked gold, much of which was found in a gold hoard within Diocletian's Camp. You come now to the southern gallery filled mainly with religious sculpture from the Temple of Baal Shamin, but look out too for the statue found in the Temple of Allat, identified with Athena, which would have held a spear in its right arm and a shield in its left. It looks like a direct copy of the statue of Athena on the Parthenon on the Acropolis at Athens.

The most noteworthy part of the museum however is the final group of rooms IV, V and VI, which contain the remarkable and distinctive funerary art of Palmyra, especially the heavily detailed busts of the deceased which were found sealing off the entrance to their tombs. These represent a highly developed style of dress, especially the ladies who had immaculate and elaborate hairstyles. Those with headdresses were thought to be married, those without unmarried. The statues also illustrate well the elaborateness of the jewellery, earrings, necklaces, bracelets and even forehead jewellery, along with the heavily embroidered clothing. In one vitrine a fragment of cloth even remains, a testimony to the dryness of the climate, but there is far more on this upstairs. In scenes of funeral banquets on the sides of sarcophagi, some are holding a cup in one hand to symbolise eternal life, while in the other hand is a leaf symbolising life coming back. The facial expressions of the statues are remarkably lifelike.

Go now to the upstairs galleries, most of which are empty, their contents having been moved to what is now the Ethnographic Museum beside the Temple of Bel, but in the one small area in the corner that is left, you will find some fascinating exhibits of mummies, fragments of papyrus with Greek and Palmyrene letters and many textile fragments, all of which were found in the tower tombs. There is a whole grouping of mummies found in the tower tombs between 1985 and 2004, and the wrapping procedure is explained whereby a pink silk was put over the face and feet as the innermost layer, then working towards the outermost layer, there were three layers of thin fine wool, then one of coarse wool, then one of purple wool, then two of coarse linen, before the final outermost layer of fine linen. Note too the leather shoe fragments in all sizes, from adult to child.

The major displays here are from the 2,000 textile fragments found in the tower tombs, one of the largest groups of ancient textiles of proven origin in the world. They all date from between the 1st-century BC and the 2nd-century AD. All the restoration work on them has been done in Syria and they are displayed only here

More than half of Syria qualifies as *badia* or steppeland, with a low annual rainfall of under 200mm. It makes good grazing for livestock however and has traditionally been home to most of Syria's sheep, whose numbers have increased five-fold since the 1950s. Overgrazing has recently been a serious problem and a project is now in place to plant hundreds of thousands of seedlings to restore the damaged steppeland, which has met with considerable success. The regeneration of the badia has had other unexpected side benefits, such as an increase in the number of valuable truffles to be found after early rainfall. These truffles are prized locally and in the Gulf and can fetch as much as US$20 a kilo. The Bedouin have quickly discovered for themselves that the reseeding provides a better return than growing barley and their fodder costs have dropped substantially as a result.

and in Damascus. There are two types of textile, the local linen, wool and cotton, and the imported silk from India and China. The textiles are of excellent quality and have sophisticated designs such as floral arabesque patterns which can be traced to architectural patterns too, and some have human and animal motifs. Maritime subject matters also show a link with the Syrian coast. Often the principles of design are Roman, brought into line with oriental taste. Weaving techniques are also illustrated in one of the vitrines. The Syro-German mission which conducted the research work on these textiles has put up an excellent series of explanatory tableaux beside the exhibits. The tower tombs where they were found evidently belonged to the high aristocracy of Palmyra, to judge from the wealth and quality of the textiles.

TALILA RESERVE Opened in 1992 and financed jointly by the Italian government, the World Food and Agriculture Organisation and the Syrian Ministry of Agriculture, this remarkable and praiseworthy project deserves to be more widely visited and publicised. It was the first in Syria and there is now just one other in Hasake in the north, called the Jebel 'Adb Al-'Aziz Reserve, named after the mountain range where it is located southeast of Hasake.

Within Talila's 72km perimeter fence there are no plastic bags, wonder of wonders, and the calm and peaceful air is broken only by birdsong. There are 380 protected gazelle and 65 oryx. Even so the caretakers say it will take a full 30 years for the land to return to its original pristine state. Syria's Ministry of the Environment is only three years old so all such schemes are in their infancy here. Asma Al-Assad, British-born wife of Bashar, opened the reserve and is also involved in sponsoring village crafts for women.

Apart from the animals themselves the reserve also has an inspired visitors' centre, very cleverly designed and put together with display boards explaining Bedouin poems and wisdom to do with their approach to nature and to life generally.

To make the visit you have first of all to find the Mudiriyat Al-Badia (Directorate of the Desert/Steppe), tucked up in a side street in Tadmur, with its yellow sign announcing: 'Range Rehabilitation and Establishment of a Wildlife Reserve in the Syrian Steppe.'

Make an appointment for later the same day and an escort from the office will then accompany you to the reserve to ensure that the gates are unlocked for you and that your access is authorised. Once inside, the sandy tracks to reach the animals are easily driveable in a saloon car. The reserve lies 35km to the southeast of Palmyra, at a clearly marked turning south off the Deir Ez-Zour road.

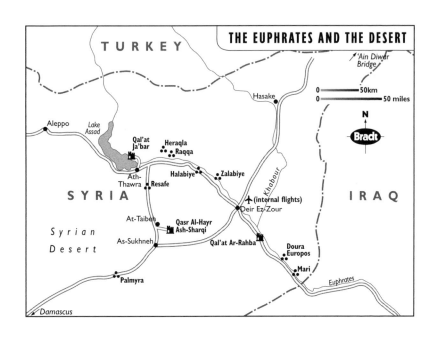

THE EUPHRATES AND THE DESERT

TURKEY

'Ain Diwar Bridge

Hasake

0 ———— 50km
0 ———— 50 miles

N

Bradt

Aleppo

Lake Assad

Qal'at Ja'bar

Heraqla

Raqqa

Ath-Thawra

Resafe

Halabiye

Zalabiye

Khabour

(internal flights)
Deir Ez-Zour

SYRIA

IRAQ

At-Taibeh

Qasr Al-Hayr
Ash-Sharqi

As-Sukhneh

Qal'at Ar-Rahba

Doura Europos

Syrian Desert

Mari

Palmyra

Euphrates

Damascus

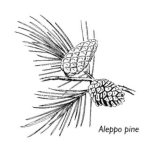

Aleppo pine

248

11

The Euphrates and the Desert

البادية والفرات

Better to ride a dung beetle than to tread on soft carpets.

The Euphrates is, along with the Tigris, one of the great rivers of the Middle East. When you first see it, its serenity, power and majesty are almost tangible. Much of this is obviously association, as it is easy to imagine life and early civilisation growing up on its banks. Rising in the highlands of eastern Turkey it then flows through southeast Turkey, its flow diminished by a succession of dams within Turkey as part of the Turkish Southeast Anatolia Project (GAP), then enters Syria northeast of Aleppo near Membij and forms the western edge of the triangular shape formed by the Tigris on the eastern side. This triangle is known in Arabic as 'Al-Jazira' and corresponds with the northern part of ancient Mesopotamia, most of which lies in today's Iraq.

GETTING THERE AND AWAY

There is an airport for domestic flights at Deir Ez-Zour (see page 255), 7km east of the city centre.

DELUXE COACH STATION Known as the 'Garagat Al-Jdaide' the Deir Ez-Zour coach station is located a longish walk just over 1km south of the town centre. Kadmous offers the most frequent services, with Damascus (via Palmyra) taking five hours, and Aleppo also five hours, with prices around S£140–180.

TRAIN STATION The train station is 3km northeast of the centre of Deir Ez-Zour, inconveniently located, but trains are so erratic you would be ill-advised to use them anyway.

FOLLOWING THE RIVER

The highlights of the drive along the Euphrates are the Byzantine walled desert city of Resafe, the Byzantine fortress city of Halabiye and the walled city of Doura Europos in its dramatic setting on a clifftop overlooking the river. The other sites are essentially minor, and Mari, though so important historically, is a bare site, its treasures all in museums. The Jazira region has only one monument of interest, the ruined Roman bridge at 'Ain Diwar, and otherwise is noteworthy for its fertile landscape of beautiful rolling hills and fields of wheat and for its very friendly Kurdish population, most of Syria's 1.9 million Kurds being concentrated here.

THE DRIVE FROM ALEPPO TO DEIR EZ-ZOUR (*Allow 4–5hrs if non-stop*) Leaving Aleppo from the western suburbs on the airport road, you embark on the long and in all honesty somewhat featureless drive along the Euphrates to Deir Ez-Zour,

Created in 1973 when the dam became operational after ten years of construction, the lake measures 80km in length, with an average width of 8km. The dual purpose of the project was to meet Syria's growing demand for electricity through the hydro-electric turbines, and to provide irrigation water to reclaim 640,000ha of desert into cultivation. It is the most ambitious construction project ever undertaken in Syria, a remarkable piece of engineering, achieved with Soviet technical and financial assistance. The dam is 4.5km long and 500m wide at its base, filled in with 41 million cubic metres of sand and gravel. Its ability to achieve its targets of electricity generation and irrigation have been severely curbed by the subsequent construction upstream of Turkey's Ataturk Dam, centrepiece of its series of dams called the Southeast Anatolia Project. A number of archaeological sites were flooded by the creation of the lake and several rescue excavations took place, as documented in the upstairs section of the Aleppo Museum. The site that can still be visited despite the lake is Qal'at Ja'bar, raised up on its own hillock and now approached on a specially constructed causeway.

where, at the time of writing, the only tourist-standard accommodation in the whole Euphrates valley is to be found. There is talk of a new hotel at Halabiye but that will be a few years off. The airport at Aleppo, which takes an increasing number of international flights, is about 10km west of the city centre, and beyond that you pass through flat, drab expanses of scrub desert.

Ath-Thawra الثورة The first place for a stop is Ath-Thawra about 150km east of Aleppo, where there is a simple shop/café with tolerably clean toilets, on the right-hand side as you enter the town on the dual carriageway approach to the centre of town. You can also stock up with soft drinks and snacks here to supplement your picnic, as there is nowhere recommended for lunch en route. Ath-Thawra itself (the name means 'The Revolution') is a hideous Soviet-style modern town, whose horrendous housing blocks are the subject of a scandalous corruption story. Built to appallingly inadequate specifications, their foundations are crumbling and vast amounts of money need to be spent on their rebuilding. The town was constructed with Soviet aid in the 1970s at the site of the Tabqa Dam that created Lake Assad. The lakeside areas are run-down and neglected with the ubiquitous plastic rubbish in evidence. In the distance is Qal'at Ja'bar, the work of the Ayyubid Nur Ad-Din, now rising on its hillock above the lake, having been flooded when the dam was constructed.

Qal'at Ja'bar قلعة جعبر (09.00–16.00 winter, 09.00–18.00 summer, closed Tue; S£75 entry fee; no WC facilities; simple restaurant on the lakeside) Qal'at Ja'bar can be reached by boat or else you can drive to it by road first crossing the dam, skirting the lake to the north for 12km, then approaching on the new causeway. Dating to the 12th century it has been the subject of extensive restoration work and now even boasts a small museum displaying Islamic ceramics and other decorative elements found on the site. There is a guardian selling tickets. Entry is by an impressive passageway cut through the rock leading out into the interior. Not much is left inside beyond the brick minaret, but the walk round the ramparts gives lovely views over the lake. The small red bricks used in the minaret and the walls are typical of the Mesopotamian style.

Shortly after the Ath-Thawra turning is the main turning right, south towards Resafe, a 25km detour off the Deir Ez-Zour road, and the perfect spot for a picnic lunch.

Resafe الرصافة (also spelt Risafe or Resafeh) (*197km southeast of Aleppo); 204km from Hama on the new road across the steppe; 194km from Deir Ez-Zour; 54km south of Raqqa; unfenced site, no entry fee; allow 1¹/₂hrs. Simple café near the far southeast entrance; basic WC facilities; there is virtually no shade on the site, so come prepared with sunhats or sunshades*) A massive walled Byzantine city in the middle of nowhere, Resafe cannot fail to impress by virtue of its sheer scale and the beauty of its construction. The stone itself is also remarkable, a sort of crystalline gypsum that looks like marble and is everywhere on the ground, glinting in the sun. This gypsum came from a quarry 12km to the north of the town.

The best place to enter is from the original main gate to the north, which is where the road arrives at the site anyway, diagonally opposite the entrance where the café is. Walk first across to the vast 550m by 400m enclosure towards what is known as the centralised church. The northern gate is marvellously decorated with an elaborate concoction of arches and columns between the two powerfully built bastions on either side. The walls total 2km in length and had a good 50 towers and bastions to add to their strength. They are best preserved along this north wall.

The original site here was established by the Romans in the 3rd century AD to defend the empire against the Persian Sassanids and as a fortified caravan town on the ancient trade route between Damascus and the Euphrates, via Dmeir and Palmyra. But by Byzantine times the city had grown in importance due to the burgeoning cult of St Sergius, a Roman soldier who refused to conduct a sacrifice to Jupiter and was duly martyred for his stubbornness in 305. As the cult grew the town was renamed Sergiopolis after the saint, and a huge basilica was constructed in his honour. The gigantic cisterns and the ramparts also date from this period, the late 5th century. In the 6th century Emperor Justinian strengthened and enlarged the rampart walls, replacing the mud brick with limestone, and generally enhancing the military aspects of the city. Justinian stationed a large garrison here, making Resafe part of a chain of frontier defences against the continuing Sassanid threat.

All this defence work turned out to be largely in vain however, as the Sassanid Persians sacked it on several occasions, and it was subsequently taken by the Arabs in the 7th century and Caliph Hisham built a palace here for himself, which the 'Abbasid caliph in 750 ordered destroyed. A major earthquake at the end of the 8th century caused great damage. A Christian population of moderate size continued to live here till the 13th century, when the Mameluke Sultan Baibars sent the remaining inhabitants off to Hama. When the Mongols arrived later in the 13th century there was little left for them to sack. For the last seven centuries it has sat here in the desert largely undisturbed, serving only as an occasional Bedouin encampment.

The bareness of the site is partly due to the encroachment of sand over the centuries, and the fact that the German excavators of the 1970s concentrated on the main churches. All the bomb-crater-like holes over the site are the result of local Bedouin digging for treasure over the centuries. The first church you come to from the north gate is the centralised church, so called because of its curved shapes bulging out from the basic rectangle of the building, as can be seen by careful examination of the ground plan. It has been dated to the 520s, making it slightly later than the bold experiments with circular shapes used at Bosra and Ezraa. Like them it probably originally had a dome. The German excavators felt this was the metropolitan church of the town because of the sarcophagi for the local bishops found here. Its columns and panelling were built of fine gypsum that seems like pink marble. Many columns and pillar bases are still scattered about.

The next area to look at is over in the southwest corner of the site, where there are three gigantic and very impressive Byzantine cisterns, the furthest one being

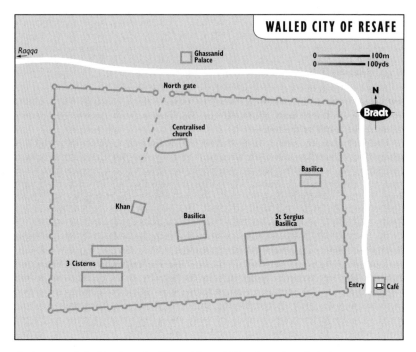

the largest of all, 50m long by 22m wide and 13m deep. Resafe had no permanent water supply so this storage capacity was necessary, collected from run-off from the nearby mountains and channelled into the cisterns. Between the cisterns and the large main basilica to the west is a ruined building imaginatively known as Basilica B, dating to the 5th century.

Moving on to the east you come now to the large basilica dated to the late 5th century but standing out as by far the most complete and impressive building on site. This has always been known as the Basilica of St Sergius, but in 1977 an inscription was found by the excavators calling it the Basilica of the Holy Cross. It has benefited in recent years from some reconstruction. It sticks to the triple symbolism of the Trinity, with three entrances, three arches and so on, and was the centre of the cult of St Sergius in the last decades of Byzantine rule. Its dedication in an inscription dates it to 559, and its huge lateral side arches were a bit too ambitious and had to be supported a little later on by two smaller arches resting on three columns to help withstand the destructive power of earthquakes. The churches at Qalb Lozeh and Bissos in Ruweiha both used similar broad lateral arches resting on thick piers. The original roof is thought to have been wooden. In the very centre of the nave are the remains of a large and complex bema, where the altar in the centre would have been covered with an ornamental stone structure called a baldachin, with side seating for 28, a throne and additional seating for the clergy arranged in a semicircle. The quality and fineness of the stonework is remarkable, especially given the remoteness of the location. The Germans found a small treasury of religious vessels and votive offerings to St Sergius buried in the atrium north of the church, now on display in the Resafe section of the Damascus Museum.

Outside the city are the remains of several other buildings, including a fragmentary palace part-buried in the sand to the north of the north gate. This is thought to be a Ghassanid palace, the Ghassanids being a tribe of Arab Christians who allied themselves in the 6th century with the Byzantines against their common enemy Rome. To the south are several further ruined palaces, thought to include the palace of Caliph Hisham, a typical Umayyad square camp-style military enclosure. Nearby are some scruffy settlements of Bedouin who have been encouraged to give up their nomadic lifestyle.

Raqqa الرقة (*193km southeast of Aleppo, 134km northwest of Deir Ez-Zour*) Returning to the main road you now follow the river all the way to Deir Ez-Zour with the fertile land heavily settled by farmers. This part of Syria should be the richest in the country, but in reality the government has difficulty getting the younger generation to take on such work which is perceived as dull and unexciting, so the fertility of the land is less exploited than it might be.

The half-hour diversion to Raqqa, north of the main Aleppo–Deir Ez-Zour road is not warranted by anyone other than a specialist in 'Abbasid times, as what was once an impressive walled city with fine buildings inside has today been swamped by the modern town. Within the walls it even has the air of a Palestinian camp or semi-slum with inhabitants unused to Western visitors and who have been known to welcome them by throwing stones.

Though originally a Greek and Roman settlement nothing remains from those periods beyond a few architectural fragments incorporated into other later Arab buildings. In its heyday the city was under the 'Abbasids when from 772 the Caliph Al-Mansur reinforced it to serve as his second capital, controlling the province of Al-Jazira ('the island', the area between the Tigris and the Euphrates), and to defend against the Byzantines. A few years later the famous Caliph Haroun Ar-Rashid also started a building programme here to symbolise 'Abbasid dominance of the region and to reinforce the frontier. Like all of these settlements it suffered the destructive wave of Mongol incursions in the 13th century and never recovered.

Raqqa has been the subject of archaeological excavations since 1906 off and on but what remains visible today is not that impressive. Much of the construction was of mud brick and therefore highly perishable. The walls were originally graced by 100 round towers built at 35m intervals all round the perimeter. The main gateway, the Bab Baghdad, is the most significant remnant of the walls, in the southeast corner. It has been renovated and has attractive decorative brickwork. Recent excavations have been ongoing by the University of Nottingham, leading a multinational team of archaeologists, in areas outside the city walls, where they have uncovered two more 'Abbasid palaces and an industrial factory site which has revealed the extent of Islamic technological advancement for its day.

Within the walls, hard to find among the modern sprawl of the town, are two major buildings worth looking at. The first is Qasr Al-Banat (Palace of the Maidens), a 9th-century building round a courtyard with a central fountain and four open *iwans*, a style not usually found outside Iran. This has been identified as the recreational summer residence of Haroun Ar-Rashid. It is kept fenced and locked, with no obvious guardian. The second is the Great Mosque, further to the north, with a tall 25m tower in Mesopotamian style and a colossal courtyard built with Arab mud brick arches. Originally it would have had a triple-aisled prayer hall and parallel gabled roofs like the Umayyad Mosque in Damascus.

The recent University of Nottingham excavations have focused mainly on the 2km-long industrial complex in use from the 8th to the 12th century, where Raqqa manufactured its glass and pottery. They have found well-preserved glass furnaces involved in the production of green, brown, blue and purple glass on a massive scale. The glass was made largely from quartz pebbles taken from the nearby Euphrates river bed, combined with the ashes of plants that grow in the surrounding semi-desert environment. The sheer scale of production confirms Raqqa as one of the Islamic world's most important glass-making centres. The artisans were both Muslim and Christian and were buried side by side in an area close to the kiln sites.

Heraqla هراقلة (*8km west of Raqqa*) Rarely visited, these unusual ruins consist of a large Arab monument thought to have been built in the 8th century by Haroun Ar-Rashid. Standing on a terrace and enclosed by a massive round stone-built wall entered by four gates, the monument, which was never completed, is thought to have been intended to commemorate Haroun Ar-Rashid's victory over the Byzantines at Herakleon. There are towers on each corner and each side is 103m long, complete with vaulted *iwan*.

Halabiye حلبية (*100km south of Raqqa, 66km north of Deir Ez-Zour. Drive from Resafe to Halabiye takes 1hr 45mins; open site, no entry fee unless the guardian appears on his motorbike; allow 1hr; no facilities*) Some 70km before Deir Ez-Zour you will start to spot in the desert the big black tents of the Bedouin who still cling to their nomadic lifestyle, following the grazing for their flocks of sheep and goats. The biggest tents cost US$3,000 and are rain resistant (see box page 269 on Bedouin lifestyle).

The site of Halabiye has great charm, dramatically perched on the hillside, its fine walls drawing a triangle from the river banks up to the summit, overlooking the broad green Euphrates, enhanced by the rather quaint French suspension road-bridge built on floating pontoons that are tied with steel rope to concrete blocks on the banks to stop them being pulled off downstream by the current. The green colour of the Euphrates is quite distinctive. Higher upstream in Turkey it is exactly the same colour. The Tigris on the other hand generally looks black, for reasons which must be connected to its mineral content. Curiously, the Euphrates with its smooth and gentle flow is grammatically male in Arabic, while the more vigorous and strongly flowing Tigris is female.

Down below within the walls at the centre of the site are the remains of two churches and the *forum* and a baths closer to the river. The walls on the river side have been largely eroded. The steep climb up to the summit is well worth the effort, for the views back over the site and the Euphrates. Towards the top over to the right the large three-storey outbuildings are the *praetorium* or imperial barracks, with gypsum and brick groin vaulting still largely intact. The fortress city was fortified originally by Queen Zenobia during her attempt to challenge the might of the Roman Empire, but the remains you see today are Byzantine from the 6th century AD, the result of Emperor Justinian's determination to secure his empire's frontier against attack from the east. In the event it was never much put to the test, as the Arabs were more interested in opening up contact with Mesopotamia, so after Byzantine power waned, the massive fortress stood largely unused, challenged only by the occasional earthquake. Even its stones were barely reused in other local building, as there was hardly any local population to carry this out. Notice the impressive construction work of the walls themselves, built of flint-grey crystalline gypsum, the same as used at Resafe. This gypsum is found in abundance along the Euphrates valley because of the particular geological similarities and was therefore frequently the building material of choice in these ancient cities.

North of the city you can follow the dirt track beside the river for about 1km to reach a cluster of ruined late Roman funerary towers and rock cut tombs.

Zalabiye زلبية Far less remains here of this twin city to Halabiye, located some 2km away downstream, but 6km away by road on the other side of the river, reached by crossing the floating bridge and turning right. This is largely due to the location on the bend of the river, exposing it over the centuries to heavy erosion. Its proximity to the Raqqa–Deir Ez-Zour railway also means that it served as a convenient quarry for ballast. Its difficult access means it is rarely visited and it is therefore most easily seen from the passing train.

The drive onwards between Zalabiye and Deir Ez-Zour is very rural and attractive, with the river to one side and irrigated fields of maize, and rows of cliffs to the left (west).

Deir Ez-Zour دير الزور *Telephone code 051*
(205km Deir Ez-Zour to Palmyra, 330km Deir Ez-Zour to Aleppo; population 185,000)

Where to stay and eat

Furat Cham Hotel (200 rooms) PO Box 219; ☎ 313800; f 312901; e chamfra@net.sy; www.chamhotels.com. Some 5km out of town in an excellent location on the Euphrates (Furat is Arabic for Euphrates). Large swimming pool on a raised terrace overlooking the river. Pergola serves drinks and meals on the terrace in warmer months. Tennis courts. Four Seasons, pleasant if expensive à la carte restaurant offering river fish. Business centre with 30 offices, used by oil companies. *US$190/160 dbl/sgl.*

Badia Cham Hotel (80 rooms) PO Box 219; ☎ 313401/4; f 310300; e chambadia@net.sy; www.chamhotels.com. Owned by the Cham Palace group this hotel is newer than the Furat Cham but it is rated four instead of five, and therefore cheaper, so many groups use it in preference. It is located closer to town, about 1km away, and is not directly on the river. Restaurant serving alcohol, coffee shop, snack bar. Swimming pool. *US$130/110 dbl/sgl.*

Oasis Hotel About 5km outside the town in the opposite direction to the Furat Cham, this hotel is very attractively set in the palmery with its own little zoo and gazelles. It is a bit run-down and has temperamental plumbing. *US$45/35 dbl/sgl.*

✗ **Four Seasons Restaurant** in the Furat Cham Hotel overlooks the river and offers Euphrates fish. La Terrace Restaurant at the Badia Cham Hotel. These are the only two places serving alcohol in town. *Lebanese wine costs S£850.*

Practicalities

Tourist information There is a small tourist office downtown on the main street, Khalid Bin Walid, with the usual maps and pamphlets.

Hospital The best hospital is the private Badri Abboud (☎ *221341*) with which the foreign oil companies have a contract for their workers, so some of the doctors speak good English.

Pharmacies There are several pharmacies in the town centre selling the usual range of prescription drugs over the counter. Again, because of the oil-worker expatriate presence, many pharmacists speak good English.

Banks The Commercial Bank of Syria has a branch downtown on 'Ali Ibn Abi Taleb St (*open 08.00–12.30 except Fri*).

Visa extensions There is an Immigration Office downtown on Ar-Rashid St (*open 08.00–13.30 except Thu*), where the process takes only half an hour or so. You will need two photos and the cost is S£25.

Post office Downtown on 8 Azar Street near the main square (*open 08.00–20.00 except Fri*).

What to see and do Deir Ez-Zour is no beauty as a town, but there are a few diversions it has to offer the visitor which are definitely worth a half day. In general it is used as a base for the two excursions to the south, Mari and Doura

Europos, both highly significant archaeological sites, and therefore requiring a stay ideally of two nights. In the evening out of the heat of the day you should find time to wander along the charming and colourfully painted French suspension bridge for cyclists and pedestrians only, though be equipped with mosquito repellent in the summer months. Built in the 1920s it is 500m long. On the other side is a popular swimming pool but only men would be advised to use it. On the river itself you may be struck by the large numbers of black moorhens and coots on the water. They are not eaten by Arabs as they are thought not to taste good, since they live on fish. Arabs prefer to eat the flesh of animals which have fed on grass and vegetables, so the coot population thrives. There are several fish restaurants in town and along the river banks, serving simple grilled river fish, but no alcohol.

In the town itself the *souk* is surprisingly traditional with arched covered walkways not unlike a miniature version of the Damascus Hamadiye Souk. The other thing worth seeking out is the interesting Armenian church opposite the Ziad Hotel, an immaculately kept haven of cleanliness and organisation in what is undoubtedly a grubby and chaotic place. The guardian or his son will show you round free of charge into the church with its extraordinarily designed monument to commemorate the Armenian martyrs of recent years, a spiral staircase leading down into an exhibition area with interesting old black and white photos. The final place which warrants a visit of at least two hours is the remarkably well put together museum.

Deir Ez-Zour Museum (*Open 09.00–16.00 winter, 09.00–18.00 summer, daily except Tue; S£150 entry fee; no facilities*) The museum opened in 1996 and its contents were organised, assembled and put on display by the Ministry of Culture in Damascus with financial help from Shell and Denimex and Daimler-Benz from Germany. The real brains behind its conception and the superb quality of its explanatory boards which are written in English and in Arabic however, belonged to the Free University of Berlin. An excellent accompanying booklet on the museum written in English by Dominic Bomnatz, Hartmut Konna and As'ad Al-Mahmoud, is now out of print and therefore unfortunately almost impossible to find. Funds having been completely exhausted, the maintenance and administration of the building is pitiful, even the toilet facilities remaining uncompleted since 1996. As a result the once grand building set in fine gardens is neglected and gradually deteriorating, no maintenance having taken place since its opening ten years ago. The staff just sit around drawing their salaries and a few dusty books are for sale if the employee whose job it is to open the vitrine can be found and happens to be on duty.

The museum follows through room by room chronologically. It has some fine reconstructions, one of a prehistoric house and another of the Temple at Mari. One of the most memorable sections though, displays the earliest examples of writing from the end of the 4th millennium in Uruk, southern Mesopotamia. The earliest type of writing was pictogram. From this, the writing progressed and developed from pictorial to abstract writing called cuneiform, created by a wedge-shaped stylus pressed onto a clay tablet. Originally there were 1,200 symbols, which were over time gradually reduced to 500. In the 1st millennium BC a simplified cuneiform developed in Ugarit on the eastern Mediterranean coast using just 30 symbols, which was the forerunner of most modern forms of writing including Arabic and Greek. The accompanying boards explain the importance of writing which was needed to count and to register ownership and to fulfil the economic and administrative demands of increasingly complex social hierarchies and specialisation in the early Bronze Age. This gradual urbanisation led to the formation of the earliest city states.

In the 'Abbasid room the economy of the Jazirah ('island', meaning the land between the Tigris and the Euphrates) is explained. It flourished with cotton from the River Khabur area, sugarcane from Sinjar, rice from Nusaybin, olive oil from Raqqa and its other products were fresh and dried fruit, honey, cheese, butter and charcoal.

In the final room the museum addresses the vexed questions of the ecological balance of the whole steppeland of northeast Syria which has been heavily disrupted over the last 100 years, due to the spread of agriculture, the use of the car, the sharp rise in the size of the cattle herds, and the competition between sheep and goat breeders. The Bedouin have been forced to abandon the Euphrates and Khabour valleys and to go deeper into the steppe. Now with motorisation flocks of sheep can be transported by lorry to remote areas in just a few hours, so everywhere can be overgrazed and nowhere has the potential to regenerate any more. The desert vegetation has been irretrievably destroyed by this, especially in years of low rainfall (see box on the *Syrian badia or steppelands*, page 247).

Hasake and the Jazira الحسكة والجزيرة The northeast of Syria, north of the Euphrates towards Hasake and framed on the eastern side by the Khabour River, makes a triangle known as Al-Jezira (the Island). An area of enormous archaeological importance, forming as it does part of the Fertile Crescent, there are over 250 tells or artificial mounds of early settlement, the two most famous of which, Tell Brak and Tell Halaf, were extensively excavated. It was here in the Tell Brak region that Mesopotamian archaeologist Max Mallowan and his wife Agatha Christie conducted their legendary digs over a five-year period, arriving each season at Nusaybin just over the border on the magnificent Orient Express (see box on page 160). Today however very few foreigners visit as there is almost nothing to be seen on the ground. Only the Roman bridge at 'Ain Diwar on the Tigris, right up in the north on the Turkish border where the Tigris itself forms the border, is worth the excursion if you have a spare half day at your disposal. Reaching it is difficult, down a rough dirt track into the wild and remote valley, and because of the proximity to the border you will be required to have a police escort. The landscape of the Jazira is pleasant with gentle rolling hills and fertile fields of wheat, and the local people, predominantly Kurds, are surprisingly friendly and welcoming.

ONWARDS TO DOURA EUROPOS AND MARI Make sure you take your passport with you on this day trip, as there is a road block shortly before Mari where you will be stopped and asked to show it.

Qal'at Ar-Rahba قلعة رحبة On the way to Doura Europos make time to call off briefly at the delightfully ruined fairy-tale castle of Qal'at Ar-Rahba, visible to the right of the main road, some 40km south of Deir Ez-Zour. The road off to the castle winds up round it from the back, arriving on a hilltop at the same height from where you can look across to it on its own rocky outcrop. Local youths are frequently to be found perched on its various crumbling walls – for them it is the local playground and social centre. The scramble down into the ditch and up the other side into its walls requires good footwear as the rocky screed may be very loose.

The remains date from the 12th century built by Nur Ad-Din, but the Mongol invasion a century later swept over the whole area and the castle was sacked and abandoned. Inside there is a series of underground passages and chambers which require a torch for a proper investigation.

Despite the potential loveliness of the setting of the castle, with the blue sky and the green fertility of the river valley beyond, the European eye is nevertheless overwhelmed by the visual pollution aspects to which the local people appear oblivious. The fields are covered in plastic bags and bottles and the mud-brick houses are covered in rusty satellite dishes. On the same high vantage point on the hill beside the castle a sensitive soul from the village has pitched a large tent and planted for himself a cluster of palm trees, as if making a statement about his views on the habitation below. Also in the area are a number of Gypsies, originally from the Qarbaat Mountains in Romania. They have no ID cards and are generally mistrusted by the locals and associated with theft and crime.

Doura Europos تل الصلحية (Arabic As-Salihiye, name of the neighbouring village) (*100km to Deir Ez-Zour; drive takes 1¹/₂hrs from Deir Ez-Zour; open 09.00–16.00 winter, 09.00–18.00 summer daily; allow 2hrs; S£150 entry fee; no WC or refreshment facilities; a totally unshaded open site, so come prepared with sunhat or sun umbrella in the hotter months and plenty of water*) The 100km drive to Doura Europos from Deir Ez-Zour takes you through endless squalid villages, scruffy markets with mud, squawking chickens, sheep carcasses and fruit. This is the richest part of Syria in oil and fertility, yet the population here is the poorest. The buildings all along the way are low-rise mud brick. Local women are dressed colourfully and have no objection to being photographed. They even find it amusing to be the centre of attention. They are at their most colourful when they are attending some occasion, like a funeral or wedding.

At first the setting of the vast Hellenistic fortress city of Doura Europos ('Doura' means fortress in Aramaic) is difficult to appreciate, as you approach from the west and cannot see the dramatic vantage point on a high clifftop overlooking the broad Euphrates to the east. Founded in Alexander the Great's reign by Seleucus Nicador in 303BC ('Europos' was the name of his birthplace in Macedonia), the city was to become, by virtue of its location on the edge of the Roman and Parthian empires, an example of supreme tolerance, with 16 temples in which pagans, Jews and Christians all worshipped together, with Parthians, Greeks, Macedonians and Palmyrenes all living here harmoniously: Archaeologically, the site is remarkable above all for the wall paintings discovered here, both in the synagogue and the churches, which, though no longer *in situ* as they have all been moved to museums in Damascus, the Louvre and Yale University, have given us new insights into early Christian and Jewish representational art, and in which art historians have even seen the origins of later wall paintings in the Romanesque churches of Europe.

After the Seleucid Empire declined, Doura became in effect a Parthian city around the 1st century BC and began to absorb Eastern influences. When the Romans then conquered Syria in 64BC, Doura was in a delicate position on the borders between the Parthian and Roman empires, but a kind of truce was maintained for nearly two centuries. By 211 it was formally declared a Roman colony by Septimius Severus. Doura's fortunes were closely linked to those of Palmyra, and when that city flourished and prospered, Doura did likewise. Palmyrene influences can be seen at Doura, not only in the temples to the Palmyrene goddesses found here, but also in the effect on the local customs and dress of the wealthy merchants, as illustrated in the art and sculpture found on the site.

You enter the city from the ticket office through an opening in the walls beside the massive Seleucid Palmyra Gate, the main entrance to the city, and should begin by climbing up onto the 9m-high ramparts, most of which are also Seleucid, to gain an appreciation of the colossal size of the site (80ha) and to see traces of the Hellenistic grid layout of the city. Protected on three sides by the river cliffs and steep wadis, the only defensive wall required was here on this western, desert side. Of the towers, 26 can still be identified. The wildlife of the site is also very rich in spring, with birds, beetles and caterpillars in great abundance and local women collecting fodder for their flocks from the rich pastureland now growing within the walls.

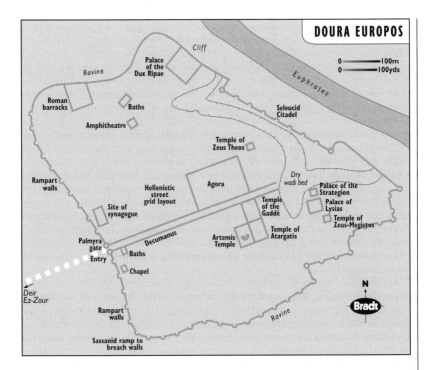

Cliff

Palace
of the
Dux Ripae

Ravine

Euphrates

Roman
barracks

Baths

Seleucid
Citadel

Amphitheatre

Temple of
Zeus Theos

Rampart
walls

Dry
wadi bed

Palace of the
Strategion

Hellenistic
street
grid layout

Agora

Palace of
Lysias

Site of
synagogue

Temple
of the
Gaddé

Temple of
Zeus-Megistos

Palmyra
gate

Decumanus

Artemis
Temple

Temple of
Atargatis

Entry

Baths

Chapel

Deir
Ez-Zour

N

Bradt

Rampart
walls

Ravine

Sassanid ramp to
breach walls

0 — 100m
0 — 100yds

It was of course here that the stunning synagogue was found, then transported piece by piece to Damascus in 1932 where it was reconstructed in the National Museum. Its magnificent richly coloured murals had been preserved in near perfect condition buried under the sands of time. This led Doura Europos to be hailed as the Pompeii of the Desert. The eastern, Parthian influences clearly had a deep effect on the Mesopotamian Jews living here, and enabled them to depart from the traditional Talmudic injunctions against human and pictorial representation, and this has in turn helped us appreciate the development of religious iconography before the Roman Empire converted to Christianity in the 4th century. Only the remnants of a few walls of the synagogue are still visible now, so after a cursory glance at the site from where the wall paintings were removed, you can move northwards along the ramparts towards the ravine.

In this area between here and the cliff was the early 3rd-century Roman barracks and military camp, as Doura's role was to protect and control trade along the Euphrates and to be part of the defensive chain of military caravan towns along the northern and eastern borders of the empire. Right on the edge of the cliff at the highest northeast point of the site is the Palace of the Dux Ripae, Commander of the River Bank. Though heavily ruined, it is possible to discern two courtyards, an arcaded corridor, and a private bath complex. The Romans heavily fortified Doura Europos as a military garrison to guard against attacks from the Persian Sassanians in the early 3rd century. With a location like this the commander's palace must have been quite stunning. The Roman military camp is almost like a self-contained military colony, with its own baths, temples and exercise area.

The Persian Sassanids did succeed in taking the city in 256 after a siege, and the point at which they entered, at the southwest gate, can still be seen from the outside of the walls, with the access ramp they built and where they undermined the walls, a technique much later used by the Mamelukes against the Crusader

11

castles (see page 190). Its fortunes declined thereafter, and the Byzantines under Justinian did not occupy it, leaving it abandoned in favour of sites like Resafe and Halabiye.

Moving over towards the cliff itself you will see for the first time the view of the impressive Seleucid citadel, sitting on its outcrop across a small wadi, defending the site from the river side. The cliffs in spring are green, even on their vertical surfaces, from the grass that manages to grow on them even as they plunge down 50m to the river. Beyond the citadel, a little to the south, is a reconstructed Doura Europos house, giving an idea of what a typical house here is thought to have looked like, located close to the house of the Franco-Syrian excavators who are still working on the site and who come every March and October for digs. The original excavations took place in the 1920s and 1930s after the accidental discovery of the synagogue wall paintings by a British expeditionary force in 1921, and were conducted by French and American teams. The murals were so well preserved purely by chance, because the Romans, in their efforts to fortify Doura against the Sassanids, built up a massive makeshift embankment of sand up against the vulnerable western desert-facing walls, burying many buildings including the synagogue and another early church with murals in the process.

Of the remains, most are heavily ruined and their exposure to the elements since the 1930s has not helped. Raised up on an acropolis you will see what is probably the most imposing building left standing in the main city, known as the Palace of the Strategion, residence of the Seleucid governor. A certain amount of reconstruction work has recently been undertaken, especially on the fine embossed façade. Behind the palace are the fragmentary remains of the Temple of Zeus-Megistos, originally in a hybrid Hellenistic/Parthian style of the 1st century BC, later adapted by the Romans in AD169. Beyond the temple are the remains of the so-called House of Lysias, which probably served as the private residence of the governor, set round a courtyard.

As you return towards the Palmyra Gate and the site entrance, following the course of the original decumanus or main east–west street, you will come, right in the centre of the city, to the left of the street, to a cluster of buildings, all barely above foundation height, which were a group of three temples. Of these, the 1st-century BC Parthian Artemis Temple is the most noteworthy because of the little *odeon* with nine tiers of seating within it, totally reconstructed like a miniature horseshoe. Artemis here is thought to have represented motherhood, fertility and hunting and was merged with her Persian equivalent Nanaia. Ceremonies and rituals must have taken place here, while the city notables, whose names are visible cut into the stone seats, looked on. Of the other temples in this cluster, one is a 1st-century AD temple to the goddess Atargatis, an ancient Syrian deity, and the other is a mid-2nd-century AD temple to the Gaddé, a double Palmyrene deity of fortune. The proximity of these mixed places of worship again illustrates how tolerant the inhabitants of Doura were to each other's religious preferences. The temples were identified from statuettes found in the excavations. On the other (northern) side of the decumanus from the cluster of temples is the large open Hellenistic *agora* or marketplace.

Completing the walk back to the site entrance you pass the remains of a bath complex just to the left of the decumanus, and then immediately to the right of the site entrance are the foundations of a small chapel, dated to 231, thereby making it one of the earliest identified Christian chapels in the world. Murals showing Adam and Eve, various New Testament miracles and a shepherd tending his flocks were discovered here, also buried under the sand abutting the western wall, and were transported to Yale University Art Gallery in the 1930s.

Mari تل الحريري (*Open daily 09.00–dusk. S£150 entry fee; allow 1hr; basic WC facilities opposite guardian's kiosk. Simple refreshments tent at entrance run by the site guardian with local handicrafts for sale plus cards and books. There is no actual food for sale so bring your picnic to eat here, which the guardian may well supplement with his own freshly baked bread and whatever else is cooking. He has four wives to help him. The Palace of Zimri-Lim is partly covered so there is some shade on the site. Distances to walk are much less than at Doura Europos, though the site is still extensive.*) Soon after heading south beyond Doura Europos en route to Mari, 26km further south, you will find a military checkpoint, where the military ask the purpose of your travel and when you plan to return. On being told you are visiting Mari and will return later the same day, they are quite happy and wave you on. It is always best to have your passport with you on these occasions to prove your identity. The checkpoint is a consequence of Mari's proximity to the Iraqi border, at this point just 12km to the south.

On this stretch between Doura Europos and Mari, the buildings at the side of the road look newer, richer and more elaborate, and many are still under construction.

Syria's most important Mesopotamian site and capital of the middle Euphrates, Mari was a 3rd-millennium BC royal city state contemporary with Ebla (see page 137), its opulent 275–365 room palace (depending on which source you read) originally on two levels, complete with treasures and archives yielding up its secrets in the course of excavations, thereby enabling us to trace early Mesopotamian history. The site at Mari, not even visible from the refreshments tent and ticket desk, is vast, far more extensive than people might expect. You begin by walking east across the flat featureless land to ascend the hillock crowned today by a concrete block, thought to be the site of a temple ziggurat, that overlooks the site from the west and which affords the best available vantage point. The local name is Tell Hariri, Silk Mound, so named because the mud is thought to be soft and silky to the touch. Underfoot is does feel quite spongy. In very hot or wet conditions this can be a problem.

This highest point is known by the excavators as the 'Massif Rouge' because of its rust-red earth and beside it were found a cluster of religious buildings, three temples in which many superbly preserved statues were found including that of the singer-dancer Ur-Nanshe, now in the Mari room of the Damascus Museum. This was also the point where the site was accidentally discovered by a group of Bedouin digging to find a gravestone for a relative. Instead they found a huge stone, weighing 300kg, which turned out to be a headless statue of Shamash, sun god and the city's patron, now in the Louvre. Excavations then began in 1933 under the French archaeologist and Sumerian specialist André Parrot, who continued to excavate here till 1974, an astonishing record of longevity. The site must have been tremendously difficult to dig, and the excavation costs were met by the Louvre, so most of the pre-war important finds can now be seen there in Paris. There is very little to see above ground as everything was so deeply buried under the accumulated debris of thousands of years that the site is now largely underground according to today's ground level. Parrot was succeeded by French anthropologist Jean-Claude Margueron, whose researches have focused on Mari's role in the Mesopotamian world, analysing its economic resources and agricultural base. The French continue to excavate each season, yet still less than half the site has so far been dug.

Mari's position here was chosen because it lies between the confluence of the Khabour and the Euphrates rivers, and the cliffs further south at Baghuz, making it a natural trade route between the Sumerian cities of lower Mesopotamia and the cities of northern Syria such as Ugarit, Ebla and Aleppo, with Sumer requiring building materials such as timber and stone passing through Mari. Abraham is also

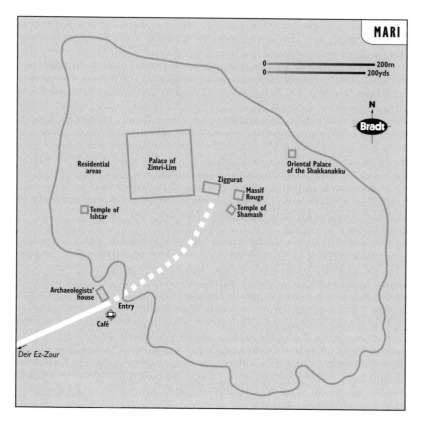

said to have passed through Mari on his way from Ur to Harran, now in southeast Turkey. The traded goods also included dates, olives, pottery, porcelain and grains as well as the tin so necessary for bronze casting, brought overland from India and Malaya where it occurred naturally. Lapis lazuli was also an important item, used in jewellery and for the pupils of the eyes of the statues, with ivory for the whites. From the elaborate hair styles and dress of the citizens of Mari as depicted in statues and murals, they were clearly part of the Mesopotamian culture, even though they were 240km upriver from Babylon. A vast array of Sumerian gods were worshipped, including Dagan, god of storms, Ishtar, goddess of fertility and Shamash, the sun god, all-knowing and all-seeing patron of the city.

To compensate for its limited agricultural potential, Mari developed a sophisticated irrigation scheme. Mari itself is built on a mound set back from the Euphrates but was originally connected to it by an 11m-wide canal, designed to bring barges in and out of the city. The purpose of this appears to have been to avert the risk of flooding, as the circular city was originally protected by a dyke, but also to provide a water supply and to control navigation on the river. Recent excavations have also shown there was a 120km navigation link from Mari to the Khabour River to the north.

First occupied in c2900BC by people of Semitic origin who were referred to as Amorites in the Old Testament and who spoke a language related to Hebrew, the city state of Mari built a great palace for its ruler, three temples and the high terrace area known as the 'Massif Rouge'. The Akkadians under Sargon of Akkad then controlled it for a time (2340–2150BC) but it then regained its independence, only to fall to the rising dynasty of Babylon in 1759BC. Their leader Hammurabi sacked Mari and set fire to the palace. It never really recovered and had only limited occupation in Seleucid and Parthian times.

Today the two most striking aspects of the site are its sheer size, 1.2km from north to south, especially the scale of the gigantic palace with its huge mud-brick walls and pillars, and the astonishingly advanced water and drainage system. As you walk round the site look out for water channels of mud brick leading into canals, which lead into cisterns, many of which were bitumen-lined, even all those thousands of years ago, one of the first uses to which the by-products of oil were put. There were also many wells.

The gigantic palace is named after Mari's last ruler Zimri-Lim (1775–1760BC), though the building pre-dated him and was enjoyed by many previous rulers. Mercifully a large chunk of the palace, which originally covered 2.5ha, has had protective roofing erected to help keep the elements at bay, and provides welcome shade. The palace walls have survived in places to a height of over 5m, thanks to Hammurabi's sacking which made the walls fall in on themselves and fill the rooms. This too preserved the 15,000 clay tablets written in Akkadian (old Babylonian) cuneiform, archives found intact inside the palace, whose subject matter covered religion, economy, diplomatic and trading activities, military matters, laws, taxes, administration and royal missions. The murals on the lower walls too were well preserved by virtue of being covered in mud from the sacking and are a fascinating record of life in Mari, depicting the investiture of kings and the taking of slaves. They have geometric motifs combined with pictorial elements such as trees and flowers inside fantastic landscapes with real or imaginary animals, gatherings of deities, ceremonies and sacrifices. These and other finds from the site are now on display in the Louvre and in the Damascus, Aleppo and Deir Ez-Zour museums.

In the centre of the palace are two open courtyards, known respectively as the palm court, thought to have been adorned with palm trees, and the larger eastern court. Immediately south of the palm court is a large hall where the statue of the water goddess pouring from a vase, now one of the chief exhibits in the Aleppo Museum, was found. South of that is a similar-sized room thought to have been

MUD OF MESOPOTAMIA

Mespotamia – in Ancient Greek, the 'land between the rivers' (Tigris and Euphrates) – was once part of what is now referred to as the 'fertile crescent' of the Middle East by Egyptologists.

Looking at the flat featureless plain and reconciling it with this fertile image of Mesopotamia is no easy matter. Robert Byron in his classic *Road to Oxiana* clearly had the same problem:

It is little solace to recall that Mesopotamia was once so rich, so fertile of art and invention, so hospitable to the Sumerians, the Seleucids and the Sassanids. The prime fact of Mesopotamian history is that in the 13th century Hulagu destroyed the irrigation system; and from that day to this Mesopotamia has remained a land of mud deprived of mud's only possible advantage, vegetable fertility. It is a mud plain, so flat that a single heron, reposing on one leg beside some rare trickle of water in a ditch, looks as tall as a wireless aerial. From this plain rise villages of mud and cities of mud. The rivers flow with liquid mud. The air is composed of mud refined into a gas. The people are mud-coloured; they wear mud-coloured clothes, and their national hat is nothing more than a formalised mud-pie.

There are about 1.9 million Kurds living in Syria today, making them the largest single minority ethnic group in the country, at roughly 10% of the population. They are concentrated in Aleppo and here in the northeast of Syria, but unlike in Turkey and Iraq where they have historically been considered a threat to internal stability, in Syria they have tended on the whole to be less troublesome. The Syrian authorities are however concerned that this may change if the Kurds here link up with the Iraqi Kurds across the border, whose position has been much strengthened by the 2003 American-led invasion and who now effectively control Kirkuk and Mosul, the oil-rich areas of northern Iraq. Much of Syria's oil too is concentrated in these Kurdish heartlands, producing considerable nervousness about local aspirations to Kurdish separatism. In the Middle East as a whole there are some 25 million Kurds. In Iraq they account for 23% of the population, 19% in Turkey and 10% in Iran. They were promised their homeland of Kurdistan after World War I but the promise was reneged on, leaving them as the largest ethnic minority group in the world without a homeland. Only those in northern Iraq now have a form of autonomy with their own province.

Originally their homeland of Kurdistan is a mountainous region south and southeast of Lake Van (in eastern Turkey) between what was Persia and Mesopotamia. Their language of Kurdish is Indo-European and occurs in two main dialects of Kermanji and Sorani. They celebrate Nawrouz as New Year's Day, 21 March, the first day of spring. Kurdish literature is banned in Syria now, but during the French Mandate period (1920–46) the Kurds were allowed to organize politically and publish books and other literature in their own language. Distrustful of the majority Arab Sunni population, the French recruited a disproportionate number of Kurds (as well as Christians, Druze and 'Alawis) into the police and military. The Kurdish nationalist movement emerged in the 1920s and lobbied for greater cultural and political autonomy, but in Syria at present there are some 300,000 Kurds without citizenship who therefore cannot vote, own property, get a government job or go to secondary school or university, whilst still not being exempt from military service. President Bashar Al-Assad has recognised the potential problems from such a situation, and in early 2006 made promises to naturalise large numbers of Syria's stateless Kurds.

the throne room, which still has an enormous slab of stone, thought to have been the base of the throne itself. The palace complex also included temples, harem baths, administrative offices, audience halls, banquet halls, storerooms, kitchen, baking ovens, royal apartments, elite residential areas, guest quarters, artisans' quarters, library, archives, school of arts for sculpturing and mural painting, study centres for the royal children and gardens. Scraps of cheese and bread were still found on the kitchen floor, with containers for olive oil and water and clay kitchen utensils. The open excavated areas of the site weather very quickly and deteriorate, because all of Mari was built simply from the river clay of the Euphrates mixed with finely chopped straw, pressed into bricks and dried in the sun.

ACROSS THE DESERT

FROM DEIR EZ-ZOUR TO PALMYRA VIA QASR AL-HAYR (*Allow 2hrs for the drive direct from Deir-Ez-Zour to Palmyra; add 3hrs extra for the diversion to Qasr Al-Hayr Ash-Sharqi. Coming from Palmyra it takes about 1hr to the turn-off, so again, the whole trip takes a minimum of 5hrs. Make sure you have plenty of water and food. The road is now tarmac* *all the way, though often in poor condition, so the trip can be done all year round.*) This drive takes you across real bleak flat desert where Bedouin are still to be found in quite large numbers. At the roadside in spring lots of sheep and goats can be seen grazing on the grass from the winter rains. Syria has at least 15 million sheep. Every year 10 million of them are exported to Saudi Arabia, as they are widely considered the best or tastiest in the world.

The only point of interest on the drive is the diversion to the early 8th-century Umayyad desert palace of Qasr Al-Hayr Ash-Sharqi (the eastern), about an hour's drive north of the main road, the much better preserved twin of Qasr Al-Hayr Al-Gharbi (the western), whose façade graces the entrance of the Damascus National Museum.

After 146km you turn off to the right, north, at As-Sukhneh (Arabic 'hot'), so called because of the hot sulphurous springs that still exist here. The town is extremely scruffy, very basic and dirty, with shops that do not sell mineral water, only soft fizzy drinks. Make sure you come well equipped with your own water and food for a picnic, as there is nowhere to buy anything the average Westerner would consider edible.

The tarmac road leading out of As-Sukhneh is only three years old but gets worse every year. At the first tarmac junction after 17km, turn right towards At-Taibeh. Progress is slow because of the pot-holes. At At-Taibeh there is a sign pointing right, east, towards Qasr Al-Hayr. This final stretch of road after At-Taibeh is the best, as it is not used so much by heavy trucks. After about 10km you will see the walls rising up from the desert, like some mirage shimmering with its towers. The total drive from Deir Ez-Zour will have taken about two and a half hours.

Qasr Al-Hayr Ash-Sharqi قصر الحير الشرقي ('Eastern Palace of the Fenced-in Garden') (*Unfenced open site; S£75 entry fee from roaming guardian; allow 1hr; no facilities*) The track leads straight up to the castles and the guardian, observing your approach from a nearby cluster of huts, will catch up with you soon after your arrival. The site is divided into two separate enclosures some 40m apart with a freestanding tall square minaret c10m high in the ground between them. The purpose of this tower was a source of confusion to many, who thought it must have some defensive role as a watchtower. If it had been built at the same time as the palaces it would have been the third-oldest minaret in the Islamic world, but exhaustive studies and investigations by American archaeologists between 1964 and 1972 concluded that it was built much later in the 13th century, when the ruins of Qasr Al-Hayr served as a staging post for nomads from the steppe, and seemed to be part of a Muslim prayer hall.

This mosque is what now occupies the southeast corner of the first palace enclosure you come to. Columns and capitals brought from Palmyra have been reused in the construction and there is even one piece of Aswan granite whose journey here you have to marvel at. Syria boasts just two of these desert palaces: this one and its western namesake Qasr Al-Hayr Al-Gharbi, which is far more heavily ruined and whose 8th century entrance gateway has been incorporated into the modern entrance to the Damascus National Museum.

Both palaces served as pleasure palaces, rural retreats for the nomadic rulers who tired of city life. Early Islam did not apply the same restrictions on lifestyle as in later centuries. The palaces also served as military outposts to help cement relations with the Bedouin who were always revolting against authority. Both were built on irrigated estates in military encampments (hence the name, Palace of the Fenced-in Garden) and on trade routes, at the time of Caliph Hisham, last statesman of the House of Umayya, under whose long reign (724–43) the Muslim Empire reached

When the Umayyads settled and made Damascus their capital and for the first time had to get to grips with administering their newly acquired empire from it, they still retained a streak of nostalgia for the nomadic life they had given up. Mu'awiya, the first Umayyad caliph, was married to a Bedouin woman called Maysoun. For her wild spirit the luxuries of Damascus held no charm and she describes her feelings in these verses:

> A tent with rustling breezes cool
> Delights me more than palace high
> And more the cloak of simple wool
> Than robes in which I learned to sigh.
> The crust I ate beside my tent
> Was more than this fine bread to me;
> The wind's voice where the hill-path went
> Was more than tambourine can be.
> And more than purr of friendly cat
> I love the watch-dog's bark to hear;
> And more than any lubbard fat
> I love a Bedouin cavalier.

Her son Yazid grew up in her mould, as a Bedouin with a love of pleasure, a distaste for piety and a reckless disregard for the laws of religion. He preferred wine, music and sport to the drudgery of public affairs. On Yazid's death (683) the Umayyad Empire threatened to fall apart. A contemporary poet sang:

> Now loathed of all men is the Fury blind
> Which blazeth as a fire blown by the wind.
> They are split in sects: each province hath its own
> Commander of the Faithful, each its throne.

The Umayyad dynasty was saved by 'Abd Al-Malik who became caliph in 685, and it needed seven years of hard fighting by him and his armies to reclaim authority and re-establish the supremacy of the Umayyads.

the limits of its expansion. Far bigger than the simple hunting lodges of the same period to be found in northern Jordan, they were more like self-contained towns with gardens, markets, populations of entertainers, servants and craftsmen. Their fortified look, with their 9m-high walls and defence towers, was possibly modelled on Roman forts, built to accommodate large armies. The outer enclosure wall, now only visible in parts, had a 22km perimeter and enclosed an area some 6km by 3km of gardens in which gazelle and rabbits were kept. The water supply came from a dam 30km away to the northwest, and this maintained the greenery and vegetation within the outer enclosure and also fed the baths inside.

The structure you come to first, to the left of the minaret, is the palace with five gateways and 28 rounded towers. At first glance the inside is just a field of ruins, but on closer inspection you will find a baths, a cistern and an open pool and olive presses, all scattered about beyond the mosque and prayer hall that lie in the southeast corner. The other second enclosure is six times smaller and is generally thought to be a caravanserai or *khan* with circular towers at its square corners. On its western side facing the minaret is the monumental gateway which is the most interesting architectural feature of the whole complex, protected by a machicolation box, set between the twin towers. This is the first known use of machicolation boxes in the world, dating from 729. They were holes in the overhang of a parapet for defenders to fire arrows or drop down liquids or projectiles on their attackers. They were much favoured by later Arab military architects, and the Crusaders copied them and took the idea back to Europe, where they first appeared in the 12th century at Chateau Gaillard built by Richard the Lionheart after his return from the crusade.

The building style of the castle in general displays an eclectic mix of influences, local, Byzantine, Mesopotamian and Persian, with many items such as Roman and Byzantine capitals clearly transported from elsewhere and recycled. Note the similarity with the façade of Qasr Al-Hayr Al-Gharbi, which now forms the entrance of the Damascus National Museum. Certainly the grandiose gateways are curiously at odds with the rather ordinary buildings inside. The lower walls are of grey limestone, while the upper levels are of Mesopotamian brick, probably added after 760, and are the earliest known use of brick patterning in Syria. The whole palace complex was abandoned after the Mongol invasions and never again resettled.

As you return to the main road and continue west to Palmyra, you can look out for the black Bedouin tents scattered about in the wild bleak landscape. The Bedouin you will find in this desert area, remote from any settlements, are the closest you will find in Syria to true nomads. Syria was one of the first lands to be inhabited by the Bedouin outside the Arabian desert and today there are still over a million living in the northern Syrian desert, all of whom are Sunni Muslims. Only some 60% are still fully migratory in lifestyle.

Totally nomadic Bedouin will break camp soon after dawn with a herd of say 60 camels, four of which are used to carry the baggage and belongings. They will travel approximately 20km before setting up camp again in the evening. It is normal to stay at the encampment a few days, moving on once the grazing around it has been exhausted. The women, heads covered against the sun but always unveiled, do the lion's share of the work, moving with that timeless ease that comes early to those who live in the desert. One woman can erect the family's huge tent (Arabic 'bait sha'r', house of hair) on her own in just 30 minutes. All the holes are then sealed against snakes and the tent inside is checked for eggs and spiders. The chicken coop is carried from place to place on the back of one of the camels, and there tends to be a collection of sheep, goats and donkeys which also trot along. Middle Eastern sheep are usually of the fat-tailed variety, the fatness of their tails showing how well-fed they are and whether there has been adequate grazing for them. At milking time the women bind them all together in two neat rows, using just one piece of rope, cleverly tied in such a way that when the milking is over, they just give one sharp tug and the whole lot unravels in a trice like a piece of knitting. The women collect dried camel dung and scrub for fuel in cooking. The ritual of coffee making, flavoured with cardamom and prepared in a traditional brass pot, is usually undertaken by the oldest male member of the family.

Men's clothing is loose, lightweight, light-coloured robes called a *thawb* or *jellabiye*, highly suited to the extreme heat, with a white or coloured square cloth, folded diagonally for the head (Arabic kaffiye), secured by a headband of camel's hair (Arabic 'iqal'). In winter or cold nights they wear a thick outer cloak of wool, called a *bisht*. Women tend to be very colourfully dressed in heavily embroidered robes of black and are unveiled. Once married, they wear heavy silver jewellery.

The black tents are divided into sections according to their status: those belonging to the most lowly have three sections, those belonging to the middle class have five, and the uppermost richest level of Bedouin have seven-section tents. When it rains the tent drips and leaks a little at first till the goat hair swells out to prevent further leaking, though if the rain is really torrential, a plastic sheet is drawn out underneath the roof to guarantee total leak-proofness. The tent partition is called a *gata*. In the simplest three-section tent, one area is for sleeping, one area for cooking and storage and one area is always kept for receiving guests, usually with an open fire.

Women do most of the labour, while men socialise and discuss plans for the group. Milk from camels, goats and sheep forms the basis of the diet, mainly in the form of yoghurt and butter. Most meals consist of a bowl of milk, yoghurt and rice, with flat unleavened bread. Dates form the dessert. Meat is reserved for special occasions like weddings, ceremonial events or feast days, when a camel, sheep or goat is slaughtered, according to the family's means, as prescribed in the Koran. The author spent a few weeks living with a Bedouin tribe some years ago and at Eid Al-Adha, the major annual Muslim feast day, was invited to get up at dawn and watch the ritual slaughter of the camels. The throat is slit with a dagger and the camel is then bled to death, pinned down by two men while it writhes. The rest of the day was spent moving ceremonially from tent to tent, from the most senior downwards, eating boiled camel's meat from the communal platters of rice (Arabic 'mansaf'). A sauce made of camel's cheese (jameed) was poured over the dish to keep it moist. By the end of the day, some 15 platefuls of camel later, it was easy to appreciate why such feasts are restricted to annual events. In the desert the Bedouin also get occasional meat in the form of lizards, sometimes over a metre long, and even the odd hedgehog, after the children have finished playing with it. Visiting friends and relations may bring a gift, such as a freshly caught hare, when they call on each other, and they will then all sit together to eat, perhaps reciting poetry, as there are still some Bedouin poets in the oral tradition of the desert. Arabs have always loved the magical rhythm of words and the man who can compose or recite poetry at the fireside enjoys great prestige.

Intermarriage between tribes is rare. Marriage is in general an expensive business in Syria, as indeed it has become in most Arab countries. It is usual but not compulsory for the bride's family to host the wedding feast. The average husband has to pay around S£200,000 (c£2,000) for his wife, usually in cash. The exact price is agreed through bargaining by the parents of the two parties, and may drop lower in poor rural areas. The money is not for the bride's father, but for the wife herself, to secure her position and to give her some money for jewellery and dresses, as well as a certain independence. This price also deters the husband from having too many wives, something he may be inclined to do if he drinks a lot of camel's milk (thought to be an aphrodisiac) and is from a rural part of the country. The wife is considered *kharban*, literally 'broken', for the man's enjoyment, once she has had children, and second wives are often very young, around 16, to ensure that they will be 'tight'. In rural and desert areas a woman is still married not for her beauty or intelligence but for her ability to bear fine children. 'Two-thirds of the boy takes after his *khal* (maternal aunt)' is the saying. After the first sum is paid over at the *kitaab* or marriage contract, there is another contract where the husband agrees to pay the girl a further sum in gold in the event of divorce, for her security. No money changes hands: it will only become payable if he divorces her. The third stage is the wedding itself, the *dukla* or entering, named after the first sexual encounter which ensues. Many Bedouin do have more than one wife, a situation the earlier wives accept and shrug their shoulders about, saying such a thing is normal for Arabs. The age gap between the wives is usually about ten years, so each has her separate role and the older ones command respect as long as they have produced male children. Though the man is master, the woman is free to choose her husband and to leave him if ill-treated.

In their purest form the Bedouin represent the most perfect adaptation to their environment. The main tribes in Syria are the Rwala, who also live in Saudi Arabia, Jordan and Iraq, the Beni Sakhr and the Beni Khaled. Today only some 60% of the million or so Bedouin in Syria are thought to be fully migratory, living in tents and moving their flocks of sheep and goats between pasture areas, while some 24% are semi-settled, living in both houses and tents. About 85% of the men are illiterate, 96% of the women. Even among the young 76% of boys are illiterate and 83% of girls. Many Bedouin have now been settled, either voluntarily or compulsorily, in government-provided housing either in the desert itself or even on the edges of cities, and the important role they used to fulfil in escorting caravans and merchants along the trade routes from oasis to oasis, protecting them from hostile tribal raids, has disappeared. Slowly therefore the Bedouin traditions are breaking down, and the supreme virtue of the Bedouin, *Sabr* (tenacity, endurance in the face of great hardship), is no longer called for. However, the spirit of the clan, *'asabiya*, remains strong and every Bedu is fiercely loyal to his tribe. If the honour of the tribe is insulted or shamed in any way, the whole tribe is implicated and no punishment is recognised other than revenge. Blood feuds have been known to last 40 years or more.

In the semi-settled areas the houses are connected to electricity which is widely used for television, refrigeration and lighting. Butane gas is used for cooking. Pure nomads use camel dung and woody shrubs for fuel. television use is the top priority for electricity use with 70% now owning television and watching it regularly. Radio is also common but less popular than television. Some 80% of Bedouin now own at least one truck or tractor, and 33% own both. With an average herd size of 400, Bedouin income is relatively high, but very seasonal, with a peak in spring through high lamb and wool sales, and a low in winter (November to February) when supplementary feed has to be bought for the sheep, often requiring credit from the feed merchant or the *jabban* (milk/cheese) merchant.

The deterioration in the fragile ecosystem of the Syrian steppes is leading inexorably to the decline in numbers of pure nomads in the country, and as lifestyles become increasingly settled, the traditional Bedouin values too are likely gradually to disappear and become mere legend, unless efforts are made by the relevant authorities to sustain the economic viability of the Bedouin lifestyle. Responsibly organised tourism could well have a positive role to play here, providing a ready market for Bedouin handicrafts, and supplementing Bedouin income through adventure holidays and camel treks. This type of holiday, living on the edge of survival and experiencing first hand the rigours of nature and the elements, is increasingly in demand now as a contrast to our Western, comfort-based lives, and helps us to regain a valuable perspective on the essentials of life.

If invited into a Bedouin tent, it is extremely rude to refuse. You must take off your shoes before stepping onto the carpet inside the tent. When sitting having tea, two glasses of tea is normal, more is greedy, fewer is impolite. It is very useful on these occasions to be able to speak some Arabic, or else have someone along who can translate, as they generally know no language beyond their own. Do not be surprised at the directness of their questions about your age, marital status and so on. It is considered normal to ask such things, not rude. As a woman, take care to sit with your legs tucked beneath you, not cross-legged unless you are wearing a voluminous skirt. Be equipped with sweets for the children or cigarettes for the adults, as gestures of appreciation. Such gifts must always be given to the men.

Money is totally out of place. The preferred vehicles for Bedouin these days are Chevrolets or GMCs. The degree of religious observance varies, but is in any event a personal matter on which you are not judged. Your personal qualities are considered far more important.

FCO TRAVEL ADVICE
know before you go
fco.gov.uk/travel

Bradt Travel Guides is a partner to the 'know before you go' campaign, masterminded by the UK Foreign and Commonwealth Office to promote the importance of finding out about a destination before you travel. By combining the up-to-date advice of the FCO with the in-depth knowledge of Bradt authors, you'll ensure that your trip will be as trouble-free as possible.

www.fco.gov.uk/travel

Appendix I

LANGUAGE

Arabic has a very complex grammar in which everything is derived from an original three-consonant root. There are then potentially up to 13 different forms of the verb derived from that root, each one with slightly different shades of meaning. Bertrand Russell said: 'Life is too short to learn Arabic', and after obtaining a degree in it and a further 30 years of study the author is inclined to agree with him. No foreigner could really presume to call him or herself fluent and new words still crop up constantly.

THE ARABIC ALPHABET

Final	Medial	Initial	Alone	Transliteration	Pronunciation
ﻝ			ا	aa	as in 'after'
ﺐ	ﺒ	ﺑ	ب	b	as in 'but'
ﺖ	ﺘ	ﺗ	ت	t	as in 'tin'
ﺚ	ﺜ	ﺛ	ث	th	as in 'think'
ﺞ	ﺠ	ﺟ	ج	j	as in 'jam'
ﺢ	ﺤ	ﺣ	ح	H	emphatic, breathy 'h'
ﺦ	ﺨ	ﺧ	خ	kh	as in the Scottish 'loch'
ﺪ			د	d	as in 'den'
ﺬ			ذ	dh	as in 'that'
ﺮ			ر	r	as in 'red'
ﺰ			ز	z	as in 'zero'
ﺲ	ﺴ	ﺳ	س	s	as in 'sit', hard 's'
ﺶ	ﺸ	ﺷ	ش	sh	as in 'shut'
ﺺ	ﺼ	ﺻ	ص	S	emphatic, strong 's'
ﺾ	ﻀ	ﺿ	ض	D	emphatic, strong 'd'
ﻂ	ﻄ	ﻃ	ط	T	emphatic, strong 't'
ﻆ	ﻈ	ﻇ	ظ	Z	emphatic, strong 'z'
ﻊ	ﻌ	ﻋ	ع	'	ghutteral stop, hardest sound for non-Arabs to make, called 'ayn.
ﻎ	ﻐ	ﻏ	غ	gh	like a gargling sound
ﻒ	ﻔ	ﻓ	ف	f	as in 'fire'
ﻖ	ﻘ	ﻗ	ق	q	like a guttural 'k'
ﻚ	ﻜ	ﻛ	ك	k	as in 'king'
ﻞ	ﻠ	ﻟ	ل	l	as in 'lady'
ﻢ	ﻤ	ﻣ	م	m	as in 'mat'
ﻦ	ﻨ	ﻧ	ن	n	as in 'not'
ﻪ	ﻬ	ﻫ	ه	h	as in 'hat'
ﻮ			و	w	as in 'will', or 'oo' as in 'food'
ﻲ	ﻴ	ﻳ	ي	y	as in 'yet', or 'ee' as in 'clean'

Short vowels are not usually shown except in the Koran for the sake of total clarity and in children's texts.

The Arabic script is the easiest thing about the language, though it may look initially daunting with the confusing shapes and dots and the right to left flow. In fact there are only 29 characters in the Arabic alphabet and there are strict rules about which ones join on to which. These characters change their shape according to their position within the word, but always follow the same rigid pattern. The process of learning the characters and their shapes is therefore purely a memory exercise which can be done in three days and thereafter just requires practice. The right to left flow is just another basic adjustment, rather like driving on the right instead of the left of the road.

Once the script is mastered, the task begins in earnest. The first conceptually difficult thing you now encounter is that only the consonants are written. You have to supply the vowels yourself, but how do you know where to put them? The answer is that you do not, or at least not until you have acquired a thorough grasp of the intricacies of Arabic grammar and word structure, which will take a good three or four months' intensive study. For this reason all beginners' texts and children's school books are fully annotated with vowel signs added in the form of dashes and dots above and below the line. Getting students to read an unvowelled text aloud is always an excellent way of assessing their level, as it instantly reveals the depth of their understanding of Arabic grammar.

Pronunciation is another area which is not as daunting as it may seem. Of the 29 consonants, 18 have direct phonetic equivalents in English such as b, d, t, l, s. The rest have no direct equivalent and range from emphatic versions of d, s, and t, transliterated as D, S and T; or s, d and t with a single dot below; or s, d and t underlined. The guttural stop or 'ayn' as it is called in Arabic, usually represented in transliteration as an inverted high comma, is probably the one that gives most trouble, sounding like a vibrating constriction of the larynx.

Arabic is, by the very nature of its structure, an extremely rich language, capable of expressing fine shades of meaning, and this is reflected in the wealth of Arabic literature, especially poetry. The average English tabloid reader is said to have a working vocabulary of 3,000 words, while the Arab equivalent is said to have about 10,000.

There are also many interesting features of the language which hint at the nature and attitudes of the Arab mind, notably the existence of only two tenses, perfect and imperfect. There is no future tense. In the Arabic concept of time there is only one distinction that matters: has something been finished or is it still going on? Another curiosity is that the plural of inanimate objects is treated grammatically as feminine singular.

GREETINGS On first meeting when travelling generally outside the cities the respectful greeting to older people is: *As-salaamu 'alaykum*, meaning literally 'May peace be upon you.' The standard reply is: *Wa 'alaykum as-salaam*, meaning 'And on you the peace.'

There are three common phrases you will hear incessantly. *In sha Allah*, meaning 'If God wills it', is used all the time in the sense of 'hopefully', because nothing is certain to happen unless God wills it. So if you say to an Arab 'See you tomorrow', he will reply '*In sha Allah*', meaning, 'Yes, if God permits it and nothing happens in the mean time to prevent it.' It can also be a polite way of avoiding commitment, conveying 'Let us hope so…'

The second phrase is *Al-Hamdou lillah*, meaning 'Thanks be to God'. This is said every time something works out the way it should have done. It also expresses relief, along the lines of 'Thank God for that!'

The third phrase is *TafaDDal*, meaning 'Please go ahead' or 'Come in' or 'After you'. It is always said by your host when you arrive and on entering the house or room and before eating. Literally it means 'Please be so good as to…'

Other greetings

Hello, welcome   *marHaba, ahlan*

Goodbye   *ma'a as-salaama* (literally, with the peace)

Open	maftouH	مفتوح
Shut	musakker	مسكر
Forbidden	mamnou	ممنوع
Police	shurTa, boulees	شرطة
Gents	rijaal	رجال
Ladies	sayyidaat	سيدات
Hospital	mustashfaa	مستشفى

USEFUL ARABIC WORDS AND PHRASES
The basics

Yes	*aiwa, na'am*
No	*laa*
Please	*min faDlak*
Thank you	*shukran*
Thank you very much	*shukran jazeelan*
Sorry, excuse me	*'afwan, muta'assif*
Hurry up, let's go	*yallah*
More, again, also	*kamaan*
Is it possible? May I?	*mumkin?*
My name is …	*Ana ismee…*
What is your name?	*Shu ismak?*
I don't understand	*Ana maa bafham*
Where are you from?	*Min wayn anta?*
There is …	*Fii…*
There is not …	*Maa fii …*
What?	*shu?*

Getting around

airport	*maTaar*
bus	*baas*
car	*sayyaara*
suitcase, bag	*shanTa*
taxi	*taksee*
ticket	*tadhkira*
petrol	*benzeen*
diesel	*maazout*
far	*ba'eed*
left	*yasaar*
right	*yameen*
near, close by	*qareeb*
straight on	*dhughri, 'alaa aT-Toul*
where?	*wayn?*
Where is the museum, please?	*Wayn al-matHaf min faDlak?*
How far is it to…?	*Kam kiiloometre ila …?*

Hotels and restaurants

hotel	*funduq, ootel*
room	*ghurfa*
soap	*Saaboun*
toilet, bathroom	*Hammam, bait mai*

towel	*manshafa*
the bill	*al-faaToura, al-Hisaab*
restaurant	*maT'am*
breakfast	*fuTour*
lunch	*ghadaa*
dinner	*'ashaa*
glass	*finjaan*
I don't eat meat	*ana ma baakul laHm*

Food and drink

bread	*khubz*
butter	*zibdeh*
cheese	*jibneh*
eggs	*bayD*
fish	*samak*
fruit	*fawaakeh*
honey	*'asl*
jam	*murabbeh*
meat	*laHm*
sugar	*sukkar*
vegetables	*khuDar*
yoghurt	*laban*
half kilo	*nuSS kiiloo*
beer	*beera*
coffee	*qahwa*
mineral water	*mai ma'daniya*
red	*aHmar*
tea	*shay*
white	*abyaD*
wine	*nabeedh*

Shopping

cheap	*rakhees*
expensive	*ghaalee*
money	*fuluus*
a lot, much, very	*kateer*
no problem	*mish mishkila*
never mind	*ma'a laysh*
shop	*dukkaan*
market	*souk*
How much (does it cost?)	*bikaam? Addaysh?*

Health

chemist	*Saydaliyeh*
dentist	*Tabeeb asnaan*
doctor	*doktoor, Tabeeb*
diarrhoea	*ishaal*
ill, sick	*mareeD*

Days and time

Monday	*Yawn al-Ithnayn*
Tuesday	*Yawm ath-Thalaatha*
Wednesday	*Yawn al-Arba'a*

Thursday	Yawm al-Khamees
Friday	Yawm al-Jum'a
Saturday	Yawm as-Sabt
Sunday	Yawm al-AHad
today	al-yawm
tomorrow	bukra

Numbers

1	waaHad	١
2	ithnayn	٢
3	thalaatha	٣
4	arba'a	٤
5	khamsa	٥
6	sitta	٦
7	sab'a	٧
8	thamaaniya	٨
9	tis'a	٩
10	'ashara	١٠
20	'ishreen	٢٠
30	thalaatheen	٣٠
40	arba'een	٤٠
50	khamseen	٥٠
60	sitteen	٦٠
70	sab'een	٧٠
80	thamaaneen	٨٠
90	tis'een	٩٠
100	mi'a	١٠٠
150	mi'a wa khamseen	١٥٠
200	mi'atayn	٢٠٠
500	khams-mi'a	٥٠٠
1,000	alf	١٠٠٠
2,000	alfayn	٢٠٠٠

Other vocabulary

bank	bank, maSraf
museum	matHaf
post office	maktab bareed
good	kwayyis, Tayyib
bad	mish kwayyis, zift
hot	Haar
cold	baarid

Appendix 2

GLOSSARY

Ablaq	patterned stone work of alternate black basalt and white limestone
Acanthus	artichoke-like, stylised leaves carved as decoration on Corinthian capitals
Agha or Aga	agha is from the Turkish meaning military commander or chief; Aga Khan is the hereditary title of the Imam (spiritual and general leader) of the Nizari Isma'ili sect which split from the Musta'liya Isma'ili sect within Shi'a Islam. The current Aga Khan is a renowned philanthropist for development projects in the Islamic world.
Agora	open market place in Greek cities, like Roman forum
Andron	meeting place for men in Greek, Roman and Byzantine times
Bab	door, gate
Bait	Arabic (and Hebrew) for house, from the original root meaning to spend the night; in Syria all houses are named after the family that lives there, irrespective of size or grandeur, so Bait such and such (eg Bait Nizam, Bait Da'dah) can be a palace or a modest home.
Bedouin	Anglicised plural of Arabic singular 'badawi', meaning desert dweller, which has come to mean desert nomads
Bema	raised area, often in a horseshoe-shape, in the chancel of a Byzantine church (from the Greek). The altar was often placed on it and sometimes there was seating for the clergy.
Bimaristan	hospital and school of medicine in the Arab world
Caliph	from the Arabic 'khalifa' meaning successor, used as the title for all Muslim leaders who succeeded the Prophet Muhammad
Cardo maximus	main street running north–south in a Roman city
Cella	sacred chamber in a classical temple containing the cult image
Chancel	raised area around the altar in a church
Cryptoporticus	semi-subterranean chamber surrounded by a portico
Decumanus	main street running east–west across a Roman city
Dervish	from the Persian meaning beggar, the term has now come to be used for a member of any Sufi Muslim religious fraternity, known for extreme poverty and austerity, similar to a mendicant friar
Diwan	administrative council for keeping public registers introduced in Umayyad times
Druze	A distinct religious community whose origins were in Shi'a Islam, though they are not considered Muslim by other Muslims. There are about 1 million worldwide, concentrated in the mountains of Lebanon and southern Syra.
Eid Al-Adha	Muslim feast at the Hajj
Eid Al-Fitr	Muslim feast at the end of Ramadan

Exedra	semicircular recess set into a wall or line of columns, often lined with benches
Forum	from the Latin meaning open meeting place or market in a Roman city (like Greek 'agora')
glacis	smooth sloping surface on the outside of a fortification wall designed to stop attackers scaling.
Hajj	Muslim pilgrimage
Hammam	Turkish bathhouse with steam room, adapted from the Roman baths though with no pool, as Muslims believe water must flow freely not sit stagnant as this is considered unhygienic
Haramlik	private family quarters in an Arab courtyard house
Hijab	from the Arabic meaning 'covering', the term in its original form means dressing modestly for women, as ordered by the Koran. Different Muslim communities have interpreted hijab many different ways, from the extreme total covering of the face and body in loose robes as in Saudi Arabia, to just a headscarf covering the hair, worn with jeans and other Western clothing. In Syria facial veiling is rare and is seen only among Saudi and Iranian visitors. In modern usage the word 'hijab' is often used to refer just to the woman's headscarf.
Hijaz	region of Saudi Arabia containing Mecca and Medina
Hijra	Arabic for 'emigration', a reference to Muhammad's emigration to Medina from Mecca in AD622 when the Islamic calendar begins.
Iconostasis	screen in an Orthodox church separating the nave from the choir, inset with icons
Iwan	roofed but open, usually north-facing, room with an arch giving directly onto the courtyard of a traditional Arab house. Iwan is the Arabic word, but the Persian 'liwan' is used interchangeably.
Jellaba	full-length robe worn by men and women as traditional dress
Jihad	from the Arabic root 'to strive, make great efforts', jihad is now frequently translated as Holy War (by Muslims against non-Muslims), but the Islamic concept of jihad is far more than just warfare. It is also an inward spiritual struggle to attain perfect faith, ie: a personal jihad, and can also be jihad by the tongue, by the pen or by the hand, not just by the sword.
Khadamlik	servants' quarter in an Arab courtyard house
khan	from the Persian, an inn and warehouse set round a courtyard close to the *souk* area of a town or city, where merchants could stay in upstairs rooms, while their goods were stored in downstairs rooms, ready for trading and taxing. All merchandise of the same type was grouped in the same *khan*, so Khan Al-Harir for example (Harir is Arabic for 'silk') is where all silk was traded.
Khanqah	building that housed a Sufi fraternity
Kohl	Arab eyeliner
Liwan	used interchangeably with 'iwan' above
Machicolation	projection from the top of a stone wall designed for dropping missiles or hot oil on the enemy below
Machicoulis	hole in a ceiling designed for dropping missiles or hot oil on the enemy below
Madrasa	from the Arabic meaning 'school', the earliest madrasas were always religious, teaching the Koran and religious law
Mahmal	richly decorated camel-borne litter sent by Islamic rulers to Mecca with the Hajj as an emblem of their independence.

Majlis	open council held by the sheikh or tribal elder where grievances were aired by other members of the tribe and then settled by the shikh
Mashrabiyya	elaborate wooden carved screen on a window or balcony of an Ottoman house, which allowed women to see out without being observed themselves
Mezze	selection of starters, hot and cold, that comprise a typical Arab meal
Mihrab	prayer niche facing Mecca in a mosque
Minbar	raised pulpit in a mosque reached by a flight of steps, from which the Friday sermon is preached
Muezzin	man who calls to prayer from the mosque minaret
Muqarnas	'stalactite' decoration in wood or stone
Nargileh	from the Persian word for water-pipe, hubble-bubble or hookah
Narthex	vestibule or entrance hall to the nave of a Byzantine church usually running the whole width of a building
Nave	central rectangular hall of a church or basilica, usually lined with colonnades to separate it from the side aisles
Noria	large waterwheel with bucket scoops for irrigation of areas lying higher than the river
Nymphaeum	monumental fountain in Roman cities built to honour the emperor and symbolise the power of the empire
Odeon	small theatre in semicircular or horseshoe shape used for concerts or public addresses
Pasha	Turkish title of respect
Peristyle	colonnaded portico round a temple or courtyard
Qa'a	enclosed reception room off the courtyard of an Arab house, unlike the iwan/liwan which is open to the courtyard
Qadi	judge
Qibla	the direction of Mecca
Praetorium	residence of the Roman governor, or a barracks
Propylaeum	monumental gateway to an important building
Salamlik	reception area for guests in an Arab courtyard house
Sheikh	elder or head of the tribe
Shi'a	the branch of Islam that split off from the Sunni orthodoxy, believing 'Ali was Muhammad's rightful successor
Sufi	Muslim mystic
Sultan	Muslim ruler
Sunni	orthodox Islam that follows the 'Sunna', the tradition.
Souk	Arab market
Talus	same as glacis above. Smooth sloping surface on outside of fortification wall designed to prevent attackers from scaling it. Best example is at Krak des Chevaliers.
Tell	mound, hill of accumulated manmade debris from earlier settlements
Temenos	sacred precinct round a sanctuary where worshippers gather
Tetrapylon	monument with four (Greek *tetra* means four) pillars marking the intersection of two Roman thoroughfares
'Ulema	Muslim scholars, religious elite
Vizier	adviser to the ruler
Vomitorium	passageway for entry and exit from a Roman theatre
Waqf	system of Islamic trusts
Ziggurat	pyramid-shaped monument originating in ancient Mesopotamia, topped with a temple from which the stars were observed

Appendix 3

FURTHER INFORMATION

BOOKSHOPS In London there are several bookshops specialising in the Middle East:

Al-Saqi 26 Westbourne Grove, London W2 5RH; ☏ 020 7221 9347; f 020 7229 7492; e alsaqi-books@compuserve.com

Daunts Books for Travellers 83 Marylebone High St, London WIM 3DE; ☏ 020 7224 2295; f 020 7224 6893. **Probsthain & Co Oriental Booksellers** 41 Great Russell St, London WCIB 3PE; ☏ 020 7636 1096

All these bookshops do worldwide mail order and you can also order direct from amazon.co.uk or barnesandnoble.com.

The British Museum bookshop within the British Museum itself on Great Russell Street, Bloomsbury, London WC1, has an excellent selection of books on the culture and history of the region.

TRAVEL WRITING AND BIOGRAPHY

Bell, Gertrude *The Desert and the Sown* Cooper Square Press, 2001. An entertaining account of her 1905 trip across the Syrian desert from Jericho to Antioch and her observations on the people she met en route.

Blanch, Lesley *The Wilder Shores of Love* Phoenix, 2004. Fascinating profiles of four Western women, Isabel Burton, Jane Digby, Aimee Dubucq de Rivery and Isabelle Eberhardt, each of whom found love and fulfilment in the East.

Brodie, Fawn M, *The Devil Drives: A Life of Sir Richard Burton*. Compelling biography of this difficult but mesmerizing man who lived in Damascus for two years as British Consul.

Burton, Isabel *The Inner Life of Syria, Palestine and the Holy Land* London, 1884. Written as a result of her two years living in Damascus as the wife of Richard Burton, with descriptions of the people and places she encountered.

Christie, Agatha *Come Tell Me How You Live* HarperCollins, 1999. Charming, light-hearted account of her time in Syria on excavations with her second husband, archaeologist Max Mallowan.

Dalrymple, William *From the Holy Mountain: A Journey in the Shadow of Byzantium* Flamingo 1998. Readable account following in the footsteps of two Byzantine monks, starting in Mt Athos in Greece and moving via monasteries in Turkey, Syria, Palestine and finishing in Egypt, looking at and analysing the remnants of eastern Christianity en route.

Joris, Lieve *The Gates of Damascus* Lonely Planet, 1996. Perceptive account of the Belgian author's year spent in Damascus with a woman whose husband had been jailed for political reasons.

Kociejowski, Marius *The Street Philosopher and the Holy Fool: A Syrian Journey* Sutton Publishing, 2006. Entertainingly written story of the author's encounter over the course of five journeys to Syria with a range of unusual characters each of whom represents an unexpected face of Syria. Moving and often hilarious.

Haslip, Joan *Lady Hester Stanhope: A Biography* Sutton Publishing, 2006. Thorough account of the life of this bold, unconventional figure who ended her days in Lebanon and was the first Western woman to reach Palmyra.

Lawrence, T E *Seven Pillars of Wisdom* Coles Pub Co, 1992. Lawrence of Arabia's classic account of the Arab Revolt during World War I.

Lovell, Mary S *A Scandalous Life: The Biography of Jane Digby* Fourth Estate, 1995. Lively and highly readable account of the highs and lows of this English aristocrat who spent the last 25 years of her life in Syria married to a Bedouin sheikh.

Lovell, Mary S *A Rage to Live: a Biography of Richard and Isabel Burton* WW Norton, 1998. A lively read of the life of the Burtons, he one of the greatest adventurers of his age, an unorthodox social outlaw, she a Victorian Catholic who never accompanied him on his ventures but who lived them all by proxy.

Severin, Tim *Crusader* Weidenfeld & Nicholson, 2001. Entertaining story of his re-creation on horseback of the Crusaders' journey from France to Jerusalem, stopping at Crusader castles en route.

Tergeman, Siham *Daughter of Damascus* University of Texas at Austin, 1994. Interesting if a little disjointed description of life in the Old City in the early 20th century.

Thubron, Colin *Mirror to Damascus* Penguin, 1996. Entertaining and learned account of his time exploring the city, often by bicycle; full of classical knowledge and personal anecdotes.

Twain, Mark *The Innocents Abroad or the New Pilgrim's Progress* Random House, 2003. The young Mark Twain sets out for Europe and the Holy Land on a paddle steamer and records his wry observations.

Wallach, Janet *Desert Queen: The Extraordinary Life of Gertrude Bell: Adventurer, Adviser to Kings, Ally to Lawrence of Arabia* Phoenix, 1996. A balanced assessment of the woman who provided the intelligence for T E Lawrence's military activities and who was generally considered the most powerful woman in the British Empire.

HISTORY

Ajami, Fouad *The Dream Palace of the Arabs* Vintage, 1998. Heartfelt appraisal of where the Arabs went wrong in the 20th century, politically and economically.

Asbridge, Thomas *The First Crusade: A New History* OUP Inc, USA. Excellent, exciting read, which clearly conveys the action and the historical background.

Butcher, Kevin *Roman Syria and the Near East* British Museum Press, 2003. Serious hardback nearly 500 pages, comprehensive and well-illustrated, but heavy to carry around.

Degeorge, Gerard *Damas: Des Ottomans à nos jours* Paris, 1994

Degeorge, Gerard *Damas: Des origins aux Mamluks* Harmattan, 1997

Degeorge, Gerard *Damascus: City of Ages* Flammarion, 2005. Trio of excellent if expensive coffee-table books with superb photographs and intelligent text.

Fedden, Robin *Syria: An Historical Appreciation* Hale, 1955. Interesting and readable survey up to the 1950s.

Glain, Stephen *Dreaming of Damascus: Merchants, Mullahs and Militants in the Near Middle East* John Murray, 2003. Arab voices from a region in turmoil. The author was Middle East correspondent of the *Wall Street Journal* and gives a poignant account of how the Arab world may collapse in the absence of badly needed reform, with militant Islam rushing to fill the vacuum.

Hitti, Philip *A History of the Arabs* Macmillan/St Martins, 2002. Classic, detailed history, first written in 1970, from the pre-Islamic age to the 1960s.

Hourani, Albert *A History of the Arab Peoples* Faber/Warner, 1992. Comprehensive and highly regarded study of the social and political history of the Arabs.

Ibn Munqidh, Usama *An Arab-Syrian Gentleman and Warrior in the Period of the Crusades* London, 1987. The extraordinary memoirs of this 12th-century Arab warrior/poet/prince, detailing his encounters with and reactions to the Frankish Crusaders, the only such record to be translated into English.

Lesch, David *The New Lion of Damascus* Yale University Press, 2005. The author examines whether Syria is a rogue state and looks at the new Syria under Bashar. Syria's inside story is told on the basis of unique first-hand access to Bashar, his family and his circle.

Leverett, Flynt *Inheriting Syria: Bashar's Trial by Fire* Brooking Institution, 2005. Former US State Department and CIA Syria expert, the author gives an authorative portrait of Syria under the Assad dynasty, particularly the strategic legacy bequeathed from Hafez Al-Assad to his son Bashar, and analyses US foreign policy towards Syria.

Lewis, Bernard The *Middle East: 2000 Years of History from the Rise of Christianity to the Present Day* Weidenfeld & Nicolson, 2001. Excellent survey of the civilisation of the Middle East, examining how history has shaped its identity.

Maalouf, Amin *The Crusades Through Arab Eyes* Al-Saqi Books, 1984. Highly readable, refreshing and original account of the Crusades from the Arab viewpoint, offering fascinating insights into forces that have shaped the Arab consciousness today. The author is a Lebanese journalist.

Madden, Thomas *The New Concise History of the Crusades*, Rowman & Littlefield, 2005. Engaging narrative of the Crusades and their contemporary relevance, focusing especially on their effects on the Islamic world and the Christian Byzantine East.

Mansfield, Peter *A History of the Middle East* Penguin, 1991. Very readable general survey covering 1800–1990, by the former Middle East correspondent of the *Sunday Times*. Good for general understanding, though not much specifically on Syria.

Runciman, Steven *A History of the Crusades* Penguin, 1991. The classic authorative work on the subject by this Byzantine scholar, in three volumes.

Said, Edward *Orientalism* Penguin, 1995. Controversial and prophetic book written 25 years ago, it has now attained the status of Penguin Modern Classic, and seems more relevant than ever. It offers profound insights into the roots of Western antagonism towards the Orient.

Seale, Patrick, *Assad: The Struggle for the Middle East*, I B Taurus, 1988. Scholarly, well-written analyses by an author who had good links into the Assad family, with much material from personal interviews.

Shaa'ban, Buthaina *Both Right and Left Handed* The Women's Press, Indiana Univeristy Press, 1988. Balanced account by the woman who is currently Syrian Minister for Immigration, of the woman's role in modern Arab society, destroying all stereotypes of the passive Arab woman, presented through a series of conversations with local women.

Tyerman, Christopher *The Crusades: A Very Short Introduction* OUP, 2004. A clear and lively discussion of the Crusades, the debates and controversies that surround them, challenging past assumptions.

Van Dam, Nikolaos *The Struggle for Power in Syria: Politics and Society under Assad and the Ba'ath Party* I B Taurus, 1996. The author worked in the Dutch Ministry of Foreign Affairs, and demonstrates a firm grasp of the complexities of Syrian politics, with extensive use of Arabic sources including previous secret documents.

ART, LITERATURE AND ARCHITECTURE

Adonis *Victims of a Map: A Bilingual Anthology of Arabic Poetry* Saqi Books, 2005. Excellent introduction to modern Arabic poetry, which has had a far greater influence on popular culture than the modern Arabic novel. Fifteen translated poems from each of the leading poets of the Arab world, Mahmoud Darwish, Samih Al-Qasim and Adonis.

Akkermans, Peter and Schwartz, Glenn *The Archaeology of Syria: From Complex Hunter-Gatherers to Early Urban Societies (16,000–300BC)* Cambridge World Archaeology, CUP, 2003. A comprehensive survey from the end of the Ice Age to the Iron Age.

Arberry, A J *Arabic Poetry* CUP, 1965. Bilingual text, an anthology of poems from the 6th century to the 20th century, with a detailed introduction and biographical notes.

Architecture and Polyphony: Building in the Islamic World Today Thames and Hudson, 2004. Critical essays considering the challenges and rewards confronting architects working in

Muslim countries, together with profiles of the winning schemes of the Aga Khan Award for Architecture.

Badawi, M M *A Critical Introduction to Modern Arabic Poetry* CUP, 1975. Covering from the latter half of the 19th century to the 1970s, this detailed book ranges across the entire Arabic-speaking world, including Arab poets who emigrated to the USA and Latin America, making links to the classical Arabic tradition.

Browning, Iain *Palmyra* Chatto & Windus, 1980. Thorough study of the site, well-illustrated, still widely available within Syria.

Burns, Ross *Monuments of Syria* I B Taurus, 1992. Excellent and thorough gazeteer on the archaeology and architecture of the sites. The best reference book around.

Burton, Sir Richard (trans) *The Arabian Nights* Modern Library of New York, 2001. Includes the most famous and representative tales from Burton's original ten-volume translation, such as 'Aladdin and the Lamp' and 'Ali Baba and the Forty Thieves'.

Eiland, Murray and son, *Oriental Carpets: A Complete Guide – the Classic Reference*, Bulfinch Press, 1998. The best and most accessible publication by far on the mysteries of oriental carpets; lavish and entertaining, with thorough and well-laid out text and richly coloured plates.

Fadel, Marie, and Schami, Rafik *Damascus: Taste of a City* Armchair Traveller, 2005 (first published in German, 2002). Curious but entertaining mix of recipes and anecdotal background.

Hillenbrand, Robert *Islamic Art and Architecture* Thames and Hudson, 1999. Wide-ranging guide to the arts of Islam, including architecture, calligraphy, ceramics and textiles, covering the whole geographic scope over a thousand-year period.

Jones, Mark Wilson *The Principles of Roman Architecture* Yale University Press, 2003. An exploration by this practising architect and architectural historian of how architects of ancient Rome approached design.

Keenan, Brigid *Damascus: Hidden Treasures of the Old City* Thames and Hudson, 2001. Beautifully photographed coffee-table book with intelligent and well-researched text, a tribute to the heritage of the Old City with its lavish but neglected palaces and private houses.

Kennedy, Hugh *Crusader Castles* CUP, 2001. Detailed study of the castles, siege warfare and the Crusader knights themselves.

Kritzeck, James *Anthology of Islamic Literature* Penguin, 1987. Comprehensive and clear account of everything Islamic literature has to offer, from pre-Islamic poetry, through the developments of the Umayyad and 'Abbasid caliphates, the Ottoman times, to the present day.

Lawrence, T E *Crusader Castles*, Michael Haag, 1986. Lawrence's PhD thesis, giving an insight into both the castles and the author as a young man.

MacDonald, William Lloyd *The Architecture of the Roman Empire: An Introductory Study* Yale University Press, 1982. Examines Roman architecture, progressing through the emperors, looking at overall urban design, arches, public buildings, tombs, forums and streets.

Michell, George *Architecture of the Islamic World* Thames and Hudson, 1978. Panoramic survey of the entire field of Islamic architecture from mosques to markets, citadels to cemeteries, with the emphasis on function and meaning rather than on chronology and style. Seven specialist authors have contributed.

Qabbani, Nizar *On Entering the Sea* Interlink Books, 1996. By far the most popular poet of the Arab world, Qabbani was born in Damascus in 1923 and published over 50 collections of poetry, celebrating love and women in the face of chaos and tragedy, agony and ecstasy. His later work became more political as he expressed his anger and rage at the forces of evil at work in the Middle East. He died in 1998.

Robinson, Francis (ed) *Islamic World: Cambridge Illustrated History* CUP, 1996. Lavishly illustrated cultural history of the Islamic world from Muhammad to the present day, demystifying Muslim civilisation and celebrating its achievements, whilst placing in perspective its role in the world today.

Savory, R M *Introduction to Islamic Civilisation* Cambridge University Press, 1976. Wide-ranging and general introduction to Islamic civilisation from its origins to the present day, examining how a single civilisation developed in a multi-ethnic, multi-cultural region.

RELIGION

A J Arberry *The Koran* Oxford World Classics, Oxford Paperbacks, 1998. Generally seen as the best English translation, along with N J Dawood's version. Arberry was Professor of Arabic at London and Cambridge universities.

Armstrong, Karen *Islam: A Short History* Phoenix, 2000. Engaging and provocative corrective to the hostile caricatures of Islam that circulate in the English-speaking world.

Bloom, Jonathan and Blair, Sheila *Islam: A Thousand Years of Faith and Power* Yale University Press, 2002. Colourfully illustrated excellent introduction to the rich history of a civilisation, examining the rise of Islam, the life of Muhammad and Islamic principles of faith.

Brenton, Robert *The Druze* Yale University Press, 1990. A thorough work giving some fascinating insights into the secretive sect. The first complete account of the Druze, with a survey of their history, traditions and society, much of it from first-hand observations.

Cook, Michael *The Koran: A Very Short Introduction* OUP, 2000. Lucid and direct exploration of the significance of the Koran in both the modern world and in traditional Islam.

Dana, Nissim *Druze in the Middle East: Their Faith, Leadership, Identity and Status* Sussex Academic Press, 2005. From an Israeli author, the book analyses the Druze in the Middle East in general, with a particular focus on the Druze relationship with Israel.

Lewis, Bernard *The Assassins: A Radical Sect of Islam* Phoenix, 1967. Sensible readable account of the sect, dispelling the drug-taking myths, giving the origins and history.

Lewis, Bernard *The Crisis of Islam: Holy War and Unholy Terror* Weidenfeld and Nicolson, 2003. Thought-provoking book that sets out to analyse the crises faced by Islam, the roots of the frustration and resentment in the Islamic world today, and the rise of terrorism.

Lewis, Bernard *The Multiple Identities of the Middle East* Phoenix, 1998. Examines and seeks to clarify how Western political concepts have altered ideas of Middle Eastern identity and how imported Western ideas have inflamed political conflicts in the region.

Pelikan, Jaroslav *Christian Tradition: A History of the Development of Doctrine: The Spirit of Eastern Christendom 600–1700* University of Chicago Press, 1977. Masterpiece of exposition which explains the divisions between Eastern and Western Christendom, the linguistic barriers, political divisions and liturgical differences which combine to isolate the two cultures from each other.

Rogerson, Barnaby *The Prophet Muhammad: A Biography* Abacus, 2003. Fascinating, thoughtful and open-minded biography, giving insights into the life of the man, leader and visionary. The book will probably change the way you think about Islam.

Ruthven, Malise *Islam: A Very Short Introduction* OUP, 1997. One of the best books for gaining understanding of modern Islam, including the overthrow of Saddam Hussein and the debates about democracy currently raging in the Arab world.

Said, Edward *Covering Islam* Vintage, 1997. Well-written examination of the basis of western stereotypes of Islam.

Sivan, Emmanuel *Radical Islam: Medieval Theology and Modern Politics* Yale University Press, 1990. Highly acclaimed book focusing on the development of Sunni Mulim fundamentalism. It reviews areas of controversy between Sunni and Shi'a Muslims and examines whether rapprochement is likely or possible.

Tripp, Charles *Islam and the Moral Economy: The Challenge of Capitalism* CUP, 2006. Thought-provoking book about how Islam copes with 20th- and 21st-century economics and the dilemmas involved in reconciling the teachings of the Koran and the Hadith with the needs of modern life.

Zernov, Nicolas *History of Religion: Eastern Christendom* Weidenfeld & Nicolson, 1961. An overview of the history of the Eastern Orthodox Church; thorough and comprehensive.

WEBSITES

www.cafe-syria.com Comprehensive website offering a range of factual information on all aspects of the whole country. Put together by a group of independent Syrians.

www.syria-guide.com Syrian-produced website complete with music, requires small payment for membership to access its hotel, restaurant and other practical information.

www.syriadaily.com Very good website for current affairs, with articles from the world's media.

www.syriagate.com Comprehensive website with everything from business information to archaeological site reports.

www.syriatourism.org Syrian Ministry of Tourism's own website with a general country profile and virtual tours.

www.syritour.com Syrian travel agency and tour operator's own website, offering reservation and guide services.

www.echosyria.com Syrian website geared to businessmen and investors, with some general information.

www.sana.org Syrian Arab News Agency's own website, good for current events and the political situation.

www.syria-net.com Syrian website for business information, with some general and cultural background.

www.fco.gov.uk British Foreign Office website for current travel safety recommendations.

www.menewsline.com Good website for latest updates on Middle East news.

www.odic.gov/cia/publications/factbook/geos/sy.html CIA factbook giving a comprehensive Syria country profile.

www.moi.syria.com Official website for the Syrian Ministry of Information with a comprehensive directory of links.

MEASUREMENTS AND CONVERSIONS

To convert	Multiply by
Inches to centimetres	2.54
Centimetres to inches	0.3937
Feet to metres	0.3048
Metres to feet	3.281
Yards to metres	0.9144
Metres to yards	1.094
Miles to kilometres	1.609
Kilometres to miles	0.6214
Acres to hectares	0.4047
Hectares to acres	2.471
Imperial gallons to litres	4.546
Litres to imperial gallons	0.22
US gallons to litres	3.785
Litres to US gallons	0.264
Ounces to grams	28.35
Grams to ounces	0.03527
Pounds to grams	453.6
Grams to pounds	0.002205
Pounds to kilograms	0.4536
Kilograms to pounds	2.205
British tons to kilograms	1016.0
Kilograms to British tons	0.0009812
US tons to kilograms	907.0
Kilograms to US tons	0.000907

5 imperial gallons are equal to 6 US gallons
A British ton is 2,240 lbs. A US ton is 2,000 lbs.

TEMPERATURE CONVERSION TABLE The bold figures in the central columns can be read as either centigrade or fahrenheit.

°C		°F	°C		°F
−18	**0**	32	10	**50**	122
−15	**5**	41	13	**55**	131
−12	**10**	50	16	**60**	140
−9	**15**	59	18	**65**	149
−7	**20**	68	21	**70**	158
−4	**25**	77	24	**75**	167
−1	**30**	86	27	**80**	176
2	**35**	95	32	**90**	194
4	**40**	104	38	**100**	212
7	**45**	113	40	**104**	219

WIN £100 CASH!

READER QUESTIONNAIRE

**Send in your completed questionnaire for the chance to win
£100 cash in our regular draw**

All respondents may order a Bradt guide at half the UK retail price – please
complete the order form overleaf.

(Entries may be posted or faxed to us, or scanned and emailed.)

We are interested in getting feedback from our readers to help us plan future Bradt
guides. Please answer ALL the questions below and return the form to us in order
to qualify for an entry in our regular draw.

Have you used any other Bradt guides? If so, which titles? . . . .
. . . .

What other publishers' travel guides do you use regularly? . . . .
. . . .

Where did you buy this guidebook? . . . .

What was the main purpose of your trip to Syria (or for what other reason did you
read our guide)? eg: holiday/business/charity etc. . . . .
. . . .

What other destinations would you like to see covered by a Bradt guide?
. . . .

Would you like to receive our catalogue/newsletters?

YES / NO (If yes, please complete details on reverse)

If yes – by post or email? . . . .

Age (circle relevant category) 16–25   26–45   46–60   60+

Male/Female (delete as appropriate)

Home country . . . .

Please send us any comments about our guide to Syria or other Bradt Travel
Guides. . . . .
. . . .
. . . .
. . . .

Bradt Travel Guides

23 High Street, Chalfont St Peter, Bucks SL9 9QE, UK
☎ +44 (0)1753 893444 f +44 (0)1753 892333
e info@bradtguides.com
www.bradtguides.com

CLAIM YOUR HALF-PRICE BRADT GUIDE!

Order Form

To order your half-price copy of a Bradt guide, and to enter our prize draw to win £100 (see overleaf), please fill in the order form below, complete the questionnaire overleaf, and send it to Bradt Travel Guides by post, fax or email.

Please send me one copy of the following guide at half the UK retail price

Title	Retail price	Half price
. . .	. . . .	. . . .	. . . .

Please send the following additional guides at full UK retail price

No	Title	Retail price	Total
. . .	. . . .	. . . .	. . . .
. . .	. . . .	. . . .	. . . .
. . .	. . . .	. . . .	. . . .

Sub total	. . . .
Post & packing	. . . .
(£1 per book UK; £2 per book Europe; £3 per book rest of world)	
Total	. . . .

Name . . . .

Address . . . .

Tel . . . .   Email . . . .

☐ I enclose a cheque for £ . . . . made payable to Bradt Travel Guides Ltd

☐ I would like to pay by credit card. Number: . . . .

Expiry date: . . . / . . .   3-digit security code (on reverse of card) . . . . .

☐ Please add my name to your catalogue mailing list.

☐ I would be happy for you to use my name and comments in Bradt marketing material.

Send your order on this form, with the completed questionnaire, to:

Bradt Travel Guides SYR1
23 High Street, Chalfont St Peter, Bucks SL9 9QE
✆ +44 (0)1753 893444 f +44 (0)1753 892333
e info@bradtguides.com www.bradtguides.com

Bradt Travel Guides

www.bradtguides.com

Africa

Africa Overland	£15.99
Benin	£14.99
Botswana: Okavango, Chobe, Northern Kalahari	£14.95
Burkina Faso	£14.99
Cape Verde Islands	£13.99
Canary Islands	£13.95
Cameroon	£13.95
Eritrea	£12.95
Ethiopia	£15.99
Gabon, São Tomé, Príncipe	£13.95
Gambia, The	£13.99
Georgia	£13.95
Ghana	£13.95
Johannesburg	£6.99
Kenya	£14.95
Madagascar	£14.95
Malawi	£13.99
Mali	£13.95
Mauritius, Rodrigues & Réunion	£13.99
Mozambique	£12.95
Namibia	£14.95
Niger	£14.99
Nigeria	£15.99
Rwanda	£13.95
Seychelles	£14.99
Sudan	£13.95
Tanzania, Northern	£13.99
Tanzania	£16.99
Uganda	£13.95
Zambia	£15.95
Zanzibar	£12.99

Britain and Europe

Albania	£13.99
Armenia, Nagorno Karabagh	£13.99
Azores	£12.99
Baltic Capitals: Tallinn, Riga, Vilnius, Kaliningrad	£12.99
Belgrade	£6.99
Bosnia & Herzegovina	£13.95
Bratislava	£6.99
Budapest	£7.95
Cork	£6.95
Croatia	£12.95
Cyprus see North Cyprus	
Czech Republic	£13.99
Dubrovnik	£6.95
Eccentric Britain	£13.99
Eccentric Cambridge	£6.99
Eccentric Edinburgh	£5.95
Eccentric France	£12.95
Eccentric London	£12.95
Eccentric Oxford	£5.95
Estonia	£12.95
Faroe Islands	£13.95
Hungary	£14.99
Kiev	£7.95
Latvia	£13.99

Lille	£6.99
Lithuania	£13.99
Ljubljana	£6.99
Macedonia	£13.95
Montenegro	£13.99
North Cyprus	£12.99
Paris, Lille & Brussels	£11.95
Riga	£6.95
River Thames, In the Footsteps of the Famous	£10.95
Serbia	£13.99
Slovenia	£12.99
Spitsbergen	£14.99
Switzerland: Rail, Road, Lake	£13.99
Tallinn	£6.95
Ukraine	£13.95
Vilnius	£6.99

Middle East, Asia and Australasia

Great Wall of China	£13.99
Iran	£14.99
Iraq	£14.95
Kabul	£9.95
Maldives	£13.99
Mongolia	£14.95
North Korea	£13.95
Oman	£13.99
Palestine, Jerusalem	£12.95
Sri Lanka	£13.99
Syria	£13.99
Tasmania	£12.95
Tibet	£12.95
Turkmenistan	£14.99

The Americas and the Caribbean

Amazon, The	£14.95
Argentina	£15.99
Bolivia	£14.99
Cayman Islands	£12.95
Costa Rica	£13.99
Chile	£16.95
Chile & Argentina: Trekking	£12.95
Eccentric America	£13.95
Eccentric California	£13.99
Falkland Islands	£13.95
Peru & Bolivia: Backpacking and Trekking	£12.95
Panama	£13.95
St Helena, Ascension, Tristan da Cunha	£14.95
USA by Rail	£13.99

Wildlife

Antarctica: Guide to the Wildlife	£14.95
Arctic: Guide to the Wildlife	£15.99
British Isles: Wildlife of Coastal Waters	£14.95
Galápagos Wildlife	£15.99
Madagascar Wildlife	£14.95
Southern African Wildlife	£18.95
Sri Lankan Wildlife	£15.99

Health

Your Child Abroad: A Travel Health Guide	£10.95

Index

Page numbers in bold indicate major entries; those in italic indicate maps.